In the Beginning

Siphrut
Literature and Theology of the Hebrew Scriptures

In the Beginning

Essays on Creation Motifs in the Ancient Near East and the Bible

Bernard F. Batto

Winona Lake, Indiana
EISENBRAUNS
2013

www.eisenbrauns.com

Library of Congress Cataloging-in-Publication Data

Batto, Bernard Frank.
   [Essays. Selections]
   In the beginning : essays on creation motifs in the ancient Near East and the
     Bible / Bernard F. Batto.
       pages cm. — (Siphrut : literature and theology of the Hebrew
         Scriptures ; 9)
     ISBN 978-1-57506-267-9 (alk. paper)
     1. Creation—Biblical teaching. 2. Bible. O.T. Genesis I–XI—Criticism,
interpretation, etc. 3. Middle East—Religion. 4. Middle Eastern literature—
History and criticism. I. Title.
   BS1199.C73B382 2013
   221.6—dc23

                                   2013009703

Contents

Introduction

The eight articles in this volume were written as independent essays. Nevertheless, they are unified in that all eight deal with some aspect of creation or with creation motifs in the Hebrew Bible and the ancient Near East, and they attempt to show how the two cultural worlds are closely intertwined. Two of these articles have never been published previously. Six have been previously published—one at least in a somewhat obscure publication. It is hoped that collecting these articles together in one place will serve a useful scholarly purpose, especially for biblical scholars who may be less familiar with the larger ancient Near Eastern context of many biblical topoi.

The eight articles included, in order, are:

1. "The Ancient Near Eastern Context for the Hebrew Ideas of Creation." Previously unpublished.
2. "Paradise Reexamined." Previously published in *The Biblical Canon in Comparative Perspective* (ed. K. Lawson Younger, Jr., William W. Hallo, and Bernard F. Batto; Ancient Near Eastern Texts and Studies 11; Lewiston, NY: Edwin Mellen, 1991) 33–66.
3. "The Institution of Marriage in Genesis 2 and in *Atrahasis*." Previously published in *CBQ* 62 (2000) 621–31.
4. "The Divine Sovereign: The Image of God in the Priestly Creation Account." Previously published in *David and Zion: Biblical Studies in Honor of J. J. M. Roberts* (ed. Bernard F. Batto and Kathryn L. Roberts; Winona Lake, IN: Eisenbrauns, 2004) 143–86.
5. "The Sleeping God: An Ancient Near Eastern Motif of Divine Sovereignty." Previously published in *Bib* 68 (1987) 153–77.
6. "The Reed Sea: *Requiescat in Pace*." Previously published in *JBL* 102 (1983) 27–35.
7. "The Covenant of Peace: A Neglected Ancient Near Eastern Motif." Previously published in *CBQ* 49 (1987) 187–211.
8. "The Malevolent Deity in Mesopotamian Myth." Previously unpublished.

The two unpublished articles serve as bookends, so to speak, to the volume. The opening article not only gives a concise overview of the various ancient Near Eastern conceptions of creation but also provides a cultural context within which to view biblical conceptions of creation and the Creator in the opening chapters of Genesis. The final essay deals with the

Mesopotamian manifestation of the eternal human quest for the origin of evil. The long Mesopotamian quest ends, much like the biblical book of Job, with a recognition that the ways of the supreme god and universal creator are inscrutable, and that the ways of this divine sovereign must be accepted as ultimate wisdom. The articles sandwiched in between explore in novel ways various creation motifs that cut across boundaries often thought to separate the Bible from the ancient Near East.

The opening article surveys the literatures of ancient Egypt, Mesopotamia, and Canaan as cultural context for the Hebrew creation accounts found in the opening chapters of Genesis. Although there is no direct dependency upon Egyptian literature evident in the Genesis narrative, there are significant motifs common to both traditions. Principal among these is the conception of a living space for both humans and animals within the void formed on the base of a solid earth underfoot and a rigid sky overhead, which together hold back the chaotic waters that engulf our "created world" on all sides. There are no extant Egyptian creation myths per se. But there are diverse texts that speak of humans being formed on a potter's wheel or as the tears of a deity; moreover, these humans were once threatened with annihilation by a flood from a deity. Canaanite mythic themes are generally absent from the Genesis creation accounts, although they abound elsewhere in the Hebrew Bible. Mesopotamia provides the closest parallels to the Genesis creation accounts, which may even be literarily dependent in part upon Mesopotamian myth. In particular, *Atrahasis*, the so-called Babylonian story of the flood, appears to have influenced the typology of the Yahwistic creation account, from a close association between the creation of humankind and the cultivation of the soil, to the sending of a universal flood to wipe out humankind as the result of human rebellion (or sin) against the god(s). Less certain, though highly probable, is the influence of the Mesopotamian combat myth tradition, especially *Enuma Elish*, upon the Priestly creation account. There can be no doubt, however, that Hebrew conceptions of creation are part and parcel of the larger ancient Near Eastern mythic tradition, as this article attempts to demonstrate.

In "Paradise Reexamined" I show that, contrary to a common scholarly opinion, biblical authors did not derive the paradise motif from Sumerian sources. A careful examination of the relevant Sumerian texts, notably the description of "pure Dilmun" in *Enki and Ninhursag* and of "Nudimmud's Spell" in *Enki and the Lord of Aratta*, reveals that not only are the alleged primeval paradisiacal conditions entirely lacking, but actually the opposite conditions prevail therein. Both myths conform to the standard Mesopotamian viewpoint that creation was progressive, with the Sumero-Akkadian civilization considered to be the culmination of a long development from originally inferior conditions. Turning to Genesis, I argue that the paradise motif was not borrowed from Mesopotamia but is an internal biblical development. The earlier Yahwistic creation account, like its Mesopotamian forerunners, assumes a progression in the primeval period from an originally inchoate creation to a better and improved creation, in that the divine creator had to tweak his handiwork multiple times in order to achieve a sustainable world and especially a workable model of humankind. It was a later Priestly writer, when he prefaced the story of "Adam and Eve" and their disobedience with the account in Genesis 1 about God originally creating everything "very good"—that is, perfect!—who transformed the primeval narrative from a story about a gradually improved creation into a story of "paradise lost." Ezekiel 28, with obvious links to the Priestly tradition, reinforces this interpretation of the primeval tradition as a story of a "fall" from perfection.

In "The Institution of Marriage in Genesis 2 and in *Atrahasis*" I attempt to settle a long-standing debate among biblical interpreters regarding the narrative about the creation of woman as a suitable companion for "the Human" (*hā-'ādām*) in Genesis 2:18–25. Some purport that the text envisions marriage and/or sex as part of the deity's original creative design for humankind in the Garden of Eden, others that sexual intercourse is a secondary element introduced only after the first couple had been expelled from Eden, and was a consequence of the sinful human condition (i.e., concupiscence) as Augustine, among others, taught. Improved readings of the relevant portions of *Atrahasis* reveal that in that Babylonian creation myth, marriage and procreation were integral to the original creative design for humankind. If my contention (argued elsewhere) is correct that the Yahwistic writer is in part dependent upon *Atrahasis* for the typology of his primeval story, then it follows that the Yahwist likewise understood the institution of marriage to be part of the creator's original design for humankind. This finding casts a positive spin upon marriage and sex. Sex may be considered connatural to the human condition and therefore something which humankind was expected to engage in from the very beginning in Eden—and not an activity now grudgingly allowed humankind because of their sinful nature.

Precisely how the Priestly writer understood God as creator is the subject of "The Divine Sovereign: The Image of God in the Priestly Creation Account." Interpreters have long observed that, compared to the Yahwistic creation account, the deity in the Priestly creation account is much less anthropomorphic. I argue that the anthropomorphism of P is merely on a different level. P chose to depict the Creator using the most theologically sophisticated conception of God available to him, the metaphor of the divine sovereign, the universal supreme deity who rules both the other gods and the physical world with its denizens. During the course of Mesopotamian history, the functions of divine leadership and the responsibility for creation were gradually consolidated in the figure of a single deity. This culminated during the Neo-Assyrian and the Neo-Babylonian empires, when virtually all authority in heaven and on earth and in the underworld, as well as all aspects of creation, were assigned to the national deity, namely, to Ashur in Assyria and to Marduk in Babylonia. As is evident from a close scrutiny of both textual evidence and ancient Near Eastern iconography, this conception of the national deity was used to undergird the authority of the kings of Assyria and Babylonia, respectively, in that the king was said to be in the "image" of the divine sovereign—in other words, his viceroy on earth; and as such, the king was responsible for maintaining the weal of the whole earth. Likely out of the experience first of Assyrian and later of Babylonian domination over Israel and Judah, the Priestly writer adapted this Neo-Assyrian/Neo-Babylonian conceit for his own theological agenda of portraying Israel's national deity "God" as the true divine sovereign who was, therefore, also the creator of all. This Priestly theologian resisted one aspect of the Mesopotamian conceit, however. With the recent experience of the disastrous policies of the kings of both Israel and Judah etched into his memory, P balked at representing the king as God's viceroy on earth. Instead, P democratized kingship by having the divine sovereign "create humankind in (his) own image," with the injunction to "rule over every living thing." In P's creation theology, every human is thus anointed to continue the agenda of the divine sovereign by working to eliminate from this world every form of oppression and injustice (chaos) so that peace and universal weal (cosmos) may prevail throughout this universe that God created "very good," indeed, perfect!

"The Sleeping God: An Ancient Near Eastern Motif of Divine Sovereignty" is a further exploration of the concept of the divine sovereign and the connection with creation theology. From an examination of Egyptian, Canaanite, and Mesopotamian texts, I posit the existence in the ancient Near East of a motif of "the sleeping god," associated especially with so-called *Chaoskampf* creation myths. This motif functioned as a symbol of the absolute rule of the divine king. At the conclusion of his victory over the forces of chaos, the divine creator is depicted as resting or sleeping in his newly constructed palace, the seat of his rule. The ability of the divine sovereign to sleep undisturbed signifies not only his completion of the work of creation but also his undisputed rule. Various writers of the Hebrew Bible appropriated this motif to express their belief in Yahweh as both the creator and the divine sovereign. The motif of the sleeping god is reversed in Isaiah 51:9–11 and in psalms of complaint, wherein the deity is asked to "wake up" and come to the aid of the supplicant in times of oppression. This expresses the Psalmist's faith in Yahweh—who "neither sleeps nor slumbers" (Psalm 121)—as the divine sovereign, eternally vigilant in maintaining right order in creation. Finally, in the New Testament the evangelists employed the motif, for example, in the story of Jesus sleeping during the storm at sea, as an epiphanic formula to reveal the divine authority of Jesus.

At first blush "The Reed Sea, *Requiescat in Pace*" might seem out of place in a volume about the creator and creation, given that the focus of this article is on the meaning of the phrase *yam sûp*, frequently translated as "Reed Sea," in the exodus narrative. I contend that this translation is incorrect and that the allied attempts to use this "Reed Sea" hypothesis to undergird arguments for the historicity of the exodus from Egypt are misguided. Rather than being derived from Egyptian *ṯwf(y)* "papyrus (reeds)," *sûp* is actually a by-form of Semitic *sôp*, "end" and the correct meaning of *yam sûp* is "sea of end," in other words, the sea located at the end of the earth (i.e., the created world). The *yam sûp* referred to what moderns call the Red Sea and included its extension into the oceans farther to the south. In the mythic thinking of the day, the created world was centered around the mountain where the creator had his earthly palace/temple (e.g., Jerusalem) and ended where the sea begins. This sea at the end of the world was fraught with connotations of non-creation (chaos), as evidenced by the psalm in Jonah 2, especially 2:6, and Psalm 18 (= 2 Samuel 22). The Priestly writer identified the sea of the exodus with the "Sea of End." By a deliberate theological stratagem, P portrayed the exodus out of Egypt as God's third and greatest act of creation: Israel's emergence out of the split waters of the Sea of End (= non-creation) to become the people of God was just as much an act of creation as the original act of creation in primeval times when God split "the deep" to create the heavens and the earth and populated them appropriately, and when (in act two of creation) God recreated the earth following the flood by drying it with his own breath/wind, prior to repopulating it.

In "The Covenant of Peace: A Neglected Ancient Near Eastern Motif," I isolate yet another primeval motif that biblical authors appropriated for their own theological agendas. Demonstrable from Egyptian, Canaanite, Mesopotamian, and biblical texts is a motif which may appropriately be called "the covenant of peace." It was grounded in the idea of an original offense (rebellion) against the creator that led to an attempt to annihilate humankind, sometimes by a flood, sometimes by other means. Once divine rule was (re)established, however, humankind was not only spared, but all of creation also participated in the benefits of the new and more perfect order characterized by peace and harmony between creator and creation. This new order manifested itself in the cooperation of heaven and earth in producing paradisiacal conditions. Moreover, the divine wrath was forever put aside because the deity bound himself under oath (= covenant) to establish peace and harmony on earth—an oath guaranteed by a sign, normally some natural phenomenon visible to deity and humankind alike (e.g., the rainbow in Genesis 9). In some instances this covenant of peace included a submotif of planting peace in the ground/earth, a symbol of divine mercy whereby the deity takes the initiative in bringing peace and harmony to a world disrupted by sin and violence. Biblical prophets, operating from a belief in the continuing wrath of Yahweh against his sinful people, projected the covenant of peace/the planting of peace into the eschatological age when God and humankind will truly be reconciled and peace will finally become reality on earth. With this development, the covenant of peace was transformed from primeval myth into eschatological hope.

The final article is a rapid survey of some of the major Sumerian and Akkadian mythic (literary) texts with a view to determining how ancient Mesopotamians viewed the origin of evil, especially when the evil seemed to originate from a divine source. Although the gods were generally considered benevolent towards humankind, at times the gods could appear capricious in their actions—and even hostile. As long as the divine realm was thought to consist of many gods, acts of divine benevolence and acts of divine malevolence could be resolved by attributing them to different gods. But once all authority and power were attributed to the national deity—Marduk in the case of the Neo-Babylonian Empire, or Ashur in the case of the Neo-Assyrian Empire—then both benevolence and malevolence had to be attributed to the same deity. Like biblical Job, the Babylonian author of *Ludlul Bel Nemeqi* is unable to resolve this dilemma and ends up acknowledging the inscrutability of the mind of the divine sovereign and praising Lord Bel for his infinite wisdom in creation.

This last article may serve as an appropriate conclusion to the volume, in that it reveals the theological sophistication of the ancients as they sought to understand their world as both God-given and yet beyond the capacity of humans to control completely. It may also serve as a reminder of our own modern dilemma. Despite great gains in knowledge about our "world"—whether of the micro-world of subatomic matter or the macro-world of a continuously expanding universe—we moderns seem no closer to obtaining ultimate answers to the questions posed by our own existence and the physical realm in which we live. Not only "creator" but also "creation" remain cloaked in mystery.

Chapter 1

The Ancient Near Eastern Context of the Hebrew Ideas of Creation

1. Introduction

The Hebrew Bible, at least in its origins, is a product of the ancient Near East. Although at this late date we can no longer reconstruct the long and complex history of composition of the Hebrew Bible in much detail, most scholars agree that the bulk of the Hebrew Bible was composed after the founding of the Israelite monarchy (ca. 1000 B.C.E.) but before Greek ideas began to pervade the Levant following Alexander the Great's defeat of the Persian Empire (332 B.C.E.). Prior to the Hellenistic period, most of the peoples of Mesopotamia, Syria, Canaan, and, to a lesser extent, Egypt shared a common culture and world view that has been designated as ancient Near Eastern. Within this larger culture, of course, individual tribes and nations had their own distinctive social organizations, laws, and religions that undergirded the institutions of their specific societies. Ancient Israel, the society whose poets and theologians gave us the Hebrew Bible, was no exception. Apart from their distinctive Yahwistic religion, the Israelites were part and parcel of the ancient Near Eastern culture.

To be sure, some would argue that the Yahwistic character of biblical religion is so distinctive as to set the religion of the Hebrew Bible in a category apart from the rest of the ancient Near East. It is true that Yahwism, grounded in the belief that the deity Yahweh had chosen the Israelites as his own people and had entered with them into a covenant requiring exclusive worship of this deity and adherence to a set of commands emphasizing ethical behavior, is unique in the ancient Near East. But when viewed more closely, much of the content of Yahwism, including ideas about both the divine realm and the human realm, is founded solidly on a common ancient Near Eastern world view.

But if the Israelites and their religion were not as distinctive as many have supposed, neither were Israel's neighbors as theologically unsophisticated as is often assumed, especially when synchronically compared. Just as the Israelites gradually moved away from polytheism and henotheism and increasingly toward monotheism in the first half of the first millennium B.C.E., so also at roughly that same time both in Egypt and especially in Mesopotamia there was a trend toward attributing all divine power to a single god, namely, the national deity.[1] Moreover, Israel's neighbors were not simplistic practitioners of a nature religion grounded in mere myth, as is often alleged.[2]

A case in point concerns the wide use of cult images across the ancient Near East versus the supposed aniconism in Israel. Despite explicit prohibitions in the Hebrew Bible against the making of images (Exod 20:3–4, 23; 34:17; Lev 19:4; 26:1; Deut 4:15–20; 5:8–9), both archaeology and the biblical record indicate that cult images were common in both the Northern Kingdom of Israel and the Southern Kingdom of Judah. Moreover, the frequent prophetic parodies of Israel's neighbors for making futile cult images (Isa 40:18–20; 41:6–7; 42:17; 44:9–20; 45:16, 20; 46:1–2; Jer 10:1–16) misrepresent the actual practices and beliefs of these neighbors. First-millennium B.C.E. texts from Assyria and Babylonia—roughly contemporaneous with Jeremiah and Isaiah—reveal a sophisticated theological understanding of the distinction between the (transcendent) deity per se and the cult image that served to focus the worship of the devotee in any given sanctuary. For a statue to represent the deity, the image first had to undergo a special ritual known as "mouth-washing" (Babylonian *mīs pî*) or, alternatively, "mouth-opening" (Babylonian *pit pî*) by which the material form of the statue was animated and enabled to manifest the presence of the deity. By the same token, a statue could also be decommissioned from use when it was no longer needed or was replaced by another image.[3]

A good visual example of such theological sophistication from the time of Nabu-apla-iddina, king of Babylon (ca. 887–855 B.C.E.), is the "Sun-God Tablet" (also known as "The Shamash Tablet") from Sippar.[4] The tablet's cuneiform text relates how for two centuries Sippar had been without an authentic image of the sun-god Shamash, because Shamash became angry and allowed the Sutu to ransack his temple Ebabbar and destroy its cultic image. In Nabu-apla-iddina's time, however, Shamash relented and allowed this Babylonian king to defeat the Sutu and rededicate Ebabbar. King Nabu-apla-iddina is credited with restoring an authentic golden cultic image of Shamash to the temple, modeled on a terra-cotta copy of the original cult statue of Shamash found (conveniently?) on the far side of the Euphrates by the priest Nabu-nadin-shum. Not surprisingly, the king also installed

---

1. See my *Slaying the Dragon: Mythmaking in the Biblical Tradition* (Louisville: John Knox/Westminster, 1992) 36–40; and chap. 4 below, "Divine Sovereign," pp. 96–138.

2. This view was popularized by G. Ernest Wright in *The Old Testament against Its Environment* (SBT 2; London: SCM, 1950); idem, *God Who Acts: Biblical Theology as Recital* (SBT 8; London: SCM, 1952). More recently, see John N. Oswalt, *The Bible among the Myths: Unique Revelation or Just Ancient Literature?* (Grand Rapids: Zondervan, 2009).

3. See Michael B. Dick, ed., *Born in Heaven, Made on Earth: The Making of the Cult Image in the Ancient Near East* (Winona Lake, IN: Eisenbrauns, 1999).

4. For the most recent, comprehensive treatment of this text, including photos, transliteration, translation, and commentary, see Christopher E. Woods, "The Sun-God Tablet of Nabû-apla-iddina Revisited," *JCS* 56 (2004) 23–103.

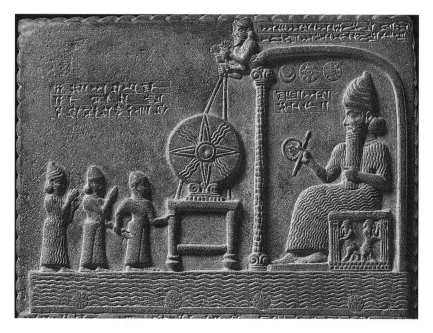

Fig. 1. "Sun-God Tablet" of Nabu-apla-iddina, from Sippar. BM 91000. © Trustees of the British Museum.

Nabu-nadin-shum as priest in charge of the temple, with extensive funds to oversee the cult.

The scene depicted at the top of the tablet (fig. 1) clearly is related to the restoration of the cult image in Sippar. Previous attempts to decode the sun-disk on the table suspended by ropes held by two adjutants perched on the temple roof have ranged from a depiction of the actual retirement of the sun-disk, a symbol that was intended to represent Shamash in the temple Ebabbar only temporarily, until a proper cult statue of the deity could be procured, to the suggestion that the suspended sun-disk represents the rising of the sun, that is, Shamash, each morning. The imagery is more theologically complex, however. The cult image(s) in the Sippar temple may not be equated in any simplistic fashion with Shamash himself—or for that matter, with other high gods. Sin, Shamash, and Ishtar are all represented through their respective symbols. True, Shamash is depicted in anthropomorphic form within the temple, but in very circumscribed fashion.

The temple is not just the earthly building in Sippar but also Shamash's cosmic or heavenly temple, as is evident from the fact that the temple rests on "the heavenly ocean," symbolized by the wavy lines underneath ("Apsu"). Shamash holds the rod-ring symbol of authority in his right hand, perhaps to confer it upon Nabu-apla-iddina, who is shown standing respectfully *outside* the temple and being ushered forward by a priest (Nabu-nadin-shum?) and a personal goddess. The priest holds Nabu-apla-iddina's wrist with one hand and with the other hand grasps the table on which rests the sun-disk, as if in a kind of ceremonial presentation of the king to Shamash (represented by his symbol, the sun-disk). All the while, the deity himself remains aloof *inside* his temple. Manifestly, this scene is designed to suggest that the deity is invisible within his heavenly temple, while what his worshipers encounter at the Sippar temple is not transcendent Shamash himself but only his external, visible symbol.

It is within ancient Near Eastern theological probing such as this that biblical ideas of creation must be examined.

The ancients, no less than many moderns, were conscious of the tenuousness of existence on earth. Accordingly, with their theories of creation they sought explanations for at least two issues: (1) how the world in which we live came to be, including not only an accounting for its physical origins but also how and why it acquired its present configuration, and (2) the origins of humankind and its relation to its "creator" and to the rest of "creation." At times, these two were treated as distinct issues; at other times, they were intimately linked.

Ancient Near Eastern peoples, despite regional differences, shared certain common assumptions about creation.[5] First, they had no concept of *creatio ex nihilo*; this idea seems to have made its appearance no earlier than the second century B.C.E. with the arrival of Hellenistic ideas in the region, after the heyday of ancient Near Eastern culture and near the end of the Hebrew Bible period. Instead, ancient Near Eastern peoples assumed either that some kind of primeval matter preexisted creation and that this primeval substance spontaneously generated into the present universe, including the gods, or that primeval matter coexisted with a divine power, with the latter transforming the former into the present universe. Second, the universe did not just happen by impersonal chance but is the result of will; that is, the universe in its present form was designed and executed by an intelligent being or beings (viz., a creator deity or deities). Indeed, in many ancient systems the world was thought to be the result of a dramatic conflict of wills, specifically, a primordial clash between a benevolent creator and a malevolent anticreator in which the creator prevailed and transformed the matter of the anticreator into the various components of the universe. Third, the product of creation is either a bipartite world (earth + the heavens) or a tripartite world (earth + the heavens + the underworld) in which humankind has an integral role. Humankind, far from being incidental within this scheme, is the focus of creation: creation theology always accounts for the existence of humankind as organized society in service of the divine creator (and other deities). Fourth, the resulting creation

---

5. See R. J. Clifford, *Creation Accounts in the Ancient Near East and in the Bible* (CBQMS 26; Washington, DC: Catholic Biblical Association, 1994) 7–10.

is tenuous in that it could go out of existence: were the creator to relax his vigilance and allow his primeval archenemy, the anticreator, to prevail, the world would revert to its former state of chaos, where meaningful life is impossible. Alternatively, humans through their own malevolence (sin) may so corrupt the creator's benevolent design that creation could be overwhelmed by chaos and thus come to an unfortunate end. Finally, to the ancients the cosmological stories they told themselves were self-evidently true. Their verisimilitude was manifest: the sun and the moon are in the sky just as the narrative proclaimed, and human society in the ancients' experience was indeed organized as the myth(s) prescribed. Discrepancies, whether between competing myths or between the myths and personal experience, were no more troublesome to the ancients than is prayer to many modern physicists.

Hebrew ideas of creation were no more unitary than those in the rest of the ancient Near East. Best known of the Hebrew creation stories, of course, is the twofold cosmogonic tale found in the opening chapters of Genesis: the account of the deity creating during six days and resting on the seventh day (Gen 1:1–2:3), and the following story of a primeval human couple in the Garden of Eden and the consequences of their eating of the forbidden fruit (Gen 2:4–3:24). This cosmogonic myth actually extends through the story of the universal flood in Genesis 6–9, to judge from similar Mesopotamian stories. Accordingly, because of limitations of space, part four of this essay will focus for the most part on Genesis 1–9 as the *locus classicus* for biblical notions of creation.

But other creation motifs can be found scattered throughout the Hebrew Bible, in various genres and in different books, from narrative books such as Exodus and Chronicles, to hymns and laments in the Psalter, to prophetic oracles in Amos and in Isaiah, to the poetic wisdom texts of Job and Proverbs. While we cannot attend to these in detail here, we will look briefly at a few examples of the use of creation motifs in other texts beyond Genesis.

As already noted, biblical ideas of creation are grounded in the cultural context of the ancient Near East, including mythic conceptions of the origins of humankind and the world that humankind inhabits. For this reason, we continue our study, in parts 2–4, with surveys of extrabiblical ideas of creation in various regions of the ancient Near East—namely, Egypt, Mesopotamia, and Canaan.

2. Egyptian Ideas of Creation[6]

Egypt, strictly speaking, was not part of the ancient Near East. But although Egypt is located on the continent of Africa and its language is

---

6. For further detail, see Jacobus van Dijk, "Myth and Mythmaking in Ancient Egypt," *CANE* 3.1697–1709.

non-Semitic, it is associated with the ancient Near East because frequently throughout its long history it attempted to extend its sway over regions to the east and northeast, with the result that its culture was greatly influenced by contact with its Asiatic neighbors, and vice versa.

In Egypt, speculation about the origins of the cosmos was not systematic. Moreover, stories changed with time and also varied from district to district. Sometimes differing explanations existed side by side. The Egyptians, like the Hebrews, were fond of deriving the origins of names, institutions, and objects through paronomasia, or punning. Despite their popularity, these puns were often far from the mark linguistically and historically. Mostly, however, explanations of the origins of the cosmos were theological: speculation centering around the creative activity of a god or gods in primordial time.

There are no extant cosmogonies from ancient Egypt; indeed, it is doubtful that any true cosmogonies were ever written. Especially in the early periods, myths were transmitted orally. Knowledge of the myths was the secret domain of specialized priests, who employed their esoteric knowledge for "practical" purposes such as healing, rituals, and funerary preparations. Reference to myths is mostly by allusion within texts of various kinds, especially the pyramid texts of the Old Kingdom (ca. 2675–2130 B.C.E.), the coffin texts of the Middle Kingdom (ca. 1980–1630 B.C.E.), and the Book of the Dead in the New Kingdom (ca. 1539–1075 B.C.E.), all of which were designed to assist the dead to make a successful transition into the next life. Our knowledge of ancient Egyptian myths is, therefore, less direct than we wish. For example, the best known myth, that of Seth and Osiris, was first written down only in the second century C.E. by Plutarch, who as a Greek outsider interpreted the myth for a non-Egyptian audience. Nevertheless, even such late sources seem to be mostly reliable; for example, the essential accuracy of Plutarch's account of the myth of Seth and Osiris seems to be confirmed by corresponding allusions to the myth in native Egyptian texts from much earlier periods.

2.1 Standard Egyptian Cosmology

Speculation about creation was carried on at all the major religious centers of Egypt, especially at Heliopolis, Memphis, Hermopolis, and Thebes. These cities vied with each other to be considered the place at which creation began, usually by claiming for their local deities the honor of being the primeval deity who was responsible for all of creation. Though the theologies developed at these regional centers were in competition with one another, there is nonetheless a fundamental unity in Egyptian thought that transcended regional differences. Basic to the Egyptian world view was a concept of the one and the many: all the many beings that constitute the divine and the human realms, including the physical world surrounding us, are diverse manifestations of one primordial substance. This world view seems to have been most fully articulated at Heliopolis, with other religious centers adding and adapting to reflect local interests rather than developing completely new systems.

Heliopolitan theology centered round the Ennead, a self-generated cluster of nine original deities: Atum, Shu and Tefnut, Geb and Nut, Osiris, Isis, Seth, and Nephthys. Of these, Atum ("He who makes complete") was considered the primeval creator—the other eight deities being emanations from this august, self-evolving god. But even before that, in the beginning there was only an undifferentiated watery substance known as Nun (primeval abyss). Although Nun was sometimes personified as a god, Nun seems more properly described as a chaotic condition associated with non-creation, a state of non-being devoid of elements necessary for life. In some sense Atum at this stage was identical with Nun, floating in this primeval abyss "in his egg,"[7] that is, he was as yet only inchoate being: inert, unconscious, unformed, but possessing a hidden potential for development.

At some point Atum began to evolve and to differentiate himself. He emerged from his watery incubation onto a primeval mound, which the Egyptians identified as a prototypical pyramid, and there he began a process of self-development, or creation. He first generated the Ennead, and then the diversity of the world as we experience it, including not only the natural elements but also social institutions and moral laws.

Atum is said to have created by masturbating and swallowing his own semen, that is, self-impregnation, thereby producing life-forces in complementary pairs.[8] He first produced Shu and Shu's sister Tefnut; from these two were born female Nut (Sky) and the male Geb (Earth) to form boundaries between the primeval abyss and the "world." (The genders of these deities are the reverse of most cultural stereotypes concerning the genders of the natural elements because in Egypt the land was fertilized not by rain but by the annual flooding of the Nile.) In the empty space between, Atum placed Shu (Atmosphere) to support the sky. Atum himself then assumed the form of his "Sole Eye," that is to say, he manifested himself as the sun-god Re. Life and Order followed in short order. Order, or Maat ($m^{\jmath}t$), was a particularly important element of creation, as it represents the eternal, divine order thought to undergird every aspect of creation, including not only what we would call the natural order but also organized human society and the norms for correct human behavior. Maat is the constant companion of Re (in some versions, the daughter of Re), helping him to establish and maintain truth, justice, and moral integrity in the world. Thus, in the midst of the primeval abyss Atum created by stages a self-contained world as a kind of protective "life bubble" within which creation could develop and wherein meaningful life could be sustained.

---

7. From Coffin Texts Spell 714, trans. James P. Allen, *COS* 1:2 (p. 6).
8. From Pyramid Texts Spell 527, trans. James P. Allen, *COS* 1:3 (p. 7).

Fig. 2. In this Egyptian conception of the world, the male earth Geb reclines in horizontal position as the ground. Arched above Geb is the female sky goddess Nut; in some representations Nut's body is covered with stars. In the space between Geb and Nut, and supporting Nut, stands the atmosphere god Shu; assisting Shu are two helper deities. Drawing by the author of a detail from the Greenfield Papyrus (Book of the Dead), Sheet 87. BM 10554.87.

Because of the centrality of this mythic world view for practically every aspect of ancient Egyptian life, it is a frequent motif in Egyptian iconography (see fig. 2). In such depictions, the god Geb lies horizontally to represent the earth. Poised vault-like above Geb is the goddess Nut (Sky), resting on tiptoes and fingertips, "with her rear in the east and her head in the west."[9] Sometimes the image of Nut as sky is carried logically further by painting stars, visible by night, over her whole body (fig. 5); in the waters above or beyond Nut there is no light, only utter darkness. The god Shu (Atmosphere) fills the space between Geb and Nut and stands supporting Nut.

Atum then manifested himself as the sun-god Re, who rises and sets in an eternally recurrent cycle. Atum-Re symbolized more than light and warmth, however. As the perpetually rising and setting sun, Re represented Atum's twin attributes of eternal Sameness and eternal Recurrence. By day, Re emerged as a distinct entity and ruled the sky, symbolizing the multiplicity of being in creation. By night, however, Re was thought to become one

---

9. From the "Book of Nut," trans. James P. Allen, *COS* 1:1 (pp. 5–6).

with Osiris, the king of the Duat (the realm of the dead, usually thought to be in the underworld, and in some aspects similar to Nun); that is to say, by night Re merged back into primordial undifferentiated sameness. In order for the primeval event of creation to continue on into the future, Re had to engage his archenemy, Apophis (the dragon of Darkness), each night in battle so that he could emerge victorious the next morning. Pictographically, Egyptian artists depicted this eternally recurrent struggle of Re in several ways: as the winged sun-disk emerging newly born each morning in the east from the vulva of Nut (or at her feet, the eastern horizon) only to be swallowed by her again each evening (figs. 3, 4), or as the god Re riding his bark from east to west across the primeval waters above the sky (fig. 5). Alternatively, since the sun god was particularly vulnerable to the power of the dragon Apophis as he entered the realm of darkness at evening, in some traditions Re was said to be assisted in this eternal struggle against Apophis by the god Seth, who spears the dragon of darkness (fig. 6).[10] In each instance, the intent is to depict certitude that the delicate world order achieved primevally will continue in perpetuity.

In the Egyptian world view, creation was tenuous also in the sense that, were the gods to fail in their designated activities, the primordial waters of Nun would flood their living space and destroy all creation.

------

10. See also the text "The Repulsing of the Dragon," trans. Robert K. Ritner, *COS* 1:21 (p. 32).

Fig. 3. The sky-goddess Nut gives birth to the sun Re each day. The disk at her vulva is the morning sun; the disk at her neck is the evening sun about to be swallowed up again. The disk at Nut's feet represents the sun rising in the east at dawn. Underside of lid of sarcophagus of Ankhnesneferibra, found at Deir el-Medina (Thebes). BM EA32 (Additional IDs: ES.32; AN1106944001). © Trustees of the British Museum.

*Fig. 4. Nut (Sky) above and
Earth below together form
a barrier to keep chaotic
waters (symbolized by
wavy lines) from invading
the living space between
them. The sun, born each
morning from the vulva of
Nut and swallowed again
each evening, illuminates
and warms this living space,
at the center of which is the
deity's temple situated in the
Nile Valley. Painted relief,
temple at Dendera, 1st–2nd
century* C.E. *Drawing by
O. Keel,* The Symbolism
of the Biblical World, *42
fig. 36; used with permission.*

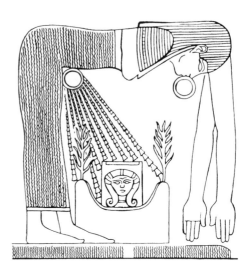

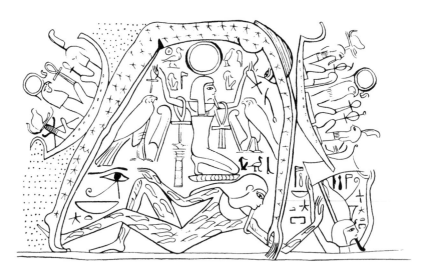

*Fig. 5. The sun-god Re traverses the heavens daily in an invisible boat. The sky
forms a barrier between the waters above the heavens and the waters below the
earth. Papyrus, New Kingdom. Louvre. Drawing by H. Keel-Leu, in O. Keel,* The
Symbolism of the Biblical World, *36 fig. 32; used with permission.*

Although itself quite late, a Roman-period painting from a temple at Dendera depicts well the Egyptians' view of the fragility of the "life bubble"
within which they lived and at the same time their confidence in the divine

Fig. 6. The sun-god Re in his boat, pulled by helpful jackal and cobra demons, traversing the underworld sea by night. The god Seth wards off the dragon Apophis, who threatens Re by night. Papyrus of Heruben, 21st Dynasty. Egyptian Museum, Cairo. Drawing by H. Keel-Leu, The Symbolism of the Biblical World, *55 fig. 55; used with permission.*

to maintain the world order (fig. 4). True to Egyptian psychology, Egypt (symbolized by the temple in the central valley) is situated at the center of the world, with mountains at both the eastern and western horizons. Living in the middle of a desert, the Egyptians were quite conscious of the tenuousness of their world; the wavy lines around the fringes (below and on the body of Nut) symbolize the chaotic waters of Nun, those ever-present destructive forces which, unless tamed, would certainly engulf creation and bring it to an end. Egypt depended for its economy upon the vivifying waters of the Nile and the fertile soil deposited by its annual flooding. Without the Nile, whose waters were thought to originate in upper Egypt by welling up from the flood under the earth, Egypt would be indistinguishable from the desert to the east and to the west, where human existence is nearly impossible to sustain. The Egyptians attributed their good fortune to divine benevolence—thus the temple in the center of the valley. A temple was less a place of worship than a palace from which the deity ruled and maintained right order in the world. In a real sense, a temple with its various parts was thought of as a microcosm. Accordingly, the temple in this scene witnesses to the Egyptian belief that their world would continue even in the face of such powerful cosmic threats. Re's life-sustaining morning rays shining forth over Egypt is similarly expressive of that confidence.

This basic Heliopolitan cosmology was modified in different ways by Memphite, Hermopolitan, and Theban theologians, sometimes by supplementation, sometimes by substitution.

Over time, theologians at Memphis began to claim for their deity Ptah, revered as the patron of sculptors and artisans, the honor of the original primeval deity. During the Middle Kingdom, the creative role of Ptah was clearly secondary to that of Atum. But by the New Kingdom, the Ptah tradition at Memphis had evolved into a full cosmological system in its own right by making Ptah to be "the father of the gods, Tatenen, eldest of the originals." Nothing came into being without him, for he determined all that is.[11] According to the "Memphite Theology," it was Ptah "who gave life to all the [other gods]" and "who creates what exists." He was the one who emerged unbegotten from the primeval waters as the great creator. Without any evolution, he appeared as Tatenen, or the primeval mound in the midst of the Nun. Then, in what may be a kind of one-upmanship on the Heliopolitan Atum who created by masturbation and self-impregnation, it is claimed that the craftsman Ptah appropriately created with "his heart" and "his lips," that is, what he conceived mentally he was able to translate into reality by fiat: with Ptah "the tongue . . . repeats what the heart plans."[12]

At Hermopolis, theologians supplemented the Heliopolitan system by speculating on the undifferentiated state of the universe before the birth of the sun, that is, the chaotic conditions before creation. They subdivided the primeval waters into four aspects, each of which was represented by a divine couple: Nun and his female partner Naunet (primordial abyss), Huh and his partner Hauhet (infinity), Kuk and Kauket (darkness), and Amun and Amaunet (concealed dynamism). From these eight gods, the Ogdoad as they were known, Atum was born and eventually self-evolved from the cosmic egg.

During the New Kingdom, Amun emerged as the great state god of the Egyptian empire. At Thebes especially, Amun, whose name means "the Hidden," was promoted as the primeval deity, the creator and ruler of all. Theban theologians attempted to reconcile this new theology with the theologies of Heliopolis, Memphis, and Hermopolis by attributing to Amun the combined functions of Atum-Re, Ptah, and the Ogdoad. The (Hermopolitan) Ogdoad, they said, was Amun's first evolution; (Memphite) Ptah is his body, in which he emerged on the primeval mound; and (Heliopolitan) Re, the sun, is his face, by which he manifests himself to millions. As Amun-Re, he is at once eternal recurrence (the rebirth of the sun each day sustaining the millions) and eternal sameness (reuniting with Osiris in the Underworld by night). Indeed, speculation on Amun-Re as the supreme and universal deity brought Egyptian theology during the New Kingdom very close to monotheism, though it never took the step of denying the existence of other gods. (Ironically, this theological position was not far from that of the prior short-lived Amarna period, when, in the mid-fourteenth century B.C.E., the "heretical" king Akhenaten caused an uproar among Egyptian intellectuals, scribes, priests, and courtiers, by promoting the wor-

---

11. From the Berlin "Hymn to Ptah," trans. James P. Allen, *COS* 1:14 (pp. 20–21).
12. From the "Memphite Theology," trans. James P. Allen, *COS* 1:15 (pp. 21–23).

ship of benign Aten, a form of the solar god, as the universal and exclusive deity.)[13]

2.2 The Creation of Humankind

First, it must be said that in the Egyptian view, the king, or pharaoh as he was called, belonged less to the realm of human beings than to the realm of the gods, because he was thought to be the incarnation of the chief god of Egypt. Throughout most of Egyptian history, this meant that the Egyptian monarch was promoted as a living manifestation of the god Horus, a form of the sun god; alternatively, the king was identified with the Heliopolitan solar deity, either as Re or as the son of Re. One papyrus contains a claim that the sun god impregnated the wife of the high priest of Heliopolis, giving birth to three future pharaohs of Dynasty V.[14] Another tradition has the divine craftsman Ptah fashioning the body of Pharaoh Rameses II out of electrum and his limbs out of copper and iron. Still other propaganda portrayed kings as born in various ways of the union of the chief god and goddess; Isis, the wife of Osiris and mother of Horus, may be depicted as holding the royal heir in her lap or nursing him at her breast. As the manifestation of the solar deity, the Egyptian king was responsible for maintaining good order in the universe—not merely justice and moral order in the land, but also the very order of the physical world. Egyptian artists depicted this cosmic function of the king by having the royal palace and the royal falcon fill the space below the heavens, or even by the king actually supporting the heavens—and by implication, the whole universe (fig. 7).[15] At death, the king was thought to become Osiris in the Under-world, and as deified royal ancestor he served as legitimator of subsequent pharaohs, thereby continuing his role of stabilizing world order.

The creation of humankind per se is but rarely mentioned in Egyptian cosmological texts. Although seldom stated, the creation of humankind was assumed to be just a part of the process by which creation unfolded as the self-evolution of the primeval god. A notable exception is Spell

---

13. On the attempt to rationalize Egypt's many gods into a single matrix, a process already under way at least two centuries before the Amarna revolution and which continued unimpeded after Akhenaten's failed initiative, see J. Assmann, *Egyptian Solar Religion in the New Kindgom: Re, Amun and the Crisis of Polytheism* (trans. A. Alcock; London: Kegan Paul, 1995), esp. pp. 102–89. For initial developments of the solar cult at the beginning of Amenhotep IV's reign, see William J. Murnane, "Observations on Pre-Amarna Theology during the Earliest Reign of Amenhotep IV," in *Gold of Praise: Studies on Ancient Egypt in Honor of Edward F. Wente* (ed. Emily Teeter and John A. Larson; Studies in Ancient Oriental Civilization 58; Chicago: Oriental Institute, 1999) 303–16.

14. George Hart, *A Dictionary of Egyptian Gods and Goddesses* (London: Routledge, 1986) 170.

15. This theme is illustrated also on a First Dynasty ivory comb from Abydos, reproduced in O. Keel, *Symbolism of the Biblical World*, fig. 19 on p. 27, in which the function of the falcon-god Re, ruling from his boat above the sky, is duplicated beneath the sky in the figure of the king, also depicted in the form of a falcon.

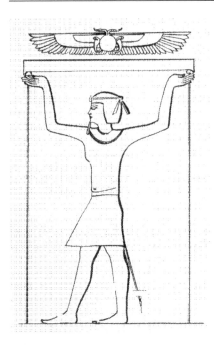

Fig. 7. Symbolic of his function of maintaining universal order, the king of Egypt holds up the sky, shown twice: once as a flat roof and once as the sun with wings. Relief at Edfu. Drawing by H. Keel-Leu, in O. Keel, The Symbolism of the Biblical World, *28 fig. 21; used with permission.*

1130 of the Coffin Texts, which explains the creation of human-kind by way of an "etymological" explanation based on the word for humankind: "humans" (*rmṯ*) are "tears" (*rmyt*) which flowed from the creator's eye.[16] The same text is also exceptional in spelling out that the norms for human behavior and social organization likewise were established at creation. No reason is given for the tears of the creator; however, a late text from the fourth century B.C.E. but based on earlier sources, hints that the tears from the creator's eye may have been caused by jealousy when the eye was replaced by another eye; a solution to the conflict was found by Atum promoting the original eye to be his uraeus on his forehead.[17]

As might be expected, Memphite theologians ascribed all of creation—"all the gods, all people, all animals, and all crawling things that live"—to Ptah, who created them by divine fiat. Upon completion of the totality of creation, Ptah, similar to God in Genesis 2:2, rested: "So has Ptah come to rest after his making everything and every divine speech as well. . . ."[18]

At Elephantine, at the boundaries of Upper Egypt, the god Khnum was believed to have fashioned gods, humankind, cattle, birds, and fish on a potter's wheel (fig. 8). Iconographically, Khnum is sometimes depicted as fashioning humans out of clay at the behest of the creator deity. Apparently, Khnum would then breathe life, or "health," into the molded figure to make it human, as in the case of the first three kings of the fifth dynasty,

---

16. "I made the gods evolve from my sweat, while people are from the tears of my Eye." Translation by James P. Allen, *COS* 1:17 (p. 27).

17. From Papyrus Bremner-Rhind, trans. James P. Allen, *COS* 1:9 (pp. 14–15).

18. From the "Memphite Theology," trans. James P. Allen, *COS* 1:15 (pp. 21–23).

according to the Westcar Papyrus.[19] (Patently, this Elephantine
theology has reflexes in the biblical story in Genesis 2, wherein
Yahweh God is said to have created humankind by molding clay
and then breathing life into it.)

2.3 The Rebellion of Humankind

Humans were supposed to conduct themselves in accordance
with the order (maat) established
in the beginning. Human misdeeds, or sin—of which social in-
equality is a prime example—were
attributed to human failing: "I
have made every person like his
fellow. I did not decree that they
do disorder; it is their (own) hearts
that break what I said."[20]

The motif of a universal human
rebellion against the deity also
appears in Egyptian theology but

*Fig. 8. At Elephantine the ram-headed
god Khnum was said to fashion all things
on a potter's wheel; here he is molding
the god Ihy. Mammisis of Nectanebo,
Dendera, Dyn. XXX. Drawing by the
author.*

mostly by allusion, so that the underlying myth itself cannot be reconstructed. The 175th chapter of the Book of the Dead makes reference to
this motif within the context of a spell designed to aid the deceased.[21] For
the deceased to enter the Duat, or Underworld, they first had to be judged
to determine whether they had lived their lives according to the norms of
maat (fig. 9). One of the duties of the divine scribe Thoth was to tally the
deeds of each person so that Osiris, king of the Underworld, could judge
their worthiness. Those found worthy were admitted into Osiris's presence
to enjoy a blessed afterlife; indeed, they became Osiris by becoming one
with the ruler of the Underworld. (In the Old Kingdom, this privilege was
restricted to the king: while alive the pharaoh was identified with Horus,

---

19. See Hart, *A Dictionary of Egyptian Gods and Goddess*, 111–12. The motif of creation
of all things on the potter's wheel could also be linked to other motifs such as the emergence of the solar deity from the primeval waters of Nun and his rebirth each morning
after overcoming Apophis; see Peter F. Dorman, "Creation on the Potter's Wheel at the
Eastern Horizon of Heaven," in *Gold of Praise: Studies on Ancient Egypt in Honor of Edward
F. Wente* (ed. Emily Teeter and John A. Larson; Studies in Ancient Oriental Civilization 58;
Chicago: Oriental Institute, 1999) 83–99.

20. From Coffin Texts Spell 1130, trans. James P. Allen, *COS* 1:17 (pp. 26–27).

21. Book of the Dead 175, trans. Robert K. Ritner, *COS* 1:18 (pp. 27–30).

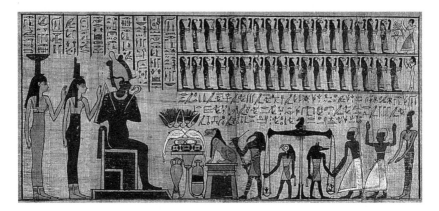

Fig. 9. Weighing of the heart. At death, each individual undergoes judgment before Osiris, king of the Underworld (seated at the left, wearing an "atef" crown, with the goddesses Isis and Nephthys standing behind him). The scene is dominated by Maat, right order, whose symbol is a feather. The goddess Maat (at far right with her head replaced by her characteristic feather) presents the deceased Hor for judgment. Above is a court of thirty-five gods, each holding a feather of Maat, serving as judges to determine the condition of the deceased's "heart" (ba). In the center, jackal-headed Anubis and falcon-headed Horus weigh the deceased's heart in the balance, normally against Maat (symbolized by a feather, but here replaced by a tiny black figure). Thoth, guardian of truth, sits atop the scale in his baboon form and also stands in his ibis form before Osiris at the left (holding a scribe's palette and reed brush) recording the calculations of the weighing of the heart. If judged worthy, the deceased is admitted into the blessed presence of Osiris, but failing the test, is immediately swallowed up by the ferocious Devourer (seated on table in the center). BM 10479,6. © Trustees of the British Museum.

son of Osiris; in death the pharaoh was thought to become Osiris. In later periods, with the gradual democratization of religion, every person was thought capable of becoming an Osiris.) Meanwhile, the unworthy suffered a fate worse than death: "the second death." As punishment for misdeeds, the "hearts" of criminals were immediately devoured at judgment by a fearsome crocodile-headed "devourer," while their souls and bodies were given over as food for the ferocious demons that dwelt in the twelve western caverns of the Underworld.[22] The Book of the Dead contained spells or magical formulae that the deceased could use to negotiate safely the perilous gates into the Underworld.

---

22. Similar ideas concerning survival after death of the individual human (soul) and subsequent reward or punishment in an afterlife, dependent upon one's merits or demerits during life, did not develop in Israel until much later, toward the close of the biblical period. Such ideas seem not to have developed at all in Mesopotamia.

Utilizing the spell in chapter 175 of the Book of the Dead, the deceased was prompted to protest his or her innocence, manifestly in an attempt to gain a favorable accounting from Thoth at judgment. At the same time, the deceased was instructed to identify with the creator Atum's dismay over a primeval rebellion of humankind:

> "O, Thoth, what is it that has happened through the children of Nut? They have made war. They have raised disturbance. When they committed evil, then they created rebellion. When they committed slaughter, then they created imprisonment. Indeed, they have converted what was great into what was small in all that I have done."

To this, Thoth suggests that the appropriate response would be for the creator to shorten the life spans of the guilty, and perhaps of all humankind: "Curtail their years, hasten their months, since they have betrayed . . . all that you have done." The spell goes on to suggest that at one point in the future, the whole of creation will revert to original chaos, seemingly as a result of human wickedness: "Then I will destroy all that I have made. This land will return into the Abyss, into the flood as in its former state"— though the innocent deceased person is promised a lifetime of millions of years with Osiris. (Perhaps in view here is a cosmic "flood" analogous to the one posited by the Priestly Writer in Genesis 6–9, which nearly wiped out humankind.)

The motif of a universal human rebellion is also found in "The Book of the Cow of Heaven."[23] Inscribed in several New Kingdom royal tombs, the myth is named after an event in the second part: when the god Re grew old and tired of governing, he commanded the goddess Hathor to turn herself into a cow so that he might retire by sitting on her back, after turning the government over to other deities such as the moon god. The myth serves as an explanation for such natural phenomena as the alternating "rule" by the sun and the moon, and the annual flooding of the Nile upon which the economy of Egypt depended. But it is the first part of the myth that interests us here.

The myth opens with the statement that Re, "king of men and the gods together," having grown old, was faced with a plot against him by humankind. Re summoned his court for advice. The decision was taken to send Re's Eye down as Hathor to smite the humans. "After slaying humankind in the desert"—or most of them— the gloating goddess interrupted her blood bath to report her initial success, intending to return the following day to complete the annihilation of humankind. At this point Re apparently relented, alarmed by the prospect that humankind would be completely eradicated, and set about finding a way to save a remnant of humankind. He quickly dispatched messengers to gather red ochre from distant upper Egypt. The red ochre was then mixed with fresh beer. Shortly before dawn

---

23. The Destruction of Mankind, trans. Miriam Lichtheim, *COS* 1:24 (pp. 36–37).

the fields were flooded "three palms deep" with the liquid. When Hathor arrived early the next morning to continue her slaughter, she mistook the red beer for human blood and, exultant, began to drink deeply of the draft. Thus inebriated, Hathor apparently failed in her mission and some humans escaped, it would appear, to repopulate the earth. Despite many differences, the tale bears some obvious similarities to the biblical story of the flood in Genesis 6–9, in that a guilty humankind is nearly wiped off the face of the earth but then spared by a relenting deity.[24]

3. Mesopotamian Ideas of Creation

Mesopotamia, with a history of creation traditions of comparable length to that of Egypt, has preserved for us much less in the way of pictographic representations but has bequeathed us a much richer literary tradition in both the Sumerian and the Akkadian languages. Though they overlap, generally speaking, the Sumerian tradition is earlier (floruit ca. 2500–1600 B.C.E.) and the Akkadian tradition later (floruit ca. 1800–500 B.C.E.). Oftentimes, Akkadian poets have taken over earlier Sumerian motifs and expanded them into full epic traditions.

3.1 Sumerian Foundations

Sumerian cosmology is still a matter of dispute, mostly because the Sumerian language is still not perfectly understood. Unlike Akkadian, which belongs to the well-known Semitic family of languages, Sumerian belongs to no known language group. Sumerologists are thus dependent upon Sumerian-Akkadian bilingual word lists—an early form of a foreign language dictionary—and upon context for deciphering Sumerian. The difficulties of interpretation of Sumerian are further compounded by the fragmentary condition of many of the clay tablets on which these cuneiform texts were inscribed; seldom are we fortunate to have a completely preserved text. As a result, specialists not infrequently find themselves in disagreement with one another not only over the interpretation of a given Sumerian myth, but even over its reading.

Sumerian economy was based upon agricultural production made possible by irrigation from the Tigris and Euphrates rivers, supplemented by pastoral production (mainly sheep). The city-states that developed along the two rivers were joined in a loose federation owing to the need for cooperation in the digging and maintenance of the system of irrigation canals on which the whole region depended. Without water, the fertile land would be no different from the nearby desert lands.

Despite the great variety of Sumerian cosmological narratives, nearly all reflect the world view of their authors living on the fringes of the desert. Some assume the preexistence of the earth, but as a wasteland. "Creation"

---

24. See further Bernard F. Batto, "The Covenant of Peace: A Neglected Ancient Near Eastern Motif," *CBQ* 49 (1987) 187–211; reprinted in this volume as chap. 7.

was the process by which water was added to this barren desert, turning it into fertile fields. At the center of such tales is Enki, the male god personifying sweet (i.e., nonsalty) underground water, who makes the land fecund through the Tigris and Euphrates rivers. "Enki and Ninhursag" contains just such a cosmological motif: Enki successively impregnates Ninhursag and her daughters, from which unions are born various elements of the world. As indicated by Ninhursag's name, which means "Lady of the mountains," Ninhursag and her daughters represent the dry highlands made fertile by irrigation. Related to this motif are texts that suggest that animals and humans originally emerged from the ground like sprouting plants.

Other texts, perhaps in acknowledgment of the vivifying power of rain, posit that earth was made fertile by a marriage between earth (Ki) and heaven (An), as for example in the introductory portion of the disputation between Tree and Reed:

> The Great Foundation made herself resplendent, her body flowered joyously.
> Vast Earth adorned her body with precious metal and lapis lazuli. . . .
> Pure Earth made herself verdant in a clean place for pure An.
> An, high Heaven, consummated marriage with vast Earth,
> He implanted the seed . . .
> Earth gave herself to the happy birth of the plants of life.
> Earth joyously produced abundance; she exuded wine and
> honey. . . .[25]

Still other texts attempt to delve even deeper into the cosmological mystery by positing a primordial time before earth and heaven were distinct. In this scheme, creation began when Enlil, the chief god of the Sumerians, sundered primeval matter in two to make a bipartite world:

> Enlil, to bring forth the seed of the land from the ground,
> Hastened to separate heaven from earth,
> Hastened to separate earth from heaven.[26]

Frequently, Sumerian cosmological speculation found its way into the genre of entertaining, instructional disputations over the relative value of specific phenomena that figured prominently in their world view, e.g., cereals versus sheep (the two foundations of Sumerian economy), reeds versus trees (important building materials), hoes versus plows (principal agricultural implements), or summer versus winter (the two principal seasons of the region). Such disputations posit that the debate between the two disputants dates from the time of creation itself, or, as the Sumerians preferred to express it, before anything existed. A prime example of the genre is the disputation between "Ewe and Wheat":

---

25. R. J. Clifford, *Creation Accounts in the Ancient Near East and in the Bible*, 26.

26. Trans. W. G. Lambert, "Myth and Mythmaking in Sumer and Akkad," *CANE* 3.1828.

When upon the Hill of Heaven and Earth
An ("Heaven," father of the gods) had spawned the divine Godlings,—
Since godly Wheat had not been spawned or created with them,
Nor had the yarn of the godly Weaver been fashioned in the Land,
Nor had the loom of the godly Weaver even been pegged out,
For Ewe had not yet appeared, nor were there numerous lambs,
And there was as yet no goat, nor numerous kids—
The very names of Wheat, the holy blade, and of Ewe
Were yet unknown to the Godlings and the greater Divinities. . . .
The godly Weaver not having been born, no royal cap was worn;
Lord herald, the precious lord, had not been born;
Shakan (god of the wild animals) did not go out to the arid lands.
The people of those distant days
Knew not bread to eat,
They knew not cloth to wear;
They went about in the Land with naked limbs
Eating grass with their mouths like sheep,
And drinking water from the ditches.
At that time, at the birthplace of the Gods,
In their time, the Holy Hill, they (the gods) fashioned Ewe and
Wheat. . . .[27]

The predications of nonexistence here, as elsewhere in Mesopotamian literature, were intended to express the inchoate conditions prior to the creation of the world with its ordered society. The gods themselves have not been fully formed, certainly not those patron gods thought to represent the effective power behind various earthly phenomena. In the Sumerian view, creation consisted as much in organizing the world and its denizens into a civilized society as in bringing them into existence. More specifically, in ethnocentric fashion the Sumerians saw their own society as the apex of creation: when the gods created the world and organized humankind into various peoples, the gods placed the "black-headed people" (the Sumerians' self-designation) at the center of the world and gifted them with a superior culture based on divine wisdom.

In addition to being the personification of fecund waters, Enki was also honored as the god of wisdom and the patron of humans. The archaic and partially incomprehensible myth *Enki and Ninmah*[28] tells of a primeval time before the creation of humankind when the senior gods made the minor gods do the work of digging the canals and irrigating the fields—the gods being conceived anthropomorphically as organized in a hierarchical society much like the Sumerians themselves. Feeling oppressed and excluded from the benefits of divinity, the minor gods revolted against Enki, who lay resting in his palace bed, and they demanded relief from their toil.

27. Trans. H. L. J. Vanstiphout, "The Disputation Between Ewe and Wheat," *COS* 1:180 (p. 575).
28. A translation by J. Klein is available in *COS* 1:159 (pp. 516–18).

Acceding to the demands of the minor gods, wise Enki, together with his mother (the mother goddess), fashioned humankind out of clay to serve as substitute laborers for the gods.

The second half of the myth seems somewhat disjointed from the first half in that Ninmah, who played only a minor role in assisting Enki with the creation of the substitute human laborers, now emerges as a major character. She challenges Enki to a contest in which the two seemingly compete to make the best human prototype. The results are pathetic, although in each case Enki manages to salvage the situation by finding a position within human society for each of the deformed or crippled "humans." Finally, Enki makes what at first sight appears to be the most defective of all, but in actuality proves to be the best of all: a human baby! The point of the myth seems to be that it took the inexperienced gods several attempts at creating before they finally came up with a true human: a self-propagating creature that goes through all the stages of life, from birth at infancy to death in old age.

A second feature of the myth is its insistence upon a theme that runs through all of Mesopotamian theology: humans were created to be the servants of the gods. Although apotheosized humans do appear occasionally in Mesopotamian literature, the common belief was that even kings—indeed, especially kings—were charged with the care and the provisioning of the gods. One of the prime obligations of humankind was to provide for the gods so that the latter could enjoy a life of leisure appropriate to their divinity.

Many of the motifs of Sumerian myths were taken over and expanded in Akkadian literature, through which they had an indirect influence upon Hebrew notions of creation. But one biblical motif that did not originate in Sumerian myth is the paradise motif. Contrary to an oft-repeated misconception, there was no "paradisiacal" period in Sumerian mythology. Rather than a golden age at the beginning, Sumerians thought of human history as a *progression* from an original primitive beginning to its zenith in a glorious age of civilization—which contemporary Sumerian society was thought to exemplify par excellence. As evidenced in "Ewe and Wheat," quoted above, Sumerians thought the original condition of humankind was one in which humans, pathetically, were scarcely distinguishable from animals: roaming the steppe naked because they didn't know how to make cloth, grazing grass in the plains and drinking water from the watering hole like sheep because they didn't know to make agricultural implements or even to use their hands. No Sumerian would ever have thought of that humble period of origins as paradisiacal.[29]

---

29. See Bernard F. Batto, "Paradise Reexamined," in *The Biblical Canon in Comparative Perspective* (ed. K. Lawson Younger, Jr., William W. Hallo, and Bernard F. Batto; Scripture in Context 4; Lewiston, NY: Edwin Mellen, 1991) 33–66; reprinted in this volume as chap. 2.

3.2 Akkadian Expansions

Beginning around 1900 B.C.E., power in Mesopotamia shifted from Sumer in the south to various Amorite dynasties farther to the north and west. By ca. 1760 B.C.E., Hammurapi of Babylon had gained hegemony over major portions of Mesopotamia. This political vigor was matched by an equally vigorous literary production in Akkadian, the language of the new Amorite rulers. Among the major compositions of the Old Babylonian period (ca. 1900–1600 B.C.E.) were the myth *Atrahasis* and the epic *Gilgamesh*. In each case the authors incorporated older Sumerian motifs, but the new compositions were innovative for the depth in exploration of philosophical issues and the literary skill with which old motifs were combined and new themes sustained at length.

Atrahasis[30] continues the theme of humans created to be substitute workers for the gods, noted already in *Enki and Ninmah*. But in *Atrahasis* the theme was expanded in various ways, including linking it with the story of a universal flood, to make it the most ambitious of Mesopotamian creation stories to that point. According to this new myth, in the beginning, before there were any humans, the senior gods forced the minor gods to labor at digging the irrigation canals and at plowing the fields. Finding themselves deprived of essential prerogatives for divinities, the minor gods revolted and raised such a din that Enlil, the ruling deity, was deprived of his sleep until wise Ea, the Akkadian version of Enki, proposed a solution that both preserved the authority of the divine sovereign and satisfied the minor deities. The ringleader of the rebel gods was slain and from his blood mixed with clay Ea fashioned seven pairs of primeval humans (*lullû*) to do the work for the gods. The creating gods failed to anticipate a serious problem, however. They did not think to provide for any natural means of death for these first human prototypes—though, like the gods themselves, they could be killed by unnatural means. Accordingly, as primeval humankind reproduced and multiplied, so the noise of their outcry increased, once again robbing Enlil of his rest, just as previously with the rebel gods. Enlil attempted to diminish the numbers of the humans by successive stratagems of plague, drought, and famine. Each time, however, Ea intervened by revealing to Atrahasis, the pious king of the primeval humans, Enlil's plan and a way to thwart that plan. Frustrated, Enlil finally decided on an ultimate solution: a universal flood that would wipe out the whole human population. Ea, reluctant to see his creation annihilated, again revealed to Atrahasis a way to circumvent Enlil's decree: build a huge boxlike boat

---

30. Text and translation by W. G. Lambert and A. R. Millard, *Atra-ḫasīs: The Babylonian Story of the Flood* (Oxford: Oxford University Press, 1969; reprinted Winona Lake: Eisenbrauns, 1999); translations by S. Dalley, *Myths from Mesopotamia* (Oxford: Oxford University Press, 1989) 1–38; B. R. Foster, *Before the Muses* (Bethesda, MD: CDL, 1993) 1.158–201.

in which Atrahasis and his family and a few representative animals[31] may survive the flood. Enlil was not pleased at being thwarted again, but finally relented of his attempt to wipe out the human race, provided that Ea establish death as a normal condition for humankind, along with other regulations that better defined the humans' mortal condition. Accordingly, the postdiluvian humans turned out to be a different species from their antediluvian ancestors. Postdiluvian humankind was programmed to die naturally. In short, the primeval period had come to an end; from this point onward humankind became truly human (*awīlu*): mortal and bound by divinely decreed regulations (*uṣurāt nišī*).

The interpretation of the myth *Atrahasis* is debated. One school claims that the myth concerns issues of overpopulation in Mesopotamia and that the purpose of the myth is to argue for population control in a region where resources were limited. An alternative interpretation seems the more likely, however—namely, that *Atrahasis* is about the proper role of humankind and its limits in relation to the divine. Humans must curb their innate tendency to want to act as gods, since their proper function is service of the gods.

According to exponents of the second interpretation, when the gods decided to make humankind from clay moistened with the blood of the rebel god, they unwittingly placed the seeds of rebellion in the human heart. Just as it was the cries (*rigmu*) and the din (*ḫubūru*) of the rebel gods that kept Enlil from resting in his palace initially, so later it was the cries and the din of primeval humankind that kept Enlil awake. The humans, no less than the minor gods, seem to have been rebelling against their assigned role of digging the canals and provisioning the gods. In other words, the humans, too, desired the prerogatives of divinity. After all, the humans did have divine blood coursing in their veins. Similarly, on Enlil's part, the attempt by the king of the gods to annihilate humankind was an attempt to restrict divine prerogatives to the gods.

Even Ea's clever preservation of Atrahasis and his family from the flood was not a universal rescue but only the salvation of a pious man, since Atrahasis is portrayed as the faithful devotee of Ea, patron god of humankind. Moreover, Atrahasis appeared to have accepted service of the gods as his proper role, since his first act after disembarking from the boat was to offer sacrifice to the gods. The gods, for their part, acknowledged that they needed the service of humankind and guaranteed their place within the universe by vowing never again to attempt to destroy humankind by a flood. Thus, during the primeval period, through a process of trial and error, the creating deities finally achieved a workable definition of humankind,

---

31. Although the mytheme of the flood hero boarding representative animals on his boat is not preserved in the fragments of *Atrahasis* published to date, one may assume with confidence that this mytheme occurred within the myth, as evidenced by its mention in the Sumerian version of the flood story and in other Mesopotamian myths.

Fig. 10. A deity slaying the Chaos monster, in the form of a horned serpent-dragon, using a bow. Assyrian cylinder seal. Berlin, VA 7951. Drawing reproduced from O. Keel, The Symbolism of the Biblical World, *52 fig. 47; used with permission.*

one that acknowledged a proper distinction between divinity and humanity, on the one hand, and allowed that humankind had a legitimate and necessary place in the universe as servants of the gods, on the other hand.

Properly speaking, *Gilgamesh* is not a creation story, but an epic tale of a heroic human in search of immortality.[32] Nevertheless, the story does touch incidentally upon several creation motifs. The epic opens with Gilgamesh, the legendary semidivine king of Uruk, without peer among humankind, disrupting the lives of ordinary humans with his excessive demands. To alleviate the pain of the ordinary humans, the gods create another superhuman, whom the gods hope will keep Gilgamesh preoccupied with battle. Their new creation is Enkidu, a shaggy *lullû*, or primeval human, of prodigious strength and awesome appearance, who is more at home with the wild animals than with (civilized) humans. Enkidu is civilized eventually, however, through contact with a woman, who not only teaches him human intercourse but also how to eat and dress like a civilized person. Indeed, she transforms Enkidu into a true human. Enkidu then proceeds to Uruk where he first challenges and then befriends Gilgamesh. The two friends then set out to accomplish grand exploits, such that the goddess Ishtar is physically attracted to Gilgamesh. But when Gilgamesh spurns her love, the angry goddess persuades her father Anu (the Akkadian equivalent of Sumerian An, here the king of the gods) to allow Enkidu to die. Confronted with the death of his friend, Gilgamesh—himself one-third human—is now haunted by the prospect of his own mortality. He embarks on a quest for immortality that leads him beyond this world, across the gulf at the edge of the world, to the mythic isle of Dilmun where the flood hero (here named Utnapishtim rather than

---

32. Translations by E. Speiser, "The Epic of Gilgamesh," *ANET* 72–99; S. Dalley, *Myths from Mesopotamia*, 39–153. For a study of this myth and its development, see J. Tigay, *The Evolution of the Gilgamesh Epic* (Philadelphia: University of Pennsylvania Press, 1982). An authoritative new edition of the whole epic has been published by A. R. George, *The Babylonian Gilgamesh Epic: Introduction, Critical Edition and Cuneiform Texts* (2 vols.; Oxford: Oxford University Press, 2003); for a less full treatment by the same scholar, see his *The Epic of Gilgamesh: The Babylonian Epic Poem and Other Texts in Akkadian and Sumerian* (New York: Penguin, 1999).

Fig. 11. *Storm god slaying the horned and clawed watery Chaos dragon with lightning bolts, assisted by two helper deities. Assyrian cylinder seal. BM. AOB, no. 374a. Drawing by H. Keel-Leu, in O. Keel,* The Symbolism of the Biblical World, *53 fig. 49; used with permission.*

Atrahasis) has been placed along with his wife. The flood hero informs Gilgamesh that the privilege of immortality that the gods granted him and his wife was unique to his situation and therefore not available to Gilgamesh. Gilgamesh has one opportunity at immortality, however, if he can obtain the plant of life from the bottom of the sea. Gilgamesh succeeds in finding the plant of life, but before he can eat it, it is stolen by a serpent. Reluctantly, Gilgamesh is forced to return without the plant of life to Uruk, to live out the remainder of his life. The moral of the epic seems to be that humans were not created for immortality; rather, they should be content in their mortality with the joys of life that the gods have destined for them.

3.3 Creation as a Struggle against Chaos

One creation motif prominent in Akkadian literature not derived from Sumerian precedents concerns the so-called Combat Myth, best represented by the "Babylonian Creation Epic" (*Enuma Elish*). The Combat Myth also figures in the myths of "Anzu" and "The Theology of Dunnu." Other versions of the Combat Myth were popular among the West Semites of Syria and Canaan, appearing perhaps in the Baal cycle at Ugarit and certainly in God's battle with the Sea in the Hebrew Bible, among others.[33]

---

33. See my paper "The Combat Myth in Israelite Tradition Revisited," delivered at the Joint Meeting of the Midwest Region of the Society of Biblical Literature, the Middle West Branch of the American Oriental Society, and the American Schools of Oriental Research, held at Olivet Nazarene University, Bourbonnais, IL, February 11–13, 2011; publication forthcoming in *Creation and Chaos: A Reconsideration of Hermann Gunkel's Chaoskampf Hypothesis*, ed. JoAnn Scurlock (Winona Lake, IN: Eisenbrauns).

Fig. 12 (right). Deity, accompanied by two helpers, slaying seven-headed Chaos monster. Rays emanating from the body of the monster further emphasized the awe-inspiring ferocity of this dangerous divinity, who despite having been slain in the past always seems to rear yet another of its ugly heads elsewhere. The multi-pronged frenzied attack of the victorious deity is depicted here by having the deity spear the monster from more than one angle. Cylinder seal from Tell Asmar. Baghdad. Drawing by O. Keel, The Symbolism of the Biblical World, *54 fig. 52; used with permission. For photo, see* ANEP, *no. 691*

Fig. 13 (above). Deity (Ninurta?) slaying the seven-headed Chaos monster. The ferocity of the monster is suggested by fire coming from its mouths and by the awesome rays emanating from its back. Drawing by the author after an engraved shell inlay plaque. Early Dynastic Period. Collection E. Borowski. For photo, see ANEP, *no. 671.*

The common theme in all versions of the Combat Myth is a battle be-tween the creator deity and his archenemy, a chaos monster, who attempts to subvert the creator's good designs for bringing about an ordered uni-verse, of which humankind is a part. Although not explicit in all versions, basically this is the story in which the creator must first slay the chaos monster—most often depicted as a water dragon (figs. 10, 11) or a fearsome seven-headed monster (figs. 12, 13, 14), though occasionally as a birdlike monster (figs. 15, 16)—and then from the carcass of the slain chaos mon-ster (= primeval substance) the creator constructs the ordered cosmos.

Enuma Elish, the Babylonian version of the Combat Myth, is best known from later Neo-Assyrian copies, but likely was composed ca. 1100 b.c.e. in Babylonia to justify Babylon's claim to political hegemony over all Meso-potamia.[34] This so-called Babylonian "Epic of Creation" is really a paean

---

34. Translations by E. Speiser, "The Creation Epic," *ANET* 60–72, 501–3; S. Dalley, *Myths from Mesopotamia* 228–77; B. Foster, *Before the Muses*, 1.351–402; idem, *COS* 1:111 (pp. 390–402).

Fig. 14 (left). Seven(?)-headed serpent-monster with attacking deity holding a severed head. Detail from bottom register of seal impression. Tell Asmar Drawing by the author, after H. Frankfort, Stratified Cylinder Seals from the Diyala Region *(Oriental Institute Publications 72; Chicago, 1955), no. 497.*

Fig. 15. Deity (Ninurta?) attacking a leonine bird-monster (Anzu?). Cylinder seal. Assyrian. Pierpont Morgan Library, New York. For photo, see D. Collon, First Impressions: Cylinder Seals in the Ancient Near East, *168 #783. Drawing by O. Keel,* The Symbolism of the Biblical World, *51 fig. 45; used with permission.*

glorifying Marduk, the patron god of Babylon; it tells how Marduk rose from the rank of a minor deity to become the universal divine sovereign, a metaphor for the political hegemony of Babylonia—the implication being that earthly politics are coterminous with heavenly politics and that an earthly polity mirrors the rank of its patron deity.

Previous Mesopotamian creation myths had begun with at least the high gods of the pantheon in existence. By contrast, the author of *Enuma Elish* began his poem before anything had been created, when all—even the future gods—was as yet only inchoate being or undifferentiated primeval substance:

> When on high as yet Heaven had not been named
> Nor below had the name Earth been pronounced,

Fig. 16. The god Ninurta pursuing the leonine bird-monster Anzu. Drawing by
A. H. Layard, A Second Series of Monuments of Nineveh *(London, 1853) pl. 5,*
after a monumental stone relief, Ninurta temple at Kalhu (Nimrud), BM 124571.
© Trustees of the British Museum.

> Only Apsu (Abyss), the foremost, their begetter,
> And creator Tiamat (Ocean), the one who bore them all,
> Were mingling their waters together . . .[35]

With these bold words the Babylonian poet-theologian blatantly claimed
priority for his version of creation over all other accounts, including the
by-now-normative creation myth *Atrahasis*. In *Enuma Elish* the path of authority would pass from the previously recognized ruler(s) straight to Marduk—or one should say, to Babylon.

According to the Babylonian theologian, creation began as an evolution
from primeval substance, chaotic waters. Later, Tiamat (Ocean) would be
identified with salt water and Apsu (Abyss) with the nonsalty waters under
the earth, but at this point they were still undistinguished. Yet from their
commingled waters—a kind of copulation—sprang successive generations
of increasingly more refined godlings, until finally the great gods Anu, Ea,
and the rest of the Mesopotamian pantheon were born. In order for these
young upstart gods to survive, however, they had to overcome a challenge

---

35. Additional discussion and justification for this translation is provided in chap. 8,
"The Malevolent Deity in Mesopotamian Myth," p. 217.

Fig. 17. The water-god Enki (Ea), god of wisdom and patron to humankind, enthroned in his palace in Apsu (on the right), surrounded by wavy lines representing water and fish swimming in the water at his shoulders. Before Ea stand two solar deities: on the left is sun-god Utu (Akkadian Shamash), with rays emanating from the shoulders and his characteristic saw in upraised hand; the deity in the middle is unidentified. Drawing by the author, after a British Museum photograph (= ANEP, no. 684) of impression from stone cylinder seal in Baghdad, Iraq Museum 14577. Ur, 9750.

by Apsu, who wanted to annihilate them—a patent metaphor for the triumph of cosmos over chaos. This was accomplished by Ea, the god of wisdom, who slew Apsu and built his palace (a symbol of divine rule) in the midst of Apsu (fig. 17).

Thus far, the Babylonian theologian had bowed to the older political paradigm by acknowledging the legitimacy of the standard Mesopotamian pantheon, which undergirded the previous system of city-states in Mesopotamia. But, the Babylonian theologian continued, this older political synthesis had become increasingly ineffective in the face of new threats to the world order (especially from recent "barbarian" invasions), and a new political order was called for. In the metaphor of *Enuma Elish*, the chaos monster Tiamat once again raised her ugly head to threaten the divine order by marrying a new husband, Qingu. This new coalition of malevolent forces was far more threatening to world order than anything previously experienced, as many of the gods were seduced to "the dark side" and joined the new coalition.[36] None of the usual high gods were able to

36. I explore this theme in detail in my article "The Malevolent Deity in Mesopotamian Myth," below in this volume, chap. 8, pp. 199–228.

take on the new "axis of evil." Even Ea proved unequal to the challenge. Fortunately, Ea's son Marduk, hitherto an insignificant deity, rose to the occasion and succeeded in capturing Qingu and slaying Tiamat. In gratitude, the other gods proclaimed Marduk their king. Translation: Babylon, a political newcomer, was claiming to be the undisputed ruler of the world.

Further glorifying Marduk, the Babylonian theologian then attributed to this new divine sovereign all the divine powers and attributes previously assigned to other deities, in particular the function of creator. From the carcass of Tiamat the victorious Marduk created the "universe." Cleaving the body of Tiamat in two "like a fish for drying," Marduk stretched out one half to form the heavens; the other half he fashioned into the earth and the underworld. Tiamat's ribs became supports to hold up the heavens. Her udders became the mountains. He pierced her eyes to form the Tigris and Euphrates rivers. He bored holes to drain the runoff, and other holes to provide springs.

Turning to Qingu, Marduk appropriated for himself the "tablets of destiny" that the rebel god had stolen from the previous divine sovereign—thereby claiming for himself the authority to decree the roles and the fates of all things. In standard Mesopotamian creation accounts Enki-Ea had been credited as the creator of humankind. In *Atrahasis* in particular, Ea devised the plan which gave rest to the gods by creating substitute human laborers from the blood of the rebel god mixed with clay. But in *Enuma Elish*, Ea is demoted to a mere artisan carrying out designs conceived by Marduk, the real creator. Marduk ordered Qingu killed and his blood mixed with clay to make humankind, who would in turn do the work of the gods. It was only appropriate that the true divine sovereign should also be acknowledged as the creator of all.

Enuma Elish itself may be taken as a paradigm for the history of creation theology in Mesopotamia. Increasingly, creation myths were turned into national epics. Older mythemes were subsumed into new mythic syntheses which served the political ends of their proponents. The function of *Enuma Elish* as propaganda to undergird not only the Babylonian world view but also the hegemony of Babylonia over all Mesopotamia is manifest. Ironically, when Babylonia's political fortunes waned and Assyria became the dominant power in the ancient Near East, Assyrian propagandists recast *Enuma Elish* as a tool of Assyrian hegemony merely by substituting the name of their own patron deity Ashur everywhere in place of Marduk. This time the identification of national interests with religious ones was even more obvious, as the name of the country (ancient Ashur) was identical with the name of the national deity (Ashur).

In keeping with long-standing Mesopotamian tradition, Babylonians and Assyrians generally thought of themselves as located at the zenith of human history and civilization—the result of gracious divine providence. Civilization was literally a gift from the gods. Mesopotamian folk believed that in "ancient" times seven divine *apkallu* (semidivine wisdom beings) had taught the Mesopotamians all knowledge and the arts, including how to live as civilized people. Kingship itself was one of these divine gifts. The Sumerian King List speaks of kingship being lowered from heaven before the flood and renewed again following the flood.[37] Another fragmentary text apparently speaks of the king as being a special creation of the gods, much like the original creation of humankind as told in *Atrahasis*.[38] But unlike in Egypt where the king was considered to be the incarnation of the divine sovereign, Mesopotamian kings presented themselves as the deity's agents for promoting the commonweal and for maintaining correct social order. Perhaps nowhere is this theme more exploited than during the reign of the Neo-Assyrian king Ashurnasirpal II (883–859 B.C.E.), who decorated his palace with numerous panels depicting himself as the earthly viceroy of the divine sovereign, maintaining order and promoting prosperity on earth through his various royal activities. For example, in the throne room of the Northwest Palace at Nimrud, located directly behind the king's throne and forming the backdrop for the throne, was a wall panel serving as a power-ful piece of propaganda. In the center of the panel stands the tree of abun-dance, above which hovers a winged anthropomorphic divinity within a nimbus, representative apparently of the Assyrian king's divinely conferred authority as the earthly viceroy of the divine sovereign. The king, assisted by a winged *apkallu*, is depicted on both sides of the tree performing a ritual ceremony of "blessing." Both the graphic imagery and the superimposed cuneiform text informed the visitor of Ashurnasirpal's central role in bring-ing about universal well-being, with divine help, of course.[39]

But such propaganda was hardly a new tactic in Mesopotamia. During the Old Babylonian period (18th century B.C.E.), Hammurapi of Babylon published his famous law code on a stele that depicts the king as receiving these decrees directly from the sun-god Shamash, the divine patron of uni-versal justice (fig. 18). Similarly, Zimri-Lim of Mari, Hammurapi's contem-porary in a sister state to the north, had his throne room decorated with a mural in which the goddess Ishtar, surrounded by other deities, is depicted as conferring upon the king his emblems of authority and rule, resulting in weal for the whole land. Similar to the situation with Ashurnasirpal II

---

37. Thorkild Jacobsen, *The Sumerian King List* (Assyriological Studies 11; Chicago: University of Chicago Press, 1958). A convenient translation by A. Leo Oppenheim can be found in "The Sumerian King List," *ANET* 265–66.

38. W. R. Mayer, "Ein Mythos von der Erschaffung des Menschen und des Königs," *Or* 56 (1957) 55–68.

39. For a detailed discussion of this theme, particularly in the palace reliefs of Ashur-nasirpal II, see my article "The Divine Sovereign: The Image of God in the Priestly Creation Account," in *David and Zion: Biblical Studies in Honor of J. J. M. Roberts* (ed. Bernard F. Batto and Kathryn L. Roberts; Winona Lake, IN: Eisenbrauns, 2004) 143–86, esp. pp. 149–63; the panel under discussion is reproduced on p. 156, fig. 10. This article is reprinted in this volume as chap. 4.

Fig. 18. Detail of the top of Hammurapi's Law Code Stele. The (standing) king is shown in an attitude of respect before the enthroned sun-god Shamash, the god of justice. Shamash extends to the king the symbols of his kingship, and by implication, the authority to issue the divinely decreed laws promulgated on the lower portion of the stele. Discovered at Susa. Louvre, Sb 8. Photo © RMN; used with permission.

at Nimrud, the so-called "investiture of Zimri-Lim" formed the central portion of a wall painting in the throne room of the palace at Mari. An upper register depicts a goddess (far left) presenting the king to the great goddess Ishtar (center) and adjutor deities. Ishtar, with her right foot upon her animal, the lion, and outfitted with her war equipment, confers upon the king his emblems of authority, the rod and ring. A lower register is suggestive of paradisiacal conditions, apparently the result of good rule. In mirror images to the right and to the left, a goddess holds a vase from which flow four streams to water the whole land. The picture is thus reminiscent of Eden in Genesis 2.[40]

Despite such royal propaganda promoting the divine origins of their authority, Mesopotamian kings were careful to present themselves as loyal servants of the gods. Approximately a millennium after Hammurapi and Zimri-Lim, the Neo-Assyrian king Ashurbanipal (668–627 B.C.E.) is shown personally carrying clay for the making of the first brick in the rebuilding of the temple Esagila in Babylon (fig. 19). The posture of Ashurbanipal depicted upon the commemorative stele, deliberately modeled after Sumerian kings of a much earlier period who had (re)built temples in their day,

---

40. For a drawing and fuller discussion of this two-panel scene, see my "The Divine Sovereign," 158-60, reproduced below, chap. 4, pp. 111–12, with fig. 13 on p. 110.

Fig. 19. Ashurbanipal, king of Assyria, carrying on his head a basket of clay for the making of the first brick for the rebuilding of the temple Esagila in Babylon. Marble stele from Marduk temple, Babylon. Height 14.5 in. BM 90864. © Trustees of the British Museum.

would appear to be blatant propaganda suggesting the piety of this Neo-Assyrian king.

4. Canaanite Ideas of Creation

Canaan may be loosely described as encompassing those West Semitic groups who occupied the eastern Mediterranean coastal lands from Syria to the borders of Egypt. Unfortunately, little of the literature of these groups has survived. Our main sources for creation traditions are (1) the Baal cycle found on six alphabetic cuneiform tablets of the fourteenth century B.C.E. from Ugarit on the North Syrian coast, and (2) mention of the divine epithet "creator of heaven and earth" in Phoenician, Punic, and Aramaic inscriptions of the first millennium B.C.E. and of the first and second centuries C.E.

Fig. 20. Presentation of offering to the god El (seated), head of the Canaanite pantheon. Drawing by the author, after stele from Ras Shamra. Aleppo, National Museum. For photo, see ANEP, *no. 493.*

Technically speaking, Ugarit probably lay outside the boundaries of ancient Canaan, but it is included here because the themes of its literature parallel those of Canaan. Mention may also be made of the third-hand summaries of Phoenician religion reported by the fourth-century Christian writer Eusebius of Caesarea, who derived his information from the *Cosmogony* written by Philo of Byblos (ca. 50–150 c.e.), which in turn was alleged to be based on an account of a certain Sakkunyaton, a Phoenician priest. But this material is eclectic at best and is often contaminated by accommodation to classical concepts, and hence it will not be considered further in this summary article. The designation Canaanite also includes the ancient Hebrews, but because of their particularistic religion and literature the Hebrews will be considered separately below.

Canaanite tradition has preserved for us no clear cosmology. The Ugaritic Baal cycle is a conflict between gods rather than a cosmology; and although it shares many features of the Combat Myth genre, it contains no account of creation per se. Ugaritic literature does ascribe to El, the head of the Canaanite pantheon (fig. 20), the epithets *bny bnwt,* "creator of creation/creatures," and *ʾb ʾdm,* "father of humankind." An eighth-century b.c.e. Phoenician king, Azitiwada from Karatepe in Cilicia, invokes El as "creator of the earth" (*qn ʾrṣ*). In Genesis 14:19 Abraham likewise invokes this Canaanite deity under the title "El Most High, creator of heaven and earth" (*ʾēl ʿelyôn qōnê šāmayim wa-ʾāreṣ*). Analogously, at Ugarit El's wife Asherah is termed *qnyt ʾlm,* "creator of the gods."

Nowhere in the Canaanite tradition are we informed of the process by which creation of either the physical universe or of humankind took place, however. Some scholars speculate that the process involved a sacred marriage between El and his wife Asherah, but this is by no means certain, as the ancient Near East contained a variety of traditions about how the gods, humankind, and the physical elements were generated.

The Ugaritic Baal cycle deserves special mention. It is usually classified as a Canaanite version of the Combat Myth, since we witness therein a struggle of the storm-god Hadad—more commonly known by his title Baal ("Lord")—to achieve control and to assert order. As the storm god, Baal was believed to control the winds and the rain, important elements in the agricultural economy of that region, where during one half of the year virtually no rain falls. Considered a matter of life and death, the cult of the storm god was immensely popular. Even so, the Baal cycle should not be understood simply as an alternate version of the Combat Myth.

Six fragmentary tablets from Ugarit tell of Baal's battles against two rivals for the throne. The one foe is Yamm, "Sea," alternatively called by his twin names Prince Sea and Judge River. Yamm is usually considered the Canaanite equivalent of Tiamat, primeval ocean. After an exhaustive battle, which Baal nearly lost, Baal finally subdued Yamm with the aid of two divinely crafted weapons—and some help from his ferocious warrior-sister Anat. After overcoming other difficulties, Baal finally was awarded a palace from which his thunder could encompass the earth. But unlike other versions of the Combat Myth, the Baal cycle is not simply a struggle for cosmic order. Like Baal, Yamm is a son of El, the divine sovereign in Canaanite belief; so the conflict between Yamm and Baal appears more a struggle to determine which of the two will succeed El as the divine sovereign. In this regard, the story resembles more a succession narrative, analogous to the struggle for the throne in Judah between the various sons of King David, than a Combat Myth wherein the creator's arch foe is chaotic primeval ocean.[41] Nevertheless, because Yamm's name as "Sea" was evocative of the antagonist in the Combat Myth, it was inevitable that the composer of this Ugaritic tale would draw upon the imagery of the Combat Myth to add color to his story and definition to its characters. Probably for this reason, combat-myth motifs may be perceived as lurking just below the surface of the Baal cycle. Similarly, in Canaanite iconography Baal is depicted variously as treading on the back of the sea or atop Mt. Saphon and wielding a club and spear (fig. 21), or as striding on a charging bull and brandishing lightning bolts.[42]

---

41. So Wayne Pitard, "The Combat Myth as a Succession Story at Ugarit," a paper delivered at the Joint Meeting of the Midwest Region of the Society of Biblical Literature, the Middle West Branch of the American Oriental Society, and the American Schools of Oriental Research, held at Olivet Nazarene University, Bourbonnais, IL, February 11–13, 2011.

42. On a stele from a temple in the Neo-Assyrian provincial capital Hadatu (Arslan Tash), the storm god strides atop a vigorous charging bull, brandishing lightning bolts in each hand. The deity's dress has been adapted to that of the Assyrian version of the storm god (Adad), revealing the staying power of this popular deity, worshipped throughout

Baal's second foe was Mot, "Death." In this episode, Baal was at first vanquished by Mot and forced to descend into the jaws of Death. In the end,
however, Baal was rescued by his powerful sister Anat, and Mot was slain.
Because the crops fail upon Mot swallowing up the storm god and then
revive when he is released from Death's jaws, this aspect of the Baal cycle is
often interpreted as the Canaanite explanation for the alternating annual
cycle of scorching dry summer months of no rain, followed by the winter
months of abundant rain clouds blowing off the Mediterranean Sea. Others
prefer to see here a metaphor for alternating years of drought followed by
years of plenty. In any case, the struggle between the storm god and Death
is but an extension of the theme of the struggle between cosmos, or creation, and chaos, or nonexistence.

5. Hebrew Ideas of Creation

Geographically and culturally, the Hebrews may be considered a branch
of the Canaanite group. The Hebrews shared many conceptions about creation in common with their Canaanite neighbors; one finds these prominently in the Psalms, in Job, and in the Prophets, especially in the second
half of the Book of Isaiah. One also finds echoes of Egyptian creation motifs
in the Bible. But for reasons not fully understood, the classic Hebrew creation account of Genesis 1–11 was most influenced by the geographically
more distant Mesopotamian creation myths, rather than by the nearby Canaanite ones. Unfortunately, there are no extant iconographic representations of Hebrew creation mythemes, thus closing off one important avenue
for reconstructing Hebrew conceptions of creation.

Like other societies in the ancient Near East, ancient Israel had its distinguishing features. Most distinctive for Israel was its Yahwistic religion,
which during most periods of Israelite history was the official state religion—though during some periods syncretism with Assyrian and especially
Canaanite Baalistic cults prevailed in the temple at Jerusalem in the southern kingdom of Judah as well as in the royal sanctuaries of the northern
kingdom of Israel, to say nothing of popular religious practices which seem
to have been even less pure. Reforming Yahwistic priests and the classical
Israelite prophets strove mightily against such syncretistic religious practices, though often without much success. Yahwism demanded exclusive
worship of Israel's national god, Yahweh. But few, if any, among Israel's religious leaders and theologians were monotheists in the philosophical sense,
that is, believing in the existence of only one God. Numerous biblical passages attest an Israelite belief in Yahweh as the supreme deity among other
gods: a divine sovereign surrounded by a host of lesser gods (for example,
Gen 3:22; 6:2; 11:7; Exod 15:11; Deut 10:17; 1 Kgs 22:19–23; Ps 136:2; Dan

---

the whole of the Syrian region since the third millennium. Louvre, AO 13092 (= *ANEP*,
no. 501; Keel, *Symbolism of the Biblical World*, 216 #294).

Fig. 21. Stele known as "Baal of the Lightning." The Canaanite storm-god Hadad holds in his raised right hand the club used to smite his foes. With his left hand he thrusts downward a spear whose top branches into either vegetation or a lightning bolt; either motif would be appropriate to Baal. He strides upon what appears to be either mountains—his palace was situated on Mt. Saphon—or, more likely, a wavy sea—he was renowned for having defeated his archrival Yamm (Sea). The small human figure standing in front of the deity upon a pedestal likely is the king of Ugarit, beneficiary of Hadad's protection. From Ras Shamra (Ugarit). Louvre, AO 15775. Photo © RMN; used with permission.

11:36). This great god had freely chosen Israel as his elect people (Deut 32:8) and entered into an exclusive covenant with them, for which reason Israel was obligated to exclusive devotion and worship of Yahweh God. Accordingly, ancient Israelite religion, at least until well into the postexilic period, may be described as henotheism (the worship of a single deity without denying the existence of other deities) or even as "practical monotheism" or "near monotheism" (acting as if there were only one powerful deity, either by demoting all other deities to the rank of lesser gods or by ignoring them as lacking any power).

Also like their neighbors in Egypt, Mesopotamia, and Canaan, Israelite theologians readily engaged in mythmaking speculation; that is, they

created new myths or reworked old ones as explanations for their belief
in Yahweh as the divine sovereign and the creator of all. Many of the motifs that we previously encountered appear also in Hebrew literature: a primeval substance from which all creation is made, whether chaotic waters
(Gen 1:1–2) or barren desert (Gen 2:4–5); a special creation of humankind,
whether out of clay infused with a divine substance (Gen 2:7) or by mere
divine fiat (Gen 1:26–28); the earth as a disk floating in primeval water,
sealed by a rigid vault to hold back the primeval waters above (Gen 1:6–10;
Prov 8:27–29); Combat Myth themes wherein the creator deity overcame
his archenemy, chaotic primeval Sea, to bring about an ordered cosmos
(Isa 27:1; 51:9–11; Hab 3:8–10; Pss 65:5–7; 74:11–17; 77:17–21; 89:9–14;
93:3–4; Job 26:12–13; 38; cf. Rev 12:3, 9; 21:1). One motif that official Yahwism avoided, however, was the theme of creation resulting from a sacred
marriage—although there is evidence for belief at the popular level of a
marriage between Yahweh and a divine consort, Asherah, in biblical literature (1 Kgs 15:13=2 Chron 15:16; 2 Kgs 21:7; 23:4, 7) and perhaps also in
extrabiblical inscriptions from Khirbet el-Qom and Kuntillet ʿAjrud.[43] The
practice, popular especially among women, of worshiping the "queen of
heaven" within the temple precincts, bitterly repudiated by the prophet
Jeremiah (Jer 7:18; 44:17–19, 25), may also have been linked to an idea of
sacred marriage.

5.1 The Yahwist's Primeval Myth

The propensity of Israelite theologians to resort to mythmaking is
perhaps nowhere more manifest than in the classic creation account in
Genesis 1–9, which actually contains two intertwined versions of creation,
which were composed at different times: (1) an original myth of creation
composed by "the Yahwist" (J), so called because of his consistent reference
to the creator deity by the name "Yahweh (God)"; and (2) a later "Priestly"
(P) revision and expansion of the primeval story, wherein the deity is con-
sistently referred to simply as "God." By keeping the two levels of the creation account separate, the process of mythmaking is easier to see, and the
creative genius of the writers is easier to appreciate.[44]

Although dating here is speculative, there is substantial evidence to
posit that the Yahwist composed his primeval myth sometime between the

---

43. See, e.g., D. N. Freedman, "Yahweh of Samaria and his Asherah," *BA* 50 (1987)
pp. 241–49; S. Olyan, *Asherah and the Cult of Yahweh in Israel* (SBLMS 34; Atlanta: Scholars, 1988); and W. G. Dever, "Ashera, Consort of Yahweh?" *BASOR* 255 (Summer 1984)
21–37. For cautious opposing views see M. S. Smith, *The Early History of God* (San Francisco:
Harper & Row, 1990) 88–94; and O. Keel and C. Uehlinger, *Gods, Goddesses, and Images of
God in Ancient Israel* (Minneapolis: Augsburg Fortress, 1998) 210–48.

44. For a more detailed study, see Bernard F. Batto, *Slaying the Dragon: Mythmaking in
the Biblical Tradition* (Louisville: Westminster/John Knox, 1992), esp. chaps. 2–3; idem,
"Creation Theology in Genesis," in *Creation in the Biblical Traditions* (ed. R. J. Clifford and
J. J. Collins; CBQMS 24; Washington: Catholic Biblical Association, 1992) 16–38.

tenth and eighth centuries B.C.E., at a time when the kingdoms of Israel and Judah were still relatively young and Israelite theologians were still working out a theology that would set their patron deity Yahweh apart from other gods. By contrast, the Priestly revision of the primeval myth likely was accomplished in the sixth century B.C.E., perhaps within the shadow of the catastrophic destruction of the kingdom of Judah at the hands of the Babylonian army.

The Yahwist's primeval myth was not so much a creation story as it was a story of origins patterned after Mesopotamian myth. Reconstructing from the stories now preserved in Genesis 1–11, the Yahwist's primeval myth began with the story of Eden (Gen 2:4b–3:24), continued with the stories of Cain and Abel and of Lamech (Gen 4), and concluded with the flood story (Gen 6–8 [where J and P texts are found intertwined]). The stories of the drunkenness of Noah (Gen 9:18–27) and the tower of Babel (Gen 11:1–9) also stem from J, but these seem not to be part of the primeval myth; they rather constitute a new period of world history linking the primeval story to the story of the Hebrew patriarchs in Genesis 12–50.

Under the influence of Christian interpreters such as St. Augustine of Hippo, the Eden story is frequently interpreted as "the fall" of the first human couple from an original state of grace and perfection to a depraved condition of sinfulness and corruption. Such an interpretation is foreign to the Yahwist's intention, however. The Yahwist was intent upon telling a story about the national god of Israel as the universal creator, analogous to the manner in which theologians from other ancient Near Eastern societies justified their own national gods as the divine sovereign and creator. In formulating this new Hebrew myth the Yahwist seems to have borrowed from prior Mesopotamian stories such as *Adapa* and *Gilgamesh*, and especially *Atrahasis*, as a comparative chart of the two narratives makes obvious.

Like *Atrahasis*, the Yahwist's primeval myth is not a story about the loss of a golden age of humankind but rather a story of origins in which humankind *progresses* by stages from an ill-conceived solitary "human" prototype, fashioned by an inexperienced creator deity, to fully defined and self-propagating humankind (male and female). I shall not attempt here to justify this partially novel interpretation of this myth—since I have done that elsewhere[45]—but merely trace the contours of the myth as I believe the Yahwist originally intended it.

The Yahwist's primeval myth opens with a barren wasteland, which the deity Yahweh transformed into productive agricultural land by "planting" a "garden" in Eden. Then, in what is clearly an etiological pun, the deity formed "the human" (or "humankind," *hā-'ādām*) from "the humus" (or

---

45. See "The Yahwist's Primeval Myth" in my book *Slaying the Dragon*, 41–72; for my rejection of the theory, popularized by S. N. Kramer, that the Yahwist incorporated into his story an alleged Sumerian "Paradise Myth," see my article "Paradise Reexamined" (cited above, n. 29).

Inchoate Creation in Atrahasis *and in the Yahwist*

Atrahasis ("The Babylonian Story of the Flood")	*J's Primeval Myth* (Genesis 2–4; 6–8)
Irrigation agriculture assumes steppe setting of Mesopotamia	Eden (located in Mesopotamia): dry wasteland becomes garden by irrigation
Igigi gods = original laborers	Yahweh = original laborer Planted a garden: Yahweh = irrigator of steppe?

Anunnaki gods enjoy privileges of divine rank	Eden = Yahweh's private garden with magic trees
	   1. tree of life
	   2. wisdom tree (knowledge of good and evil)

lullû (Proto-humans) created as substitute laborers for gods
  • modelled from clay + rebel god's blood
  • implicitly immortal (no natural death)
	Primeval human (*hā-ʾādām*) created to work and care for Yahweh's garden
	  • modelled from clay + divine breath
	  • implicit immortality (tree of life)

Institution of marriage	Institution of marriage

lullû revolt against the divine sovereign
  • their "din" and "cries" = rebellion
  • inherit "spirit" and "plot" of rebel god
	hā-ʾādām aspires to divine status, eats from the wisdom tree reserved for deity
	  • wisdom makes one "like gods"

Successive outbreaks of "din"/rebellion	Cain, Lamech, "sons of the gods" all increase sin
Punishment—life diminished by: (1) plague, (2) drought, (3) famine	Punishment—life diminished by expulsion from garden and tree of life
Flood	Flood (with obvious similarities to *Atrahasis*)

Atrahasis = pious wise king
  • sacrifice = provisioning of gods
	Noah = righteous (and wise?, see Ezek 14:14)
	  • sacrifice = provisioning of deity

Gods smell sacrifice and bless survivors
  • Enlil reconciled and accepts situation
	Yahweh smells sacrifice and swears oath
	  • Yahweh reconciled to flawed humankind (evil from youth onward)

"Regulations for people": limitations on life
  • provisions for natural death
  • *lullû* become (normal) humans
	Limitation of 120 years placed on each individual (Gen 6:3)
	  • *hā-ʾādām* become (normal) humans

Sign: Nintu's fly necklace	Sign: duration of the earth and its seasons
[End of myth]	[Primeval period ends at Gen 8:22]

"the ground," *hā-ʾădāmâ*) "to till and to take care" of the garden. With his own divine breath, the deity had animated "the human" whom he molded from clay. Given the similarities in typology to *Atrahasis*, it would appear that the deity's intention was to create for himself a substitute laborer who would work "the garden of Yahweh" (Gen 13:10; cf. Isa 51:3; Ezek 28:13; 31:8–9). The deity failed to anticipate all the attendant problems, however. First was the loneliness of this solitary creature, which the deity attempted to solve by molding additional creatures from the clay. But these new "animals," though fashioned from the same material substance as "human-kind," proved to be incompatible as proper companions. The deity was forced back to the drawing board, so to speak, to redesign "humankind." Casting the creature into a deep sleep, the deity remodeled "humankind" by dividing him to form a complementary couple, "man" and "woman," suitable for marriage.

But if "humankind" had thereby been defined as a separate, self-prop-agating species distinct from animalkind, a second issue remained to be resolved, namely, its relation to the deity. Humankind had been animated with divine "breath," which is to say, humankind was similar to the de-ity in that it possessed divine spirit. The creator seemingly recognized the potential for confusion between divinity and humanity, which led to the deity forbidding the man and the woman access to the "tree of knowledge" (wisdom).

The "serpent," a semidivine creature with wings and feet like the ser-aphs of Isa 6:2, whose function was to guard sacred persons and sacred objects such as the tree of divine wisdom, recognized the fallacy in the deity's words and advised the man and the woman that wisdom does not bring death but instead a godlike condition. Desiring to be "like gods," the man and the woman partook of the forbidden fruit. The deleterious consequences were immediate—though not instant death, as the serpent had correctly foretold. The deity expelled the man and the woman from the garden of God, apparently in an attempt to prevent humankind from usurping further divine prerogatives (i.e., immortality, by eating of the tree of life), since the deity's action was consequent upon discovering that the man and the woman had indeed "become like one of us (gods)"! In further acknowledgment that the creator's plan had gone awry, he declared that the original natural bond between humankind and the humus had been strained to the breaking point and that henceforth the ground would be "cursed" because of humankind and would yield its produce only with great difficulty (Gen 3:17–19).

The disruption in nature extended also to the humans themselves, frac-turing the harmonious relationship that was supposed to exist between them and spreading like a cancer among their descendants, as illustrated in the following stories of Cain killing his brother Abel and of Lamech griev-ously avenging a mere bruise. The ground that was supposed to be served by the creation of humankind was instead cursed still further by brother spilling brother's blood (Gen 4:10–12). Indeed, the more humankind in-creased, the more the cancer spread—to the point where it reached even to the heavens and threatened to corrupt the lesser gods ("the sons of the gods," Gen 6:1–4).

The Yahwist's story is reminiscent of *Atrahasis*. In response to human-kind's attempted usurpation of divine prerogatives, the creator "regretted" making humankind and determined to send a flood to purge the face of the earth of rebellious humans. As in *Atrahasis*, a single righteous man and his family, together with a representative portion of animalkind, was saved by a divine instruction to build an "ark." And also like the Mesopotamian flood hero, immediately upon disembarking the ark at the conclusion of the flood, Noah offered a "sweet-smelling" sacrifice to the deity (Gen 8:20). By this sacrifice, Noah manifestly accepted the deity's design of a bond between humankind and the "ground" (Gen 5:29); in other words, this pious representative of humankind acknowledged by his actions that the proper posture of humankind vis-à-vis the deity is that of servanthood.

Appeased, the deity relented and vowed never again "to curse the ground because of humankind." At the same time, the deity resigned himself to coexistence with a humankind that will never be totally submissive, since he recognized in humankind an inherent proclivity to rebellion (Gen 8:21–22). Such coexistence must not be in competition with the deity, however. Even though humankind is guaranteed a place within creation, immortality is placed beyond human reach. Henceforth the human lifespan will be limited to one hundred and twenty years (Gen 6:3).

At this point the Yahwist's primeval story of origins, like *Atrahasis*, reached its conclusion—though the Yahwist continued his epic with additional stories of the development of the nations and of the Hebrew patriarchs (in Genesis), and concluded with Moses mediating a covenant between Yahweh God and his elect people Israel in the wilderness (in the books of Exodus and Numbers). But the Yahwist could end his primeval myth of human origins with the flood story because by its conclusion the essential definition of humankind had been achieved. By that point, humankind had been successfully defined as male and female, each complementing the other; as sharing attributes in common with both animalkind and with the divine, yet constituting a unique species distinct from either; as creatures whose proper function as divine servants has been worked out; and as mortals whose newly circumscribed lifespan would be the common experience of humankind from that day forth. Moreover, though creation may have been achieved by a circuitous route involving false starts and blind alleys, a now wiser creator had grown to love his less-than-perfect creatures and a chastened humankind had matured to accept their creaturehood—a relationship that would culminate eventually in the covenant between Yahweh and the Israelites at Sinai.

5.2 The Priestly Revision of the Primeval Myth[46]

The Yahwist's myth may have been heady stuff in the early days of the monarchy, when the Israelites were first working out a cosmic role for their patron deity. But the Yahwist's myth, with its allowance for a creator who

---

46. See chap. 3 of my *Slaying the Dragon*, 73–101, for a fuller presentation.

required several tries to achieve a workable model of creation, lost some of its appeal following the catastrophic destruction of Jerusalem and the temple in 587 B.C.E. by the powerful Babylonian army and the resulting exile to Babylonia. The stinging taunts of the Babylonian conquerors about the superiority of their national god Marduk over the Israelites' deity (for example, Ps 74:4–8, 18–19, 23; cf. 2 Kgs 18:28–35) cut to the quick and caused many to lose faith in Yahweh (Jer 44:15–19; Ezek 16:29; 23:14–21). Israel's theologians, among them the anonymous prophet of Isaiah 40–55 ("Second Isaiah"), attempted to bolster the sagging faith of the exiles with bold assurances that Babylon's god was powerless before the true divine sovereign, the creator, who is none other than Israel's own patron deity Yahweh (see Isa 41:21–29; 42:5; 44:6–20, 24; 46:1–10).

There is good evidence that the Priestly writer also wrote out of this calamitous situation. One may postulate that the Priestly writer, like Second Isaiah, attempted to shore up the faith of his fellow Israelites by portraying the character of God in ever more powerful images. To an Israelite whose faith in the universal power of their patron deity had been deeply undermined by the Babylonian catastrophe, the Yahwist's legacy of Yahweh God as a naïve and bumbling creator was anything but reassuring. What these discouraged exiles needed was reassurance that their God was indeed the universal divine sovereign who had the world and its affairs firmly under control according to a master plan. Such reassurance the Priestly writer sought to provide for his audience through a twofold strategy: (1) to revise the Yahwist's primeval myth in such a way as to show that the creator's work was perfect in design, and (2) to subvert the claims of the Babylonians that their god was the universal divine sovereign by attributing to Israel's God the very cosmic powers the Babylonians claimed for their national god Marduk.

The first thing the Priestly writer did was to preface the Yahwist's primeval myth with an additional account of creation (Gen 1:1–2:3), which could serve as a corrective lens through which to view the rest of the story of creation. This is the well-known story of God masterfully creating the world in six days by divine fiat ("Let there be *x*, and so it happened!") and at the conclusion noting that everything that was made was "very good," that is to say, perfect in every aspect! Commentators have often noted how the six days of creation are artfully arranged so that the on the first three days the deity created light, the firmament (heavens), and dry land with its vegetation; on the second three days the creator populated these different regions with their proper denizens: the heavenly lights, the sea creatures and birds, and the beasts and humans, respectively. Even the creation of woman was not an afterthought in P's retelling; rather from the very first God designed humankind to be male and female, with both created in the deity's own "image and likeness." Such marvelous design and perfect execution were not the work of a naïve and unsure beginner but the work of a master craftsman (cf. Ps 8; Prov 8:22–31). If one now finds imperfections in creation, it is not because of any flaw in the original divine creation.

By prefacing the Yahwist's primeval myth with this account of an originally perfect creation, the Priestly writer transformed the following story of the man and the woman in the garden of Eden from a story of continuous progression in creation to one of a "fall" of humankind from perfection to sin. Likewise, Cain's murder of his brother Abel and Lamech's murderous seventy-sevenfold avenging of a mere bruise may now be understood as the exponential growth of sin among humans, further debasing God's originally perfect creation. Moreover, the flood story was transformed through its new Priestly additions (notably Gen 6:9–22 and 9:1–17) from the self-defensive reaction of a threatened deity to the salvific purging of earth of the excessive "violence" of humankind, a kind of cosmic cleansing prior to repopulating the earth with the seed of the righteous flood hero and the establishment of an "everlasting covenant" of peace "with all flesh."[47]

One may imagine that the Israelites, whose world had been shattered by the Babylonian atrocities, found solace in this new Priestly portrait of God. Surely the all-powerful creator who acted so decisively to save his good creation at the beginning of human history—and again during the exodus from Egypt by drowning Pharaoh and his army in the Red Sea—will act just as decisively again in the present day to smash the Babylonian hordes and to restore his covenanted people to their rightful place.[48]

The Priestly strategy of subverting the Babylonian boast of their patron deity Marduk as the divine sovereign is less obvious. Neither Babylon nor Marduk ever appears in the Priestly composition. For that matter, many would argue that the motifs of the Babylonian version of the Combat Myth, *Enuma Elish*, are also lacking. It may be granted that they are subtly developed, but they are not lacking.[49]

Similar to *Enuma Elish* (and some Egyptian creation accounts), Genesis 1 opens at a time prior to creation when there was as yet only the divine spirit and chaotic watery primeval substance (*těhôm*, "abyss"), completely devoid of form and light. Etymologically, *těhôm* is akin to Tiamat, "Ocean," the archfoe of Marduk in *Enuma Elish*. There is no battle against the abyss in Genesis 1—though a battle motif is recognizable in the very similar text of Psalm 8 (especially v. 3). Nor is the abyss personified—though such personification is attested elsewhere in the biblical tradition (for example, Hab 3:10; Isa 51:10; Pss 77:17; 106:9). Nevertheless, there are enough mo-

---

47. See n. 24, above.

48. For a study of the Priestly retelling of the exodus out of Egypt as a continuation of the battle against chaos, see Bernard F. Batto, *Slaying the Dragon*, chap. 4, "The Exodus as Myth"; see also my article "The Reed Sea: *Requiescat in Pace*," *JBL* 102 (1983) 27–35, reprinted herein as chap. 6.

49. See my paper "The Combat Myth in Israelite Tradition Revisited," cited above ad n. 33.

tifs common to both Genesis and *Enuma Elish* to suggest a subtle polemic against the latter by the Priestly writer: the appearance of light prior to the creation of the sun and the moon, the power of the divine word, the splitting of the abyss and the formation of a "firmament" as a part of the creation of dry ground, the capping of creation with the creation of humankind, and the resting by the deity at creation, among others.

Perhaps most telling of all, however, is the motif of the deity's placing of his war bow in the sky—visible as the rainbow—following the flood (Gen 9:8–17). In the Priestly writer's retelling of the flood story, the flood is viewed as an intrusion of the abyss once again into God's creation, not unlike Tiamat's renewed aggression with her cronies, first Apsu and then Qingu, against Marduk and the good gods. When Marduk finally subdued Tiamat and her allies, Marduk hung his war bow in the sky as the "bow star" to shine forever as a symbol of his unchallenged divine sovereignty. The Priestly writer likewise used the symbol of the deity placing his war bow in the sky. This motif makes little sense in the Priestly account, however, unless one recognizes it as a symbol of God's absolute control over all creation, including any negative forces that would threaten his absolute divine sovereignty, such as the chaos monster. The motif of the divine sovereign's war bow as a heavenly phenomenon is known in the ancient Near East only from *Enuma Elish* and Genesis 9 (and derivative biblical passages). This can hardly be coincidence; rather it points to the Priestly writer's strategy of undermining Babylonian claims of hegemony by attributing the role of divine sovereign to Israel's God.

On one significant issue, however, the Priestly writer departed radically from his Mesopotamian counterpart, namely, on the question of how God exercises his divine sovereignty on earth.[50] Mesopotamian kings, or at least their propagandists, understood the king to function as the divinely appointed viceroy of the divine sovereign on earth. The king's actions and decrees were treated as if they were those of the deity himself. In Israel, too, some apologists for the Davidic dynasty tried to make similar claims for the kings of Judah, espousing a view that has come to be known as "royal theology of Zion," or more simply, "Davidic theology." One finds this viewpoint in royal psalms such as Psalms 2, 89, and 110, among others. Psalm 2, for example, boldly asserts that the Davidic king is literally God's own specially created son. In verses 6–7 the Psalmist has God declare, "I myself created my king on Zion, my holy mountain," to which the king responds: "Let me tell of Yahweh's decree. He said to me: 'You are my son; today I have begotten you.'"

The Priestly writer, however, would have none of such royal theology— or, more accurately, propaganda. Writing out of the shadow of the Babylonian destruction of Jerusalem, brought on in large measure by the excesses

---

50. See my article "The Divine Sovereign: The Image of God in the Priestly Creation Account," in *David and Zion*, 143–86; reproduced in this volume as chap. 4.

of Judah's kings, the Priestly writer rejected any notion that kings were invested with divinely infused knowledge and power, to say nothing of privilege. Instead, in a kind of democratization of kingship, the Priestly writer declared that all humans are created in God's image and likeness. Accordingly, all humans are entrusted with power to rule over the earth (Gen 1:26–28). After an initial ordering of chaos, God has turned over the duty of maintaining peace and harmony in the world to humans, who as the deity's representatives have been charged with promoting the welfare of creation. It is the duty of each person to actualize and maintain this world in the perfection that the divine sovereign intended from the beginning. Heady creation theology indeed!

6. Conclusion

From this rapid survey of ancient Near Eastern conceptions of creation it is obvious that Egypt, Mesopotamia, and Canaan shared certain basic assumptions about creation, even as each society produced its own unique creation traditions. Moreover, there were regional differences within each society, and in some instances there was more than one mythic paradigm operative in the same place at the same time. More often than not, this variety in creation stories was motivated by each locality, in ethnocentric fashion, promoting its own patron deity and, implicitly at least, also the superiority of its own community. Each locale tended to rewrite the creation traditions into new mythic paradigms in which the local patron deity was exalted either as the divine sovereign or as the wise creator, or both. This was accomplished in large part by ascribing to the patron deity attributes previously ascribed to other gods, as well as completely new powers.

Despite local variations, one may discern certain characteristics common to most ancient Near Eastern conceptions of creation. (1) Creation did not happen by accident but was willed by a wise deity, often over the opposition of a nearly equally powerful force that would have subverted the creator's cosmic designs, if possible. (2) The present world is derived from preexisting inchoate matter, a primeval substance that at times was thought of as a dark, untamed, destructive flood or as a completely barren wasteland. (3) The creator either coexisted eternally with this primeval substance or self-evolved from within its midst and eventually succeeded in ordering it into a habitable cosmos. (4) Within this cosmos, humankind occupies a central position and serves an essential function of servanthood. (5) The future of this cosmos is not guaranteed in that the creator's masterful designs may still be subverted in a moment of weakness by his primeval archenemy, especially if abetted by humans revolting against their divinely ordained roles. (6) Knowledge of the creator's design for creation and of humankind's proper roles within that creation may be discerned from the dramatic myth(s) in which the story of creation is told.

Israelite conceptions of creation found in the Hebrew Bible are part and parcel of this general ancient Near Eastern pattern. Many themes that derived from extrabiblical myth occur in the Hebrew Bible. But the classic biblical account of creation found in the opening chapters of Genesis is so similar in places to the Mesopotamian stories of *Gilgamesh, Atrahasis,* and *Enuma Elish,* among others, that even direct borrowing cannot be excluded. In any case, the Israelites, no less than their ancient Near Eastern neighbors, engaged in speculative mythmaking to express their belief that their patron deity Yahweh was the divine sovereign and the creator of the world. Moreover, analogous to the function of creation myths elsewhere, the Hebrew creation myth was placed as a preface to Israel's national epic and thus served to undergird that community's belief in itself as the creator's elect people.

Chapter 2

Paradise Reexamined

Were Milton still living today and conversant with contemporary biblical scholarship, he might feel compelled to write a sequel to his earlier two compositions, and entitle it "Paradise Reexamined." The belief that human existence on this planet began with an idyllic existence in "paradise"—a kind of "Golden Age"—which was subsequently "lost" through demonic jealousy and human hubris has a long history in Jewish and Christian tradition, a tradition that Milton brilliantly exploited in creating one of the great masterpieces of literature. Nonetheless, the very existence of a paradise motif in the Bible must be reexamined in light of cognate cuneiform literature.

Although the garden of Eden story in Genesis 2–3 has been traditionally read as a story of "Paradise Lost," the recovery of various Mesopotamian myths makes it increasingly difficult to hold that such was the original meaning of these Genesis chapters. To be sure, Mesopotamian literary parallels have been alleged in the past to exactly the opposite end, namely to claim that not only is Genesis 2–3 a paradise story but also that the biblical author was dependent upon prior Mesopotamian traditions about human history having begun with an original paradisiacal existence, comparable to the so-called Golden Age of Hesiod. In Hesiod's myth of the five races, the first, the golden race in the time of Kronos, had neither toil nor disease. In the prior but evidently complementary tale Hesiod links the advent of every manner of evil into the human condition with the creation of woman (Pandora).[1] A comparable primeval "golden age" motif has been

---

Originally published in *The Biblical Canon in Comparative Perspective: Scripture in Context IV* (ed. K. Lawson Younger, Jr., William W. Hallo, and Bernard F. Batto; Lewiston, NY: Edwin Mellen, 1991) 33-66. To my knowledge there have been no challenges to the thesis presented in this article, nor have there been any studies published since which would cause me to alter the conclusions reached in this study. There has been a major new study of *Enmerkar and the Lord of Aratta*, including a new edition of the text with an extensive commentary, published in 2009 by Catherine Mittermayer (see n. 37), which would suggest a slightly different translation for portions of this Sumerian text, but does not require any significant modification to my thesis. Also, I call attention tthroughout to other minor corrections and additional studies by way of supplementary notes.

1. Hesiod, *Works and Days*, 42–201. See G. S. Kirk, *Myth: Its Meaning and Functions in Ancient and Other Cultures* (London: Cambridge University Press / Berkeley: University of California Press, 1970) 226–38.

posited for Mesopotamia. But as with Genesis 2–3, a closer examination of the Mesopotamian texts in question reveals that the paradise motif had no true home in Mesopotamian tradition either.

Lest I be misunderstood, let me define more exactly what I mean by "paradise motif." As understood in this paper, "paradise motif" refers to a belief or concept that at some time in the distant past, a period usually identified as primeval, humankind lived in idyllic conditions in which there was peace and harmony between humankind and deity, and between humankind and the rest of creation, such that in humankind's experience there was no hostility of any kind; and death and aging and illness were virtually non-existent. Since this obviously is not the human condition of experience, there is often a corollary theme, namely, some story which tells how those pristine conditions were altered—often by human frailty— to arrive at the present situation wherein hostility, death, illness, and the like, became normative in the human condition. Note that this definition excludes from consideration texts that may posit a primeval period before death became normative to the human experience, e.g., *Adapa* and *Atrahasis*. The lack of death by itself is insufficient to establish an authentic paradise motif as proven by *Atrahasis*, wherein primeval humankind was created to be substitute laborers for the gods. Note, too, that by this definition we are concerned with *human* conditions and *human* experience, whether historical or imaginary. Thus the "paradise motif" as defined here does not extend to possible idyllic conditions for transcendental beings such as gods and angels or the like, whether these are imagined to have existed on earth or in some extraterrestrial space such as heaven.

This study will proceed in two parts. The first part will examine the evidence for a paradise motif in Mesopotamia, particularly in Sumerian literature. The second part will survey the evidence for a paradise motif in the opening chapters of Genesis.

1. Was a Paradise Motif Known in Mesopotamia?

To my knowledge there are no Akkadian texts which have been adduced as evidence for a paradise motif in Mesopotamian tradition. All alleged attestations of the motif come from Sumerian texts. The most important texts are (1) the description of Dilmun in *Enki and Ninhursag*, lines 1–30, and (2) "Nudimmud's spell" (NAM.ŠUB) in *Enmerkar and the Lord of Aratta*, lines 136–55. Certain additional texts are sometimes cited in this context, namely, the various "King Lists," e.g., the Sumerian King List in conjunction with the unhumanly long lifespans attributed to antediluvian and early postdiluvian kings; or the "Rulers of Lagash" with its attribution of 100 years spent in childhood and another 100 years spent in youth; and finally a mythic fragment (UET 6.61) which duplicates elements of texts nos. 1 and 2 above.

Sumerologists are in disagreement over the interpretation of these texts, and in particular about whether a paradise motif is present in Sumerian literature. The two poles in this debate may be represented by Samuel N. Kramer and Bendt Alster, respectively. On the one hand, Kramer in numerous publications has popularized the view that Sumerian literature contains significant precedents for the biblical stories of paradise and Babel, of a golden age when there was no killing or enmity among either humans or beasts and when all of humankind spoke but a single language.[2] Alster, on the other hand, has argued that a paradise motif is completely absent in Sumerian literature.[3] Alster has failed to attract much of a following, although the evidence supports his position. It is therefore necessary to consider the evidence anew and in a more thorough fashion to establish the absence of a paradise motif in Sumerian literature.

A. *The Myth of* Enki and Ninhursag

In 1915 Stephen Langdon published a Sumerian myth which he entitled "Sumerian Epic of Paradise, the Flood, and the Fall of Man."[4] Langdon's interpretation gained considerable popularity, despite the fact that the scholars scored Langdon's translation as generally unreliable and pointed out that the myth in question "had nothing to do with paradise, did not mention the flood, and said nothing about the fall of man."[5]

The first reliable edition of this myth was published by S. N. Kramer some thirty years later.[6] However, Kramer subtitled his edition "A Sumerian 'Paradise' Myth," thereby perpetuating the notion that a paradise motif is a major aspect of this composition. In Kramer's interpretation *Enki and Ninhursag* is a forerunner of the biblical paradise story. Dilmun is said to be both a land and a city, a place "in which there is probably neither sickness nor death"; it is a paradise for the gods and immortal heroes. Among the parallels to Genesis 2–3 suggested by Kramer are Enki's eating of the plants and his subsequent cursing by Ninhursag, to be compared to "Adam and Eve" eating of the fruit of the tree of knowledge of good and evil and

---

2. For a representative sample, see Samuel N. Kramer, *Enki and Ninhursag: A Sumerian 'Paradise' Myth* (BASOR SS 1; New Haven: ASOR, 1945) 8–9; "The 'Babel of Tongues': A Sumerian Version," *JAOS* 88 (1968) 108–11; *From the Tablets of Sumer: Twenty-five Firsts in Man's Recorded History* (Indian Hills, CO: Falcon's Wing Press, 1956), esp. chap. 17 "Paradise," pp. 169–75, repeated in *History Begins at Sumer* (Garden City: Doubleday, 1959) 110–13. This interpretation is maintained in the recent joint volume of S. N. Kramer and John Maier, *Myths of Enki, the Crafty God* (Oxford: Oxford University Press, 1989) 22–30.

3. Bendt Alster, "An Aspect of 'Enmerkar and the Lord of Aratta,'" *RA* 67 (1973) 101–9; "Enki and Ninhursag," *UF* 10 (1978) 15–27; "Dilmun, Bahrain, and the Alleged Paradise in Sumerian Myth and Literature," in *Dilmun: New Studies in the Archaeology and Early History of Bahrain* (ed. Daniel T. Potts; BBVO 2; Berlin: Dietrich Reimer Verlag, 1983) 39–74.

4. PBS X 1.

5. S. N. Kramer, *Enki and Ninhursag*, 3.

6. Ibid.

the resulting curses; Enki's watering of the Dilmun, compare the *'ēd* which watered Eden; and the goddesses' effortless birthing of offspring, compare the curse which caused Eve to birth children in pain. Most suggestive for Kramer, however, is a supposed analog for Eve's creation from a "rib" of Adam.[7] Kramer's interpretation has held sway over the years, in part because his translation was reiterated in the widely used anthology, *Ancient Near Eastern Texts Relating to the Old Testament.*[8]

Fortunately, additional help for interpreting *Enki and Ninhursag* is now available in the form of a new edition by P. Attinger[9] and a fresh translation by T. Jacobsen.[10] However, there is no agreement about the meaning and function of this myth among the various scholars who have tried their hand at deciphering it. Formerly, Jacobsen regarded it as a nature allegory which attempts to find a causal unity between the disparate phenomena of nature and a common origin in a conflict of two principles, earth and water, expressed mythopoeically as Ninhursaga (Mother Earth) and Enki (the god of fickle waters).[11] More recently, however, Jacobsen would separate the myth into two parts having little in common with each other. The relevant passage occurs at the beginning of the first part, which Jacobsen interprets as an etiology of the foundation of Dilmun as an emporium or trading center.[12] Y. Rosengarten interprets Sumerian myths as attempts at providing "rational" explanation for existent forms and essences; in this case Dilmun's importance as a city is explained through the marriage of Earth (Enki) and Water (Ninhursag) which produced grain and other valuable plants.[13] G. S. Kirk, working from a structuralist interpretation, saw in this myth a code for advocating a middle course between the two excesses of sexual regularity and sexual irregularity, which has consequences both in human fertility and in natural or geographical fertility.[14] Alster claims that once its mythic code is deciphered, *Enki and Ninhursag* is essentially a creation myth which focuses on the creation of the first ordinary males and females capable of propagating themselves.[15] Attinger says that the myth proscribes incest and makes a socially regulated sexuality the foundation

---

7. Ibid., 4 and 8–9.

8. *Ancient Near Eastern Texts Relating to the Old Testament* (ed. James B. Pritchard; 3rd ed.; Princeton: Princeton University Press, 1969) 37–41. Little has been changed from the first edition in 1950.

9. P. Attinger, "Enki et Ninhursaga," *ZA* 74 (1984) 1–52.

10. Thorkild Jacobsen, *The Harps That Once . . . : Sumerian Poetry in Translation* (New Haven: Yale University Press, 1987) 181–204.

11. T. Jacobsen, in *The Intellectual Adventure of Man* (ed. H. Frankfort et al.; Chicago: University of Chicago Press, 1946) 157–59.

12. T. Jacobsen, *The Harps That Once . . .* , 181–85.

13. Yvonne Rosengarten, *Trois aspects de la pensée religieuse sumérienne* (Paris: Boccard, 1971) 7–38.

14. G. S. Kirk, *Myth: Its Meaning and Functions in Ancient and Other Cultures*, 91–98.

15. B. Alster, "Enki and Ninhursag."

and guarantee of a well-functioning society.[16] Fortunately for our purposes, it is not necessary to decide among these conflicting and often mutually exclusive interpretations of the myth as a whole.

The only passage that bears directly upon the question of a paradise motif is the description of Dilmun in the opening scene (lines 1–30). In Jacobsen's translation, it reads:[17]

> Pure is the city—
>   and you are the ones
>   to whom it is allotted!
> Pure is Dilmun Land!
> Pure is Sumer—
>   and you are the ones
>   to whom it is allotted
> Pure is Dilmun Land!
>
> Pure was Dilmun land!
>   Virginal was Dilmun land!
> Virginal was Dilmun land!
>   Pristine was Dilmun land!
>
> When all alone
>   he had lain down in Dilmun,
> the spot where Enki
>   had lain down with his spouse,
> that spot was virginal,
>   that spot was pristine!
> When all alone
>   he had lain down in Dilmun,
> the spot where Enki
>   had laid down with Ninsikila (Ninhursag)
> that spot was virginal,
>   that spot was pristine!
>
> In Dilmun the raven
>   was not (yet) cawing,
> the flushed partridge
>   not cackling.
> The lion slew not,
> the wolf was not

---

16. Attinger, "Enki et Ninhursaga," 5. [In a recent study, Keith Dickson ("Enki and Ninhursag: The Trickster in Paradise," *JNES* 66 [2007] 1-32) likewise sides with Alster against Kramer and argues that the opening lines of the myth, rather than depicting paradisiacal conditions, constitute a prolepsis of what wil be—a creation in latency (pp. 4-7).]

17. T. Jacobsen, *The Harps That Once* . . . , 185–86. For other translations see S. N. Kramer, *ANET*, 38; B. Alster, "Dilmun, Bahrain, and the Alleged Paradise," 61–63.

carrying off lambs,
the dog had not been taught
to make kids curl up,
the colt had not learned
that grain was to be eaten.
When a widow had spread out
malt on the roof,
the birds were not eating
that malt up there,
the dove was then not tucking
the head (under its wing).

No eye-diseases said there:
"I the eye disease."
No headache said there:
"I the headache."
No old woman belonging to it
said there:
"I old woman."
No old man belonging to it
said there:
"I old man."
No maiden was as she in
her unwashed state
in the city.
No man dredging a river said there:
"It is getting dark!"
No constable made the rounds
in his border district.
No singer was singing
work songs there,
and no wailings were wailed
in the city's outskirts
there.

At first blush Kramer would certainly appear justified in seeing here the description of an idyllic place. Dilmun is described as a pristine place in which there would appear to be no enmity or disease or even aging. Yet Alster can claim the support of other Sumerologists who increasingly are in agreement that this description of Dilmun cannot be separated from other Mesopotamian primeval texts containing a similar series of negative statements: There was no x, there was no y.[18] In other texts such statements

---

18. See, among others, M. Jastrow, "Sumerian Myths of Beginnings," *AJSL* 33 (1916) 107; M. Lambert and R. Tournay, "Enki et Ninhursag," *RA* 43 (1949) 105–36, esp. p. 123; Y. Rosengarten, *Trois aspects*, 7–41, esp. p. 16; J. van Dijk, "La 'confusion des langues': Note sur le lexique et sur la morphologie d'Enmerkar, 147–55," *Or* 39 (1970) 302. P. Attinger

clearly are not intended to describe a positive condition, that is an existing idyllic state of affairs; rather they describe a lack of existence which is then remedied by a creative act on the part of the appropriate deity or deities. Jacobsen sees this as "an initially inchoate world" before it has received its final form, its present mode of being.[19]

In this regard the Sumerian myth *Ewe and Wheat* (or Lahar and Ashnan)[20] is typical in the way that it begins with a series of statements of non-existence of things with a "creation" context:

> Upon the Hill of Heaven and Earth
> When An had spawned the divine Godlings,
> Since godly Wheat had not been spawned with them, not created with
>   them,—
> Nor had been fashioned in the Land the yarn of the godly weaver,
> Nor had the loom of the godly Weaver even been pegged out—
> And Ewe did not drop her triplet kids,
> The names even of Wheat, the holy blade, and of Ewe
> Were unknown to the Godlings and the great Divinities.
> There was no wheat-of-thirty-days;
> There was no wheat-of-forty days;
> There was no wheat-of-fifty-days;
> Nor small wheat, nor mountain wheat, nor wheat of the goodly villages.
> Also there was no cloth to wear:
> The godly Weaver had not been born, so no royal cap was worn,
> And lord Herald, the precious lord, had not been born;
> Shakkan did not go out to the arid lands.
> The people of those distant days,
> They knew not cloth to wear;
> They went about with naked limbs in the land,
> And like sheep they ate grass with their mouth,
> Drinking water from the ditches.

("Enki et Ninhursaga," 33–34) says that lines 13–14 constitute not a description of Dilmun as a paradise but a depiction of Dilmun before any form of life or civilization. In this regard, one is reminded of Egyptian creation texts which also begin with a description of the condition of things "before such and such existed/was"; see discussion and bibliography in C. Westermann, *Genesis 1–11* (Minneapolis: Augsburg Publishing House, 1984) 43–46.

19. Jacobsen, *The Harps That Once . . .* , 182.

20. Originally published by E. Chiera (*Sumerian Religious Texts* [Crozer Theological Seminary Babylonian Publications 1; Upland, PA, 1924] 26–32 no. 25), the text is best known in the translation of S. N. Kramer (*From the Tablets of Sumer: Twenty-five Firsts in Man's Recorded History* [Indian Hills, CO: Falcon's Wing Press, 1956] 144–45, and repeated in *History Begins at Sumer* [3rd ed.; Philadelphia: University of Pennsylvania Press, 1981] 108–10). The text has been studied most recently by B. Alster and H. Vanstiphout ("Lahar and Ashnan: Presentation and Analysis of a Sumerian Disputation," *ASJ* 9 [1987] 1–43), from which the translation of the opening twenty-seven lines given here is taken. [For Vanstiphout's more recent, slightly revised translation of these lines, see "The Disputation Between Ewe and Wheat" (*COS* 1:180 [p. 575]).]

At that time, and at the birth-place of the Gods,
In their own home, the Holy Hill, they fashioned Ewe and Wheat.

The predications of non-existence here, as elsewhere in Sumerian literature,[21] are inseparable from the creation topos. In context it is clear that the poet means to depict a sorry state of affairs, a time prior to the domestication of animals and the cultivation of cereals, since their "forms" (the gods thought to embody their essences) have not come into being. What is more, the early humans—perhaps the attribution of "human" is too generous in this situation—were virtually animals. They wore no clothes and apparently had not yet learned to walk upright (on two legs).[22] Neither had they as yet learned to use their hands to feed themselves; rather they browsed on grass "like sheep," and lapped or slurped water from watering holes as would an animal. To the Sumerian way of thinking there is nothing in these depictions of "those distant days"—what we refer to as the primeval period—which could be termed idyllic or paradisiacal.

The only hesitation at this point for an outright rejection of a paradisiacal motif in *Enki and Ninhursag* arises out of the fact that a number of the predications of non-existence in the description of Dilmun appear to concern things that we normally consider undesirable or "bad." The non-predication of killing (the lion and the wolf), illness ("eye-disease" and "headache"), aging (no "old woman" nor "old man"), sadness ("wailing in the city's outskirts"), and perhaps others besides,[23] all could suggest idyllic conditions. I shall return to this question later in conjunction with the discussion of *Enmerkar and the Lord of Aratta*. For the present it is enough to note that other of these statements of non-predication concern conditions which we would consider desirable or "good": there were no herding dogs; colts did not know how to eat (and hence there would be no horses); there was no singing; and the like. Any assessment of these predications of non-existence must take into consideration that desirable as well as undesirable elements did not exist at that time. It is unlikely, therefore, that statements such as

the lion slew not,
the wolf was not carrying off lambs

---

21. E.g., W. W. Hallo, "Antediluvian Cities," *JCS* 23 (1970) 56–67, esp. pp. 65–66, with the corrections of B. Alster, *RA* 64 (1970) 189–90. See also A. Heidel, *The Babylonian Genesis* (2nd ed.; Chicago: University of Chicago Press, 1951) 62, line 8.

22. T. Jacobsen, "The Eridu Genesis," *JBL* 100 (1981) 513–29, esp. p. 517 n. 7.

23. Rather than the usual interpretation that birds were stealing malt placed on the roof to dry, William W. Hallo has suggested to me privately that lines 19–20 may concern child exposure, i.e., the vultures were not eating the infant which the widow places upon the roof, since the word translated "malt" (Sumerian MUNU₆) is written with a sign that can equally well be translated "foster-child, adopted child" (Sumerian BULUG₃).

can be interpreted to mean that there once was a primeval period when the lion and the wolf were non-carnivorous, or that these predators ate grass like lambs instead of preying on other animals. Rather than predicating a primordial idyllic age, these statements are poetic ways of imagining a time before the world in its present form came into being. Jacobsen's characterization of the relevant lines in *Enki and Ninhursag* seems to be exactly correct: "It begins in primeval Dilmun . . . where everything is still in the bud, pristine and unformed; nothing has yet settled into its final being or behavior"; it is a description of "an initially inchoate world achieving, or being given, its present mode of being."[24]

Something similar must be said about the [fact that the] adjectives used to describe Dilmun—KÙ, SIKIL, ŠEN, DADAG—all have essentially the same meaning: "pure," "clean," "bright," "shining," or in cultic contexts, "holy."[25] Certainly the multiplication of these terms is a bit excessive and designed to connote that Dilmun is indeed a special place. But of themselves these terms do not imply paradisiacal conditions. In this same passage not only Dilmun but also Sumer is said to be "pure" (line 3). All temple sites are by definition supposed to be "pure" places.[26] As David Wright has shown, purity in cultic contexts primarily means that all traces of the demonic and the unbecoming have been expelled. Statements about purity serve primarily a theological function of surrounding the numinous with a protective aura which sets them apart from the profane.[27] These are, then, not so much statements about paradisiacal conditions as about the suitability of the place as a cultic center.[28] One may observe that the myth concludes with the birth of Ensak,[29] the patron deity of Dilmun, so that in the end the patron deity and his sanctuary are properly wedded.[30]

---

24. Jacobsen, *The Harps That Once* . . . , 181–82, with n. 3.

25. Compare *CAD* E 4: "While *ebbu* (DADAG) often appears in literature (Sum. and Akk.) in parallelism with *ellu* (SIKIL), the latter never refers to physical cleanliness. . . . *ebbu* mostly describes animals, objects and materials for cultic purposes."

26. See, for example, the statement in the Sumerian Flood Story, lines 6′–8′: "May they come and build cities and cult places, that I may cool myself in their shade; may they lay the bricks for the cult cities in pure spots, and may they found places for divination in pure spots!," trans. Jacobsen, *The Harps That Once* . . . , 145.

27. David Wright, *The Disposal of Impurity: Elimination Rites in the Bible and in Hittite and Mesopotamian Literature* (SBLDS 101; Atlanta: Scholars Press, 1987).

28. Compare the similar statement in *Enki and the World Order*, 236–37: [kur(?) Dilm]un-na mu-un-sikil mu-un-zalag / [^{d}ni]n-sikil-la zà-ba nam-mi-in-gub "He cleansed and purified Dilmun. He installed Ninsikila in its sanctuary." Translation slightly modified from Kh. Nashef, "The Deities of Dilmun," *Akkadica* 38 (1984) 1–33, esp. p. 22.

29. *Enki and Ninhursag*, 267–68: šeš-gu$_{10}$ a-na-zu a-ra-gig zà-gu$_{10}$ ma-[gig] / ^{d}en-sa$_6$-ag im-ma-ra-an-[tu-ud] "'My brother, what part of you hurts you?' 'My side hurts me!' She gave birth to Ensak out of it." Trans. Jacobsen, *The Harps That Once* . . . , 204.

30. *Enki and Ninhursag*, 277: [^{d}en-sa$_6$-a]g en-dilmun-na ḫé-a "May Ensak become lord of Dilmun." Trans. Jacobsen, *The Harps That Once* . . . , 204.

In any case, as Rosengarten[31] has clearly seen, the "pure" Dilmun being described in the opening lines of *Enki and Ninhursag* is the mythic Mount Dilmun (KUR DILMUN[ki]) where the gods live, and not the historical city (URU) of Dilmun; the latter does not enter the picture until lines 26 and 30. At that point Ninsikala complains to Enki, "A city you will give me, a city you will give me which you have not (yet) given." With Rosengarten, the verbs here should be translated in the future tense. Enki's gift is incomplete at this point because the city does not have any life-sustaining water as yet. In short, the historical Dilmun is at this time only an idea existing in the mind of Ninsikila which must still be brought into reality. Subsequently Enki does provide water, which may suggest that the poet had in mind the huge freshwater springs that well up from the bottom of the Persian Gulf at Bahrain and provide that island with an abundant water supply.

Indeed, the function of this composition would appear to be an etiology of the founding of Dilmun as an emporium.[32] Dilmun's importance as a trading center linking Mesopotamia to the east is well attested in texts from all periods. Through this port there flowed into Mesopotamia all kinds of exotic merchandise. So suggestive to the Sumerian mind was Dilmun's fame as emporium of exotic merchandise that an Ur duplicate text (UET 6.1) added a whole section extolling Dilmun as the port through which the precious gems and rare wood and finest dyed cloth from the fabled lands of Meluhha and Maggan could be exchanged for grain, the production of which Sumer excelled in.[33]

Although Dilmun enjoyed a reputation for the exotic and the fabulous, it was nonetheless known to the Sumerians as a real place to which some of their number traveled and returned. The location of historical Dilmun is a matter of dispute, since the inscriptional evidence is ambiguous. Most scholars identify Dilmun with the island Bahrain, though acknowledging that in certain periods Dilmun may have also included the neighboring mainland coastal area.[34]

Whatever the precise identity of historical Dilmun, it is to be distinguished from its mythical analogue, the "pure" or "holy" Mount Dilmun

---

31. Rosengarten, *Trois aspects*, 10–16.

32. Alster, "Dilmun," 58–60. Jacobsen (*The Harps That Once* . . . , 181–82) divides the myth of *Enki and Ninhursag* into two originally discreet stories with but a marginal connection; the first of these, the section with which we are concerned, according to Jacobsen "deals with how Dilmun was supplied with fresh water" en route to becoming "an emporium for neighboring regions."

33. This is lines 51–70 in Jacobsen's translation (*The Harps That Once* . . . , 188–89).

34. On Dilmun and the problems of identification associated with different historical periods see bibliography compiled by Brian Lewis, *The Sargon Legend* (ASORDS 4; ASOR, 1980) 84 n. 179; and the various articles in Daniel T. Potts, ed., *Dilmun: New Studies in the Archaeology and Early History of Bahrain* (BBVO 2; Berlin: Dietrich Reimer V, 1983); and the review article of this volume by Theresa Carter, "Dilmun: At Sea or Not at Sea," *JCS* 39 (1987) 54–117.

(KUR DILMUN). The latter is encountered also in "The Sumerian Flood Story."
According to the Sumerian version of the deluge, at the conclusion of the
flood the gods blessed the flood hero Ziusudra with immortality and removed him to live forever on Mount Dilmun:

> Ziusudra, being king,
>   stepped up before An and Enlil
>   kissing the ground,
> And An and Enlil after hono[ring him]
> were granting him life like a god's
> were making lasting breath of life, like a god's
>   descend into him.
> That day they made Ziusudra,
>   preserver, as king, of the name of the small
>   animals and the seed of mankind,
> live toward the east over the mountains in Mount Dilmun.[35]

Jacobsen's translation of the last line does not bring out the full mythic import of Mount Dilmun.[36] Mount Dilmun is clearly not located within the
human realm. It lies *beyond* the mountains, at the place where Shamash (the
sun) rises in the east. The Akkadian *Gilgamesh* epic confirms this mythical
understanding of Dilmun. In this Akkadian version the name of the place
where the immortal flood hero now resides is not given, but it is clearly the
same as Mount Dilmun in "The Sumerian Flood Story." It is located beyond
the historical world. To reach it Gilgamesh had to accomplish superhuman
feats patently impossible for ordinary mortals. He crossed mountains upon
which no human had previously set foot to reach the edge of the world,
going beyond even the orbit of Shamash's (the sun's) rising and setting,
and beyond that he still had to traverse the forbidding Waters of Death at
the impossible expanse of sixty leagues before finally reaching the shores
of that distant isle on which the flood hero now resides with his wife and
boatman.

Clearly the Dilmun tradition cannot be used to posit the existence of a
paradise motif in Mesopotamian tradition. From the double witness of *Enki
and Ninhursag* and "The Sumerian Flood Story" it is clear that the historical
Dilmun must be distinguished from Mount Dilmun. Only the latter has
any possibility of being the object of a paradise search, and even that is
doubtful. In any case, Mount Dilmun lies outside the orbit of human existence. It may be a place where gods and the divinized flood hero reside,
but there is no indication that humans, even primeval humans, ever lived

---

35. Trans. Jacobsen, *The Harps That Once . . .* , 149–50. [These lines of Jacobsen's translation are reproduced in *COS* 1:158 (p. 515).]

36. See also P. Michalowski, "Mental Maps and Ideology," The Origin of Cities (ed.
Harvey Weiss; 1986), esp. pp. 133–35. Regarding the last line, note that M. Civil translates
simply "in Dilmun" (apud Lambert and Millard, *Atrahasis: The Babylonian Story of the Flood*
[Oxford: Clarendon Press, 1969] 145).

there with the lone exception of the divinized flood hero—an exception which proves the rule.

B. *"Nudimmud's spell" in* Enmerkar and the Lord of Aratta

The second passage which is alleged to describe paradisiacal conditions is "Nudimmud's (another name for the god Enki) spell" (NAM.ŠUB) in the epic *Enmerkar and the Lord of Aratta*.[37] The connection of this passage to the rest of the epic is a matter of debate. For that reason it is necessary to consider briefly the structure of the epic.

Enmerkar and the Lord of Aratta is part of a series of epics involving Uruk with its rulers Enmerkar and/or Lugalbanda, on the one side, and the rival city of Aratta with its ruler, on the other side. In *Enmerkar and the Lord of Aratta* the king of Aratta remains anonymous, although in the related epic "Enmerkar and Ensuhkešdanna," he bears the name of Ensuhkešdanna.[38] The location of Aratta is uncertain, but is probably to be identified as a city in eastern Afghanistan. All the epics of this series emphasize the superiority of Uruk over its rival.

---

37. S. N. Kramer, *Enmerkar and the Lord of Aratta: A Sumerian Epic Tale of Iraq and Iran* (Philadelphia: Museum Monographs, 1952). A new edition was prepared by Sol Cohen, *Enmerkar and the Lord of Aratta* (Ph.D. Thesis; University of Pennsylvania, 1973). For a recent translation see T. Jacobsen, *The Harps That Once . . .* , 275–319. [A new critical edition, together with an extensive commentary, has been published by Catherine Mittermayer: *Enmerkara und der Herr von Arata: Ein ungleicher Wettstreit* (OBO 239; Fribourg: Academic Press / Göttingen: Vandenhoeck & Ruprecht, 2009); the alleged "Golden Age" text is treated in section 4.1, pp. 57-62, and in the commentary, pp. 241-45. Mittermayer also summarizes and assesses other recent studies by C. Uehlinger (1990), H. Vanstiphout (1994), J. Klein (2000), and C. Wilcke (2003). Mittermayer argues that this passage (lines 136-55) is not an amplification of Enki's NAM.ŠUB mentioned in line 135, but rather is the poet's aside to the audience explaining how Enmerkar and the Lord of Aratta were able to communicate with one another, since his audience would know that in the present day (the time of the poet and his audience) different languages are spoken in the two countries. The poet quotes a passage from the Sumerian Flood Story that tells how in the distant past—in what may be termed the "good ol' days" (*gute alte Zeit*), in the time of Enmerkar and his rival—people did speak a common language, before Enki confounded their languages. Mittermayer adopts Jacobsen's view that the Sumerian Flood Story, like other Sumerian texts, does not depict early humankind as living in a "golden age," as Kramer had argued, but rather as living in an *uncivilized* world where both positive conditions (humankind had no enemies) and negative conditions (humans were little better than animals) were present. Because the author's purpose was to explain the situation whereby in Enmerkar's day a common language prevailed, our poet chose to cite only the positive elements, leaving aside the negative ones. Mittermayer leaves many questions unanswered, but manifestly she does not assume the existence of a primeval paradisiacal motif within Sumerian literature.]

38. See Adele Berlin, *Enmerkar and Ensuhkeshdanna: A Sumerian Narrative Poem* (Philadelphia: Occasional Publications of the Babylonian Fund, 1979). Cf. also C. Wilcke, *Das Lugalbandaepos* (Wiesbaden: Harrassowitz, 1969); W. W. Hallo, "Lugalbanda Excavated," *JAOS* 103 (1983) 165–80; T. Jacobsen, "Lugalbanda and the Thunderbird," *The Harps That Once . . .* , 320–44.

The plot of *Enmerkar and the Lord of Aratta* is clear enough. Enmerkar, seeking to aggrandize the temple of Inanna in Kullab, an old cult center which had by this time been incorporated into Uruk, needed lapis lazuli and special woods that must be obtained from distant Aratta. In later times it would have been possible to obtain these materials by trade through the emporium Dilmun; however, the poet says, Dilmun as yet did not exist. The only avenue seemingly open to Enmerkar was to force Aratta into submission so as to deliver the necessary materials as tribute. For this the approval of Inanna was necessary, since Inanna was worshiped in Aratta as well as in Uruk. With Inanna's blessing, Enmerkar dispatched a messenger to the Lord of Aratta demanding his submission with the promise that Aratta would be spared destruction. "Nudimmud's spell" (NAM.ŠUB) forms the conclusion of Enmerkar's message. The Lord of Aratta naturally refused submission, unless Enmerkar could prove his superiority by a match of wits. Enmerkar was able to best the Lord of Aratta in this context, and in the course of these exchanges even to come up with several innovations or inventions. However, the time consumed in this battle of wits provided the Lord of Aratta with a reprieve in the form of much needed rain which in turn produced the food that Aratta required in order to hold out against the demands of Enmerkar. With matters now at a stalemate, an old (and patently wise) woman suggested a way out that would work to the benefit of both Uruk and Aratta. Let Uruk send barley, of which it had an abundance, to Aratta in exchange for lapis lazuli and precious woods, which Aratta possessed in goodly supply. In the course of the story one encounters what appear to be etiologies for the production of barley malt and the invention of writing. It has been suggested, further, that the myth itself is an etiology for the invention of trade.

With this background we can now turn to a consideration of "Nudimmud's spell" (lines 132–52) with its alleged paradise motif. For convenience I quote it here in Jacobsen's translation (with slight modifications as noted):[39]

> In those days,
>   there being no snakes,
>   there being no scorpions,
> there being no hyenas,
>   there being no lions,
> there being no dogs or wolves,
>   there being no(thing) fearful

---

39. Jacobsen, *The Harps That Once . . .* , 289–90 [and reproduced in *COS* 1:170 (pp. 547-48)]. Kramer's most recent translation of this passage is to be found in S. N. Kramer and John Maier, *Myths of Enki, The Crafty God*, 88–89. This passage is also the subject of a study (with transliteration and translation) by B. Alster, "An Aspect of 'Enmerkar and the Lord of Aratta,'" *RA* 67 (1973) 101–9; and again in "Dilmun, Bahrain, and the Alleged Paradise in Sumerian Myth and Literature," 57–58.

or hair-raising,
mankind had
no opponents—
in those days
in the countries of Subartu,
Hamazi,
bilingual[40] Sumer
being the great country
of princely office,
the region Uri (= Akkad)
being a country
in which was
what was appropriate,
the country Mardu (= Amurru)
lying in safe pastures,
(in) the (whole) compass
of heaven and earth
the people entrusted (to him)
could address Enlil,
verily, in but a
single tongue.

In those days,
the neighbor[41] lord,

---

40. On the meaning of EME.ḪA.MUN see Åke W. Sjöberg and E. Bergmann, *The Collection of the Sumerian Temple Hymns* (TCS III; Locust Valley, NY: J. J. Augustin, 1969) 83–84. Sjöberg says that EME.ḪA.MUN means "(of) different tongue"; he understands this passage to say "that in spite of the fact that Šubur, Hamazi, Kenge, Akkad, Amurru and all peoples in the entire world spoke (an) EME.ḪA.MUN, they gave praise to Enlil 'in one tongue,' i.e., 'in one spirit.'"

41. Jacobsen's translation as "(Enki having) lordly bouts, princely bouts, and royal bouts" follows J. van Dijk ("La 'confusion des langues,'" 305–9), who relates A.DA to Sumerian A.DA.MIN = Akkadian *tēṣētu* "to go one against another," "contention" "bout" and compares the "potlach"; see *CAD* A/1 95 s.v. *adammû* "battle," "onslaught." S. N. Kramer ("Enki and His Inferiority Complex," *Or* 39 [1970] 103–10, esp. p. 110) translates similarly on the assumption that ADAMIN means "two contestants"; in Kramer's view this text points to Enki as a "Junior Enlil" always in unsuccessful contention with Enlil for the preeminent position within the Mesopotamian pantheon. Alster ("Dilmun," 58) now also translates similarly: "(Enki) the contending lord, the contending prince, the contending king," although he formerly (*RA* 67 [1973] 104 n. 1) translated A.DA as "at the same time," thus "(Enki) who at the same time is lord, aristocrat, and king." Jacobsen's translation at this point has been modified in favor of a suggestion (private communication) of W. W. Hallo that A.DA may mean "neighbor"; compare DA.A = "neighbor" in Home of the Fish, line 23 (M. Civil, Iraq 23 [1961] 156-57; C. Wilcke, *ZA* 59 [1969] 86); and LÚ.DA = *itûm* in *ana ittišu* for the owner of a neighboring field (so F. R. Kraus, *Vom mesopotamischen Menschen der altbabylonischen Zeit und seiner Welt* [Amsterdam, London: North Holland, 1973] 58–59); compare TCL 2.5481: géme-bau . . . é-A.DA-a-ka ì-ná-àm "When Geme-Bau . . . slept in the house of a neighbor(?)" (B. J. Siegel, "Slavery During the Third Dynasty of Ur," *American Anthropologist* 49 [1947] no. 1, part 2, p. 41 considers A.DA a personal name,

the neighbor prince, the neighbor king,
(did) Enki, the neighbor lord, the neighbor king,
    the neighbor lord,
    the neighbor prince, the neighbor king
did Enki, lord of abundance,
    lord of effective command,
did the lord of intelligence,
    the country's clever one,
did the leader of the gods,
did the sagacious
    omen-revealed
lord of Eridu
estrange the tongues
    in their mouths
    as many as were put there.
The tongues of men which were one.

I leave aside the numerous problems of translation in order to concentrate upon the overall interpretation of this passage. The first issue concerns the relationship of this passage to the rest of the epic *Enmerkar and the Lord of Aratta*.

Jacobsen[42] claims that its presence here is gratuitous and that it "plays no role whatever in the plot. Most likely it was a separate, independent myth added by some copyist who thought it might fit." Even were one to grant this, one would still be compelled to account for its function in the present form of the epic.

Alster's[43] treatments of this passage have the advantage of attempting to deal with "Nudimmud's spell" in context. Alster notes that this passage forms the second part of Enmerkar's message demanding submission of the Lord of Aratta. In other words, were the Lord of Aratta to recite "Nudimmud's spell," he would implicitly be accepting Enmerkar's demand that Aratta submit to Uruk. That the Lord of Aratta recognized this implication

---

"in the house of Ada"); Code of Ur-Nammu #11 (B: #10): tukum-bi dam-guruš a.da úr-ra ná-a lú ì-da-lá "If a man accused the wife of a *guruš* of lying in the lap of a neighbor (i.e., of adultery) . . ." (compare J. J. Finkelstein, *ANET*, 524; differently O. R. Gurney and S. N. Kramer, "Two Fragments of Sumerian Laws," *Studies in Honor of B. Landsberger* . . . [AS 16; Chicago: University of Chicago Press, 1965] 14); Code of Ur-Nammu #28 (B: #37): tukum-bi a-šà-gán-lú lú a.da (!?) bí-rá(?) a-šà 1 [iku] 3 še-[gur] ì-ág-gá "If a man flooded the field of a neighbor(?) man, he shall measure out 3 *gur* of grain per *iku*." Hallo suggests, further, that ADAMIN may mean "a two-sided affair" rather than "two contestants." It is unclear to me whether the attribute as "neighbor" has reference to Enki as a "junior Enlil," i.e., Enlil's "double"; or to Enki in his traditional role as a patron of humankind, i.e., as one close to humankind and concerned for its progress. The latter would certainly be appropriate for the interpretation of "Nudimmud's spell" developed here.

42. *The Harps That Once* . . . , 288–89 n. 25.

43. B. Alster, "An Aspect of 'Enmerkar and the Lord of Aratta,'" 101–9; and "Dilmun . . . ," 57–59.

is evident in that he subsequently refused Enmerkar's messenger's invitation to recite the spell (lines 206–17) with the defiant retort: "How then should Aratta submit to Uruk? That Aratta should submit to Uruk—it is absolutely impossible!—say that to him!" (lines 225–26). In this matter Alster is certainly correct.[44]

In his original treatment of this passage Alster, noting that Sumerian grammar lacks tenses per se, argued that the verbs should be translated by the future tense and that the whole passage referred to an ideal time that Enki will bring about in the future. At that time the god of wisdom will bring the diverse and often warring populations of the earth together in harmony and will change their many languages into one.[45] The implication is that Enki would cause Uruk and Aratta to speak the same language, i.e., Sumerian! In short, Aratta should acknowledge Uruk as its superior.

More recently, however, Alster has wisely backed away from that earlier interpretation, noting that the introductory formula u_4.NE (u_4.BA) "in those days" points to the past. Nonetheless, Alster still maintains that the passage implies an ideal situation in the future: "there would be no point in reciting an incantation if it did not somehow apply to the future. This text proves that a Golden Age was a possibility within the mind of the Sumerians, but only in connection with the ideal kingship."[46]

Alster's position that "Nudimmud's spell" (NAM.ŠUB) must be understood within the Sumerian ideal of kingship is confirmed by a small fragment of a mythic text from Ur (UET 6.61). Jacobsen, who first called attention to this fragment, claims that it is a special Ur version of "The Sumerian Flood Story," or in Jacobsen's terminology, of "The Eridu Genesis."[47] "The Sumerian Flood Story" itself, like the parallel Akkadian myth of *Atrahasis*, is less a story of a flood than a story of the origins of humankind. Although the only known (Old Babylonian Nippur) tablet of "The Sumerian Flood Story" is badly damaged, the preserved portions reveal that the creation of humankind (lines 12′–13′) culminated with the institution of kingship (lines 33′–40′).[48] This same pattern of creation culminating in kingship is present in the mythic fragment (UET 6.61):[49]

1′ ꞌnamꞌ-l[ú-ùlu   ]
    an-edin-[na   ]
    u_4-ba ꞌídꞌ [nu-dun-ne]

---

44. So also S. Cohen, *Enmerkar and the Lord of Aratta*, 31–32.

45. Alster, "An Aspect of 'Enmerkar and the Lord of Aratta,'" 104–5.

46. B. Alster, "Dilmun, Bahrain, and the Alleged Paradise in Sumerian Myth and Literature," 58.

47. T. Jacobsen, "The Eridu Genesis," 516–17, with n. 7.

48. Text cited according to the edition of T. Jacobsen, *The Harps That Once . . . .* , 145–50; for a more complete treatment see Jacobsen's article, "The Eridu Genesis" (above, n. 22).

49. Text as restored and translated by Jacobsen, "The Eridu Genesis," 516–17, with slight modifications. See also Alster, "Dilmun," 56–57.

e-pa₅-r[e⁽!?⁾ šu-luḫ nu-ak-ke₄]
5′ ᵍⁱˢapin-ur[u₁₃ ùku-sì-ga-šár-a nu-gar]
kur-kur-re a[b-sín-na nu-gub-bu]
nam-lú-ùlu ᵣu₄ᵣ-[dal-a-ke₄-ne]
ᵈšakan bar-rim₄-[ma la-ba-ra-è-àm]
túg-sag šu-tag-[du₁₁-ga nu-mu-un-zu-uš]
10′ nam-lú-ùlu [su-bi mu-DU-DU]
u₄-ba muš nu-[gál-àm gír nu-gál-àm]
ur-maḫ nu-gá[l-àm KA nu-gál-àm]
ur-gir_x(ZÌ) ur-[bar-ra nu-gál-àm]
nam-lú-ùlu [gaba šu-gar nu-tuku]
15′ ní-te-gá [su-zi-zi-i nu-gál]
lú k[i⁽?⁾   ]
lugal [   ]

1′ Humankind . . .
the high plain [was not yet tilled] [50]
In those days [no] cana[ls were opened],
[no dredging was done] at dikes [and ditches on dike tops].
5′ The seeder plough [and ploughing had not yet been instituted
for the knocked under and downed people.]
[No (one of)] all the countries [was planting in] fur[rows].
Humankind of (those) [distant] da[ys],
since Shakan (the god of flocks) [had not (yet) come out on]
dry land,
[did not know arraying themselves in] prime cloth;
10′ humankind [walked about naked.]
In those days, [there being] no snakes, [being no scorpions,]
be[ing] no lions, [being no hyenas],
[being no] wol[ves],
humankind [had no opponent,]
15′ fear [and terror did not exist.]
. . . [   ]
King [   ]

The restoration of the final two lines is uncertain, but presence of the word
"king" and the parallel lines in "The Sumerian Flood Story" makes it clear
that the text invokes the Sumerian tradition about kingship as the culminating act of creation by the wise gods who designed humankind. UET

---

50. Jacobsen's ("The Eridu Genesis," 516 n. 7) restoration of lines 1–2 as about the
non-flooding of the high plains cannot be correct. Since much of the text parallels "The
Rulers of Lagash," lines 1–2 should be compared to "The Rulers of Lagash," obv. i 30–31;
that is, humankind had not yet learned to cultivate the high plains. See E. Sollberger, "The
Rulers of Lagash," *JCS* 21 (1969) 279–91.

6.61 is thus describing the sorry condition of "primeval" humankind, prior to the time when the wise gods gave humankind the various institutions of civilization (the ᴍᴇ's), including kingship, through which humans truly "became human."

The subhuman character of "primeval humankind" is even clearer in "The Rulers of Lagash." The setting for this text is the reestablishment of society following upon the universal deluge. All human institutions, including kingship, had to be (re-)revealed after the flood. The prologue described the condition of primeval humankind prior to the institution of kingship in dismal terms.

6	When An (and) Enlil,
	the name of humankind having been called
	and rulership established,
10	as they had not (yet) sent forth from above
9	kingship, the crown of the city;
	they had not yet instituted for the country's living people,
	the knocked under and downed people,
	Nin-Girsu (the god of the spade), the spade, the hoe,
	the wielding of the basket and the seeder plough.
	In those days a child spent a hundred years
15	in diapers (lit. "in \<bits\> of the wash");
	after he had grown up he spent a hundred years
	without being given any task (to perform).
	He was small, he was dull witted; his mother watched over him.
	His straw-bedding was laid down in the cow-pen.
20	In those days, because the water of Lagash was held back
	there was hunger in Girsu.
	No canals being opened,
	no dikes and ditches on dike tops being dredged,
	. . . .
26	humankind relied on rain!
	Ashnan did not grow the dappled barley.
	The furrow was not opened;
	it bore no yield.
30	The high plain was not tilled;
	it bore no yield.[51]

Here again the "natural" condition of humankind, i.e., without the benefits of kingship, is a far cry from being idyllic. Without the wise and firm leadership of a king, the extensive canal system necessary for the agricultural life of Mesopotamia remained undug. In Mesopotamia canals served the dual functions of providing irrigation where rain was lacking and of

---

51. E. Sollberger, "The Rulers of Lagash," 279–91; Sollberger's translation has been modified on the basis of Jacobsen, "The Eridu Genesis," 516–17 n. 7, and 520–21.

draining off excess water in marshy regions so as to prevent the salination of the soil which retarded plant growth. The primeval humans are depicted as lacking even the most elementary agricultural knowledge necessary to feed themselves and prevent starvation.

Far from enjoying any semblance of ideal conditions, these primeval humans were imbeciles who barely qualify as human beings. Their development was retarded, they spent a hundred years in diapers and another hundred years as dim-witted children who required constant supervision and who could not be entrusted with even the simplest responsibilities. Jacobsen's[52] interpretation, namely that this is merely a case of slow development and thus of a piece with the long lives of the antediluvian and postdiluvian kings, would appear to miss the mark. Those long-lived kings were themselves wise, and had benefit of wise counselors (*apkallu*'s). That is, those kings lived *after* the period of those dull-witted primeval humans who had plodded along without benefit of wisdom or even a wise ruler. These original "humans" were virtual animals. They lived not in houses but lay down in the midst of (filthy) animal enclosures. And like the animals they were completely dependent upon the rains to provide them their food.

The situation described in "The Rulers of Lagash" should be interpreted in light of the myth of *Ewe and Wheat*, which we considered previously. In that text original humankind was depicted as virtually indistinguishable from animalkind. Primeval humans like the animals wore no clothes and apparently walked about on all four limbs. Moreover, they had not yet learned to use their hands in a human fashion; they browsed on grass "like sheep" and drank water from watering holes in a manner similar to (other) animals. The original condition of humankind in "The Rulers of Lagash" is much closer to the "humans" of the myth *Ewe and Wheat* than to the later civilized humankind who had benefit of kingship; they were more animal than human at that stage of their "creation."

Let us return to the fragmentary text UET 6.61. It is obvious that this text must be seen against the backdrop of the other primeval texts we have considered. Accordingly, its statements that "in those days" there were no fearsome beasts (snakes, scorpions, lions, hyenas, or wolves), juxtaposed with statements that humankind knew not fear or terror, can only mean that humans had nothing to fear from the "wild beasts" because humankind and animalkind were as yet indistinguishable. These two species had not as yet learned to fear one another. The element of fear would come only after humankind had learned to be human and to set itself in opposition to animalkind. With the advent of civilization necessarily came a mutual hostility between animalkind and humankind. The introduction of agricultural practices automatically put animals and humans in com-

---

52. Jacobsen, "The Eridu Genesis," 520–21.

petition for the same territory; the land plowed up for cultivation was the former grazing range of the wild animals. Moreover, the domestication of animals required that humans subdue animals which formerly ran wild. With domestication the tamed animals lost the ability to hold their own against their untamed cousins, such that human protection was now required. And humans themselves, having given up their former animalistic ways, took to driving away and even killing the "wild beasts" that threatened their new way of life.

This interpretation of UET 6.61 is confirmed by the figure of Enkidu in the *Gilgamesh* epic.[53] In his original state Enkidu was less than human. Indeed, he is depicted as a virtual animal, shaggy and covered with hair over his entire body. In this "naked" condition he ranged over the steppes with the wild beasts and shared their ways, even to the extent of eating grass and drinking from the same watering hole. Subsequently, the harlot Shamhat taught Enkidu how to wear clothes, and how to drink water and to eat bread using his hands. Through Shamhat, who served as much as a midwife as a mate, Enkidu acquired a new being. The text makes the point explicitly, Enkidu "had become human" (*awēliš iwē*, OB Gilg. P. iii 25, and *kīma muti ibašši* "he is like a human," 27). Accordingly, when the new "human" Enkidu tried to return to his old ways, he discovered both that he no longer had the ability to keep up with the wild beasts and that the wild beasts no longer accepted him as one of them. At first Enkidu lamented his loss of identification with the animals. But wise Shamhat consoled him with the assurance that the loss was actually his gain: "You are beautiful,[54] you have become like a god," she told him, for he had acquired wisdom (I iv 29), the gift of the gods. The final stage in Enkidu's humanization came with his induction into urban society organized under kingship, the apex of civilized life according to Mesopotamian belief. The prostitute led Enkidu to the walled city of Uruk (i.e., civilization) where he became the friend and inseparable companion of the legendary king Gilgamesh.

This long and tortuous detour has been necessary because the mythic fragment UET 6.61 contains the hermeneutical key to unlocking the meaning of "Nudimmud's spell" (NAM.ŠUB) in the myth *Enmerkar and the Lord of Aratta.* "Nudimmud's spell" is structurally composed of three parts, each beginning with the formula u_4.BA "in those days" (lines 136, 141, and 147). The first of these parts shares in common with UET 6.61 (1) a primeval setting "in those days," (2) a non-predication of similar wild beasts (snakes, scorpions, lions, wolves, and likely hyenas), and (3) the statement that humankind had no opponent and was without fear. "Nudimmud's spell"

---

53. See J. Tigay, *The Evolution of the Gilgamesh Epic* (Philadelphia: University of Pennsylvania Press, 1982) 198–209.

54. Maureen Gallery Kovacs (*The Epic of Gilgamesh* [Stanford University, 1989] 9) notes that "a recently published Akkadian fragment from Anatolia confirms the restoration 'beautiful'" instead of the well-known reconstruction as "wise."

lacks the additional statements about the subhuman conditions of primeval humankind, but it seems impossible to avoid the conclusion that it invokes the same primeval tradition as UET 6.61. Accordingly, "Nudimmud's spell" is not about a primeval "golden age" of humankind, but about an inchoate primeval stage when humans were as yet barely distinguishable from beasts.

Unless one assumes a change in mood and function, then the other two parts of "Nudimmud's spell" must also fit within this same typology of inchoate primeval conditions. There is nothing in the text to warrant such an assumption, however. All three parts of "Nudimmud's spell" are set in the same inchoate primeval period. The second part tells of a time when all humankind spoke a common language. The third part tells how wise Enki changed their speech into the disparate languages which we know in our world of experience. The question is whether this was considered a change for the better or for the worse. Those who posit an original "golden age" of course assume that this was a change for the worse, citing the biblical Tower of Babel story (Gen 11:1–9) as corroborating evidence. However, the internal evidence from the text itself actually points in the other direction.

The author of the text seems not to have shared our modern bias that a common language for all of humankind would be a good thing. Given a context of the primeval period as a time before humankind had attained a "civilized" condition, the statement that in that period all people addressed the king of the gods Enlil in but a single tongue must imply that the dearth of language was an undesirable condition as well. The present "bilingual" or "polygot" (EME.ḪA.MUN) character of the land of Sumer was a matter for pride, not embarrassment. No doubt the author had in mind the great accomplishments of the combined Sumero-Akkadian civilization of southern Mesopotamia, which set them apart from their less civilized neighbors such as the Martu (Amorites) who even yet "lie down in the meadows," i.e., who have not yet progressed to building houses in which to live.[55] The second part of "Nudimmud's spell" thus is in agreement with the first part, the primeval condition was not idyllic at all; it was rather a time before humankind attained its fully human (civilized) stature.

If this line of reasoning is correct, then the statement that wise Enki changed the one speech of humankind into many must be understood as a *positive* step in the progression of humankind from an original subhuman condition to full humanity. Jacobsen's translation as Enki "estranged the tongue in their mouths" is unnecessarily prejudicial. It is based upon his conjecture that the multiplication of languages is to be linked to the *Atrahasis* myth, i.e., that the multiplication of languages was a clever stratagem on the part of Enki to avert the anger of Enlil who planned to wipe

---

55. On the multiple references in Mesopotamia to the uncivilized character of the Amorites (Martu), see J. Tigay, *The Evolution of the Gilgamesh Epic*, 200–202.

out humankind because of the noise made by a proliferating humankind.[56] However, there is nothing in this piece to suggest that humankind is in any way a nuisance to the gods or that Enlil is angry. Because of the lack of divine anger, it is difficult to suggest an original setting similar to the biblical story of the confusion of tongues, either. What is clear, as Jacobsen has seen, is that Enki's action—"and particularly so as Nudimmud, man's creator"—must stem from his characteristic role as the patron of humankind.[57] The multiplication of languages here is understood not as human regression but as progress, similar to the donning of clothes, the building of houses, the adoption of irrigation agriculture, and the like.

In short, a contextually consistent reading of "Nudimmud's spell" suggests that the apogee of human condition came not at the beginning of human history but at the end. That is, it conforms to the normal Sumerian view that the full human condition was reached only with the advent of (Sumerian) civilization, with its advanced knowledge of irrigation agriculture, urban comforts, and justly famous literary tradition in both Sumerian and Akkadian, all organized under the leadership of a divinely appointed king.[58]

2. Is There a Paradise Motif in Genesis?

Elsewhere I have developed at length my views concerning the interpretation of the opening chapters of Genesis.[59] Accordingly, I can be relatively brief here. Basically, I accept the view that Genesis received its present form at the hands of the so-called Priestly Writer (P), a Judahite theologian who wrote out of the exilic experience, that is either during or after the exile. This Priestly Writer did not create his composition totally *de novo*. Much of the priestly legal tradition he took over wholesale from an earlier corpus. In addition, Frank Moore Cross would appear to be correct in saying that P never existed as an independent narrative; rather it was written to supplement an older "Israelite epic" tradition (J/E); indeed, P depends upon the Yahwistic narrative to flesh out its narrative structure.[60] However,

---

56. Jacobsen, *The Harps That Once . . .* , 289 n. 25.

57. Ibid.

58. C. Uehlinger's massive monograph (*Weltreich und "eine Rede": Eine neue Deutung der sogenannten Turmbauerzählung (Gen 11, 1–9)* [OBO 101; Fribourg: Editions universitaires; Göttingen: Vandenhoeck & Ruprecht, 1990]) appeared too late to be considered in this study, but does not alter the conclusions reached herein. Uehlinger's interpretation of "Nudimmud's spell" (pp. 409–34) founders at exactly the same point as other primeval ideal world hypotheses: "Nudimmud's spell" describes an inchoate world, not an ideal world.

59. See chaps. 2 and 3 of my book, *Slaying the Dragon: Myth-Making in the Biblical Tradition* (Louisville: Westminster/John Knox Press, 1992).

60. F. M. Cross, *Canaanite Myth and Hebrew Epic* (Cambridge: Harvard University Press, 1973) 293–325.

the Priestly revision so radically altered the shape and meaning of the prior "Israelite epic" that P deserves to be called the author of the "Tetrateuch" (Genesis–Numbers).

This diachronic reconstruction of the history of composition of Genesis implies in turn that a study of the paradise motif in Genesis must begin not with P but with the older Yahwistic literary strand.

A. *The Yahwist's Primeval Myth*

A common interpretation of the opening chapters of Genesis is that it is a story of "the Fall." That is, it is the story of a gracious and loving God who created a perfect world. This perfect world or "paradise" was corrupted by human sin, which in turn necessitated divine intervention by this gracious deity to salvage a creation gone astray. In a more theological idiom, it is supposed to be the story of sin and redemption. According to this interpretation, the Yahwist prefaced his "history of salvation" with a story of "the Fall" and its disastrous aftermath. In Yahweh God's original design, as related in Genesis 2:4–25, the world was created as an idyllic garden in which there was neither death nor illness nor any form of enmity whatever, whether between the divine and the human realms or between the human and the animal realms. This paradise was created explicitly for the enjoyment of humankind, itself the apex of God's creation. Genesis 3 tells how this originally perfect creation was subsequently "lost" to humans through their own fault in disobeying the divine command and eating the forbidden fruit. This "Fall," or "original sin," resulted in alienation of humankind from their God, from their world, and even from each other. Once introduced, sin continued to grow like a cancer, corrupting God's perfect work. Such are the stories in Genesis 4 of Cain and Abel, which relate how brother turned against brother, and of Lamech, wherein murder and vengeance become the rule. The flood (Genesis 6–8) was supposed to wash this cancer from the face of the earth but failed to achieve its desired result, as evidenced in the disrespect Ham exhibits toward his father Noah (Gen 9:20–27) and the presumptuous pride of humankind in building the tower of Babel (Gen 11:1–9). Stymied at every turn by a recalcitrant humankind "whose every imagination of the thoughts of his heart was only evil continually" (Gen 6:5; cf. 8:21), the gracious Creator finally embarked upon another plan by which he elected one man and his descendants to bring about blessing for the others (Gen 12:1ff.).

This common interpretation of the opening chapters of Genesis is quite distant from the story intended by the Yahwist, however. The Yahwist's primeval myth is not about a "fall" at all, but about *continuously improved* creation. Like the Mesopotamian creation myths generally and *Atrahasis* in particular, the Yahwist's myth purports to explain the proper place of humankind within the cosmos by showing that our "world" is the result of a series of inchoate creations and adjustments to these creations by the creator as he struggled to achieve a workable creation; in the process the proper roles of deity and humankind are likewise worked out.[61]

The Mesopotamian roots of the Yahwistic primeval myth are clearly evident. The place names, insofar as they can be identified are all Mesopotamian, e.g., Cush (i.e., the territory of the Kassites, as in Gen 10:8),[62] Assyria, and the Tigris and the Euphrates rivers which surround Eden (2:13–14). Upon leaving Eden the humans are said to arrive in Shinar (Sumer) where they build with brick (11:2–3). Mesopotamian origins are also evident in the use of various loanwords in the primeval story: *ʾēd* "river(?),"[63] *ʿeden*,[64] and others.

Following the typology of *Atrahasis*, the Yahwist assumed that the pre-creation state was a barren wasteland, a desert, which required irrigation in order to be turned into an inhabitable realm. Yahweh God himself irrigated this wasteland and turned it into a paradisiacal garden by planting all kinds of wonderful trees. Contrary to common opinion, this garden in Eden was not intended as a paradise for humankind. Rather, it was the deity's private preserve. As with the *lullû* (primeval humans) of *Atrahasis*, humankind in the Yahwist's telling was created to relieve the deity of the burden of working the garden himself and the labor of providing his own sustenance. In short, humankind was created to be the servant(s) of the deity. The human vocation is also revealed in the pun involving humankind's name and origins: the "human" (*hā-ʾādām*) was taken from the "humus" (*hā-ʾădāmâ*) which (s)he was ordained to till. The human cultivator and the cultivated humus are correlative terms. Even after expulsion from the garden, the humans' vocation as cultivators of the soil remains (3:17–19, 23), though more honored in the breach than in the keeping (4:2–3+10–11; 6:7). Not until the time of Noah did humankind accept its vocation (5:29), and even

---

61. For the details of this interpretation, which are presupposed here, see my *Slaying the Dragon* (above n. 59, chapters 1 and 2).

62. See E. A. Speiser, "The Rivers of Paradise," *Festschrift Johannes Friedrich* (Carl Winter Universitätsverlag, 1959) 473–85, reprinted in *Oriental and Biblical Studies: Collected Writings of E. A. Speiser* (ed. J. J. Finkelstein and Moshe Greenberg; Philadelphia: University of Pennsylvania Press, 1967) 23–34.

63. The meaning of the word *ʾēd* is uncertain. The translation "primeval flood" assumes that the Hebrew vocable is cognate to Akkadian *edû*, a Sumerian loanword; see E. A. Speiser, "*ʾEd* in the Story of Creation," *BASOR* 140 (1955) 9–11, reprinted in *Oriental and Biblical Studies*, 19–22. For a discussion of other possible meanings, see C. Westermann, *Genesis 1–11: A Commentary*, 200–201.

64. It has been suggested that the name Eden is derived from Sumerian EDIN, meaning "steppe," "plain." However, the name Eden was more likely derived from the Semitic root *ʿdn*, which has a base meaning of "abundance," "luxury," or the like. The garden of Eden, then, would literally have been a place of abundance, a "paradise"—though maintained for the deity rather than for humankind. The root *ʿdn*, previously known in Hebrew (Neh 9:25) and Syriac, has most recently turned up in the Aramaic version of a ninth-century B.C.E. bilingual inscription from the site of Tell Fakhariyeh in northeastern Syria. See A. R. Millard, "The Etymology of Eden," *VT* 34 (1984) 103–6.

then with questionable integrity (9:20). Noah's piety in offering sacrifice at
the conclusion of the flood is surely linked to the notion that humankind
has finally accepted its proper function as cultivator of the soil and servant
of the god, just as in the case of the Mesopotamian flood hero's sacrifice to
the gods. [65]

The naïveté of the creator is evident in other ways as well. As in *Atrahasis*, the full creation of humankind proceeded by stages. At first Yahweh
created only a solitary human (*hā-ʾādām*)—actually a protohuman since it
was neither male nor female, apparently. When the solitude of this protohuman was discovered to be a problem, Yahweh at first tried to solve
the problem by creating animals. Since *hā-ʾādām* has been created out of
clay inspired with divine breath, Yahweh molded additional figures from
clay; the resulting animals proved unsatisfactory companions, however. A
second try proved more successful; Yahweh redid the human by dividing it
and making one half into a male and the other half into a complementary
female.

Further, Yahweh apparently had not counted upon the proclivity of humankind to rebel against its maker and to usurp divine prerogatives. Genesis 3 suggests that by eating of the "tree of knowledge of good and evil"
humankind was aspiring to the divine prerogative of wisdom, which had
been declared off limits to humankind. Attempting to prevent still further
encroachment upon the divine realm by humankind ("indeed, humankind
has become like one of us!," Gen 2:22), the deity expelled the humans from
his garden.

The tree of life is yet another symbol that the deity had not reckoned
fully with the implications of the human condition. The deity seems not
to have anticipated any problem with humankind having access to "immortality." But once the deity perceived that humans were illicitly aspiring
to divine status, he barred their access to the tree of life, thus establishing a clear demarcation between the divine and the human realms, the
one immortal, the other mortal. But the imposition of mortality itself was
only slowly accomplished. The vitality of humankind as measured by their
lifespans was gradually decreased until at the onset of the flood Yahweh
imposed an upper limit of 120 years (6:3). As in *Atrahasis*, it would appear

---

65. In *Atrahasis* the sacrifice of the flood hero is patently presented as the act of a faithful devotee, which is contrasted with the rebellious actions of the impious generation that
brought on the flood through their refusal to carry out their function of provisioning the
gods. For further discussion see Batto, "The Covenant of Peace: A Neglected Ancient Near
Eastern Motif," *CBQ* 49 (1987) 187–211 [reprinted in this volume as chap. 7].

Recognition of this motif may also provide the explanation as to why Cain's offering
was not acceptable to Yahweh (Gen 4:3–5). Since Cain is portrayed as continuing the sin of
his parents, it was necessary to state that the offering which this "tiller of the soil" brought
forward "from the fruit of the soil" was inherently unacceptable. Cain was rebellious in his
attitude of cultivating the soil and provisioning the deity.

that the imposition of death and a limitation upon the vitality of humankind was an afterthought occasioned by unexpected human encroachment
upon the divine.

The flood itself was another implicit admission of original failure. In
Atrahasis the decision to send a flood to annihilate humankind and the decision to save a pious remnant proceeded from two distinct divine parties,
represented by Enlil and by Enki respectively. The Yahwist did not have this
option, since all divine power was attributed to Yahweh alone. This presents something of a contradiction in the Yahwistic story. On the one hand
Yahweh "regretted" having made humankind and determined to "blot out
humankind whom I have created from the face of the ground—(everything) from humankind to the beasts to the creeping things and even to
the birds of the sky; for I regret that I made them!" (6:7). On the other hand
Yahweh spared Noah because he "found favor in Yahweh's eyes" (6:8). In
any case, a remnant was saved and the earth repopulated.

In Mesopotamian tradition the deluge marked a vast divide in the history of humankind. Postdiluvian humankind was markedly different from
the antediluvian species, symbolized most graphically in the postdiluvians'
(almost) "normal" lifespans.[66] In *Atrahasis* the gods reconvene the divine
creative pair, Enki and Nintu, and have them adjust "human nature" by
imposing additional "regulations for people" (*uṣurāt nišī*). These additional
regulations were not so much population control measures, as sometimes
suggested,[67] as the imposition of mortality as a natural condition upon
humankind.[68] With this adjustment the final definition of humankind was
apparently achieved. Humankind's place in the universe was now assured
and, appropriately, this "creation myth" or "myth of origins" concludes at
this point.

The Yahwist, too, seems to have thought of the primeval period as concluding with the flood story, more specifically with Yahweh's vow never
again to attempt to destroy humankind off the face of the earth (Gen 8:21–
22).[69] As in Atrahasis, the Yahwist appears to understand the full definition

---

66. See, for example, "The Sumerian King List."

67. See Anne D. Kilmer, "The Mesopotamian Concept of Overpopulation and Its Solution as Reflected in Mythology," *Or* 41 (1972) 160–77; W. L. Moran, "Atrahasis: The Babylonian Story of the Flood," *Bib* 52 (1971) 51–61; T. Frymer-Kensky, "The Atrahasis Epic
and Its Significance for Our Understanding of Genesis 1–9," *BA* 40 (1977) 147–55; V. Fritz,
"'Solange die Erde steht'—Vom Sinn der jahwistischen Fluterzählung in Gen 6–8," *ZAW*
94 (1982) 599–614.

68. W. G. Lambert ("The Theology of Death," in *Death in Mesopotamia* [ed. B. Alster;
Mesopotamia 8; Copenhagen: Akademisk, 1980] 54–58) is surely correct in restoring *Atrahasis* III vi 47–48, on the basis of *Gilgamesh* X vi 28–32, as follows: [*at-ti ša-a*]*s-sú ba-ni-a-at
ši-ma-ti* / [*mu-ta šu-uk-ni*] *a-na ni-ši* "(Enki opened his mouth / and addressed Nintu, the
birthgoddess,) '[You, bi]rthgoddess, creatress of destinies, / [Create death] for the people.'"

69. See W. M. Clark, "The Flood and the Structure of the Pre-patriarch History," *ZAW*
83 (1971) 184–211, esp. pp. 205–11.

of humankind to have been finally achieved only at this point. The vitality of humankind has had limits placed upon it. A clear line of demarcation has been established between humankind and deity, on the one hand, and between humankind and animalkind, on the other. The species has been defined as male and female and their complementarity confirmed in the institution of marriage (2:23–24).[70] In the person of Noah, the progenitor of a new generation, humankind has accepted its role as servant. From the other direction, humankind's right to existence is also assured, having been guaranteed by divine oath.

The Yahwist's primeval story in Genesis 2–8 is evidently a myth of origins. It has the same basic mythic typology as *Atrahasis* and contains many of the same theological conceptions because the Yahwist actually patterned his own primeval myth on this Akkadian myth. Like *Atrahasis*, the Yahwistic primeval myth is about humankind. It "established" the place of humankind within creation. It not only defined the proper relationship of humankind to the divine and to the rest of creation, it also accounted for the origins of human institutions such as marriage and cities and agriculture.

Although the Yahwist was not concerned with "theology" in a strict sense, i.e., with defining "God" and/or the attributes of God, nonetheless, a portrait of the divine does emerge from the story. From one perspective the portrait was unflattering to the God of Israel. As I have reconstructed the portrait, Yahweh is revealed as an inexperienced, naïve, even bungling creator who required several attempts to "get it right." This is certainly a long way from the omniscient and omnipotent deity of later Judaeo-Christian theology. But from another perspective "Yahweh God" does develop into a lovable and loving god in the course of the epic. In the initial chapters Yahweh God comes across as concerned only for himself and his own rights: he created humankind to take an agricultural burden off himself (Gen 2:8); he expelled the humans from the garden for encroaching upon (his) divine prerogatives (3:22); and still later he wantonly

---

70. To my knowledge, no one has remarked upon the fact that in *Atrahasis* at the corresponding position in the myth the institution of marriage is established, which provides additional confirmation to my thesis that the Yahwist's primeval myth is patterned on Atrahasis. Gen 2:24 speaks of a man leaving his parents to cleave to his wife so that the two "become one flesh." The comparable passage in *Atrahasis* occurs in a damaged section and must be restored from several fragments (texts E, S, and R, as designated by Lambert and Millard, the latter misplaced by the editors). Improving upon the restorations by C. Wilcke ("Familiengründung im Alten Babylonien," in *Geschlechtsreife und Legitimation zur Zeugung* [ed. E. W. Müller; Veröffentlichungen des Instituts für Historische Anthropologie e. V., 3; Freiburg/München: Alber, 1985] 295–98), I read "(When) a young woman [develops breasts on] her chest, / a beard [appea]rs [o]n the cheek on a young man, / [in gar]dens and in the streets / [let them choo]se one another the wife and her husband" (I 271–76). [I have since treated this topic more fully in my article "The Institution of Marriage in Genesis 2 and in *Atrahasis*," *CBQ* 62 (2000) 621-31; reprinted in this volume as chap. 3.]

annihilated all living creatures for the sins of one group.[71] Nevertheless, another side of Yahweh God's character has begun to emerge by the conclusion of the primeval myth. A tinge of solicitude may have motivated the deity to create a companion for the solitary human (2:18). Likewise, the deity's clothing of the human couple with skin clothing (3:21) is often attributed to divine compassion, though I prefer to read this as an investiture of humankind with the symbol of their humanness.[72] But by far the most important scene is the concluding one, in which Yahweh God reconciles himself to his flawed creation and accepts an imperfect humankind on its own terms. In striking contrast to the deity's previous determination to annihilate by flood all animate life because of the perpetual human impulse to evil (6:5–7), after the flood the deity commits himself under solemn oath to work with this imperfect creation, no matter how evil the impulse which beats within the human breast (8:21–22).[73] To use the current jargon from parenting manuals, a "bonding" of the Creator to his creatures had been achieved. The "child" may not be perfect but it is his; like a good parent Yahweh accepts humankind "as is," warts and all.

This latter image of Yahweh was of course the one that the Yahwist expanded upon in the remainder of his work. This was the gracious deity whom Israel celebrated in worship and in literature as having chosen her as his people and then cementing that commitment through an unbroken covenant, despite Israel's own sordid record of covenant infidelity.

B. The Priestly Revision of the Primeval Myth[74]

The Priestly Writer (P) apparently wrote out of the catastrophic experience of the Babylonian exile. Confronted with an audience which was in danger of losing its own socio-religious identity, this author set out to reaffirm the traditional Yahwistic faith of Israel. Paradoxically, in order to retain Israel's traditional Torah stories, P found it necessary to create radically new

---

71. The theme of divine caprice is present also in the parent Akkadian myth. In the derivative version of the flood story preserved in *Gilgamesh* XI 180 Enki reproaches Enlil for annihilating the innocent along with the guilty: "On the sinner lay his sin; on the transgressor lay his transgression." [For a fuller treatment of the theme of divine caprice, see now my "The Malevolent Deity in Mesopotamian Myth," chap. 8 in this volume.]

72. See above, pp. 38–39 and 45–50 [in this volume, pp. 60–61 and 69–75]. Robert A. Oden, Jr. ("Grace or Status?: Yahweh's Clothing of the First Humans," in his *The Bible Without Theology: The Theological Tradition and Alternatives to It* [New York: Harper and Row, 1987] 92–105) is mistaken in claiming that the original nakedness is an approximation of the divine status. He is correct, however, in seeing the clothing of the man and the woman in Genesis 3 as a symbol of their becoming fully human.

73. The motif of the creator reconciling himself to creation after a human sin and attempted annihilation of humankind occurs in several forms and a variety of texts in the ancient Near East; see my article, "The Covenant of Peace," *CBQ* 49 (1987) 187–211 [reprinted in this volume as chap. 7].

74. Additional evidence for positions adopted in this section is presented in my *Slaying the Dragon*, chapter 3; see above at n. 59.

settings for them. Such was the case for the by-now-traditional Yahwist's primeval myth. P composed a new creation account (Gen 1:1–2:3) which he placed at the head of his composition. In so doing he radically altered the meaning of the older Yahwistic primeval myth. In effect P created a paradise story where none had existed previously.

Apparently unhappy with the portrayal of Yahweh God as something of an incompetent creator in the Yahwistic primeval myth, P felt it necessary to stress the absolute sovereignty of the Creator and that his work was perfect. If there was anything wrong with creation, it was not to be attributed to the Creator. From the old Semitic Combat Myth P borrowed the theme of creation as a struggle between the creative power of the Divine Sovereign, on the one hand, and the nihilistic power of Chaos, on the other. Perhaps partially as a polemic against the Babylonian captors, P borrowed motifs from the Babylonian version of the Combat Myth, *Enuma Elish*, and transformed them in service of Israel's God (*'ĕlōhîm*). Israel's God, not the Babylonian god Marduk, was the Divine Sovereign who had overcome Chaos (in Hebrew: *tĕhôm* "Abyss") and by his creative word had brought the world into being.[75]

The Priestly Writer stressed that the world created by God was perfect. Six times in the course of creation the author says that God paused to reflect on the quality of his work and "saw that it was good" (*kî tôb*). At its completion God paused again to survey his creation and found that "it was exceedingly good!" ("perfect!" *tôb mĕ'ōd*, Gen 1:31).

However, for two works, the firmament and humankind, the author studiously avoided having God pronounce them "good." The reason for this is obvious. The firmament will later prove defective when it allowed the waters of Chaos (the Great Abyss) to come cascading through at the time of the flood (7:11). Humankind, too, will prove defective, indeed in the very next episode (Genesis 2–3). P used the older Yahwistic stories of Eden and the flood to show how through human sin the nihilistic power of Chaos was allowed an opportunity to rear its ugly head again and to threaten the divine order in creation. Even so, the creative will of the Divine Sovereign cannot be thwarted, and so divine order was reestablished.

---

75. [I have since treated the topic of God as Divine Sovereign in "The Divine Sovereign: The Image of God in the Priestly Creation Account," in *David and Zion: Biblical Studies in Honor of J. J. M. Roberts* (ed. Bernard F. Batto and Kathryn L. Roberts; Winona Lake, IN: Eisenbrauns, 2004) 143–86; reprinted in this volume as chap. 4. I have recently reexamined the controverted issue of the presence of Combat Myth motifs in Genesis 1 and elsewhere in the Hebrew Bible in a paper presented at the Joint Meeting of the Midwest Region of the Society of Biblical Literature, the Middle West Branch of the American Oriental Society, and the American Schools of Oriental Research, held at Olivet Nazarene University, Bourbonnais, IL, February 11–13, 2011; publication forthcoming in *Creation and Chaos: A Reconsideration of Hermann Gunkel's Chaoskampf Hypothesis*, ed. JoAnn Scurlock (Winona Lake, IN: Eisenbrauns).]

Set within this new mytho-theological framework the Eden story (Gen 2:4–3:24) acquired a radically new interpretation. Instead of a story of inchoate creation wherein the definition of humankind vis-à-vis the deity and animalkind was but gradually worked out, the Eden story became a story of a world created perfect gone awry. Created in the image of God, humankind had been the crowning achievement of the Divine Sovereign; the whole of creation had been placed under the rule of these nearly divine creatures (Gen 1:26–28). In this setting the garden in Eden took on the connotation of a paradise created for the enjoyment of humankind. Their presence in the garden was no longer as substitute laborers for the deity but to "rule" in a garden of delights. Access to the tree of life guaranteed their immortality and nearly divine nature. All of this was lost, however, when in an act of hubris these magnificent beings forgot their creaturehood and attempted to usurp divinity itself.

Confirmation of this thesis, namely, that the Priestly Writer intended to portray primeval humankind as perfect and that this portrait depended upon seeing the Eden story in a new frame, is vividly confirmed by the Oracle against Tyre in Ezekiel 28. In language apparently drawn from the completed Priestly redaction of Genesis 1–3, the prophet condemned the hubris of Tyre in a satirical tirade. The prophet accused Tyre of pretending to divinity and (divine) wisdom (28:2–5). He then likened Tyre to the creature(s) in Eden:

> . . . full of wisdom and perfect in beauty,
> You were in Eden, the garden of God,
> every precious stone your clothing . . .
> You were perfect in your ways
> from the day of your creation
> —until iniquity was found in you! . . .
> Your heart became proud because of your beauty;
> you spoiled your wisdom for the sake of your splendor. (28:12–17)

Ezekiel's portrayal of "the human" in Eden as perfect and divine-like, luxuriating in opulence, confirms that this "garden of God" was understood as a paradise, a paradise which was lost through human hubris.

For reasons which I cannot detail here, it would appear that Ezekiel borrowed his imagery here from P. In any case, Ezekiel, written in the first half of the sixth century B.C.E., provides a *terminus a quo* for the development of the paradise motif in biblical literature. Given the obvious literary dependency between Ezekiel and P and assuming that these two compositions were approximately contemporaneous, then one may conclude that the paradise motif is an internal biblical development of approximately the sixth century B.C.E. There is no evidence that the paradise motif was borrowed from extrabiblical literature.

3. Conclusion

Contrary to a common scholarly opinion, biblical authors did not borrow the paradise motif from Mesopotamian sources. The motif is lacking in Mesopotamian literature. Moreover, the earliest biblical traditions do not contain such a motif. The motif is present in later biblical literature, but by way of internal biblical development rather than from external borrowing.

Mesopotamian literature apparently lacked an authentic paradise motif. By paradise is meant a place or time in human history—usually during a primeval period—wherein humankind lived an idyllic existence free from hostility, fear, sickness, and possibly even death. There is no attestation for the motif in Akkadian literature. Sumerian literature has been alleged to contain such a motif, which in turn was the source of a biblical paradise story. However, this investigation has sustained Alster's view that the alleged paradise motif is in fact wanting in Sumerian literature also.

The two principal texts which are alleged to contain a paradise motif are (1) *Enki and Ninhursag*, particularly its description of "pure" Dilmun, and (2) "Nudimmud's spell" in the myth of *Enmerkar and the Lord of Aratta*. Predications of the non-existence of wild beasts or sickness or of the lack of fear by humankind refer not to some positive, idyllic period in human history but to an inchoate primeval period before things received their ultimate definition. Far from pointing to an ideal period of human existence, these texts are witness to a standard Mesopotamian view that the definition ("creation") of humankind occurred in stages and that in the early period humankind lived a subhuman existence virtually indistinguishable from animalkind.

The assumption, then, that the ancient Israelite author(s) of Genesis borrowed the paradise motif from Mesopotamia is simply wrong. Since the motif is not attested in Akkadian literature, the normal channel by which Mesopotamian traditions found their way into biblical literature, scholars should have been wary of suggesting literary dependency upon the still older Sumerian literature! Biblical authors could not have borrowed a paradise motif from Mesopotamia because Mesopotamia lacked such a motif.

In fact, the development of the paradise motif in the opening chapters of Genesis is an internal biblical development. The earliest version of the primeval myth, the Yahwistic version, was not a true paradise story at all. The magnificent garden in Eden was planted for the benefit of the deity, not humankind. The humans were placed there to work the garden for the deity. When they attempted to usurp divine prerogatives, they were expelled from Eden. Like the Akkadian myth of *Atrahasis* upon which it was patterned, the Yahwistic primeval myth was a story of inchoate creation in which the definition of humankind was only gradually achieved.

It is only through the juxtaposition of the Priestly creation account (Gen 1:1–2:3) and the Yahwistic creation account (Gen 2:4–3:24) that the Eden story can be interpreted as a paradise story. The notion that the world was originally perfect is found only in the Priestly literary strata. When read within this Priestly framework, the Eden story is transformed into a paradise story, that is a place of perfect happiness created by God for the benefit of humankind. This perfect world was subsequently lost to humankind through their own fault.

The Priestly Writer appears to have been quite deliberate in rewriting the Israelite primeval myth. Ezekiel 28, from approximately the same time and with patent links to the Priestly tradition, confirms that the Eden story was understood as a fall from perfection. Under the Priestly hand the Eden story was transformed from a story of inchoate creation into a story about the loss of paradise because of human sin.

Were Milton to write his masterpiece today, he might not choose to alter his masterpiece in the least. But he might also add a footnote crediting an ancient Israelite writer as the literary genius who first created the theme of a "Paradise Lost."

Chapter 3

The Institution of Marriage in Genesis 2 and in Atrahasis

Throughout the centuries the majority of biblical commentators have assumed that Gen 2:18–25, and v. 24 in particular, either directly or indirectly touches upon the institution of marriage. Some, with an understanding of this text which is analogous to that of Jesus (Matt 19:3–9; Mark 10:2–12), have even claimed this text as the foundation of monogamy.[1] In modern times some scholars have compared marriage in Genesis 2 with marriage in matriarchal societies or *erēbu* marriages in an effort to account for the unexpected statement in Gen 2:24 that "for this reason a man forsakes his father and mother and clings to his wife," a statement which seems out of keeping with the normal patriarchal and patrilocal marital patterns of ancient Israel.[2] Other commentators find in Gen 2:24 still other ideal conceptions of marriage, for example, that marriage creates a bond of kinship which transcends both death and divorce,[3] or that marriage creates a covenantal relationship between spouses.[4]

Originally published in *CBQ* 62 (2000) 621–31. To my knowledge, there have been no challenges to the thesis presented herein, nor any new data which would incline me to change the conclusions I reached when writing this article.

1. Among others, Franz Delitzsch, *A New Commentary on Genesis* (2 vols.; New York: Scribner & Welford, 1889) l. 145; August Dillmann, *Die Genesis* (Kurzgefasstes exegetisches Handbuch zum Alten Testament 11; 3rd ed.; Leipzig: Hirzel, 1875) 79; Roland de Vaux, *Ancient Israel* (2 vols.; New York: McGraw-Hill, 1961) 2. 24; Kenneth A. Mathews, *Genesis 1–11:26* (New American Commentary 1 A; Nashville: Broadman 1996) 222–24.

2. W. Robertson Smith, *Kinship and Marriage in Early Arabia* (new ed.; London: Black, 1903; reprint, New York: AMS, 1979) 9–30; Cyrus Gordon, "*Erēbu* Marriage," in *In Honor of Ernest R. Lachemann on His Seventy-Fifth Birthday, April 29, 1981* (ed. M. A. Morrison and D. I. Owen; Studies on the Civilization and Culture of Nuzi and the Hurrians 1; Winona Lake, IN: Eisenbrauns, 1981) 155–61.

3. Gordon J. Wenham, *Genesis 1–15* (WBC 1; Waco, TX: Word, 1987) 70–71.

4. Victor P. Hamilton, *The Book of Genesis: Chapters 1–17* (NICOT; Grand Rapids: Eerdmans, 1990) 181. Similarly, Mathews, *Genesis 1–11:26*, 222. Angelo Tosato ("On Genesis 2:24," *CBQ* 52 [1990] 389–409) finds that although Gen 2:24 does indeed address directly the issues of marriage, it is not an integral part of the story of the creation of man and woman but is rather a gloss from the Persian period. Tosato (p. 409) thinks that it was added to "justify the new norm which was generically antipolygamous and implicitly

In the twentieth century, however, with an increased awareness of comparative data and social-scientific interpretation, various scholars have challenged the assumption that Gen 2:18–25 must be understood in terms of marriage. Gunkel, in his ground-breaking commentary on Genesis, written in 1901, vociferously rejected the notion that Genesis 2 is concerned with the institution of marriage, much less with monogamy; Gen 2:24 in particular, Gunkel argued, is an ancient attempt to explain the mutual sexual attraction between man and woman as the yearning of the two, originally one, to become one again.[5] Moreover, the first humans did not engage in sex in Paradise, for in their childlike innocence that had not yet recognized their sexual differences; the first sexual intercourse occurred outside Paradise, when Adam "knew" his wife and she conceived Cain (Gen 5:1).[6] Claus Westermann, in his exhaustive commentary on Genesis approves of Gunkel's opinion, though he nuances it considerably. For Westermann, the thrust of Gen 2:18–24 is the formation of "personal community between man and woman in the broadest sense—bodily and spiritual community, mutual help and understanding, joy and contentment in each other," not "the foundation of monogomy [*sic*]," for the author "is not concerned with the foundation of any sort of institution, but with primeval event" and thus "is not talking about marriage as an institution for the begetting of descendants, but of the community of man and woman as such."[7] Westermann concludes that "the primary place is not given to propagation or the institution of marriage as such," and that "the love of man and woman receives here a unique evaluation."[8]

Similarly, Bruce Vawter cautions against positing here the ideals of monogamous marriage, since "the kind of interpersonal relationship of which [the Yahwist] was speaking was also conceivable within the institution of polygamy."[9] Gerhard von Rad parses the passage as an etiological explanation of the "extremely powerful drive of the sexes to each other,"[10] a

---

antidivorce (Lev 18:18; cf. Mal 2:13–16), and perhaps also the new restrictive norms in the area of incestuous and mixed marriages (Leviticus 18 and 20; cf. Mal 2:10–12)."

5. Hermann Gunkel, *Genesis* (HKAT 1/1; 3rd ed.; Gottingen: Vandenhoeck & Ruprecht, 1910) 13, where he says, "Der Mythus ist oft mißverstanden; er redet nicht von der 'Ehe'; auch davon, da er die Einehe als normal hinstellen wolle, ist nicht die Rede; vielmehr schafft Gott nur ein Weib, weil er nichts überflüssiges tut: ein Mann und ein Weib können die ganze Menschheit zeugen." O. Procksch (*Die Genesis übersetzt und erklärt* [KAT 1; Leipzig: Deichert, 1913] 30) adopted a similar position: the institution in question is "nicht eine Rechtssitte, sondern eine Naturgewalt."

6. Gunkel, *Genesis*, 41.

7. Claus Westermann, *Genesis 1–11: A Commentary* (3 vols.; trans. John J. Scullion; Minneapolis: Augsburg Publishing House, 1984–86) 1. 232.

8. Ibid., 233, 234.

9. Bruce Vawter, *On Genesis: A New Reading* (Garden City, NY: Doubleday, 1977) 75–76.

10. Gerhard von Rad, *Genesis: A Commentary* (trans. John H. Marks; OTL; Philadelphia: Westminster, 1961) 82–83.

drive that the Yahwist thought to be "implanted in man by the Creator himself."[11] The list of recent commentators adopting similar positions could be extended.[12]

This debate over the question whether the author of Gen 2:18–25 envisions the institution of marriage or not can now be settled in the affirmative on the basis of comparative evidence, hitherto overlooked, from the Mesopotamian myth of *Atrahasis*.[13]

In my book *Slaying the Dragon: Mythmaking in the Biblical Tradition*, I argued that the Yahwist—to whom scholarly consensus attributes Gen 2:18–25—was in large measure dependent upon the myth of *Atrahasis*, both for the basic structure of his primeval myth of origins in Genesis 2–8,[14] as well as for many of its specific themes.[15] Specifically, I noted that the Yahwist's primeval myth parallels *Atrahasis* in broad outline: from an original setting in a dry wasteland, to the deity (god, or gods) creating humankind out of clay to serve as substitute laborers for the deity's garden or fields, to a revolt against the divine sovereign leading to an attempt to annihilate the human population through a flood in which but a single man and his family survived, to an offering to the deity by the pious survivor of the flood and a reconciliation of deity and humankind. But while I listed the institution of marriage as one of the parallels between *Atrahasis* and the Yahwist's primeval myth, I provided no evidence for that.[16] Indeed, to my knowledge no commentator on either the biblical text or the Mesopotamian text has discussed this parallel. For that reason, it is incumbent upon me to redress that omission now.

1. The Institution of Marriage in Atrahasis

The failure to notice a parallel between Gen 2:23–24 and *Atrahasis* can be explained in part by the fragmentary condition of the text of *Atrahasis*. An additional factor is that Lambert and Millard, in their magisterial edition of newly assembled text of *Atrahasis*,[17] misplaced one fragment.

---

11. Gerhard von Rad, *Old Testament Theology* (2 vols.; trans. D. M. G. Stalker; New York: Harper, 1962–65) 1. 150.

12. See, for example, O. H. Steck, *Die Paradieserzählung: Eine Auslegung von Genesis 2,4b–3.24* (BibS[N] 60; Neukirchen-Vluyn: Neukirchener Verlag, 1970) 95; Phyllis Trible, *God and the Rhetoric of Sexuality* (OBT; Philadelphia: Fortress Press, 1978) 104; Peter Weimar, *Untersuchungen zur Redaktionsgeschichte des Pentateuchs* (BZAW 146; Berlin/New York: de Gruyter, 1977) 120.

13. For a very different approach to this same conclusion see Helgo Lindner, "Spricht Gen. 2,24 von der Ehe?" *TBei* 19 (1983) 23–32.

14. Or *her* primeval myth, should Bloom (in David Rosenberg and Harold Bloom, *The Book of J* [New York: Grove Weidenfeld, 1990]) be correct in his thesis that J was a royal woman in the court of Rehoboam, son of Solomon.

15. Bernard F. Batto, *Slaying the Dragon: Mythmaking in the Biblical Tradition* (Louisville: Westminster/John Knox, 1992), esp. chap. 2, "The Yahwist's Primeval Myth," pp. 41–72.

16. Ibid., 52.

17. W. G. Lambert and A. R. Millard, *Atra-ḫasīs: The Babylonian Story of the Flood* (Oxford: Clarendon Press, 1969).

The relevant passage in *Atrahasis* comes in the main text at I 249–308. In this scene, Ea and Belet-ili (Mami), in the presence of the birth goddesses, shape fourteen pieces of clay to create humankind: seven *pairs* of males and females. Unfortunately, the main text is broken at this crucial point so that the story line is difficult to follow. An Assyrian text of *Atrahasis* from Ashurbanipal's library (text S), itself fragmentary, helps to fill in the gap. The Assyrian version is so different, however, that only the ideas, not the specific wording, can be used to reconstruct the main (Old Babylonian) version.

In the course of the lengthy article on the institution of the family in Babylonia, Claus Wilcke offers an improved reading of this particular section of *Atrahasis*, with a new translation in several places.[18] In particular Wilcke has improved the reading of I 273–74:

> [*in-nam-ma-a*]*r? zi-iq-nu* / [*i-n*]*a le-et eṭ-li*
> [*i-na ki*]-*ra-ti ù šu-li-i* / [*li-iḫ*]-*ti-ru aš-ša-tum ù mu-us-sà*
>
> When a beard appears on the cheeks of a young man,
> In gardens and byways let them choose one another as husband and
> wife.

When a young man begins to grow a beard, it is obvious that he has reached the age of sexual maturity and, thus, is ready to marry. At Mari, Shamshi-Addu repeatedly attempted to shame his son Yasmah-Addu into joining his older brother Ishme-Dagan on a campaign against their common enemy with the words "Are you still a boy? Are you not yet a grown man (*eṭlu*)? Is there no hair on your cheeks?" (ARM 1, texts 61.10–11; 73.43–44; 108.6–7; 113.7–8). Or again, the Old Babylonian series, *ana itti-šu*, under the verb *eṭēlu*, describes the proper treatment of an adopted son by his legal father: "He did not strike him. He reared him. He taught him the scribal art. He caused him to become a man [Sumerian: "to grow hair on his cheeks"]. He acquired a wife for him."[19]

Just as the appearance of a beard is the sign of a young man's sexual maturity, so the development of breasts and the growth of pubic hair are the sign of a young woman's sexual maturity and readiness for marriage. In a bal-bal-e song celebrating the goddess Inanna's wedding to Utu, Inanna's girlfriends rejoice in Inanna's and their own sexual maturity in these words:

> Now our breasts stand up!
> Now our parts have grown hair!

---

18. Claus Wilcke, "Familiengründung im alten Babylonien," in *Geschlechtsreife und Legitimation zur Zeugung* (ed. Ernst W. Müller; Veröffentlichungen des Instituts für Historische Anthropologie e.V. 3; Freiburg/Munich: Alber, 1985) 213–317, esp. 295–98.

19. Ibid., 241–42. This passage (*ana itti-šu* 7.3.16–21) has been published in Sumerian and Akkadian, with a German translation, by B. Landsberger, *Materialien zum sumerischen Lexikon 1: Die Serie* ana ittišu (Scripta Pontificii Instituti Biblici; Rome: Biblical Institute Press, 1937) 100–101.

Going to the bridegroom's loins, Baba,
  let us be happy for them!
Dance! Dance!
Baba, let us be happy
  for our parts!
Dance! Dance!
Afterward they will please him,
  they will please him. [20]

This is a motif common to many cultures, of course, rooted in the universal experience of the way in which human bodies naturally develop. It is to be found in the Bible as well. In Ezek 16:6–8 Yahweh reproaches Israel for her infidelity under the metaphor of a foundling girl whom Yahweh has lovingly reared and eventually married:

> Then I passed by and saw you weltering in your blood. I said to you: Live in your blood and grow like a plant in the field. You grew and developed, you came to the age of puberty; your breasts were formed, your hair had grown, but you were still stark naked. Again I passed by you and saw that you were now old enough for love. So I spread the corner of my cloak over you to cover your nakedness; I swore a covenant with you; you became mine, says the Lord GOD. (*NAB*)

The image of breasts as a sign of sexual maturity and readiness for marriage also lies behind the dialogue between the bride and her older brothers in the Cant 8:8–10:

> Brothers: Our sister is little
>   and she has no breasts as yet.
>   What shall we do for our sister
>   when her courtship begins?
>   If she is a wall,
>   we will reinforce it with a cedar plank.
> Bride: I am a wall,
>   and my breasts are like towers.
>   So now in his eyes I have become
>   one to be welcomed. (*NAB*)

Thus, the presence of the word *i-ir-ti-ša*, "her chest," in *Atrahasis* I 272, followed in the next line by a reference to a beard growing on a young man's cheeks, allows us confidently to posit a context about the sexual maturation of young men and women as the time for choosing marriage partners. This is also the import of the small fragment, text R, which Lam-

---

20. Translation by Thorkild Jacobsen, *The Harps That Once . . . : Sumerian Poetry in Translation* (New Haven/London: Yale University Press, 1987) 18. See also Wilcke, "Familiengründung," 243. For the Sumerian text (N 4305 rev. 2.1–3), see Samuel Noah Kramer, "Cuneiform Studies and the History of Literature: The Sumerian Sacred Marriage Texts," *Proceedings of the American Philosophical Society* 107 (1963) 508, 521.

bert and Millard mistakenly placed at the conclusion of the myth, in tablet 3.[21] To judge from Asshurbanipal's Assyrian text S, which partially parallels the Old Babylonian text and which also has reference to similar "regulations for humankind" (*uṣurāt nišī*) at this point, text R must be fitted in the break in the main text between lines 260 and 271.[22] Accordingly, *Atrahasis* I 271–72 must be restored approximately as

[*a-na ar-da-ti tu-le*] / [. . . *i-na*] *i-ir-ti-ša*
When on a young woman breasts / [develop?] on her chest

Improving upon Wilcke, the whole complex of lines 271–76 may be restored and translated as follows:

(271–72)	[*a-na ar-da-ti tu-le*] / [. . . *i-na*] *i-ir-ti-ša*
(273–74)	[*in-nam-ma-a*]*r zi-iq-nu* / [*i-n*]*a le-et eṭ-li*
(275–76)	[*i-na ki*]-*ra-ti ù šu-li-i* / [*li-iḫ*]-*ti-ru aš-ša-tum ù mu-us-sà*

(271–72)	When on a young woman breasts [develop?] on her chest,
(273–74)	When a beard appears on the cheeks of a young man,
(275–76)	In gardens and byways let them choose one another as wife and husband.

At this point Belet-ili, the mother goddess, apparently suspends her dictation of these "regulations for humankind" (*uṣurāt nišī*), while she completes the creation of the humans by resorting to some kind of ritual birthing process (I 277–90). After she has "given birth" to humankind, she continues with the "regulations for humankind," which now have to do primarily with the procreation process itself. Again utilizing Wilcke's emendations, I 291–306 should be restored and translated as follows:

(291) *a-li a-li-it-tum ú-ul-la-du-ma*
   um-mi še-er-ri / *ú-ḫ*[*a-ar*]-*ru-ú ra-ma-an-ša*
   9 u_4-[*mi l*]*i-na-di li-bi-it-tum*
(295) *i tu-uk-ta-bi-it* ᵈ*nin-tu sa-as-sú-ru*
   ᵈ*ma-mi* [x] x-*sú-nu i-ta-ab-bi*
   i-ta-[x x x *s*]*a-as-sú-ra* / *i-ta-ad ke-ša*
   i-na b[*i-ti-šu-nu i-n*]*a na-de-e e-er-ši*
(300) *li-iḫ-ti-*[*ru aš-ša*]-*tum ù mu-sá*
   i-nu-ma aš-š[*u-ti*] *ù mu-tu-ti*
   i-na bi-it [x x] x *i ta-aḫ-du iš-tar*
   9 u_4-*mi liš-šá-ki-in ḫi-du-tum*
   iš-tar [*li-*(*it-*)*ta-a*]*b-bu-ú* ᵈ*iš-ḫa-ra*

21. Lambert and Millard, *Atra-ḫasīs*, 104.

22. John Van Seters (*Prologue to History: The Yahwist as Historian in Genesis* [Louisville: Westminster/John Knox, 1992] 53) has also noticed the misplacement of fragment R, but I do not find convincing his further suggestion to interpret *uṣurāt nišī* and its variant *uṣurāte nišīma* as "shapes or figures of humans" instead of Lambert's "regulations for humankind."

(305) *i-na* [x x x (x)] x-*ti si-ma-nu ši-im-ti*
[x x *a*]*tʾ-tu-n*[*u*ʾ (i) *t*]*a-ab-bi-*[*a-n*]*i*[*m*ʾ]

(291) Wherever a pregnant woman gives birth,
the mother of the infant delivers herself,[23]
for nine days let the (birthing-)brick lie in place.
(295) Let Nintu the birth goddess be honored.
She shall call Mami their [(?)].
She shall [invoke(?)] the birth goddess.
She shall place down the mat(?).
In their house, at the establishing of her bed,
(300) let a wife and her husband choose one another![24]
Whenever (anything) of marriage (is done),
let Ishtar rejoice in the house of [(?)].
For nine days let there be celebration;
let them proclaim Ishtar Ishhara.
(305) . . . . . at the fixed time of destiny . . .
let her name me (?) . . .

The rest of the "regulations" and the conclusion of the scene are lost in the break. Nevertheless, enough is preserved to make it clear that the myth posits a certain symmetry between the divine creative act and the human procreative act:

A.   Ea & Belet-ili mold humanoid clay figures in complementary pairs while they recite an incantation
B.   The *uṣurāt nišī* define the pairing of human couples in real life.
A'. The deity "gives birth" to the human couples by using a paradigmatic ritual
B'. The *uṣurāt nišī* are resumed, explicating the paradigm to be followed in procreation.

Wilcke treats this text not under the heading of "marriage" but under the heading *Geburt von Kindern*, "birth of children"; he calls it a "mythic account about the divine ordering of procreation and birth."[25] It is this, and more. The primary emphasis in the text is on the pairing of humankind into stable communities which we call marriage. According to *Atrahasis*, the institution of marriage and its corollary of procreation were part of the creator's design for humankind (*uṣurāt nišī*).

This is not simply a matter of physical attraction or a celebration of love between men and women. In the text one finds frequent use of terms denoting the institution of marriage: "a wife and her husband" (*aššatum u mussa*), and "wifehood and husbandhood" (*aššāti u mutūti*). The latter

---

23. See Benjamin R. Foster, *Before the Muses: An Anthology of Akkadian Literature* (2 vols.; Bethesda, MD: CDL, 1993) 1. 167 with the note on p. 200.
24. [B. Foster's (ibid.) translation, "Wife and husband were blissful," misses the normative and paradigmatic function of this text for humankind as the institution of marriage.]
25. Wilcke, "Familiengründung," 295.

phrase is itself a hendiadys indicating "marriage." Although Lambert's and Millard's translation of 1.301 as an explicit statement about the institution of marriage is unwarranted, they are on target, nonetheless, in understanding the intention of the Babylonian poet at this point. Marriage is quintessential to the human condition.

2. Implications for Genesis 2:23–24

One of the first points to notice is that Gen 2:23–24, with its reference to man and woman joining together to form "one flesh," comes at exactly the same point in the Yahwist's primeval myth as the "regulations for humankind" in *Atrahasis*, namely, at the very moment of the creation of the human species as male and female. Of course, in *Atrahasis* the human species is equally divided between males and females from the very beginning, while in Genesis 2 the human species is at first created androgynous, a fact which necessitates a second creative procedure by the deity in order for the human species to be appropriately divided into complementary halves, male and female. Both texts, however, end with the human species divided by divine design into complementary genders and ordained to choosing each other as husband and wife (*Atrahasis*), or to abandoning their parents in order to cling to each other (Genesis 2).

Precisely because of such paralleling of structure and theme in the two texts, *Atrahasis* provides an important hermeneutical key for unlocking the meaning of Gen 2:23–24. Although some maintain that v. 24 is a secondary addition to the narrative in 2:18–23,[26] v. 24 is an integral part of this narrative. Indeed, the narrative reaches its climax in v. 24; in that verse is the goal to which the whole scene has been tending. Humankind was divided into male and female so that the one might have companionship with an *'ēzer kĕnegdô*, a helpmate appropriate to itself. That companionship achieves its realization, according to v. 24, in the union of husband and wife as "one flesh." Male and female taken separately are incomplete; each naturally tends toward the other. Marriage is the bond that reunites them into a natural community of wholesomeness.

Gunkel clearly was wrong in claiming that this text is not about the institution of marriage. There is more involved than the physical attraction of men and women to each other. Westermann is closer to the mark when he writes, "The purpose of the narrative is to lead to a new understanding of the creation of humanity. God's creature is humankind only in community, only when human beings interact with each other."[27] But even this is too restrictive. Speaking of v. 24 specifically, Westermann writes, "The significance of the verse lies in this that in contrast to the established

---

26. For a history of this interpretation, see Tosato, "On Genesis 2:24," 389 n. 1. For Tosato's own position, see above, n. 4.

27. Westermann, *Genesis 1–11*, 192.

institutions and partly in opposition to them, it points to the basic power of love between man and woman."[28] Given the parallel in *Atrahasis*, however, the Yahwist surely intended v. 24 as the equivalent of *uṣurāt nišī* in *Atrahasis*, that is, as a universal law regulating the normative behavior of the sexes within a community of marriage. The leaving of one's mother and father to join with one of the opposite sex so that the two become "one flesh" can hardly be seen as anything other than a reference to marriage.

Granted that there are differences between *Atrahasis* and Genesis. The author of *Atrahasis* employs the abstraction *aššāti u mutūti*, "wifehood and husbandhood." The Yahwist uses concrete but more ambiguous terms: *'îš*, "man" or "husband," and *'iššâ*, "woman" or "wife." The author of *Atrahasis* has the regulations given in a single scene of two contiguous pronouncements of action: a first which has only to do with the pairing of the males and females into marriage partners at the time of puberty, and a second in which the human couple extend the marriage community through the procreation of children. The Yahwist has a comparable duality of pronouncements of action, but only the first, the pairing of husband and wife as one flesh, is associated directly with the moment of creation of humankind as male and female in Gen 2:18–24; the pronouncement concerning childbirth is delayed until the curse of the woman in Gen 3:16. Even so, Genesis 2 and Genesis 3 are but complementary scenes in which the full definition of humankind is being worked out.[29] Nevertheless, by delaying the mention of children until a later scene the Yahwist does seem deliberately to drive at least a small wedge between marriage *per se* and procreation; procreation, thus, is reduced to a secondary end of marriage. By divine design, a design grounded in creation itself, humankind finds its fulfillment in marriage. In marriage both the human desire for community and the natural complementarity of the sexes achieve their intended goals.

Finally, evidence from *Atrahasis* helps to decide another old debate: whether or not the first couple engaged in sexual intercourse in Eden before they ate of the "tree of knowledge of good and evil" and before "the eyes of the two of them were opened" (Gen 3:6–7). If the Yahwist was indeed following the basic pattern of *Atrahasis*, it would appear that he also assumed that the primeval couple enjoyed sex as a natural part of their existence in the garden. Coitus is explicitly mentioned for the first time in Gen 4:1, where it serves the function of introducing a story about the next generation and its contribution to the primeval story. But as we have already noted, the Yahwist apparently saw a distinction between marriage and procreation. The first act of procreation was not necessarily the first act of sexual intercourse. As in *Atrahasis*, the Yahwist assumed that the couple experienced sexual desire as part and parcel of their being, from the mo-

---

28. Ibid., 233.
29. See Batto, *Slaying the Dragon*, 41–72.

ment of their creation. In Gen 3:16c the new element is not the woman's desire for her husband but the fact that now her husband will not return her desire in complementarity; he will attempt to dominate her instead. The first clause, "Your desire is for your husband," is a verbless clause which may be understood as a temporal or continuing condition. Only the second clause, "But he for his part shall rule you," contains a future-tense verb. Neither for *Atrahasis* nor for the Yahwist was sexual desire introduced by sin or concupiscence (contrary to an opinion dating back to Augustine and beyond).[30] Sexual desire, like marriage, is part and parcel of the creation of humankind.

3. Conclusion

When *Atrahasis* 1.249–308 is properly read, it provides an important parallel to Gen 2:18–24. *Atrahasis* thus provides an important hermeneutical tool for understanding the Yahwist's message and Gen 2:18–24 in particular. The Yahwist follows his source, *Atrahasis*, in positing that the institution of marriage is grounded in the very design of creation itself, but unlike the author of *Atrahasis*, who links marriage and procreation closely as if to suggest that the primary function of marriage is procreation, the Yahwist seems to distance marriage somewhat from procreation. For the Yahwist, the communitarian, affective function of marriage takes precedence over the procreative function of marriage.[31]

---

30. Taking issue with other commentators of his day, Augustine (*De Genesi ad litteram* 9.3–11 §§5–19) opined that Eve was created to be a helpmate for Adam precisely in the matter of procreation, and, therefore, that the primal couple eventually would have had coitus in Paradise, even had they not sinned. Such "honorable nuptial union and the bed undefiled" would have been totally rational and perfectly controlled by the will, however, without any ardor of passion or concupiscence. For this, see *St. Augustine, The Literal Meaning of Genesis* (2 vols.; trans. John Hammond Taylor; ACW 41–42; New York/Ramsey, NJ: Paulist Press, 1982) 73–83; see further 11.1 §3 (p. 135) and 11.32 §42 (pp. 164–65).

31. Whether and how the Yahwist's view in this matter may be reconciled with the priestly theology of humankind's obligation to "be fruitful and multiply and fill the earth" (Gen 1:28) are questions best left to another forum.

Chapter 4

The Divine Sovereign:
The Image of God in the
Priestly Creation Account

It is commonplace among critical biblical scholars to contrast the two creation accounts in the opening chapters of Genesis by asserting that the first account, the Priestly account, is much less anthropomorphic in its depiction of the deity than is the following, Yahwistic account. Indeed, outside of "actions" such as "making," "saying," "naming," and the like, the only other supposedly anthropomorphic characterization of אלהים "God" in Gen 1:1–2:3 is that on the seventh day he "rested" (שבת, 2:2); and even this term can be translated more neutrally as "he ceased (from working)."[1] So without any explicit description of the deity, can one "flesh out"—to continue the metaphor of anthropomorphism—the Priestly Writer's conception of the deity?

Moreover, to shift the focus slightly, in Gen 1:26 the Priestly Writer says that God proposes נעשה אדם בצלמנו כדמותנו "let us make humankind in our image according to our likeness" and in Gen 1:27, acting on that proposal, ויברא אלהים את־האדם בצלמו "God created humankind in his image." Clearly, here P suggests that the deity is imaged at least partially through human form or human attributes, as many commentators from ancient to

Originally published in *David and Zion: Biblical Studies in Honor of J. J. M. Roberts* (ed. Bernard F. Batto and Kathryn L. Roberts; Winona Lake, IN: Eisenbrauns, 2004) 143-86.

Author's note: This paper is dedicated to J. J. M. Roberts, whose friendship extends back to my graduate school days at The Johns Hopkins University, where he first introduced me to Amarna Akkadian and later directed my 1972 dissertation, *Studies on Women at Mari: Politics and Religion*—his first directed dissertation but certainly not his last. His judicious use of Assyriology to shed light on the Hebrew Bible inspired me to attempt a similar path in my own career.

1. Use of the vocable ברא "to create" is generally not considered an anthropomorphism because this vocable "is never used in the Hebrew Old Testament with other than God as its subject"; so Bruce Vawter (*On Genesis: A New Reading* [Garden City, NY: Doubleday, 1977] 39), echoing the nearly unanimous voice of modern commentators. Gerhard von Rad (*Genesis: A Commentary* [OTL; 2nd ed.; London: SCM, 1963] 47) goes so far as to claim, mistakenly, that ברא implies *creatio ex nihilo*.

modern times have recognized. There is little agreement among these commentators, however, about how humans actually image the deity.[2]

In this paper I will argue that one can put a humanlike form to P's conception of God, namely, that of the divine sovereign. P may have been conscious of the theological limitations inherent in this anthropomorphism. Nevertheless, within P's world view, divine sovereignty was the most transcendent characterization of God available, and P readily employed it to further his theological agenda.[3] Corollary to P's characterization of God as the divine sovereign is P's further point that God created humans to serve as his regents in administering this world. If God is the divine sovereign, then humankind is his viceroy on earth. (The ambiguity in the phrase "the image of God"—referring to the Priestly portrayal of the deity per se as well as to humankind being created in the deity's image and likeness—is therefore intentional in the title of this paper.)

Given P's parsimonious language regarding the deity, one is forced to use an oblique method in teasing out P's conception of God. Thus, in developing my thesis I will proceed along three auxiliary lines of argument: (1) an examination of ancient Near Eastern literature and iconography wherein creator and creation are presented as constituent elements or subsidiary metaphors of a more fundamental metaphor of divine sovereignty, (2) comparative evidence from cognate biblical texts concerning God's kingship in relation to creation, and (3) an analysis of the Priestly creation account itself for indications of an implied image of God.

1. Divine Sovereignty in the Ancient Near East

In the ancient Near East, the concept of divine sovereignty had reference to the absolute and universal rule of the chief deity over heaven and earth. Since early in the second millennium B.C.E. at least, the concept of one deity's being supreme over the other gods and controlling the cosmos was well established across the ancient Near East, even if the identity of this divine sovereign varied from region to region and from period to period, for example, in Egypt: Atum, Horus, or Amun-Re; in Mesopotamia: Anu, Enlil, Enki-Ea, Marduk, or Ashur; in Canaan: El or his associate Baal.

---

2. [For a survey of biblical scholarship concerning "the image of God," see G. Jonsson, *The Image of God: Genesis 1:26-28 in a Century of Old Testament Research* (Lund: Gleerup, 1988).]

3. It is a pleasure to acknowledge J. J. M. Roberts's important contributions to the question of God's kingship, including his most recent article "The Enthronement of Yahweh and David: The Abiding Theological Significance of the Kingship Language of the Psalms," *CBQ* 64 (2002) 675–86. His earlier essays are now conveniently collected in his volume *The Bible and the Ancient Near East: Collected Essays* (Winona Lake, IN: Eisenbrauns, 2002); from these on the kingship of Yahweh note in particular his essay "Zion in the Theology of the Davidic-Solomonic Empire," 331–47, esp. pp. 332–37 (originally published in *Studies in the Period of David and Solomon and Other Essays* [ed. T. Ishida; Winona Lake, IN: Eisenbrauns, 1982] 93–108).

In Israel and Judah, of course, the role of divine sovereign was ascribed to Yahweh, also known as אלהים "God."

A. Creator as a Subsidiary Metaphor of the Divine Sovereign

The metaphor of the divine sovereign involved a number of associated subsidiary metaphors. Principal among these was that of *creator*. The association between the divine sovereign and the creator has a long history in ancient Near Eastern tradition.

In Mesopotamia, since at least the third millennium B.C.E., myths involving divine sovereignty have been used to undergird the political hegemony of particular city-states over neighboring states, without necessarily involving a subsidiary metaphor of creation per se. The Sumerian myth *Enmerkar and the Lord of Aratta*, in which Inanna is said to favor Kulab in Uruk over a rival sanctuary, served to justify Uruk's preeminence within the Sumerian confederation. The Akkadian myth of *Anzu* served a similar function for the city-state of Girsu; by defeating the chaos monster Anzu, Ninurta, the god of Girsu, was able to rescue the "tablets of destiny" and restore order in the world.

To judge from its wide distribution and long life, the Old Babylonian myth Atrahasis may be regarded as the standard Mesopotamian cosmology from the Old Babylonian period through the Neo-Assyrian period (from ca. 1700 to ca. 600 B.C.E.). The story of Atrahasis opens with a rebellion of the worker gods against Enlil, recognized as the divine sovereign in this text, as frequently in ancient Mesopotamia.[4] To satisfy the lesser gods' grievances, Enlil directed Ea, the god of wisdom noted for his craftsmanship, to devise a substitute for the worker gods; the result was the creation of primeval humankind from clay mixed with the blood of the principal rebel god. The primeval humans, however, like the rebel god from whose blood they were partially made, seem not to have acknowledged the authority of the divine sovereign. The latter, in turn, attempted in various ways to wipe them out, ultimately by means of a flood. Enlil relented only when a solution was found by recasting humankind as a naturally mortal species. Though Ea was the craftsman, the plan ultimately had to have Enlil's stamp of approval. Here the divine sovereign motif is closely linked to that of the creation of humankind. The creation of the physical universe is not addressed in this myth, however, since it assumes the preexistence of a world populated only with divine beings, divided into two classes: a small cadre of ruler deities and a large group of lesser, worker gods.

The development of the motif of the divine sovereign in Mesopotamia underwent a dramatic shift with the rise of the nation-states of Babylon and Assyria during the second millennium B.C.E. and continuing into the first millennium B.C.E. In each case the national deity, namely, Marduk in Babylon and Ashur in Assyria, were touted by their respective devotees as

---

4. See my "Sleeping God: An Ancient Near Eastern Motif of Divine Sovereignty," *Bib* 58 (1987) 153–77. [Reprinted in this volume as chap. 5.]

the supreme deity, with the obvious purpose of justifying their country's political ascendancy as the ruler of the "world." In the Old Babylonian period, when Babylon first rose to prominence under the aggressive West-Semitic Hammurabi (ca. 1792–1750 B.C.E.), Babylonian propagandists were not so bold as to claim that Marduk had displaced Anu or Enlil, the traditional two contenders for the role of head of the Mesopotamian pantheon. Nevertheless, according to the prologue to the Law Code of Hammurabi (i 1–26), both Anu and Enlil did cooperate in elevating Marduk to preeminence among the Igigu gods, giving Marduk "supreme power over all the peoples" and establishing for him at Babylon an "eternal kingship whose foundations are as fixed as heaven and earth."[5] Succeeding generations of Babylonians were not so restrained, however. In a kind of incipient monotheism, literature was rewritten and hymns composed that ascribed to Babylon's patron deity most of the important functions and the major attributes of the other gods. This process is perhaps most explicit in a Babylonian text that equates Marduk with all of the other gods and their functions:

Ninurta (is)	Marduk of the pickaxe
Nergal (is)	Marduk of battle . . .
Enlil (is)	Marduk of lordship and consultations
Nabu (is)	Marduk of accounting
Sin (is)	Marduk who lights up the night
Shamash (is)	Marduk of justice
Adad (is)	Marduk of rain

(CT 24, 50; BM 47406, obverse)[6]

And so on.

The campaign to promote Babylon's patron deity to the rank of divine sovereign is most blatant in the Babylonian theogonic myth *Enuma Elish.*[7] Borrowing heavily from the traditions of Anzu[8] and Atrahasis, the author of *Enuma Elish* gave expression to a new religiopolitical paradigm. This myth tells how Marduk became the divine sovereign when the older, established gods of Mesopotamia failed to meet new threats to world order.[9]

---

5. Trans. Martha Roth, "The Laws of Hammurabi," *COS* 2:131 (p. 336).

6. Translation by W. G. Lambert, "Historical Development of the Mesopotamian Pantheon: A Study in Sophisticated Polytheism," in *Unity and Diversity: Essays in the History, Literature, and Religion of the Ancient Near East* (ed. Hans Goedicke and J. J. M. Roberts; Baltimore: Johns Hopkins University Press, 1975) 191–200, esp. pp. 197–98.

7. See my "Creation Theology in Genesis," in *Creation in the Biblical Traditions* (ed. Richard J. Clifford and John J. Collins; CBQMS 24; Washington, DC: Catholic Biblical Association, 1992) 16–38, esp. pp. 25–26.

8. "The direct borrowing in *Enuma elish* from the *Myth of Anzu* in effect makes Marduk not only the new Anu, Enlil, and Ea, but the new Ninurta as well." So Richard J. Clifford, *Creation Accounts in the Ancient Near East and in the Bible* (CBQMS 26; Washington, DC: Catholic Biblical Association, 1994) 85.

9. For this interpretation of *Enuma Elish,* see T. Jacobsen, *Treasures of Darkness: A History of Mesopotamian Religion* (New Haven: Yale University Press, 1976) 163–91.

The former authority of those gods is acknowledged by allowing that one of their number, namely Ea (Sumerian Enki), had been successful previously in establishing a kind of primeval order. Ea had defeated Apsu, the first husband of Tiamat (Primeval Ocean), and built a palace within Apsu as a symbol of his power to control chaos. But when Tiamat reemerged in an even more threatening form—symbolized by her new marriage to the even more ferocious Qingu—Ea and the older gods proved unequal to the task. Thereupon Marduk—here, for obvious propagandistic reasons, said to be Ea's own fulgent son—offered to subdue Tiamat and Qingu in return for the right to be the divine sovereign. Marduk not only vanquished Tiamat and her cohorts, he went one better over the old regime. Out of the carcasses of the slain gods, Marduk created the world and peopled it with humans who are to act as servants to the gods, thereby allowing the gods the rest or leisure befitting their divine status.[10] In short, *Enuma Elish* claims to supplant all previous cosmologies by reaching back before them to the very beginning of existence to tell the true story of how the whole of creation came to be: the physical universe, humankind, even the origin of the gods. And in this new story Marduk demonstrates his superiority over all the gods; he alone was able to overcome the threat of annihilation by turning chaos into the completed cosmos, which includes the establishment of the human realm. The other gods gratefully acknowledged Marduk as their divine sovereign by proclaiming his fifty titles of kingship.

When *Enuma Elish* reached Assyria, Neo-Assyrian theologians appropriated this myth of divine sovereignty for their own national god simply by substituting everywhere the name of Ashur in place of Marduk. Much like Babylonian theologians did for Marduk, Assyrian theologians elevated Ashur to the rank of divine sovereign, at first somewhat tentatively by modeling Ashur on the pattern of Enlil during the second millennium and then more aggressively under Sennacherib by replacing the cult of Marduk with a cult of Ashur as head of the pantheon.[11]

The Ugaritic myth of Baal and Anat is also a myth of divine sovereignty, though of a different kind. In the Ugaritic versions of the Combat Myth, Baal does not so much replace the elder El as the king of the gods as he becomes El's associate in ruling the world. In one version Baal overcomes Death (Mot); in another version Baal subdues Sea (Yamm), alternately called River. Either way, Baal wins the right to build his palace from which he rules with thunderous voice, the symbol of his divine authority.

The ancient Near Eastern motif of the divine sovereign could be fleshed out with considerably more detail and through additional examples.[12] But

---

10. On the motif of divine rest as a symbol of divine authority, see my article "The Sleeping God," 153–77 [pp. 139–157 in this volume; see n. 4 above].

11. See J. J. M. Roberts, "The Davidic Origin of the Zion Tradition," 326–27; W. G. Lambert, "The God Aššur," *Iraq* 45 (1983) 82–86, esp. p. 86.

12. Egypt is ignored here for several reasons: (1) There are no extant Egyptian cosmologies; our knowledge of Egyptian myth is limited to allusions in various texts. Moreover,

enough has been said to allow a sketch of some of the principal features of the motif. The divine sovereign was the deity who as king of the gods ruled both heaven and earth. How he became the divine sovereign varies according to myth type. In cases such as Anu and Enlil in Sumer, Atum in Egypt, or El in Canaan, the deity seems to have been acknowledged as head of the pantheon through long-standing tradition. In the Combat Myth type, however, a deity earned the rank of divine sovereign by defeating in battle the chaos-dragon, usually symbolized as primeval Sea, though others were also possible, for example, Death, Desert, and Night or Darkness.[13] One consequence of this victory is that the divine sovereign was thought to be responsible for making an inhabitable world possible. In Babylon Marduk was made out to be the principal architect of creation, the controller of all destinies. Should this divine sovereign ever relax his authority, the forces of anticreation could win out and the world would fall into the realm of chaos.[14] In Assyria this same function was assigned to Ashur. At Ugarit Baal kept the powers of noncreation at bay in a precariously balanced world. Meanwhile, in Egypt similar powers were ascribed to Horus/Re. But whatever the country, in the ancient Near East creation—the displacement of absolute chaos with cosmic order—was usually understood to be a primary function of the divine sovereign. "Creator," accordingly, may be considered a submotif (subsidiary metaphor) of the divine sovereign motif (metaphor).

---

it is likely that knowledge of such myths was the secret domain of specialized priests who used them in healings, rituals, and funerary preparations. (2) Each major religious center had its own mythic tradition revolving around its own deity, even if at core they shared certain common features. Also, traditions even at the same center often evolved considerably over Egypt's long history. Such diversity makes generalizations difficult. (3) While one may attribute the role of divine sovereign to Amun, Amun-Re, or Aten-Re, or to Horus as a manifestation of Re, there is no unanimity in Egyptian tradition about either the creator or the process of creation. (4) Although Egyptian influence is patent in other biblical texts, for example, Psalm 104, there is no clear evidence that Egyptian ideas directly influenced the Priestly creation account. (5) The creation of humankind is a minor theme in extant Egyptian literature. See Clifford, *Creation Accounts in the Ancient Near East and in the Bible*, 99–116; B. Batto, "The Ancient Near Eastern Context of the Hebrew Ideas of Creation," see chap. 1 in this volume, pp. 7–53. Regarding (4), Jon D. Levenson (*Creation and the Persistence of Evil: The Jewish Drama of Divine Omnipotence* [San Francisco: Harper & Row, 1988] 59–65) argues for a trajectory from the Egyptian "Hymn to Aten" to Psalm 104 to Genesis 1; assuming Levenson is correct, any Egyptian influence upon P has been mediated through Psalm 104.

13. *Death*: for example, Mot in the Ugaritic myth of Baal and Anat. *Desert*: for example, in the second part of the Sumerian myth of Enki and Ninhursag, water (Enki) penetrates and makes fertile the arid land (Ninhursag). For the latest edition of this myth, see P. Attinger, "Enki et Ninhursaga," *ZA* 74 (1984) 1–52. For another translation, see T. Jacobsen, *The Harps That Once . . . : Sumerian Poetry in Translation* (New Haven: Yale University Press, 1987) 181–204. *Night or Darkness*: for example, in the Egyptian text known as "The Repulsing of the Dragon"; see S. Morenz, *Egyptian Religion* (Ithaca, NY: Cornell University Press, 1973) 167–69.

14. See Batto, "The Sleeping God," esp. pp. 163 and 169–72 [pp. 147 and 152–54 in this volume].

Fig. 1. Watercolor painting by W. Andrae of fragmentary glazed polychrome tile from Ashur.

B. The King as Viceroy of the Divine Sovereign

Throughout the ancient Near East human kingship was viewed as complementary to divine sovereignty. The human king ruled on earth in the name of the gods, and more specifically, in the name of the divine sovereign. This was nowhere more evident than in Egypt, where the pharaoh was put forth in life as the embodiment or incarnation of Horus—later, Amun-Re—and in death as the embodiment of Osiris. Accordingly, the decrees of the king had the force of the divine will. Though less explicit elsewhere, similar conceptions prevailed throughout the ancient Near East. Here I shall confine consideration just to Mesopotamia and within Mesopotamia principally to Assyria during the Neo-Assyrian period, which provides perhaps the closest extant parallels to ancient Israel.

The Assyrian King as Viceroy of the Divine Sovereign

Discussion of the Assyrian king as viceroy of the divine sovereign may begin with consideration of the winged anthropomorphic figure that hovers within a fiery nimbus since, as will be demonstrated, that figure represents the divine power working through the king. Perhaps the best-known instance of the winged anthropomorphic figure is a fragmentary polychrome glazed tile from Ashur found in the Anu-Adad Temple (fig. 1), dating to the time of Tukulti-Ninurta II (890–884 B.C.E.).[15] This fragmentary polychrome tile was found in a garbage dump, probably discarded in ancient times because of its broken condition. It depicts a winged anthropomorphic figure within a nimbus, surrounded by heavy storm clouds[16] and holding a drawn bow. The figure hovers above the Assyrian army, only the heads of which are preserved in the fragmentary lower portion of the tile. The figure within the nimbus is depicted in human form from the waist upward. Faint

Fig. 2. Broken obelisk (drawing of central panel). Drawing by the author.

markings indicate that it wears the horned cap symbolic of divinity. From the waist downward the figure terminates in a broad feathery tail. Likewise upon his back are large feathered wings that extend well beyond the circular nimbus. Together with fiery flames erupting outward from the nimbus, the multicolored feathers of amber, blue, and white project an atmosphere of awesome brilliance—the graphic equivalent of *melammu*, that "awe-inspiring radiance" surrounding deities and kings, the sight of which can cause enemies to capitulate and throw down their weapons in surrender.[17] The form of the projectiles that the anthropomorphic figure shoots cannot be made out. Given the storm clouds, however, O. Keel is perhaps correct in positing that the projectiles that the figure shoots are lightning bolts, as in a relief from the palace of Ashurnasirpal II (883–859 B.C.E.).[18]

---

15. BM 115706. See Walter Andrae, *Farbige Keramik aus Assur und ihre Vorstufen in altassyrischen Wandmalereien* (Berlin: Scarabaeus, 1923) 13, pl. 8; reproduced in *ANEP*, no. 536.

16. The clouds that surround the deity are more than "rain clouds," as suggested by the excavator; more likely the artist's intention was to portray storm clouds containing huge hailstones, a conventional component of a storm god's arsenal (Josh 10:11; Pss 18:13–14 [Heb.]; 78:47–48; 148:8; Isa 30:30; Job 38:22; cf. Isa 28:2; Hag 2:17).

17. On this concept, see A. Leo Oppenheim, "Akkadian pul(u)ḫ(t)u and melammū," *JAOS* 63 (1943) 31–34; Elena Cassin, *La splendeur divine: Introduction à l'étude de la mentalité mésopotamienne* (Civilisations et sociétés 8; Paris: Mouton, 1968).

18. Othmar Keel, *The Symbolism of the Biblical World: Ancient Near Eastern Iconography and the Book of Psalms* (New York: Seabury, 1978; repr. Winona Lake, IN: Eisenbrauns, 1997) 215, with drawing on p. 217, fig. 296, reproduced from B. Meissner, *Babylonien und Assyrien* (Heidelberg: Carl Winter, 1925) 2:40, fig. 10. Keel is followed by Martin Klingbeil, *Yahweh Fighting from Heaven: God as Warrior and as God of Heaven in the Hebrew Psalter and*

Fig. 3. Ashurnasirpal at War (scene no. 1). BM 124555 (Room B, slab 3a). Used by permission of the British Museum.

Fig. 4. Detail of the scene in fig. 3, showing anthropomorphic figure and king; drawing by the author.

In the past this winged anthropomorphic figure within the nimbus has often been mistakenly identified as Ashur, the national god of Assyria. I will return to the question of the identity of this figure below, after consideration of additional examples.

The earliest instance of an anthropomorphized sun disk is the "broken obelisk" from tenth-century Nineveh (see fig. 2).[19] Herein four enemies hunker submissively before an unidentified Assyrian king. In the left hand, the king displays his ring and mace (scepter), traditional symbols of divinely conferred sovereign authority. The king extends his open right hand as a symbol of magnanimous pardon and gra-

Ancient Near Eastern Iconography (OBO 169; Fribourg, Switzerland: Éditions Universitaires / Göttingen: Vandenhoeck & Ruprecht, 1999) 260–62.

19. BM 118898; from Kuyunjik. Photo in E. A. W. Budge and L. W. King, *Annals of the Kings of Assyria* (London: British Museum Dept. of Egyptian and Assyrian Antiquities, 1902) 1:xi; *ANEP*, no. 440.

*Fig. 5. Ashurnasirpal at war (scene no. 2). BM 124540 (NW Palace, [Throne]
Room B, slab 11a). Used by permission of the British Museum.*

ciousness. At the top of the panel appear the symbols of the principal high
gods, indicating divine approbation. In the midst of these heavenly symbols is an anthropomorphized sun disk. There is no human figure per se,
but two hands project downward from the sun disk. The left hand holds
a relaxed (i.e., undrawn) bow, the right hand is extended open, as if in
blessing. The relaxed bow symbolizes a cessation of hostilities, as I will
demonstrate below. The intention, therefore, seems to be to suggest that
(cosmic) peace and weal has been achieved through the king's use of divinely conferred authority.

A fully anthropomorphized sun disk does not appear in Assyria until the ninth century. Apart from seal impressions, the anthropomorphic
winged figure occurs only on the wall reliefs and paintings in the palaces
of three Neo-Assyrian kings, Tukulti-Ninurta II, Ashurnasirpal II, and Shalmaneser III.

The most instructive reliefs come from the northwest palace of Ashurnasirpal II at Nimrud (Kalhu). In two different reliefs depicting similar
scenes (figs. 3, 4, 5), Ashurnasirpal attacks the fortified city of an enemy.[20]
Appropriate to royal propaganda, the Assyrian king dominates the scene.
Riding in his war chariot, he leads the charge with drawn bow. In both reliefs just over the head of Ashurnasirpal or slightly in front of him hovers
the winged anthropomorphic figure in his nimbus, in form and posture almost identical to that of the figure on the polychrome tile discussed above.
The horned cap of a divinity is clearly visible. A fiery radiance issuing

---

20. Figure 4 is my drawing, providing details of similarities between the anthropomorphic winged figure and the Assyrian king. For another interpretation of these scenes,
see George Mendenhall, *The Tenth Generation* (Baltimore: Johns Hopkins University Press,
1973) 46–47.

Fig. 6. Ashurnasirpal returning from battle. BM 124551 (Room B, slab 5a). Used by permission of the British Museum.

Fig. 7. Anthropomorphic winged figure (detail from fig. 6). Used by permission of the British Museum.

forth from the nimbus is not drawn, however, though it most likely is implied. But this time one can see a detail that was lost in the broken portion of glazed tile. The Assyrian king's actions are replicated almost exactly in the actions of the winged anthropomorphic figure. It holds a drawn bow and shoots a three-pronged (lightning) bolt at the enemy, just as does the human monarch. One is reminded of the boasts by Assyrian kings such as Ashurnasirpal ("I thundered against them like the god Adad of the Devastation (and) rained down flames upon them. With might and main my combat troops flew against them like the Storm Bird")[21] or Shalmaneser III ("By the ferocious weapons which Ashur, my

21. A.0.101, translation by A. Kirk Grayson, *Assyrian Rulers of the Early First Millennium b.c.* (Royal Inscriptions of Mesopotamia, Assyrian Periods 2/1; Toronto: University of Toronto Press, 1991) 1:210. Similarly, in the "standard inscription" of Ashurnasirpal: "With the help of the gods Shamash and Adad, the gods my supporters, I thundered like the god Adad, the devastator, against the troops of the land of . . ." (ibid., 1:275; followed by John Malcolm Russell, *The Writing on the Wall: Studies in the Architectural Context of Late*

Fig. 8. Ashurnasirpal receiving official. BM 124549 (Room B, slab 7b). Used by permission of the British Museum.

lord, has presented to me, I inflicted a defeat upon them . . . descending upon them like Adad when he makes a rainstorm pour down")[22] or Tiglath-pileser III ("I pursued them, and in the very course of the march I swept over them like a downpour of the god Adad").[23]

Another relief (figs. 6, 7) depicts Ashurnasirpal returning victorious from battle, carrying a "relaxed" or undrawn bow at his side in a nonthreatening posi-

Fig. 9. Detail from fig. 8. Used by permission of the British Museum.

tion. Here, too, the winged anthropomorphic figure in his horned cap is depicted accompanying the king, hovering over and a bit to the fore, as if leading the king home in triumph. Partially replicating the action of Ashurnasirpal, the winged anthropomorphic figure carries at his side in the left hand a relaxed bow, exactly as does the king. His open right hand is extended in blessing, however, whereas the king displays two arrows in his extended right hand, apparently symbolic of "purified" weapons that

---

Assyrian Palace Inscriptions [Mesopotamian Civilizations 9; Winona Lake, IN: Eisenbrauns, 1999] 25).

22. Trans. A. Leo Oppenheim, in *ANET*, 277.

23. [Trans.] Hayim Tadmor, *The Inscriptions of Tiglath-Pileser III King of Assyria* (Jerusalem: Israel Academy of Sciences and Humanities, 1994) 73.

Fig. 10. Ashurnasirpal purifying sacred tree. BM 124531 (Room B, slab 23). Used by permission of the British Museum.

Fig. 11. Detail of fig. 10. Used by permission of the British Museum.

have received divine approval.[24] As in the battle reliefs, there is near identification between the king and the winged anthropomorphic figure, even though patently the former is still "human" while the latter is "divine."

Yet another relief (figs. 8, 9) depicts Ashurnasirpal receiving an official, perhaps a subdued enemy king, after the battle.[25] The king holds "purified" arrows in his right hand; in his left hand he holds his relaxed bow at his side. The winged anthropomorphic figure hovers above and slightly forward of the king. Although the hands of the figure are in the same position as those of the king, in this case neither hand of the winged anthropomorphic figure fully replicates the king's action. Rather, here the winged anthropomorphic figure indicates complete divine approbation of the king, since, facing in the same direction as the king (i.e., having a similar "outlook") it extends

24. On the symbolism of "purified" weapons, see Ursula Magen, *Assyrische Königsdarstellungen: Aspekte der Herrschaft* (Baghdader Forschungen 9; Mainz am Rhein: von Zabern, 1986) 81–91.

25. See also Samuel M. Paley, *King of the World: Ashurnasirpal II of Assyria 883–859 B.C.* (New York: Brooklyn Museum, 1976) 102, pl. 18a.

the open right hand in blessing and holds in the left hand the ring symbolizing divinely bestowed royal authority.

But the most important relief of all is one that served as the backdrop to the throne, thus dominating the throne room and setting its theme. As in the preceding cases, there is both identity and distance between

Fig. 12. Seal of Mushezib-Ninurta (BM 89135). Used by permission of the British Museum.

the king and the winged anthropomorphic figure. It portrays Ashurnasirpal before a "sacred tree" (figs. 10, 11).[26] The king, flanked by a winged genius (*apkallu*) that sprinkles him with a purifying cone, is depicted on both sides of a sacred tree (i.e., he ritually circles it) in a gesture of reverence. The king's pointer finger of his right hand is extended in the traditional position of humble supplication (*ubānu tarāṣu*).[27] Above the tree hovers the winged anthropomorphic figure within its characteristic nimbus—this time with erupting flames clearly drawn—and wearing its horned cap to emphasize its divinity. It again holds in the left hand the ring while extending the right hand outward in a gesture of blessing, indicating divine approbation of the king's actions. This scene is replicated in a Neo-Assyrian cylinder seal (fig. 12), except that in this case water flows forth in a double stream from the winged nimbus to either side of the sacred tree.[28] This flowing stream is a frequent motif in Neo-Assyrian cylinder seals. The meaning is the same in both cases: the abundance and well-being that the king has effected

---

26. Commenting on this relief, J. M. Russell (*The Writing on the Wall*, 12–13) observes that "the images of the king and a winged deity are shown twice, symmetrically flanking a stylized palm tree (called the 'sacred tree' in modern literature). Variations of this motif, which must represent the role of the king in assuring the prosperity of Assyria, are repeated in the palace decoration of later kings. In the corners of the throne room and beside doorways are more images of sacred trees and winged deities." A nearly identical scene, preserved in fragmentary condition, is found on slab 13, also in Room B. Moreover, in some rooms in the Northwest Palace the "sacred tree," often attended by *apkallus*, is itself the dominant theme of the wall reliefs, contributing to the ornamentation of what has been called a "rhetoric of abundance" in Assyrian royal propaganda; see Irene J. Winter, "Ornament and the 'Rhetoric of Abundance' in Assyria," *ErIsr* 27 (Hayim and Miriam Tadmor Volume; 2003) 252*–64*.

27. See Magen, *Assyrische Königsdarstellungen*, 45–55.

28. See Dominique Collon, *First Impressions: Cylinder Seals in the Ancient Near East* (London: British Museum Publications, 1987) 76–77, pl. 341.

*Fig. 13. Central panels from the Throne Room of the palace at Mari. Drawing by
J. Lauffray (Syria 18 [1937] pl. 39, fig. 8). Used by permission of Institut Français
d'archéologie du Proche-Orient.*

throughout the kingdom, which in Assyrian royal rhetoric includes the
whole world. Taken as a whole, Ashurnasirpal's "acts," especially his removal of every threat to the realm has resulted in (re)establishing peace
and cosmic order in an otherwise chaotic world. The resultant blessings

flow not only to the Assyrian homeland but also to the whole world.[29]

This motif had a long life and appeared in many forms. Naturally one is reminded of the Yahwistic primeval myth in which a stream arising in Eden issues forth into a fourfold river that encircles all the lands (Gen 2:10–14). But nearly a thousand years prior to Ashurnasirpal II, in the Old Babylonian kingdom of Mari, Zimri-Lim's artists decorated his palace walls with a (partially preserved) depiction of idyllic harmony and abundance, at the center of which is a two-paneled fresco (fig. 13).[30] In the upper panel the goddess Ishtar invests the king with his symbols of authority. In the lower panel to either side stands a goddess with a vase from which flows a fourfold stream. It is doubtful that two goddesses and two streams are intended. Rather, through the symmetry of a flowing vase on either side with their respective streams conjoined at the center of the panel, the intent is to suggest a mythical four-branched stream encircling the whole of the inhabitable land to water it, exactly as in Genesis 2. This interpretation seems to be confirmed by the single statue of a woman (goddess) found in the adjoining courtyard; the woman holds a vase from which water apparently flowed, to judge from the bored hole that runs from the base of the statue through the center of the statue and opens into the vase (fig. 14).[31] Etched on the torso of this statue are a series of wavy lines suggesting

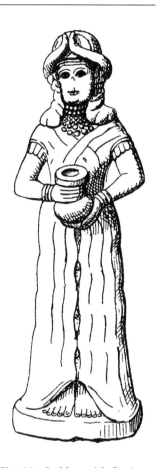

Fig. 14. Goddess with flowing vase. Aleppo National Museum no. 1659. Mari palace. Drawing by M. Barrelet; used with permission.

---

29. For additional discussion of the winged nimbus in conjunction with the sacred tree, see Klingbeil, *Yahweh Fighting from Heaven*, 211–16.

30. Mari, third campaign, 1935–36; see A. Parrot, *Syria* 18 (1937) 335–46; see also Marie-Thérèse Barrelet, "Une peinture de la cour 106 du palais de Mari," in *Studia Mariana* (ed. A. Parrot; Leiden: Brill, 1950) 16, fig. 4; *ANEP*, no. 610.

31. Drawing from Barrelet, "Une peinture de la cour 106 du palais de Mari," 32, fig. 12c, after *Syria* 18, pl. 12. For photos, see E. Strommenger, *Fünf Jahrtausende Mesopotamien* (Munich: Hirmer, 1962) pls. 162–63; André Parrot, *Nineveh and Babylon* (trans. S. Gilbert and J. Emmons; London: Thames & Hudson, 1961) 74–75, pls. 82, 83; or *ANEP*, no. 516 (partial view only).

flowing water, through which fish swim upward toward the source vase, similar to the depiction in the lower panel of the fresco. The point is that kingship itself implies peace, security, and fruitfulness in the earth, and this weal stems ultimately from the sovereignty of the deity, effected through the earthly king as viceroy.

The identity of the anthropomorphic figure within the nimbus has been the subject of considerable discussion. Among the proposals are (1) a specific deity—namely, Ashur, the national deity of Assyria, the sun god Shamash or his vizier Bunene, Ṣalmu, or Ninurta; (2) a representation of the awe-inspiring brilliance of Ashur; and (3) an iconographic depiction of the sunlike alter ego of the Assyrian king.[32] Ruth Mayer-Opificius has demonstrated that this winged anthropomorphic figure is interchangeable with the more ancient and more common winged sun disk and that the roots of this artistic convention go back to older Egyptian depictions of the solar deity. Although the sun disk originally was the symbol of the sun god, with time the sun disk acquired additional meanings. Because of an increasing "cosmic competence" attributed to the solar deity, the sun disk came to symbolize universal divine power and as such could be used to signify the beneficent presence of the highest deity. In the process the winged sun disk came to be used in three ways: (1) as a simple representation of the heavens, (2) as a symbolic representation of the relationship between the solar god in the heavens and the fruitfulness of the earth, and (3) to suggest a constellation of *sun god–king–sacred tree* involving religious implications for the office of kingship.[33]

Thomas Podella has taken this insight even further to demonstrate that the winged anthropomorphic figure within the nimbus is a specific adaptation of this solar imagery by Assyrian kings of the ninth century B.C.E. Podella has made a careful study of this figure in the northwest palace of Ashurnasirpal II at Nimrud, where the wall reliefs are relatively well preserved, thereby allowing the Assyrian adaptation of this motif to be studied in context. The anthropomorphic winged figure occurs in scenes depicting major phases in the life of the king. The anthropomorphic winged figure replicates exactly the actions of the Assyrian king in the attack of a city (figs. 3–5) and at the conclusion of a successful military campaign and return from battle (figs. 6–9). The figure also appears in a cultic context hovering over the sacred tree (figs. 10–11). The figure does not appear in less significant scenes such as in the hunting of wild animals or at the crossing of a river. From such discriminate employment by the Assyrian artists,

---

32. For a discussion of the identity, see Thomas Podella, *Das Lichtkleid JHWHs: Untersuchungen zur Gestalthaftigkeit Gottes im Alten Testament und seiner altorientalischen Umwelt* (FAT 15; Tübingen: Mohr Siebeck, 1996) 26–31, 132–54. See further Ruth Mayer-Opificius, "Die geflügelte Sonne: Himmels- und Regendarstellungen im alten Vorderasien," *UF* 16 (1984) 189–236; P. Calmeyer, "Fortuna-Tyche-Khvarnah," *JdI* 94 (1979) 358 with n. 26; S. Dalley, "The God Ṣalmu and the Winged Disk," *Iraq* 48 (1986) 85–101.

33. T. Podella, *Das Lichtkleid JHWHs*, 147.

Podella concludes that the anthropomorphic winged figure in the nimbus represents a symbiotic and thoroughgoing equivalence between the king and the highest deity. This anthropomorphic winged disk is thus an expression of the power of the king as the nexus between heaven and earth wherein peace, security, and the weal of the kingdom are accomplished.[34]

The anthropomorphic winged figure in the nimbus thus represents the power of the Assyrian king to mediate heavenly realities to his earthly realm, that is, to make the divine order present on earth. Analogous to the physical sun's rays bringing beneficence daily to the whole earth, the king as a kind of double of the solarized (or highest) deity was believed to be responsible for ensuring the weal of the kingdom. The king was said to be the "image" of the divine sovereign.[35] One may recall also the epithet of the king, *šamšu ša nišēšu / šamšu kiššat nišē* "sun of his people / sun of all the people."[36] It is no wonder that the "standard inscription" engraved

---

34. Ibid., 134–40. Podella follows the reconstructed order of the panels in the throne room in Janusz Meuszyński, *Die Rekonstruktion der Reliefdarstellungen und ihrer Anordnung im Nordwestpalast von Kalhu (Nimrūd)* (Baghdader Forschungen 2; Mainz am Rhein: von Zabern, 1981). Caution should be exercised, however, not to assume that this new symbolism of the winged anthropomorphic figure was adopted in a univocal manner by all artists, even within Assyria. A Neo-Assyrian seal from the time of Sargon II (Seal ANE 130865 in the British Museum) seemingly employs the winged anthropomorphic figure as a novel equivalent of the (older and more universal) winged sun disk. In this instance the winged anthropomorphic figure is supported by a humanoid genius flanked by two bull-men in a manner equivalent to the way the winged sun disk (symbolizing the solar deity) is supported outside of Assyria by bull-men and a humanlike genius or by a single genius; see the discussion below (esp. n. 74, with figs. 15–17). It is significant that, although the provenance of Seal ANE 130865 is Nimrud, its maker was apparently a transplanted Babylonian seal cutter; so Dominique Collon, "Seals of Merodach-Baladan," in *ErIsr* 27 (Hayim and Miriam Tadmor Volume; 2003) 10*–17*, esp. p. 16*, fig. 7. [Similarly Simo Parpola, "The Assyrian Tree of Life: Tracing the Origins of Jewish Monotheism and Greek Philosophy" (*JNES* 52 [1993] 161-208, esp. pp. 165-69.]

35. In the Tukulti-Ninurta Epic it is said of Tukulti-Ninurta I that this heroic king was formed in the divine womb (I A 17′); he was "the eternal image of Enlil (*ṣalam* ᵈE), attentive to the voice of the people, to the counsel of the land" (I A 18′); translation by P. Machinist, *The Epic of Tukulti-Ninurta I: A Study in Middle Assyrian Literature* (Ph.D. diss., Yale University, 1978) 67–69; followed by Benjamin R. Foster, *Before the Muses: An Anthology of Akkadian Literature* (2 vols.; Bethesda, MD: CDL, 1993) 1:213. The epic goes on to say (I A 19′–20′) that Enlil had exalted Tukulti-Ninurta as if he were Enlil's own son, second only to Enlil's firstborn son (i.e., the god Ninurta; so Machinist, *Epic of Tukulti-Ninurta I,* 206–7). See also Podella, *Das Lichtkleid JHWHs,* 255. The idea that the king was the son of the (chief) deity was not limited to Mesopotamia; such a conception figured even more prominently in Egyptian royal propaganda; see W. H. Schmidt (*Die Schöpfungsgeschichte der Priesterschrift* [WMANT 17; Neukirchen-Vluyn: Neukirchener Verlag, 1964] 127–48) and H. Wildberger ("Das Abbild Gottes, Gen 1:26–30," *TZ* [1965] 245–59, 481–501), cited by Claus Westermann, *Genesis 1–11*: A Commentary (trans. John J. Scullion; Minneapolis: Augsburg Publishing House, 1984), 152–53. ["Vice-regent (*iššakku*) of Ashur" was a traditional epithet given to the king as "intermediary between the god and the community," so M. T. Larsen, *The Old Assyrian City-State and Its Colonies* (Copenhagen: Akademisk Forlag, 1976) 119.]

36. *CAD* Š/1 337, s.v. *šamšu* 1.e.b′.

repeatedly on the walls of Ashurnasirpal's palace and on the base of his throne proclaims him to be the "viceregent of Ashur" and "king of the universe."[37]

During the Neo-Assyrian period, when Assyrian hegemony extended across the whole of the eastern Mediterranean, use of the anthropomorphic winged figure spread to the Levant, where it manifestly also influenced both popular religion and the royal cults of the kingdoms of Judah and Israel. Perhaps through this channel P also was influenced by the motif, albeit in an indirect fashion.

Summary

Conceptions of divine sovereignty varied in the ancient Near East from society to society and from period to period, and to a great extent mirrored developments in the political realm. In earlier periods, divine power was thought to be distributed between several gods. But with the advent of Babylonian hegemony over Mesopotamia and even over the whole of the ancient Near East at times during the second and first millenniums B.C.E., new theological conceptions evolved, according to which one deity, namely the patron god of Babylon, came to be regarded as the sole, absolute ruler of heaven and earth. Meanwhile, Assyrian propagandists similarly promoted the god Ashur as the divine sovereign, particularly in the first millennium B.C.E. during the period of Neo-Assyrian hegemony. To judge from the Babylonian myth *Enuma Elish*, one of the principal functions of the divine sovereign was to bring order into the midst of chaos, to establish conditions under which meaningful existence was not only possible but even guaranteed both for gods and for humans—or in equivalent Priestly terminology, to "create the heavens and the earth." Creation was a function of divine sovereignty. To be the divine sovereign is also to be the creator. The divine sovereign does not rule the world directly, however. Instead, he normally governs the human realm through divinely established kingship. The human king was the "image" of the divine sovereign, his viceroy on earth, charged with perfecting the divine sovereign's work of creation by promoting right order, justice, and the human weal.

2. Yahweh's Kingship in the Hebrew Bible

A. The Vocabulary of Yahweh's Kingship

In the Hebrew Bible the concept of divine sovereignty is usually referenced under the rubric the "kingship" of God/Yahweh, from the frequent appellation of Yahweh using the vocable *melek* "king" and from the related phrase in the Psalter *yhwh mālak*, variously rendered with a durative

---

37. Russell, *The Writing on the Wall*, 24. Russell (pp. 41–47) notes that despite much writing throughout Ashurnasirpal's palace there was only one basic inscription, repeated over and over with small variations. Note, too, that one of the gates in Ashurbanipal's palace was named "Long live the viceroy of Ashur" (p. 160).

meaning, that is, "Yahweh is king," or with an ingressive meaning, that is, "Yahweh has become king." Reference to the absolute and universal rule of Yahweh is sometimes also made without use of the root מלך, for example, in expressions such as "God of heaven" and "enthroned on the cherubim," or even in conceits such as the divine council and the judge of the other gods.[38] The term "king" need not imply universal rule, however. Ancient Near Eastern peoples, including biblical authors, often conceived of a national deity's authority as confined to the territorial boundaries of that nation (e.g., Deut 8:32; Judg 11:24; 1 Sam 26:19; 2 Kgs 5:17; 18:33; Mic 4:5). Accordingly, when Yahweh/God is given the appellation "king of Israel" (Isa 44:6; Zeph 3:15), "king of Jacob" (Isa 41:21), or "your king" (1 Sam 12:12; Isa 43:15), there is not necessarily any implication of Yahweh's being the divine sovereign. When Yahweh overcomes and judges the gods of other nations, the assumption is that these gods are powerful rulers in their own national territories who may even be willing to concede to Yahweh the right to govern his own people but not sovereignty over the other gods (e.g., Exod 12:12; Num 33:4; Jer 49:1–3; Isa 24:21).[39] Because of these possible limitations on the terms "king" and "kingship," the terms "divine sovereign" and "divine sovereignty" are to be preferred to express P's conception of Yahweh's absolute rule over heaven and earth.

The kingship of God/Yahweh in the Hebrew Bible has been the subject of numerous studies.[40] Particularly controversial has been Mowinckel's hypothesis concerning the cultic actualization of Yahweh's kingship during an annual Israelite enthronement festival, analogous to the ritual enactment of the kingship of Marduk during the Babylonian New Year *akitu* ritual.[41] Some have tried to illuminate Israel's conception of Yahweh's kingship by comparing how the kingship of various national gods was conceived of in other ancient Near Eastern societies.[42] Still others have tried to illuminate what "God is king" meant by examining this metaphor in terms of human kingship within ancient Israel. T. N. D. Mettinger has posited that the root metaphor for God in the official cult of Judah was *basileomorphic*, combining characteristics of Canaanite El and Baal.[43] M. Z. Brettler finds

---

38. Simon B. Parker, "The Beginning of the Reign of God: Psalm 82 as Myth and Liturgy," *RB* 102 (1995) 532–59.

39. Ibid., 548–52.

40. See the recent surveys by Keith W. Whitelam, "King and Kingship," *ABD* 4.40–48; Henri Cazelles, "Sacred Kingship," *ABD* 5.863–66.

41. Sigmund Mowinckel, *Psalmstudien II: Das Thronbesteigungsfest Jahwës und der Ursprung der Eschatologie* (Amsterdam: Schippers, 1961); *The Psalms in Israel's Worship* (trans. D. R. Ap-Thomas; 2 vols.; Nashville: Abingdon, 1961–79).

42. Werner Schmidt, *Königtum Gottes in Ugarit und Israel* (BZAW 80; Berlin: Alfred Töpelmann, 1961); Gary V. Smith, "The Concept of God/the Gods as King in the Ancient Near East and the Bible," *TJ* 3 (1983) 18–38.

43. In contrast to the Northern Kingdom of Israel, where covenant served as the root metaphor; see T. N. D. Mettinger, "The Study of the Gottesbild: Problems and Suggestions," *SEÅ* 54 (1989) 133–45; Martin Klingbeil, *Yahweh Fighting from Heaven*, 26.

the metaphor "God is king" to be the predominant relational metaphor for God in the Hebrew Bible, with which were associated a number of subsidiary metaphors such as "shepherd," "master," and "judge" that helped to flesh out what this basic metaphor meant according to the ancient Israelite way of thinking. [44] For the purpose of this essay such issues need not be decided, because my concern is less with Israel's precise conception of Yahweh's kingship than with the principle of Yahweh's universal kingship within P's theology.

There are many expressions of Yahweh's divine sovereignty in the Hebrew Bible. Constructs using מלך as the nomen rectum include מלך הגוים "king of the nations" (Jer 10:7), מלך עולם "everlasting king" (Jer 10:10; Ps 10:16), מלך כל־הארץ "king of the whole earth" (Ps 47:8; cf. Zech 14:9), and מלך שמים "king of heaven" (Dan 4:34). [45] Ps 95:3 asserts that אל גדול יהוה ומלך גדול על־כל־אלהים "Yahweh is a great god, a great king [46] over all the gods." [47] Surprisingly, the term "king of kings," while used of human overlords (Ezek 26:7; Ezra 7:12; Dan 2:37), is never applied to God in the Hebrew Bible. [48]

Yahweh's divine sovereignty is at times also expressed through the epithet אלהי השמים 'the God of heaven' (Gen 24:3, 7; Jonah 1:19; Ezra 1:2; Neh 1:4, 5; 2:4, 20; 2 Chr 36:23). [49] "God of heaven" is a shorthand for the ruler of all that is, both in heaven and on earth, as witnessed by the interchangeability of "God of heaven" with "God of heaven and (God of) earth" (cf. Gen 24:3 and 24:7; Ezra 5:11 and 5:12) and by the frequent declarations

---

44. Marc Zvi Brettler, *God Is King: Understanding an Israelite Metaphor* (JSOTSup 76; Sheffield: Sheffield Academic Press, 1989) 160. By contrast, M. Klingbeil (*Yahweh Fighting from Heaven*) argues that the root metaphor for God in ancient Israel was not king but warrior.

45. The phrase "King of heaven" continued in popularity into the Apocrypha (1 Esd 4:46, 58; Tob 13:7, 11); note also the occurrence of the phrase "the kingdom of heaven" in the Gospel of Matthew rather than "the kingdom of God" found in the other New Testament gospels.

46. Kings of powerful ancient Near Eastern countries, especially those who subjugated lesser nations and made vassals of their kings, were referred to as "great kings" (using either the adjective גדול [Jer 25:14; 27:7; Ps 136:17; Eccl 9:14] or the adjective רב [Jer 50:41; Dan 2:10; cf. Hos 5:13; 10:6]). Because in Hebrew רב is normally used quantitatively (in the sense of "many") rather than qualitatively (i.e., "great"), it is likely that the phrase *melek rab* is a calque of the Akkadian *šarrû rabû* "great king," mediated through a Northwest Semitic language (see M. Brettler, *God Is King*, 30–31). In 2 Kgs 18:19, 28 = Isa 36:4, 13, Rabshakeh, in the name of his master, "the great king (מלך גדול), the king of Assyria," boasts of the invincibility of the Assyrian army. It was almost inevitable that Israel's theologians should ascribe the epithet "great king" to Yahweh, whether using the adjective גדול (Mal 1:14) or the adjective רב (Ps 48:3).

47. The phrase "King of the gods" is also found in Add Esth 14:72.

48. But see in the New Testament: "the Lamb will conquer them, for he is the Lord of lords and the King of kings" (Rev 17:16).

49. Variants include Heb. אל השמים (Ps 136:26); Aram. אלה שמיא (Ezra 5:11, 12; 6:9, 10; 7:12, 21, 23) or, alternatively, האלהים בשמים 'the God in heaven' (Deut 4:39; Ps 115:3; Eccl 5:1; 2 Chr 20:6; cf. Josh 2:11; 1 Kgs 8:23; Ps 115:3; 2 Chr 6:14).

that the God of heaven directs the affairs of all the nations throughout the earth (e.g., Josh 2:11; 2 Chr 36:23; Ezra 1:2). The implication is that there is only one such deity (Deut 4:39) and that this incomparable majestic deity controls everything, both in heaven and on earth.[50]

B. Yahweh as the Divine Sovereign in the Hebrew Bible

Biblical authors were right at home in the mythic world of the divine sovereign. They also readily linked their belief in Yahweh's universal rule to the myth of the divine sovereign's having slain the chaos dragon in primeval time and to the defeat of national enemies in their own day. Psalm 74, for example, links Yahweh's kingship to his having slain the many-headed chaos dragon in primeval time. This psalm was clearly composed in the shadow of the destruction of the temple by the Babylonians. This exilic psalmist's anguished cry, "How long, O God is the foe to scoff?" is an appeal to Yahweh to defend his honor as divine sovereign by vanquishing the present Babylonian foe as he defeated its counterpart Leviathan in primeval days. The psalmist then abruptly turns to recounting God's acts of creation:

> Yours is the day, yours also the night;
>> you established the luminaries and the sun.
> You have fixed all the bounds of the earth;
>> you made summer and winter. (Ps 74:16–17, NRSV)

The linking of Yahweh's kingship here with creation motifs (vv. 15–17) is particularly noteworthy since creation per se does little to advance the psalmist's case; their presence seems to derive solely from the fact that creation is part and parcel of the divine sovereign metaphor. The defeat of chaos and the establishment of order is an acknowledged function of the divine sovereign.

A similar condition prevails in other Psalms. In Psalm 93 the theme of Yahweh's kingship (v. 1) is linked with the establishment of an orderly world (v. 1) and the subjugation of the chaotic Sea (vv. 3–4). In Psalm 89 Yahweh's kingship is not explicitly mentioned, but it is implied in the

---

50. Rahab, the Canaanite prostitute, reflecting on how Yahweh had already defeated Egypt and the two Transjordanian kingdoms of Sihon and Og, spoke not only for herself but all "the nations" in acknowledging how useless it was to resist the Israelites because "Yahweh your God is indeed God in heaven above and on earth below" (Josh 2:11). By putting this statement of faith in the mouth of an outsider, the Deuteronomist emphasizes the universality of Yahweh's rule. Other biblical theologians employ this same literary conceit of having outsiders acknowledge Yahweh as the God who controls both heaven and earth and as the one who empowers them: Cyrus (2 Chr 36:23; Ezra 1:2), Artaxerxes (Ezra 7:21 + 23); Nebuchadnezzar (Dan 2:18 + 47; cf. 4:1–3, 34–37 [note "King of heaven" as Yahweh's title in v. 37]). Patently, the God of heaven is the divine sovereign. The phrase "God of heaven" retained its currency throughout the intertestamental period and into the New Testament; e.g., Tob 10:11; Jdt 5:8; 6:19; 11:17; 3 Macc 6:28; 7:6; Rev 11:13; 16:11. See also C. J. Labuschagne, *The Incomparability of Yahweh in the Old Testament* (Leiden: Brill, 1966).

statement that Yahweh is incomparable within the divine council (vv. 6–9), "great and awesome above all that surround him" (v. 8). First to be mentioned among his mighty deeds are the conjoined themes of the defeat of chaotic Sea (vv. 10–11) and the "founding" of "the world and all that is in it" (vv. 12–13). Indeed, in the 16 psalms in which reference to Yahweh's kingship is either explicit or implicit,[51] creation themes are found in 8, or exactly one-half. Such a high degree of consistency, when compared with other themes, argues well for my thesis that the creator metaphor is but a subsidiary aspect of the divine sovereign metaphor.

A similar situation prevails also in Second Isaiah. This anonymous exilic prophet appealed to the cosmogonic myth of the divine sovereign to give hope to the discouraged Jewish exiles. Yahweh is "the Creator of Israel, your King" (Isa 43:15; cf. 43:1). Israel can have confidence in Yahweh because as divine sovereign he defeated chaotic Sea in primeval time (Isa 44:27; 50:2; 51:9–10) and is "the Creator of the ends of the earth" (Isa 40:28) and "of the heavens" (42:5; cf. 45:18). It is he who placed humankind upon the earth (45:12). He is the creator of absolutely everything, even light and darkness, weal and woe (45:7). Only Yahweh has such power; he has no rival among the gods, who in the final analysis are nothing more than worthless idols (Isa 41:21–24; 44:6–20). Yahweh confers human kingship upon whom he wills, even the mighty Persian Cyrus, in order to further Yahweh's purpose (Isa 41:25–26; 44:28). Thus, Yahweh is not just Israel's king (41:21; 43:15; 44:6; cf. 51:22), but also the very divine sovereign (52:7). Even now the divine sovereign is preparing a new creation and a new exodus (e.g., Isa 41:17–20; 43:16–21; 52:11–12; et passim) in which he will reestablish control over the forces of chaos and recreate Israel as his special people. It is Yahweh's power to create at will, then, which proves that he is the divine sovereign, the absolute ruler of all.[52]

Jeremiah 10 similarly links Yahweh's sovereignty with his role as creator. In a scathing attack on the gods of the nations as powerless idols, Jeremiah proclaims Yahweh's incomparability among the gods as "the king of the nations" (10:7) and as "the living God and the everlasting King" (10:10) precisely in his role as the creator. In contrast to the gods "who did not make the heavens and the earth," Yahweh is "he who made the earth by his power, who established the world by his wisdom" (10:12). "None of these

---

51. Explicit: 5:3; 10:16; 44:5; 47:3, 7, 8, 9; 74:12; 84:4; 93:1; 96:10; 97:1; 98:6; 99:1; 146:1; 149:2; as listed by Klingbeil, *Yahweh Fighting from Heaven*, 31, and correcting the typographical error from 145:1 to 146:1. Implicit: "great," "our Lord (above) all gods," 135:5; "God of gods" and "Lord of lords," 136:2, 3; "alone . . . exalted," "above earth and heaven," 148:13.

52. I explored these themes at length in "The Motif of Exodus in Deutero-Isaiah," (paper presented at the Fifty-Seventh General Meeting of The Catholic Biblical Association of America, University of San Diego, San Diego, CA, August 13–16, 1994, in the Task Force "Theology of the Hebrew Bible/Old Testament").

is like Yahweh . . . the one who formed all things" (10:16). For Jeremiah, too, Yahweh's sovereignty is self-evident from the fact that he is creator of heaven and earth.

Additional evidence could be adduced.[53] But even from the limited data presented here it is clear that in the Hebrew Bible, as in the ancient Near East generally, creation and divine sovereignty are frequently linked, with the metaphor of the creator being an aspect of the divine sovereign metaphor.

3. The Image of the Deity in the Priestly Creation Story

As already observed, within the primeval story the Priestly Writer provides no description whatever of God (אלהים) or his characteristics. Nevertheless, the Priestly Writer's conception of God may be gleaned indirectly from various clues in the passages traditionally attributed to P. In one way or another they all support the portrait of God as the divine sovereign.

A. God as the Divine Sovereign

One of the contributions of a comparative literary approach to the Bible is the recognition that, contrary to traditional renderings, Gen 1:1 is a temporal clause grammatically connected with v. 2, rather than being an independent sentence that summarizes the work of creation to be presented in greater detail in following verses.[54] Together, these first two verses lay out the state of things when the creator began to create.

> In the beginning when God created the heavens and the earth, the earth was a formless void and darkness covered the face of the deep, while a wind from God swept over the face of the waters. (Gen 1:1–2, NRSV)

The Priestly Writer thus follows a typical pattern of ancient Near Eastern cosmologies such as *Atrahasis* and *Enuma Elish*, both of which begin with a temporal clause describing conditions prior to the events that led the divine sovereign (Enlil in *Atrahasis* and Marduk in *Enuma Elish*) to inaugurate the whole chain of activities that established the cosmos as it is now constituted. Ever since Gunkel proposed the theory that a common "Combat Myth" (*Chaoskampf*) underlies both *Enuma Elish* and Genesis 1,[55] scholars have debated whether or not the Priestly creation story is dependent upon the Mesopotamian myth. Heidel's further outline of structural similarities in *Enuma Elish* and Gen 1:1–2:4a was particularly influential in convincing a whole generation of biblical scholars that the biblical account was in

---

53. See, among other texts, Gen 14:19; Deut 10:14; 2 Kgs 19:15; Jonah 1:9; 1 Chr 29:11; 2 Chr 2:11.

54. For a concise discussion of the controversy surrounding the interpretation of this verse, see Gordon J. Wenham, *Genesis 1–15* (WBC 1; Waco, TX: Word, 1987) 11–14.

55. Hermann Gunkel, *Schöpfung und Chaos in Urzeit und Endzeit: Eine religionsgeschichtliche Untersuchung über Gen 1 und Ap Joh 12* (Göttingen: Vandenhoeck & Ruprecht, 1895).

part dependent upon the Babylonian myth.[56] More recently the pendulum has swung in the opposite direction, however, with claims that P is devoid of such mythic conceptions, or at minimum that P deliberately rejected them.[57] The reality seems to lie somewhere in between these two poles: like other biblical theologians and poets, P's world view was grounded in the cultural idiom of a common Semitic Combat Myth,[58] even as he manifestly struggled to find his own distinctively "Yahwistic" voice—part of which involved muting as much as possible competing theological ideas from both within and without Israel, especially any suggestion that Yahweh's absolute control over heaven and earth was compromised by the existence of other deities wielding even limited power over specialized domains.

It is important to recognize that the Priestly creation account does not stand alone as an isolated pericope but is part and parcel of the larger Priestly primeval narrative (Genesis 1–9) that concludes with God establishing a covenant with all flesh, following the cosmic Flood. Failure to recognize the integrity of this narrative unit is one of the principal reasons why a number of scholars have been misled into denying too facilely the presence of Combat Myth motifs in the Priestly creation account. Combat Myth motifs are readily evident in, among others, the breaking out of the Great Deep from its divinely imposed bounds (1:6–10; cf. Job 38:8–10; Ps 104:6–9) during the cosmic flood (7:11), and the deity's subsequent (re)mastery over the chaotic waters by means of his storm wind (8:2; cf. 1:2), and the deity's retirement of his war bow (9:13–17). Whether there is any direct dependency running from *Enuma Elish* to P is unclear, but there seems to be at least indirect influence because the structure and motifs in the Priestly primeval story are closer to *Enuma Elish* than to any other extant form of the Combat Myth.

---

56. Alexander Heidel, *The Babylonian Genesis* (2nd ed.; Chicago: University of Chicago Press, 1951) 82–140, with diagram on p. 129, followed by, among others, E. A. Speiser, *Genesis* (AB 1; New York: Doubleday, 1969) 10.

57. E.g., W. G. Lambert, "A New Look at the Babylonian Background of Genesis," *JTS* 16 (1965) 287–300; Wenham, *Genesis 1–15*, 8–9. Westermann (*Genesis 1–11*, 132 et passim) takes a middle approach, suggesting that P manifests both "originality" and "its place in the stream of tradition" within the ancient Near East.

58. Jon D. Levenson (*Creation and the Persistence of Evil*) does a masterful job of showing the pervasiveness of the Combat Myth throughout the whole of the Hebrew Bible, although in my opinion he attempts to demythologize too much P's use of Combat Myth themes. The idea of a Combat Myth as an explanation of the cosmos—itself seen as delicately balanced between existence and nonexistence, between creation and noncreation, between order and chaos—was widely diffused in the Ancient Near East, forming part of a common cultural world view. To postulate that P—or any biblical writer, for that matter—could have been ignorant of such conceptions flies in the face of everything we know about the ancient Near East. The Combat Myth was as pervasive of ancient Near Eastern world views as are "Darwinian" theories of evolution at the beginning of the twenty-first century, even if individuals reject these as authentic explanations of "the origin of the human species." See my essay, "The Ancient Near Eastern Context of the Hebrew Ideas of Creation," chap. 1 in this volume.

True, P lacks an actual battle against a chaos dragon. Nevertheless, similarities between Genesis 1 and Psalm 8, where the vestigial battle motif is even more obvious,[59] as well as P's conscious efforts to mute Combat Myth themes by depicting a divided (i.e., ordered) תהום "Great Deep" and the tamed התנינים גדולים "great sea dragons" (compare the taming of Leviathan in Job 41 and of Egypt in Ezek 29:3–4), confirm that the Combat Myth was never far from the mind of the Priestly Writer as he rewrote his primeval story; neither was the metaphor of God as the divine sovereign, one of the foundational themes of the Combat Myth.

This explains the presence of the bow motif in Gen 9:10–17. In *Enuma Elish*, when Marduk "hangs up" his bow after defeating the last of his enemies, the symbolism is clear. Since every foe, including Tiamat, has been vanquished, Marduk no longer has need of weapons, so he is able to place his powerful bow in the heavens as the "bow star"—perhaps to be identified as the constellation Sirius—where it will forever shine as a symbol of Marduk's everlasting sovereignty. In the Priestly account the Great Deep has not yet been fully subdued by the end of chap. 1, even though God "rests," in keeping with the traditional divine sovereignty motif. In the Priestly telling, the flood is a resurgence of the Great Deep. Like the seven-headed chaos monster that it symbolizes, the Great Deep breaks out of its prison to challenge once more the divine sovereign's creative will (compare Gen 1:2, 6, 9 with 7:11 and 8:2). At the conclusion of the flood the Great Deep has been fully mastered, however, and the divine sovereign can permanently retire his bow by setting it in the sky where it can be seen as the nonthreatening rainbow—a symbol of cosmic blessings that come with this "covenant of peace" newly established with "all flesh."[60] With this act God demonstrates that he is firmly in control as the divine sovereign, similar to the actions of Marduk in *Enuma Elish*.

One may now also suggest additional symbolism for the Assyrian scenes mentioned previously. There the king, the earthly counterpart of the heavenly high god, has put aside his war bow used to subdue the enemy (figs. 3–5) and carries it in a "relaxed" condition as a symbol of triumph following the battle (figs. 6, 7). But in the cultic scene before the sacred tree suggestive of the universal weal that pervades in the kingdom after the enemy has been vanquished (figs. 10, 11), there is no need of such a bellicose symbol as the war bow. In "the covenant of peace" tradition that I have written about elsewhere, the divine sovereign, after an initial period of enmity with unruly humankind, ultimately lays aside his war equipment and establishes cosmic peace in the earth and with humankind. Examples of

---

59. Note especially, "You built a fortress for your habitation, having silenced your adversaries, the foe and the avenger" (Ps 8:2); see M. Dahood, *Psalms I* (AB 16; Garden City, NY: Doubleday, 1965) 45–51.

60. Bernard F. Batto, "The Covenant of Peace: A Neglected Ancient Near Eastern Motif," *CBQ* 49 (1987) 187–211. [Reprinted in this volume as chap. 7.]

this "covenant of peace" tradition can be adduced from Mesopotamian, Canaanite, and Egyptian mythic texts.[61] It is just to such a tradition of cosmic peace that Assyrian royal propagandists apparently were appealing in portraying the Assyrian king and his divine alter ego before the sacred tree. As the agent of the divine sovereign, the Assyrian king establishes universal weal within the realm, such that there is no longer any need of war equipment.

In Genesis the goal of cosmic weal is the same. In Gen 9:14 the deity says, "Whenever I bring a cloud over the earth, the bow will appear in the cloud." At first blush the deity's remark might seem to flow from the metaphor of God as creator, in this case as creator of atmospheric conditions. But when viewed from within the tradition of the divine sovereign who rides upon clouds, with its subsidiary metaphor of God as warrior, who uses storm clouds as a vehicle or, alternatively, as a weapon, God's statement in 9:14 takes on a different meaning.

At Ugarit, one of the principal epithets for Baal is "cloud-rider." Within biblical tradition Yahweh, similarly, is a cloud-rider. In Ezekiel's vision (Ezekiel 1) Yahweh appears in a storm cloud. In Psalm 18 (= 2 Sam 22):10–22 the deity is depicted as "soaring on the wings of the wind," with "thick (clouds) under his feet" and shrouded in darkness (= black clouds). Other passages also describe God's epiphany in equally ominous meteorological terms (e.g., Exod 15:7–10; Judg 5:4–5; Ps 68:7–8; Hab 3:3–5). Gen 9:14, too, should be understood within this storm epiphany tradition. In the immediately preceding flood scene God has just used his wind (8:2; cf. רוח אלהים, 1:2) to subdue the chaotic Great Deep (8:3). The reference to the "wind of God" hovering over the Deep in Gen 1:2 likely should also be understood as the deity using his storm winds as a weapon with which to bring the chaotic water into submission.[62] If elsewhere P's God is accustomed to using meteorological phenomena as personal equipment, then also in Gen 9:14 God's "bringing" of a "cloud over the earth" very likely stems from this same tradition of the divine warrior who from the midst of his storm cloud overwhelms the foe. In Gen 9:13–17, however, the appeal is not to that part of the tradition in which the deity overcomes his foe. That has already been accomplished twice over, in the subduing of the chaotic waters in Genesis 1 and again in the flood story in Genesis 8. Rather, in Genesis 9 the appeal is to the establishment of cosmic peace that results from the divine sovereign's victory. God enters into a covenant of peace with "all flesh." Since there is no longer any foe to overcome, God converts his bow from

---

61. Ibid.

62. Compare the description of Yahweh's employing a hail storm to defeat the enemy in Josh 10:11, "Yahweh hurled huge stones from heaven . . . so that more died from the hail stones than the Israelites killed with the sword." Not unrelated is the scene depicted in the aforementioned Assyrian polychrome tile (fig. 1), where the winged anthropomorphic figure, as the earthly counterpart of the heavenly highest god(s), fights from the midst of storm clouds, reminiscent of Adad's "thundering" against the enemy.

an implement of war into a symbol of the covenant of peace. From now on, whenever the divine sovereign makes an appearance on earth from within his majestic cloud, the bow—visible now as a rainbow—will serve as a reminder of this covenant of peace. Just as the bow has been transformed from a threatening implement of war into a symbol of hope and comfort, so also an epiphany of the "Cloud-rider" henceforth will be an event of cosmic joy rather than of dread. When the divine sovereign appears, it will not be as a warrior but as one whose presence causes peace to flourish in the earth.

Corollary to this passage is Gen 2:1–3, with its notation that upon completion of a perfect creation in six days, God "rested." It is now well accepted that this scene has implications of temple-building.[63] Like Baal after his combat with Yamm, Ea-Enki after his victory over Apsu, and Marduk after vanquishing Tiamat (and Qingu), so God after dividing *těhôm* appears to rule his newly ordered cosmos from a cosmic temple, his palace—one more bit of evidence that P thinks of God as the divine sovereign.

Elsewhere I have shown this "rest" to be an aspect of the "sleeping god" motif, which is yet another subsidiary metaphor of the divine sovereign metaphor. Just as retiring the war bow is an aspect of the metaphor of divine sovereignty, so also is the sleeping or resting deity.

The motif of the divine sleep is double edged, however. On the one side are texts that describe sleep as the prerogative of the divine sovereign. In *Enuma Elish*, Marduk rested after slaying the chaos monster Tiamat. He next built his palace Esagila on Temenanki ("the foundation of heaven and earth"), not only as the abode of his own enthronement but also as a place of rest for all the gods. In *Atrahasis* the lesser gods disturb Enlil's sleep by their outcries, which is tantamount to challenging his authority. In Egyptian Memphite theology, after creating humankind, Ptah rested. In Zion royal theology Yahweh desired Zion as "his place of rest" (Ps 132:13–14). But on the other side are texts that claim that the divine sovereign does not, or ought not, sleep. Thus, the psalmist calls upon Yahweh to "wake up" because the enemy is at the door (Ps 44:24; note that Yahweh is called king in v. 4). The divine sovereign may not "rest" because the foe is still at large. Deutero-Isaiah makes much the same plea in the so-called Ode to Yahweh's Arm (Isa 51:9–11).

If God rests in Gen 2:1–3, therefore, it is because, as divine sovereign who has just completed a perfect world, there are no threats to his authority.[64] No palace or throne is mentioned here, but a "resting place" or a throne seems to be implied nonetheless.

---

63. See Jon D. Levenson, *Creation and the Persistence of Evil*, 78–99, and the bibliography cited there. See also Victor (Avigdor) Hurowitz, *I Have Built You an Exalted House: Temple Building in the Bible in Light of Mesopotamian and Northwest Semitic Writings* (JSOTSup 115; JSOT/ASOR Monographs 5; Sheffield: Sheffield Academic Press, 1992) 242.

64. For details of this metaphor, see my "Sleeping God," 153–57 [pp. 139–143 in this volume]. It is important to keep in mind that in the Hebrew Bible the term היכל "temple/

It may be suggested, further, that P envisions God as "enthroned upon the cherubim" (Ps 80:2; 99:1), similar to Ezekiel's vision of Yahweh seated on a cherub throne (Ezek 1:26; 10:1). Because P seems to allow absolutely no other deity into this creation story, one wonders to whom God is talking when he says, "Let us create humankind in our image, according to our likeness" (Gen 1:26). As with Deutero-Isaiah (41:28), P's God has no counselor and needs none. All of his works are perfect. Nevertheless, in biblical tradition the divine monarch is never alone. In Isaiah 6 he is attended by seraphs with whom he deliberates: "Whom shall I send, and who will go for us?" (Isa 6:8). In 1 Kgs 22:19–23 Yahweh, seated on his throne in the presence of כל־צבא השמים "the whole heavenly host," deliberates with various "spirits" about how best to get rid of Ahab in Israel. Jeremiah, too, knows of such deliberations within the divine council (Jer 23:18, 22). A heavenly court is also much in evidence in the prologue of Job (1:6–27; cf. 38:7). Westermann claims that P "was not familiar with the idea of a heavenly court," because "angels or any sort of intermediary beings are found nowhere in P."[65] But P's emphasis upon Yahweh's uniqueness does not necessarily exclude divine attendants, as evident from Ezekiel where God, despite being characterized by a similar transcendence, is never alone but always borne about by his cherubim attendants. In Ezekiel's vision the cherubim, like Yahweh himself, have humanlike forms. If Ezekiel is dependent upon P for his imagery, as I argue in the following section, then one may take a cue from Ezekiel and assume that for P also the divine sovereign both possesses a humanlike form and speaks to anthropomorphic cherub attendants when he proposes, "Let *us* make humankind in *our* image, according to *our* likeness" (Gen 1:26).[66]

---

palace" is used equally of both the deity's "house" and the royal residence, as was Akkadian *ekallu* (Sum. é.gal) in Mesopotamia.

65. Claus Westermann, *Genesis 1–11*, 144–45. Westermann's own preferred explanation of the plural constructions here and elsewhere as a "plural of deliberation" is unconvincing, because the examples proffered as evidence may be better explained otherwise. The alternation between singular and plural in Isa 6:8 ("Whom shall *I* send, and who will go for *us*?") may be construed as the deity deliberating not with himself but with the seraph attendants mentioned in the immediately preceding verses. Similarly, the shift from plural to singular in David's choice of a punishment in 2 Sam 24:14 ("Let *us* fall into the hand of the Lord . . . but let *me* not fall into human hands") may be motivated by the scope of the referent: in the first case "three days of pestilence" would afflict the entire nation, while in the second case "three months of pursuit before your foes" would affect primarily David himself. A third alleged attestation of a plural of deliberation, from Gen 11:7, is even less persuasive; the deity's remark ("Come, let *us* go down. . . .") is from the Yahwistic tradent, which contains additional allusions to the deity's speaking with or interacting with other divine beings (e.g., "like gods" ‖ "like one of us" [Gen 3:5, 22]; "the cherubim" [2:24]; "the sons of the gods/God" [6:2, 4]).

66. Similarly Jon D. Levenson, *Creation and the Persistence of Evil*, 5.

B. Ezekiel's Vision of God's Majesty and
Its Significance for Understanding P

Because Ezekiel and P appear to share some common traditions and in particular overlapping traditions regarding creation, Ezekiel has the potential to confirm or to negate at least partially the Priestly portrait of God that I have been sketching. Ezekiel 28 and Genesis 2–3 share mythical elements of a common primeval story, for example, the Garden of God/Eden, precious stones, a primeval humanlike figure, who though innocent on the day of creation became presumptuous in a desire to be Godlike, and guardian cherub(s) who drive out the protagonist, "fallen" because of hubris. A strong case can be made, as well, for identifying the wise serpent of Genesis 3—a kind of seraph[67]—with the condemned proud cherub of Ezekiel 28. Because Ezekiel 28 seems to presuppose elements not only of the Yahwistic primeval story but also the idea of perfection imposed upon this story through the secondary Priestly frame of Genesis 1, it seems necessary to conclude that Ezekiel 28 is subsequent to and dependent upon the completed P+J version of Genesis 1–3, rather than being a completely independent tradition.[68]

A close relationship between Ezekiel and the Priestly primeval story can also be discerned from Ezekiel's vision of God—more exactly, of Ezekiel's vision of "the glory of Yahweh" (v. 28)—in Ezekiel 1. First, apart from late passages (Pss 19:2; 150:1; Dan 12:3) that seem to be derivative from Genesis 1 or Ezekiel 1, the word רקיע 'firmament/dome' occurs in the Bible only in the P creation story of Genesis 1 and in Ezekiel's vision of God's glory or majesty in Ezekiel 1 and the related vision in 10:1. Second, the Ezekielian phrase to describe the deity, דמות כמראה אדם "a likeness like the appearance of a human" (1:26), patently bears some relationship to the Priestly statement in Gen 1:26 that God created אדם "humankind" בצלמנו כדמותנו "in our image, according to our own likeness." The Ezekielian metaphor of God's having a human likeness is the reverse of the Priestly statement that God created humankind in the likeness of God. Third, Ezekiel's likening of the brilliance of Yahweh's majesty to "the appearance (מראה) of the bow (הקשת) in a cloud (בענן) on a rainy day" (Ezek 1:28) is reminiscent of the Priestly conclusion to the primeval story, that after the flood God placed his bow in the cloud(s) as a perpetual sign of the covenant between himself and the earth/all flesh (Gen 9:13–17). This cloud is to be seen not only by the deity but also by those on earth. "When I bring cloud(s) over the earth, the bow in the cloud will be visible" (נראתה הקשת בענן, 9:14). This

---

67. On the serpent as a seraph, see my *Slaying the Dragon: Mythmaking in the Biblical Tradition* (Louisville: Westminster John Knox, 1992) 59–60 with n. 46, and pp. 95–96.

68. For this interpretation of Ezekiel 28 and its relation to Genesis 1–3, see ibid., 94–97, with the documentation there.

bow motif does not appear elsewhere in the Hebrew Bible.[69] Moreover, in
9:14 the difficult phrase בענני ענן על־הארץ, usually translated "when I bring
clouds over the earth," may be more literally translated "when I cloud a
cloud over the earth" and probably means approximately "when I bring
my storm cloud over the earth." If correct, then this is another reference
to God as the cloud-rider who appears in his storm cloud as he maneuvers
across the sky, just as in Ezekiel 1 "the heavens opened" and in his "visions
of God" (1:1) the prophet saw רוח סערה מן־הצפון ענן גדול "a storm wind ap-
proaching from the north, an awesome cloud" (1:4).

Clearly, there is intertextuality functioning between Ezekiel and Genesis.[70] Their shared viewpoints make it legitimate, therefore, to use Ezekiel 1 as a key to unlocking P's understanding of the deity in the Genesis
narrative.

Ezekiel's own conception of the deity needs elucidation first, however,
because the prophet makes it very clear that he is not giving a literal description of Yahweh or even of the throne of Yahweh and the four "living
creatures" that bear up the throne—identified finally as cherubs in 10:1.
Repeatedly Ezekiel tells the reader that his descriptions are only approxi-
mate, "something like X," where X is itself only a point of comparison. The
visual and auditory imagery that the prophet employs may be difficult for
moderns to comprehend but is not outside the range of symbolism attested
in the ancient Near East. Moshe Greenberg[71] correctly notes that much of
Ezekiel's vision derives from stock ancient Near Eastern descriptions. The
closest literary analogue is Ps 18 (= 2 Sam 22):8–14, where in response to
the psalmist's cry for help,

> The earth quaked and trembled . . .
> [God] tilted the sky and came down
> Thick clouds were under his feet
> He rode on a cherub and flew
> He appeared [var. soared] on wings of wind
> He put darkness about him as his pavilion . . .
> In the radiance before him fiery coals burned
> Yhwh thundered from heaven
> The Most High gave forth his voice.[72]

---

69. The bow as an aspect of the motif of God's throne does reappear again in the New
Testament in Rev 4:3 and 10:1; cf. Sir 43:11; 50:7.

70. Determining in which direction the dependency flows is more difficult, though I
argue that Ezekiel is dependent upon the completed P+J primeval story rather than the
other way round. If so, then Ezekiel would be one of the first commentators on the Priestly
primeval story, and nearly contemporary in time. I addressed this issue in an unpublished
paper, "Intertextuality and the Dating of the Primeval Creation Accounts" (presented at
the Fifty-Ninth General Meeting of the Catholic Biblical Association of America, University of St. Thomas, St. Paul, MN, August 10–13, 1996).

71. Moshe Greenberg, *Ezekiel 1–20: A New Translation with Introduction and Commentary* (AB 22; Garden City, NY: Doubleday, 1983) 52–58.

72. Translation by Greenberg, ibid., 53.

The motif of a deity riding upon cherubs or composite animals is commonplace both in the Bible and in the ancient Near East. Ezekiel is very insistent that the cherubim in his vision had humanlike bodies (v. 5), despite having three additional faces of various animal forms and four wings (v. 6). They have human hands (v. 8) and straight—that is, human—legs (v. 7), not like some "cherubs" of this ancient world having bull-like or lionlike bodies with the characteristic "hooked" rear legs of bulls or lions.[73] Eze-

Fig. 15. Bull-men and humanoid genius support winged disk, from eighth-century Karatepe. Drawing by the author.

kiel's cherubim thus bear greater resemblance to the tradition of the semidivine creatures that bear up the winged sun disk (figs. 15 [middle figure], 16, 17).[74] By insisting upon the humanoid features of the cherubs, Ezekiel perhaps intended to suggest a degree of likeness between these bearers of כבוד יהוה "the majesty of Yahweh" and Yahweh himself, who is described in 1:26 as having a partially humanlike form: דמות כמראה אדם "a likeness of appearance of a human."

The continuing depiction of the deity in v. 27 is further veiled in very guarded language. The syntax of this verse is convoluted and difficult to

---

73. For representative examples, see *ANEP*, nos. 500, 501, 522, and 534.

74. Fig. 15: drawing by the author of three genii—a humanoid flanked by two bull-men—supporting a winged disk (*ANEP*, no. 855). For a similar Neo-Assyrian example, except that the winged disk has been "modernized" into a winged anthropomorphic figure within the nimbus, see Seal ANE 130865 (British Museum) from Nimrud, published by Max Mallowan (*Nimrud and Its Remains* [3 vols.; New York: Dodd, Mead, 1966] 1:48 #12); repr. Dominique Collon (*First Impressions*, 78 #352) and most recently restudied by idem, "Seals of Merodach-Baladan," in *ErIsr* 27 (Hayim and Miriam Tadmor Volume; 2003) 10*–17*, esp. p. 16* fig. 7. For another example (from tenth-century Ain Dura in Aleppo National Museum) of a humanoid genius similarly flanked by two bull-men supporting a now missing sun disk, see André Chouraqui, *L'univers de la Bible*, 3.537; for a scene of just two bull-men supporting the winged disk, minus the humanoid in the center, see M. von Oppenheim, *Tell Halaf* (ed. Anton Moortgat; 4 vols.; Berlin: de Gruyter, 1955) vol. 3, pl. 98 (A 3,171). Fig. 16: drawing by the author of winged humanoid genius with uplifted arms, presumably supporting a now missing deity, from Tell Halaf, ninth century; see photo in M. von Oppenheim, *Der Tell Halaf: Eine neue Kultur im ältesten Mesopotamien* (Leipzig: Brockhaus, 1931) 152, pl. 32a. Fig. 17: drawing by the author of a winged disk supported by a four-winged humanoid genius with an eagle's head, from Tell Halaf, ninth century (= *ANEP*, no. 653).

Fig. 16. *Humanoid genius with uplifted hands. Drawing by the author.*

Fig. 17. *Eagle-headed humanoid supporting winged disk. Drawing by the author.*

ascertain; the author seemingly deliberately avoids straightforward descriptions here in order to protect the transcendence of the deity. Nevertheless, one aspect of the vision is clear, namely, the radiance of the divine being. As Greenberg notes, the basic structure of v. 27 is chiastic:

> I saw X / from his loins up
> From his loins down / I saw Y,

where X is "the like of *ḥašmal*" (amber?) and Y is "the semblance of fire." In other words, the whole of the humanlike figure upon the throne is completely shrouded in brilliance.[75]

Ezekiel's portrait of Yahweh is intentionally opaque—an unfocusable but searing glimpse of the majestic deity enthroned above the (heavenly) dome (v. 26), engulfed in awesome brilliance and surrounded by a radiant rainbow. But even this limited vision of כבוד יהוה "the majesty of Yahweh" is so overwhelming that the prophet's only defense is to fall upon his face in reverence (v. 28).

On one key point, however, Greenberg has missed the mark. He compares Ezekiel's vision of Yahweh's majesty to the winged anthropomorphic

---

75. Greenberg, *Ezekiel, 1–20*, 50–51. See also the similar conclusion on the basis of ancient Near Eastern iconography of Othmar Keel and Christoph Uehlinger, *Gods, Goddesses, and Images of God in Ancient Israel* (trans. Thomas H. Trapp; Minneapolis: Augsburg Fortress, 1998) 296–97.

figure in the previously mentioned fragmentary polychrome glazed tile from Ashur found in the Anu-Adad Temple from the time of Tukulti-Ninurta II (fig. 1). Greenberg, following the lead of a number of other scholars, incorrectly identified the figure within the nimbus as the god Ashur and assumed, therefore, that as a representation of the Assyrian god the winged anthropomorphic figure may be used to elucidate the Ezekielian conception of God's majesty.[76] As noted above, however, the winged anthropomorphic figure is not so much the divine sovereign himself, as it is the manifestation of the divine sovereign's power exercised through his human viceroy, the Assyrian king.

Nevertheless, the winged anthropomorphic figure may illustrate Ezekiel's image of the deity indirectly. If the Assyrian winged anthropomorphic figure is symbolic of the Assyrian king as the representative or image of the divine sovereign on earth, then the corollary is that the divine sovereign himself bears some resemblance to the earthly king and especially to the anthropomorphic figure in the nimbus. Ezekiel seems to depict the "majesty of Yahweh" as a similarly anthropomorphic portrayal of a totally transcendent deity. Insofar as the deity can be apprehended by human senses at all, it is possible to do so only indirectly through recognizing the divine image as manifested in human form. Something similar seems to have been the view of the Priestly Writer; the deity's statement "Let us create humankind *in our image*" would seem to imply that the human form images something of the deity and the beings that surround the deity.[77]

C. The Democratization of Kingship in the Priestly Creation Account

If it is correct that for P the deity is first and foremost the divine sovereign, then the fact that humvankind bears the divine image must mean that P understood humans to be the earthly embodiment of the divine sovereign. In other words, on earth humankind serves as viceroy of the divine sovereign, similar to the way that in Assyria the king was understood to be the divine sovereign's viceroy. According to P, הָאָדָם "humankind" was given authority over all the earth to *subdue* (כבשׁ) it and to *exercise dominion* (רדה) over the animals (Gen 1:26, 28). This is of course royal language and royal ideology.[78]

---

76. Greenberg, *Ezekiel, 1–20*, 54.

77. For a survey of the many interpretations of the phrase "image of God," see Westermann, *Genesis 1–11*, 147–58; and more recently, Wenham, *Genesis 1–15*, 29–32. [For a more recent, comprehensive treatment, see J. Richard Middleton, *The Liberating Image: The Imago Dei in Genesis 1* (Grand Rapids: Brazos Press, 2005); see also my additional discussion of Middleton in the postscript to this article, below.]

78. On this widely recognized aspect, see the discussion, with references to previous scholarship, in Westermann, *Genesis 1–11*, 151–54, 159; and Victor P. Hamilton, *The Book of Genesis: Chapters 1–17* (NICOT; Grand Rapids: Eerdmans, 1990) 137–38. S. G. F. Brandon (*Creation Legends of the Ancient Near East* [London: Hodder and Stoughton, 1963] 1150,

In the ancient Near East ultimately the goal of cosmogonic myth was the creation of humankind. Moreover, in Mesopotamian myth at least, kingship was a necessary part of—even the apex of—the creation of humankind.[79] In royal propaganda everywhere, kingship was divinely instituted, the divine instrument for maintaining justice and right order in the earth—as Lipit-Ishtar and Hammurabi stated so eloquently in the prologues to their respective law codes,[80] and as expressed in various Neo-Assyrian benedictions over the king.[81]

Not unrelated is the well-attested literary and iconographic conceit that the king is "master of the animals." Assyrian kings are often depicted killing ferocious lions and wild bulls. To take just the example of Ashurnasirpal II, one notes that in the throne room of the Northwest Palace at Nimrud, two contiguous slabs (B-19 and B-20) in their upper panels depict the king killing lions in the one case and wild bulls in the other. In the panels immediately below, the king is shown standing over a slain lion and a slain wild bull, respectively, holding his hunting bow in his left hand and a libation bowl in his raised right hand, indicative of a successful hunt (fig. 18).[82]

followed by Westermann [*Genesis 1–11*, 159], suggests that the point of the Genesis account here is that humans are being liberated, so to speak, from the servile burden imposed upon them by the Mesopotamian mythic creation tradition "to bear the yoke of the gods." This may be true, but it misses the full import of humankind's royal function being developed here by P.

79. W. R. Mayer, "Ein Mythos von der Erschaffung des Menschen und des Königs," *Or* 56 (1987) 55–66. For English translations of this text, see Clifford, *Creation Accounts in the Ancient Near East and in the Bible*, 69–70; and Alasdair Livingstone, "A Late Piece of Constructed Mythology Relevant to the Neo-Assyrian and Middle Assyrian Coronation Hymn and Prayer," in *COS* 1:146 (pp. 476–77).

80. Lipit-Ishtar of Isin (2017–1985 B.C.E.) claimed that the high gods An and Enlil appointed him king of Sumer and Akkad "in order to establish justice in the land, to eliminate cries for justice, to eradicate enmity and armed violence, to bring well-being to the lands of Sumer and Akkad" (The Laws of Lipit-Ishtar 1.1–37 [trans. Martha Roth, in *COS* 2:154 (p. 411)]; similarly in the epilogue, 21.5–17). For his part, Hammurabi of Babylon (1792–1750 B.C.E.) claimed that Anu and Enlil promoted Marduk and his city Babylon "and made it supreme within the regions of the world" and that "Anu and Enlil, for the enhancement of the well-being of the people, named me by my name: Hammurabi . . . to make justice prevail in the land, to abolish the wicked and the evil, to prevent the strong from oppressing the weak, to rise like the sun-god Shamash over all humankind, to illuminate the land" (The Laws of Hammurabi 1.27–49 [trans. Martha Roth; *COS* 2:131 (p. 336)]; see also the epilogue, 47.9–780). Ur-Namma (2112–2095 B.C.E.), founder of the Third Dynasty of Ur, earlier had claimed that the gods had similarly commissioned him to establish justice in the land (The Laws of Ur-Namma 104–13 [idem, *COS* 2:153 (p. 409)]).

81. Representative examples from coronation prayers include prayers for Tukulti-Ninurta I ("May Assur give you authority, obedience, concord, justice and peace!" [trans. Alasdair Livingstone; *COS* 1:140 (p. 472)]) and for Ashurbanipal ("May eloquence, understanding, truth and justice be granted him [Ashurbanipal] as a gift! . . . May concord and peace be established in Assyria!" [idem, *COS* 1:142 (p. 473)]). Likewise, in a hymn to Shamash, Ashurbanipal prays for himself: "May he constantly shepherd over your peoples, whom you gave him, in justice" (idem, *COS* 1:143 [p. 474]).

82. Fig. 18: drawing by Halina Lewakowa, in J. Meuszyński, *Die Rekonstruktion der Reliefdarstellungen*, fig. 1.3. The reliefs themselves are, for the upper panels, BM 124534

Fig. 18. Ashurnasirpal killing lions (B-19) and wild bulls (B-20). Drawing of bas reliefs on walls of the throne room of the Northwest Palace at Nimrud. Used by permission of R. P. Sobelewski, Polish Mission to Nimroud/Iraq/Polish Center of Archaeology.

Also, four of the sixteen bronze bands on Ashurnasirpal's gate in the Temple of Mamu at Balawat (ancient Imgur Enlil) were dedicated to showing the king hunting lions and wild oxen; the accompanying text reads "wild oxen by the Euphrates, I killed" and "Lions by the Balih River, I killed."[83] Moreover, the inscription chiseled on the base of Ashurnasirpal's throne in his (Northwest) Palace at Kalhu diverges from the "standard text" on the walls by adding accounts of the king hunting wild beasts and breeding herds of them.[84] Undoubtedly there was an element of the thrill of hunting wild animals involved, and the Assyrian artists are careful to show the

---

(B-19a, killing lions), and BM 124532 (B-20a, killing wild bulls); for photos, see *Assyrian Palace Reliefs*, fig. 26 [= *ANEP*, no. 184] and fig. 27, respectively. The lower panels are BM 124535 (B-19b, the slain lion), and BM 124533 (B-20b, the slain wild bull; photo in Paley, *King of the World*, 102, pl. 18b). Photos of B-19a, B-19b, and B-20a are also available in Strommenger, *Fünf Jahrtausende Mesopotamien*, pl. 202. The theme of the king hunting wild animals is even more extensively depicted in the reliefs of Ashurbanipal; see Paley, figs. 55–104. For a systematic listing and discussion of the theme of the king as hunter, see Magen, *Assyrische Königsdarstellungen*, 29–36.

83. Russell, *The Writing on the Wall*, 55–57.

84. Ibid., 42–44. In addition, other scenes depict animals brought as tribute from far-flung parts of the empire or captured on hunting expeditions; regarding these Russell comments: "Viewing these animals, [Ashurnasirpal's] subjects would be reminded in a very direct way of the king's role as shepherd, and may well have seen in these heterogeneous animals from diverse regions, brought together in the capital and cared for by the king of the realm, a metaphor of the various peoples of the empire, united and protected by that same authority" (p. 44).

skill and the daring of the monarch.[85] But there is more involved, because these scenes also convey the image of the king as the lord and master of the animals, the one who protects the land from every threat, including the threat of wild animals that might ravage the land and take away its security.[86] A threat of attack by wild beasts can be as debilitating as the threat of an armed enemy.

Lev 26:5–6 speaks of the security that God bestows in precisely these terms: "I will grant peace in the land and you shall lie down, and no one shall make you afraid; I will remove dangerous animals from the land, and no sword shall go through your land" (NRSV). Ezekiel (34:25–31) in speaking of the eschatological covenant of peace that God will establish on earth echoes similar sentiments: "I will make with them a covenant of peace and banish wild animals from the land, so that they may live in the wild and sleep in the woods securely. . . . They shall no longer be plunder for the nations, nor shall the animals of the land devour them; they shall live in safety, and no one shall make them afraid. . . . You are my sheep, the sheep of my pasture and I am your God, says the Lord God" (Ezek 34:25–31; cf. Hos 2:20[2:18]).[87] When kings killed wild beasts, symbolically they were acting in place of the divine sovereign, divinely appointed shepherds ridding the earth of threats to the divinely willed peace.[88]

In creating humankind, P says, God gives humankind mastery over all the animals, both domesticated and wild (Gen 1:26, 28); in Gen 9:2, the writer elaborates on this motif, saying that animals will be in "fear and dread" of humankind, apparently because humans bear the "image" of God (9:6). Others have noted that the "fear and dread" that humankind wreaks upon the animal kingdom is analogous to the *puluḫtu* that Meso-

---

85. In the case of Ashurbanipal, where text and image are coordinated on the same relief, the element of sport in the lion hunt is acknowledged; see ibid., 201–2. The coordination of text and image in the same panel is a novel practice begun with Ashurbanipal (ibid., 216); for earlier kings, motives must be inferred.

86. Commenting on two similar Neo-Assyrian seals that depict a deity/hero with his foot resting upon a domestic animal and defending it from an attacking lion, Othmar Keel (*The Symbolism of the Biblical World*, 58) says: "The foot placed upon the weaker animal expresses 'dominion' (cf. Ps 8:6). As in the case of the king, however, this dominion consists not only in holding subject, but also in defense of the weaker animal against the attacking lion."

87. For the linkage between the themes of removal of wild beasts and the establishment of security in the land, see Katherine M. Hayes, "Lord of the Animals: God and ʾādam" (paper presented at the Sixty-Third General Meeting of the Catholic Biblical Association of America, Loyola Marymount University, Los Angeles, CA, August 5–8, 2000) 1–40; see also my "Covenant of Peace," 187–211 [reprinted in this volume as chap. 7; note esp. pp. 176–77].

88. That the killing of wild animals was intimately linked with the establishment of cosmic weal is graphically represented on an ivory bed-head from Nimrud whereon the king is depicted slaying a wild bull, amid other panels decorated with various motifs indicating universal harmony and abundance; see Max Mallowan, *Nimrud and Its Remains*, 2:491–92 ##385–87.

potamian kings generated in their foes.[89] But in P's revisioning of creation, kingship has been democratized. Not just kings but all humans bear this royal badge of divinity.

Perhaps the best commentary on P's vision of all humankind's being imbued with royal divine status is Psalm 8, which, as noted above, bears obvious similarities to Genesis 1. This psalm opens with hymned praise of God as the divine sovereign (אדון): "How majestic is your name in all the earth!" It then moves quickly to the divine sovereign's role as creator but dwells on humankind as the culmination of the deity's creative design:

> You have made [humankind] barely lower than God,[90]
> crowning them with glory and honor.
> You have given them dominion[91] over the works of
> your hands.
> You have placed all things under their feet:
> all sheep and oxen,
> and also the wild beasts,
> the birds of the sky and the fish of the sea—
> whatever courses through the sea.

The psalmist then reiterates his opening line praising the divine sovereign for his marvelous works "in all the world." As in P, the divine sovereign has made אדם "humankind" his viceroy and given it responsibility for this world and everything in it.

One cannot help but contrast Psalm 8 with royal psalms such as Psalms 2, 89, and 110. In Psalm 89 the psalmist extols the divine sovereign for choosing David and his descendants to bear the mantle of royal divinity. The king is imbued with the status of divine sonship and entrusted with the deity's own work of maintaining order in a threatening and chaotic world:

> I will set his hand on Sea,
> and his right hand on Rivers.
> He shall cry to me, "You are my Father,
> my God, and the Rock of my salvation!"
> I will make him the firstborn,
> the highest of the kings of the earth. (Ps 89:26–28)

According to this royal psalm, the Davidic king alone wears the mantle of the divine sovereign and exercises divine rule on earth. In a burst of

---

89. Despite a reputation for "calculated frightfulness," Ashurnasirpal II, like other Neo-Assyrian kings, used a careful balancing of carrot and stick to assure the submission of vassal kingdoms; see Barbara N. Porter, "Intimidation and Friendly Persuasion: Re-evaluating the Propaganda of Ashurnasirpal II," in *ErIsr* 27 (Hayim and Miriam Tadmor Volume; 2003) 180*–91*.

90. Or: "gods" (אלהים).

91. A different root (משל) is used here than in Gen 1:26 + 28 (רדה, כבש), but the meaning is identical.

poetic exuberance, the psalmist claims that God has even commissioned the king to have dominion over the powers of chaos (ים "Sea" ‖ נהרות "Rivers"), a role traditionally reserved for the divine sovereign alone, as in Ps 24:1–2, where Yahweh is celebrated as the king of glory, who subdues these waters of chaos:

> To Yahweh belong the earth and its fullness,
> The world and those who dwell therein;
> For he has founded it upon Sea,
> And established it upon Rivers.

Prior to the psalmist, the Canaanite author of the Baal epic celebrated Baal as king of the gods by virtue of his victory over Prince Sea ‖ Judge River.[92]

Psalm 2 is no less expansive in asserting that the divine sovereign has exalted the Davidic king alone. Scholars have long considered v. 7 ("You are my son; today I have begotten you") a statement of adoptive divine sonship for the Davidic king, presumably pronounced at his coronation. Recently, however, Jeffrey Tigay has recognized in v. 6 a formula of divine creation of the king through a special נסך "casting" by the deity. Although unique in biblical literature, similar claims that the king was specially created in a divine "casting" are found in Mesopotamian, specifically Assyrian royal propaganda.[93] Accordingly, Psalm 2 appears to go beyond a mere claim of adoptive or fictive sonship for the king to assert instead that the Davidic king is literally God's own specially created son:

> "But I myself created my king on Zion, my holy mountain."
> Let me tell of Yahweh's decree;
> He said to me: "You are my son;
> Today I have begotten you." (vv. 6–7)

Given such credentials, it is no wonder that the psalmist warns the nations against conspiring "against Yahweh and his anointed," since the two form but a single ruling unit. Ps 110:1 similarly claims that the divine sovereign has seated the king at his right hand and placed his enemies under his feet as a footstool.

Psalm 8, then, with its democratization of kingship is a radical departure from the royal psalms. In Psalm 8 the whole of humankind has been "crowned with glory and honor" and given "dominion" over creation because the divine sovereign has "put all things under their feet." Similar

---

92. On the connection between Psalm 24 and the Baal epic, see the perceptive commentary by J. J. M. Roberts, "The King of Glory," *PSB* n.s. 3/1 (1980) 50; reprinted in idem, *The Bible and the Ancient Near East*, 104–9. I have diverged from Roberts's translation of Ps 24:2 by reading ימים "Sea" (ים + enclitic *mem*) and נהרות "River" instead of "the seas" and "the rivers," respectively; the lack of the definite article in each case convinces me that more rather than less of the older mythological tradition has been retained in this poetic formulation. Compare Ps 89:26.

93. Jeffrey H. Tigay, "Divine Creation of the King in Psalms 2:6," *ErIsr* 27 (Hayim and Miriam Tadmor Volume; 2003) 246*–50*.

to P, however, Psalm 8 has toned down the mythical imagery of creation. Gone, for example, are references to subduing the chaos dragon Sea-Rivers, replaced instead by more secular references to ruling "whatever courses through the sea." Psalm 8 echoes conceptually and theologically P's view that all humans were created in the image of the divine sovereign.

P evidently writes out of the shadow of the Babylonian exile, by which time the shortcomings of not only the Israelite monarchy but also the Davidic monarchy in Zion-Jerusalem have been made patently evident. Hence in Genesis 1, P seeks to ground the divine image elsewhere than in the king, as the royal Zion theology would have it. Humankind itself may be flawed, as P will make clear in subsequent chapters. Indeed, the divine image is already greatly tarnished by Genesis 5, because P puts some distance between Adam's descendants and God's image by noting that Adam's sons were begotten in Adam's image rather than in the image of God, as Adam himself had been (5:1–3). Nevertheless, tarnished as the divine image in humankind may be, it is still the divinely willed avenue by which to apprehend the transcendent deity. The divine sovereign has delegated his authority to humankind. This is both privilege and duty, it would appear. Every human is anointed to continue the agenda of the divine sovereign by working to eliminate from this world every form of oppression and injustice (chaos) so that peace and universal weal (cosmos) may prevail throughout this universe that God created "perfect" (טוב מאד).[94]

4. Conclusion

When cultural clues within the Priestly primeval story are pursued, it becomes obvious that P's God exhibits many of the characteristics of the high gods observable in other ancient Near Eastern societies. God is clearly the creator of heaven and earth. But Near Eastern cosmologies, especially those of the latter part of the second millennium and the first millennium, attribute the work of creation primarily to the king of the gods, that is, to the divine sovereign. Moreover, creation frequently involved a clash of wills, the divine sovereign against an archfoe—which conflict is of cosmic proportions, that is, what Gunkel dubbed a *Chaoskampf*. Such Combat Myth motifs are downplayed in P but not wholly absent. P's deity is the divine sovereign who rules from his temple above the heavens. At especially critical junctures when his creation is threatened God emerges from his transcendent abode amid awesome clouds to (re)impose order over chaos and to (re)establish a kingdom befitting this majestic divine sovereign. Because of his totally transcendent nature, however, it is difficult to observe the divine sovereign directly. The divine sovereign is always "on duty," so

---

94. The Priestly tradition recognized that humankind frequently fell short of its royal vocation, however. For this reason the Priestly tradition posited the necessity of priesthood for bridging the gap between the sinful manner in which humans act and their royal vocation.

to speak, but after an initial ordering of chaos, he has turned over the duty of maintaining peace and harmony in the world to humans, who as the deity's representatives have been charged with promoting the welfare of creation.

The Priestly Writer used the primeval narrative to introduce God as universal ruler. The ancient Near Eastern metaphor of the divine sovereign provided the Priestly Writer with an excellent foundation upon which to build a theology in which both the transcendence and the universality of the deity clearly emerge. But at the same time this exalted deity is very close to his world. His providence extends to all things and all beings, whether in heaven or on earth. Nevertheless, the divine sovereign chooses to exercise his dominion on earth largely through humankind. There is no attempt to link any of this either to the king or to Zion, however, because in P's new universalizing theology each person is endowed with the divine image and each person is charged with actualizing and maintaining this world in the perfection that the divine sovereign intended.

*   *   *   *   *

Postscript

In a major new study of the *imago dei* in Genesis 1, J. Richard Middleton has come to many of the same conclusions as I concerning the Priestly characterization of the deity and the portrayal of humankind as the image of God. Writing approximately at the same time and working independently, Middleton likewise finds (1) that the Priestly writer depicts God as "sovereign over the cosmos," (2) that God consults with "a divine council or court of angelic beings," and (3) that "humanity is created *like* this God, with the special role of representing or imaging God's rule in the world."[95] This interpretation of the *imago dei* not only derives from but also is confirmed by the symbolic world of the ancient Near East, particularly its royal ideology.

Middleton's methodology is similar in that he bases his conclusions not only on an analysis of texts in the Hebrew Bible itself but also upon an examination of extrabiblical written and iconographical data from the ancient Near East, especially Mesopotamia. Although Genesis 1 never calls God "king," God nonetheless is portrayed therein as a king with absolute power, whose word is law. This is similar to the pattern of ancient Near Eastern mythopoeic models, like the Egyptian god Ptah bringing creatures into being by speaking with his heart and tongue, or Marduk who creates and destroys by a mere word.[96] Moreover, the deity's actions creating the

---

95. J. Richard Middleton, *The Liberating Image: The* Imago Dei *in Genesis 1* (Grand Rapids: Brazos Press, 2005); these summary quotations are from p. 26.

96. Ibid., 66.

cosmos should be understood as temple building, followed by rest, similar to Ugaritic and Mesopotamian patterns.[97] Furthermore, while it cannot be proved that the writer of Genesis 1 knew or was influenced by the text of *Enuma Elish*, there is "an intriguing similarity of ideas here," and to other Mesopotamian texts as well.[98]

Middleton argues that the author of Genesis 1 has framed his creation account in opposition to the Mesopotamian world view, which was based upon three elements: (1) Mesopotamian royal ideology, according to which the king is the image of God; (2) a mythic claim that humans were created to serve the gods; and (3) the *Chaoskampf* idea, according to which creation (the cosmos, including humankind) was grounded in primordial violence.

So it is with a bit of inconsistency that Middleton rejects my view (expounded in older publications) that Combat Myth motifs, even in a demythologized form, are present in Genesis 1, even though he admits their presence elsewhere in the Hebrew Bible (for example, Job 26:7-14; Pss 74:12-17; 89:5-14). Middleton's primary reason seems to be theological rather than comparative, however. Mesopotamian creation accounts, he says, devalue humankind in that humans were created to serve gods, thus relieving them of their burdens. Middleton ignores my thesis that much the same motif is found in the older Yahwistic account of creation in Genesis 2.[99] Even more important for Middleton, however, is his conviction that creation-by-combat would justify human violence. In this he follows Ricoeur, among others, who argues that to admit *Chaoskampf* in Genesis promotes a misguided, "negative" value system justifying human violence and the domination of others in society, as "violence is inscribed in the origin of things, in the principle that establishes while it destroys."[100] Middleton fails to appreciate that in ancient Near Eastern thought the function of the Combat Myth was actually positive, not negative. Rather than suggesting that creation is founded on violence, the function of the Combat

---

97. Ibid., 81.

98. Ibid., 131-36, esp. p. 131.

99. See my discussion in "Paradise Reexamined," in *The Biblical Canon in Comparative Perspective: Scripture in Context IV* (ed. K. Lawson Younger, Jr., William W. Hallo, and Bernard F. Batto; Lewiston, NY: Edwin Mellen, 1991) 33-66, esp. pp. 51-53 (reprinted in this volume as chap. 2); and *Slaying the Dragon*, chap. 2, "The Yahwist's Primeval Myth," esp. pp. 50-51. According to Middleton, in the biblical view no such menial tasks are envisioned for humankind, as Genesis 1:26-28 states that humankind was created to rule over God's creation. Such a judgment is possible only by lumping all Mesopotamian texts together, despite their varying ages and local differences, as if they represented one homogenous theology or ideology, on the one side, while carefully distinguishing Genesis 1 from all other competing biblical viewpoints, on the other side. A more even-handed, diachronic analysis of both Mesopotamian and biblical texts reveals that the two cultures share more similar views than Middleton allows; see chap. 1 above, "The Ancient Near Eastern Context of the Hebrew Ideas of Creation"; and also my book *Slaying the Dragon*, esp. chaps. 1-3.

100. Middleton, *The Liberating Image*, 250-60.

Myth was to proclaim that creation—more precisely, human existence—is possible because the deity has removed, and continues to remove, those threats which preclude or threaten human well-being (*šālōm*), or to use more theological language, the establishment of the kingdom of God.

Although Middleton and I travel at times by different paths, we do arrive at the same overarching conclusion, namely that behind the concept of humankind as the *imago dei* in Genesis stands Mesopotamian royal theology, in a deliberately modified form. Whereas in Mesopotamian royal theology the human king alone was said to be the representative and intermediary of the deity in maintaining order in a divinely organized world, in Genesis 1 the Priestly author has deliberately democratized such royal propaganda to proclaim boldly that all humans are "called to be the representative and intermediary of God's power and blessing on earth."[101]

---

101. Ibid., chap. 3, "An Ancient Near Eastern Background for the *Imago Dei*," esp. p. 121.

Chapter 5

The Sleeping God:
An Ancient Near Eastern Motif
of Divine Sovereignty

The psalms appear to give contradictory images of God in relation to sleep. Psalm 121 says that Yahweh never sleeps, that he is eternally vigilant in protecting his people from all evil. Psalm 44:24[23] gives exactly the opposite picture, however. The psalmist calls upon God to wake up and save his people from the wicked who threaten to devour them. Similar images of God asleep while his people perish can be found in Ps 7:7, 35:23, and 59:5–6.

Previous commentators have usually explained the image of God sleeping in various ways. One group considered it to be a metaphor for the apparent inattentiveness of God (*deus absconditus*) to the prayers of his people, especially in times of distress.[1] As such, it was considered to be one of the bolder anthropomorphisms found in the Bible, employed more for psychological effect than any theological significance.[2] A second group, taking its cue more from the word *qûmâ* "Arise!" sometimes found in parallel cola,[3] understood the psalmist's cry "Wake up!" to be a plea to God to ascend his divine throne to render judgment against wicked enemies who unjustly persecute the faithful.[4] Opinions have differed as to whether

---

Originally published in *Bib* 68 (1987) 153–77.

1. So, among others, C. A. Briggs, *A Critical and Exegetical Commentary on the Book of Psalms* (2 vols.; ICC; Edinburgh: T. & T. Clark, 1906) 1.382; E. Kalt, *Herder's Commentary on the Psalms* (Westminster, MD: Newman Press, 1961) 24, 165; M. Dahood, *Psalms I* (AB 16; Garden City: Doubleday, 1965) 267–68; and A. A. Anderson, *Psalms* (2 vols.; New Century Bible; London: Attic Press, 1972) 1.345, 436.

2. See H. H. Rowley, *The Faith of Israel: Aspects of Old Testament Thought* (London: SCM, 1956) 75; W. Eichrodt, *Theology of the Old Testament* (2 vols.; OTL; Philadelphia: Westminster, 1961–67) 1.211–14; Anderson, *Psalms*, 1.284. Specifically on Ps 44:23–24, W. O. E. Oesterley (*The Psalms* [London: SPCK, 1939] 248) opines that the psalmist's words are a taunt to God (cf. 1 Kgs 18:27) intended to stir him from his inattentiveness or inaction.

3. See below, n. 47.

4. So B. Duhm, *Die Psalmen* (Kurzer Hand-Commentar zum Alten Testament 14; Freiburg: Mohr [Siebeck], 1899) 25; J. J. S. Perowne, *The Books of Psalms: A New Translation with Introduction and Notes* (2 vols.; Andover: W. F. Draper, 1901) 1.121. B. Bonkamp (*Die*

this judgment theophany was expected in the present time,[5] or only es-
chatologically.[6] Some commentators have felt it sufficient to juxtapose Ps
121:4 with a passage like Ps 44:24, as if the assurance of the former that the
"keeper of Israel neither slumbers nor sleeps" proves that the sleeping of
the deity in the latter must be understood only metaphorically.[7]

There have also been attempts to explain the sleep of God from an ancient Near Eastern cultural context. Relying on a very questionable interpretation of Canaanite religion, some have professed to find in Ps 121:4 a
Yahwistic polemic against the Canaanite Baals who as fertility gods were
alleged to die and rise annually, which in turn supposedly was portrayed as
sleeping and awakening (cf. 1 Kgs 18:27).[8] G. Widengren,[9] followed in part
by H.-J. Kraus,[10] proposed that the cultic shout "Awake!" was a vestige of
the cult of Tammuz, the dying and rising vegetation god, which Widengren
claimed was widely practiced in the royal ritual of the ancient Near East.
Widengren's hypothesis has rightly been rejected, however, both because
of the now discredited myth and ritual basis upon which it was built and
because the motif of God's sleep in biblical tradition does not fit the typology of the Tammuz liturgy.[11]

A much more compelling proposal has been put forward recently by
M. Weippert.[12] Comparing ancient Near Eastern texts which portray the

---

Psalmen, nach dem hebräischen Grundtext übersetzt [Freiburg: W. Visarius, 1949] 69 n. 4, and
277 n. 5) explains the call to awaken from the presupposition that such judgment sessions
began at dawn.

5. So Briggs, *Psalms*, 1.58; Anderson, *Psalms*, 1.96. A. Weiser (*The Psalms* [OTL; Philadelphia: Westminster, 1962] 68) claims that this theophany was expected to occur within
the context of the annual covenant festival.

6. So H. Gunkel, *Die Psalmen* (HKAT II 2; Göttingen: Vandenhoeck & Ruprecht, 1926)
24; Oesterley, *The Psalms*, 138.

7. E.g., Briggs, *Psalms*, 1.382; Dahood, *Psalms I*, 268; H.-J. Kraus, *Psalmen* [2 vols.;
BKAT 15; Neukirchen-Vluyn: Neukirchener Verlag, 1959–60] 1.58; A. Cohen, *The Psalms:
Hebrew Text, English Translation and Commentary* (Hindhead, Surrey: Soncino Press, 1945)
139; Anderson, *Psalms*, 1.436.

8. So H. Schmidt, *Die Psalmen* (HAT 15; Tübingen: Mohr [Siebeck], 1934) 222; Oesterley, *Psalms*, 504.

9. G. Widengren, *Sakrales Königtum im Alten Testament und im Judentum* (Stuttgart:
W. Kohlhammer, 1955) 63–66; "Early Hebrew Myths and Their Interpretation," *Myth, Rit-
ual and Kingship: Essays on the Theory and Practice of Kingship in the Ancient Near East and in
Israel* (ed. S. H. Hooke; Oxford: Clarendon Press, 1958) 149–203, esp. pp. 191–93.

10. Kraus (*Psalmen*, 1.58), although accepting Widengren's hypothesis about the myth
and ritual origins of the cultic shout "Awake!," maintains that any connection with the
cult of the dying and rising vegetation deity has been lost when applied to Yahweh within
the biblical tradition. A. Weiser (*The Psalms*, 39) holds a similar position but is even more
cautious about connecting this cultic shout with the Tammuz-type liturgy.

11. See W. Moran, "Review of *Myth, Ritual, and Kingship*," *Bib* 40 (1959) 1026–28; Dahood, *Psalms I*, 267–68.

12. M. Weippert, "Slapende en ontwakende of stervende en herrijzende goden?" *NedTT*
37 (1983) 279–89; "Ecce non dormitabit neque dormiet qui custodit Israhel: Zur Erklärung
von Psalms 121:4," *Lese-Zeichen für Annelies Findeiss* (ed. C. Burchard und G. Theissen;
Dielheimer Blätter zum Alten Testament 3; Heidelberg: Carl Winter, 1984) 75–87.

great gods as not exercising their divine jurisdictions during the night while they sleep,[13] Weippert suggests that some within Israel thought of Yahweh too as sleeping when the wicked were allowed to oppress the innocent. Nonetheless, the more authentic Israelite impulse affirms that Yahweh is always vigilant (Ps 121:4). Although such religious psychology may account partially for biblical portrayals of God sleeping, it is not the complete story.

It is the contention of this writer that the biblical images of God sleeping and awaking are grounded in a hitherto unrecognized ancient Near Eastern motif of the sleeping god. Accordingly, the purpose of this paper is twofold: 1) to outline the content and use of this neglected motif from ancient Near Eastern extrabiblical texts, and 2) to demonstrate that in appropriating this motif as their own biblical authors found a powerful and effective vehicle for theologizing about their own God as creator and savior.

1. The Motif within Its Ancient Near Eastern Setting

To judge from the literature of the ancient Near East, the motif of the sleeping deity actually involves several related concepts which for convenience may be grouped under two headings: A) rest as a divine prerogative, and B) sleeping as a symbol of divine rule.[14] As would be expected, the motif is never formally stated in any ancient Near Eastern text but must be reconstructed from its deployment in diverse literary texts from Mesopotamia, Canaan and Egypt. Moreover, these texts are all concerned with the origins of the cosmos and its ordering, so that one may suspect *a priori* that the motif of divine sleep ultimately is connected with the concept of the deity as creator.

A. Rest as a Divine Prerogative

Widespread in the history of religions is a motif of the leisure (*otiositas*) of the creator god. This leisure belongs to the very nature of the creator. Creation is a unique, primeval event that cannot be repeated. The divine rest that follows creation is, as it were, a statement that the creative activity is complete and that the work of the creator is perfect.[15]

---

13. In particular, *Atrahasis* I 57–84 (see W. G. Lambert and A. R. Millard, *Atra-ḫasīs: The Babylonian Story of the Flood* [Oxford: Oxford University Press, 1969; reprinted Winona Lake: Eisenbrauns, 1999] 46) and the Old Babylonian "Prayer to the Gods of the Night" (see *ANET*, 390–91).

14. In addition, one commonly encounters the anthropomorphism that the gods required their regular physical sleep each night for refreshment and revitalization, such as Homer depicts for the Greek gods (*Iliad* i 605–11). Their retirement at night and their arising in the morning may be accompanied by cultic rituals (see A. L. Oppenheim, *Ancient Mesopotamia: Portrait of a Dead Civilization* [Chicago: University of Chicago Press, 1964] 183–98; A. Erman, *The Literature of the Ancient Egyptians* [trans. Aylward M. Blackman; London: Methuen & Co., 1927] 12). The notion that the gods did not exercise their normal jurisdictions while they slept ("Prayer to the Gods of the Night"; see n. 13) is derived at least partially from this anthropomorphism.

15. See R. Pettazzoni, "Myths of Beginnings and Creation-Myths," in *Essays on the History of Religions* (Numen Suppl. 1; Leiden: Brill, 1954) 24–36, esp. pp. 32–34.

This motif of divine leisure is found in a straightforward manner in the Egyptian text known as "the Theology of Memphis."[16] This text attempts to supplant the authority of older, recognized creator gods by portraying the Memphite god Ptah as the real creator, prior in time and principle to all the other gods. After describing how Ptah brought into being everything that exists, including the other gods, the text states, "And so Ptah *rested*[17] after he had made everything, as well as all the divine order." In a text so explicitly self-conscious about justifying every facet of Ptah's role as creator, this statement is a clear witness to the belief that a creation account should conclude with a description of the creator resting. The creator may relax because his work is finished, perfect.

The theme of leisure for the divine creator seems also to have been part and parcel of the common Semitic *Chaoskampf* myth.[18] In the Ugaritic version, the weather god Baal, the Canaanite embodiment of prosperity and order, was for a time swallowed up by the underworld god Mot (Death). During that time the earth languished for lack of rain and prosperity perished, i.e., chaos reigned. But Baal's sister Anat came to the rescue and freed Baal from the clutches of Mot. The god El, head of the Canaanite pantheon, subsequently had a dream of the heavens raining down oil and the wadis flowing with honey, and so El knew that Baal was truly alive and functioning. Among the Canaanites it was El, not Baal, who was regarded as the creator.[19] Accordingly, El's reaction to his dream is noteworthy. Once Baal had been revivified and order returned to the earth, El rejoiced and announced:

> Now I can sit and rest,
> Even my inmost being can rest. (*CTA* 6 iii.18–19)[20]

16. *ANET*, 4–5; M. Lichtheim, *Ancient Egyptian Literature. Volume I: The Old and Middle Kingdoms* (Berkeley: University of California Press, 1973) 51–57.

17. Following Wilson's (*ANET*, 5 n. 19) alternative translation. Fearing that they were being too much influenced by the parallel in Gen 2:1–3, some scholars have preferred to translate more neutrally, "so Ptah was satisfied"; see J. Wilson in *The Intellectual Adventure of Man* (ed. H. Frankfort et al.; Chicago: University of Chicago Press, 1946) 59. The translation "rested" has been accepted by, among others, C. Westermann (*Genesis 1–11* [Minneapolis: Augsburg Publishing House, 1984] 167) and H. Brunner (*Near Eastern Religious Texts Relating to the Old Testament* [ed. W. Beyerlin; OTL; Philadelphia: Westminster, 1978] 4–5).

18. Representatives include the Babylonian myth of *Enuma Elish*, the Ugaritic Baal epic, the Canaanite/Israelite myth reconstructed from diffuse allusions in the Bible, the Egyptian stories of "Astarte and the Sea" and "the Repulsing of the Dragon," and the Hittite Illuyankas myth.

19. The controversial issue of El as creator has been discussed most recently by J. Day, *God's Conflict with the Dragon and the Sea: Echoes of a Canaanite Myth in the Old Testament* (University of Cambridge Oriental Publications 35; Cambridge: Cambridge University Press, 1985) 17–18.

20. *atbn.ank.wanḫn wtnḫ.birty.npš*. These identical words are also found in the mouth of Danel at the birth of his heir (*CTA* 17 ii.12–13). In both cases the speaker implies that he can relax because his task is successfully completed.

The creator, father of the gods and humankind, could relax and rest because the cosmos was in order once more.

The motif of divine leisure is encountered again in the Mesopotamian stories of *Atrahasis* and *Enuma Elish*.[21] In both of these texts leisure is viewed as a divine prerogative, a right of all the gods and not just the creator. Indeed, *Atrahasis* takes its departure from this very theme, as the opening lines attest:

> When the gods like men[22]
> Bore the labor, suffered the toil,
> The toil of the gods was immense,
> The work heavy, the distress severe.
> The Seven great Anunnaki
> Were making the Igigi suffer the labor (I 1–6)

The implication is that there was something amiss in this situation. The high gods (Anunnaki) had imposed virtual slavery upon the lesser gods (Igigi). While the lesser gods bore the total burden of producing food for all the gods, the high gods lounged in comfort. In short, the lesser gods were not able to participate in the divine prerogative of rest. Accordingly, when the lesser gods subsequently revolted against Enlil, their king, there was justification for their mutinous conduct.

The solution is illuminating for what it reveals of the Babylonian conception of the divine vis-à-vis the human realm. The rebels' ringleader was killed and humankind fashioned from his blood mixed with clay. Henceforth humans would bear the burden of providing food for the gods; thus would all the gods enjoy rest like Enlil and the other high gods. In short, the lesser gods were to acquire full divine status; no longer would they have to slave like humans.

A reflex of this theme is encountered again in *Enuma Elish*. After Marduk defeated Tiamat, he split her lifeless body in twain to form the heavens and the earth. Then, in a scene imported from *Atrahasis*, Marduk also slew Qingu (Tiamat's husband-king and henchman) and from his body and blood fashioned humankind. As in *Atrahasis*, the stated purpose for

---

21. Composed during the Old Babylonian period (1950–1500 B.C.E.) out of prior Sumerian traditions, *Atrahasis* is the older of the two mythological texts and represented the standard or "pan-Mesopotamian" view of creation. *Enuma Elish*, probably composed around 1100 B.C.E., was a specifically Babylonian adaptation of the creation myth designed to promote Babylon's own god Marduk as head of the pantheon (see W. G. Lambert, "The Reign of Nebuchadnezzar I: A Turning Point in the History of Ancient Mesopotamian Religion," *The Seed of Wisdom: Essays in Honour of T. J. Meek* [ed. W. S. McCullough; Toronto: University of Toronto Press, 1964] 3–13).

22. Alternatively, "When the gods (still were) human . . ." For a survey of the scholarly debate over this controversial line and important observations on its implications, see R. Oden, Jr., "Divine Aspirations in Atrahasis and in Genesis 1–11," *ZAW* 93 (1981) 197–216, esp. pp. 199–200.

creating humankind was that the humans might "bear the toil of the gods so that they may rest (*lu pašḫū*)" (*En. El.* VI 8, 36, 131). Once again it is emphasized that the proper "posture" for deity is to be at ease.

B. The Sleeping Deity as a Symbol of Divine Rule

Divine rest or leisure was closely connected with a second theme, namely, sleep as a symbol of divine authority. Because rest was a divine prerogative, it was attributed to the head of the pantheon in a preeminent manner. The ability of the divine king to sleep undisturbed was accordingly a symbol of his unchallenged authority as the supreme deity. A corollary concept was also present: to interrupt or to disturb the sleep of the supreme deity was tantamount to rebellion against his dominion.

This aspect of the sleeping deity motif may be illustrated from *Atrahasis*. It is no accident that the revolt of the lesser gods against their divine king was set in the dead of night. These gods marched on Enlil's palace, their mutinous cries rousing the divine king from his peaceful sleep.

This challenge to the divine king's authority was supposed to have ended with the creation of humankind to do the toiling for the gods. However, as the humans multiplied on earth, so did Enlil's problems:

> Twelve hundred years had not yet transpired
> Before the country expanded and the people multiplied.
> The country was bellowing like a bull;
> The god was disturbed by their din (*ḫubūru*).
> Enlil heard their cries (*rigmu*)
> And addressed the great gods,
> "The cries of humankind have become too much;
> Because of their din I am unable to sleep." (I 352–59 & //s)

According to one theory now fairly widespread, Enlil was deprived of his sleep because of excessive noise generated from an overpopulated earth[23] and even that Enlil's actions were wholly capricious.[24] But is it most unlikely that the Babylonian poet-theologians meant to suggest that the flood happened as the result of an arbitrary and malicious decision by their chief deity, especially over such a petty reason as the loss of physical sleep.

Key here is the meaning of the human outcry which prevented Enlil from sleeping. According to the overpopulated earth theory, this outcry was understood to mean the noise generated by an excessive number of people on earth. But noise is not the primary characteristic intended by the ancient Babylonian poets. Rather, the Akkadian terms *rigmu* and *ḫubūru* indicate the *cries of rebellion* of humankind against the authority of the

---

23. See A. Kilmer, "The Mesopotamian Concept of Overpopulation and Its Solution as Reflected in Mythology," *Or* 41 (1972) 160–72; and W. Moran, "Atrahasis: The Babylonian Story of the Flood," *Bib* 52 (1971) 51–61.

24. See T. Frymer-Kensky, "The Atrahasis Epic and Its Significance for Our Understanding of Genesis 1–9," *BA* 40 (1977) 147–55.

deity.[25] In the prior revolt by the lesser gods Enlil's sleep was also interrupted by a similar outcry from the rebel gods. The humans are thus portrayed as carrying on in the spirit of the slain rebel god out of whose flesh and blood they were created. Indeed, in the scene describing the creation of the first humans, it is said that humankind will possess the slain god's ghost (*eṭemmu*), as well as his capacity to scheme or plot (*ṭēmu*).[26] Having inherited the rebellious spirit of their divine "ancestor," the humans duplicated the actions of the rebel god(s). Instead of promoting divine rest, they violated their mission by preventing the deity from sleeping. Accordingly, in this Mesopotamian story, as in Genesis, the divine decision to send the deluge was occasioned by human transgression against divine authority.

These same themes are present also in *Enuma Elish*.[27] In the opening scene Tiamat and Apsu, the progenitors of the gods, are being disturbed by the actions of their offspring, the young gods. Apsu complains,

> Their behavior distresses me.
> By day I cannot rest; by night I cannot sleep.
> I will destroy, put an end to their behavior
> That quiet may reign. Let us have sleep. (I 37–40)

The interruption of Tiamat's and Apsu's sleep by the young gods' behavior should be understood as a denial of the former's authority. This disturbance was not merely a matter of youthful frivolity. Such an interpretation is rejected within the myth itself. As Apsu deliberated over how to deal with the young upstarts, Tiamat at first suggested indulgence, "Their behavior is indeed sickening (*šumruṣat*), yet let us attend(?) kindly" (I 46). But there could be no indulgence. As the vizier Mummu warned Apsu, the young gods' actions constitute an act of insurrection:

> Do destroy, my father, the mutinous[28] ways.
> Then you shall rest by day, sleep by night. (I 49–50)

---

25. See Oden, "Divine Aspirations," 201–10. I discuss this issue further in my article, "The Covenant of Peace: A Neglected Ancient Near Eastern Motif," *CBQ* 49 [1987] 187-211 [reprinted in this volume as chap. 7].

26. See W. Moran, "The Creation of Man in Atrahasis I 192–248," *BASOR* 200 (1970) 48–56; Oden, "Divine Aspirations," 202–3.

27. They may also be present in the Egyptian text, "Astarte and the Tribute of the Sea," *ANET*, 17–18. This hybrid tale, often compared to *Enuma Elish* and the Canaanite Baal myth, apparently recounts how the Egyptian gods appealed to the goddess Astarte to free them from the oppression of the Sea. Interestingly, the messenger to Astarte was instructed to wake her from her sleep —perhaps another example of the theme that the deity cannot sleep while chaos threatens right order. Any interpretation is uncertain, however, due to the extremely fragmentary condition of the text.

28. Because *ešītu* "confusion/disorder," is used (frequently in conjunction with terms signifying anarchy or rebellion) to describe situations involving political unrest, the Akkadian vocable seems to carry a connotation of mutiny or sedition; cf. *CAD* E 365–66.

However, in attempting to follow Mummu's counsel, Apsu lost both his crown and his life. The god Ea used his magical skill to cast a spell[29] upon Apsu and then killed him. After stripping off the divine tiara, Ea crowned himself king in Apsu's stead. Significant for our motif, the text says of Ea after he had vanquished his foe, "[Ea] rested in ease (*šupšuḫiš inūḫma*) within his private chamber," i.e., in his new palace (*En. El.* I 75). The contrast between the former divine king being unable to rest and the new divine king taking his rest is surely intentional. Once again kingship and rest or sleep are linked concepts.

As was the case with Ea's victory over Apsu, so also in the later description of Marduk's victory over Tiamat and her forces there is a conscious attempt to portray Marduk as taking over the symbols of kingship. By taking "the tablets of destiny" away from Qingu (Tiamat's latest king-husband) and fastening them upon his own breast, Marduk overtly claimed for himself supreme authority. As confirmation of Marduk's kingship, the gods built him a palace (= Esagila in Babylon) and proclaimed his fifty titles—a litany of Marduk's powers as the supreme deity.

Within this context, so explicitly conscious of portraying Marduk as the ultimate authority in heaven and earth, it behooves one to pay closer attention to the first words acknowledging Marduk's victory over Tiamat (IV 133–36):

> His fathers (the gods) watched, joyful and jubilant;
> They brought gifts of homage, they to him.
> Then the lord rested, surveying her [Tiamat's] cadaver,
> How to cleave the monstrosity and make ingenious things.

Previously little significance has been placed upon the statement here that Marduk rested (*inūḫ*). Indeed, one well-known translation totally obscures the idea of rest, "Then the lord paused to view her dead body."[30] Resting is integral to the scene, however, as it is part and parcel of the Mesopotamian symbol of divine kingship.

Nevertheless, at this point in the story Marduk's rest had to be momentary. Only after the monster of chaos has been transformed into an ordered and inhabitable cosmos will the deity be able to enjoy absolute rest.

The handling of this absolute rest is delicately done in *Enuma Elish*. On the one hand it is implied that such rest was achieved. The celebration following Marduk's triumph over Tiamat was more than an enthronement of

---

29. Ea's powerful incantation put Apsu into a sleep-trance and turned his vizier Mummu into a zombie: "Sleep came upon him, he slept soundly. / [Ea] caused Apsu to sleep, sleep having overtaken (him). / Mummu the counselor though awake was in a daze" (*šit-tu ir-te-ḫi-šu ṣa-lil ṭu-ub-ba-tiš / ú-šá-aṣ-lil-ma* ABZU *ri-ḫi šit-tu / ᵈmu-um-mu tam-la-ku da-la-piš ku-ú-ru* [I 64–65]). It is clear from the context that this "sleep" is of a very different nature than the restful sleep of the supreme deity with which we are concerned in this paper.

30. So E. A. Speiser, *ANET*, 67.

Marduk; it was also a celebration of the arrival of the true order of things. From the gods' perspective, one of the most important was the securing of their right to rest. Marduk assigned each of the gods a shrine so that each god would have his own place of rest (VII 10–11). But in addition there was Esagila. As Marduk's personal temple-palace, Esagila was "the Babylonian Mount Olympus." It was the seat of all authority, the place where the gods assembled for their divine councils. Esagila was always open to the other gods to come and rest by night, especially at the times of their assemblies (VI 121–30; VII 51–59). Thus, Esagila was at one and the same time the symbol of Marduk's kingship and the place of supreme rest. Once again divine kingship and divine rest appear as linked concepts. On the other hand, it is not said that Marduk himself actually rested along with the other gods. This appears deliberate. From one point of view Marduk's work was complete. The image of Marduk literally hanging up his bow (VI 82–90) is as graphic a symbol as possible that Marduk will never have to face another challenge; the order of the cosmos was secure. In traditional terminology, Marduk could now rest and enjoy undisturbed sleep. But from another point of view, the battle against chaos could be considered a perpetual struggle. Human experience certainly taught just how fragile was the order in the world.

A conception of this perpetual struggle was certainly present in the Egyptian text known as "the Repulsing of the Dragon"; each day the sun-god Re arose out of the primeval ocean Nun to repulse anew Apophis, thus daily dispelling darkness and chaos from the world.[31] Similarly at Babylon the annual New Year Festival, during which Marduk's kingship was celebrated and *Enuma Elish* recited (in the Neo-Babylonian Period at least), may have been conceived partially as a periodic renewal of Marduk's triumph over Tiamat.[32] Certainly one passage near the conclusion of *Enuma Elish* suggests that the Babylonians believed Marduk's battle with Tiamat to be an ongoing conflict. Tucked within Marduk's forty-ninth title is the prayer:

> May he vanquish Tiamat, constrict and shorten her life,
> Until the last days of humankind, when even days have grown old,
> May she depart, not be detained, and ever stay far away. (VII 132–34)

The tension between story (myth) and experience (history) is a common phenomenon within the history of religions. The ancients surely believed the "salvation" proclaimed in the myth to be true, even though experience taught them that the promised transformation of their everyday world was at best still being worked out. A recognition of this tension between myth

---

31. See S. Morenz, *Egyptian Religion* (Ithaca, 1973) 167–69.

32. This is not an endorsement of the ritual theories of myth which have been justly criticized by, among others, G. S. Kirk (*Myth: Its Meaning and Functions in Ancient and Other Cultures* [Berkeley: University of California Press, 1970] 8–31) and J. W. Rogerson (*Myth in Old Testament Interpretation* [BZAW 134; Berlin: de Gruyter, 1974] 66–84).

and history restrained the Babylonian composer of *Enuma Elish* from concluding the epic with the expected statement that Marduk himself rested or slept.

To recapitulate briefly the ancient Near Eastern usage, the motif of divine sleep often was bound together with that of divine rest or leisure. The latter stemmed from the notion that it was proper for god(s) to enjoy leisure. This theme was conjoined to creation in two ways, one suggesting that the purpose of creation was to afford the gods their rightful rest, the other suggesting that the creator himself enjoyed rest upon the completion of his "work." Further, the explicit portrayal of the creator sleeping functioned as a statement of the deity's status as the supreme ruler of heaven and earth. The ability to sleep undisturbed was the symbol of the deity's absolute dominion over the heavens and the earth and the underworld. The most vivid image of this dominion was that of the creator-king subduing the chaos monster and then retiring to his chamber to sleep peacefully without fear of interruption.

2. Biblical Appropriations of the Motif of Sleeping Deity

The P creation account concludes (Gen 2:2–3) with God resting after completing the work of creation. Even so, the presence of a theme of God resting has been questioned by some who argue that *šābat* primarily means "to cease" or "to stop,"[33] thus yielding the translation, "(God) ceased from all his work."[34] Nevertheless, the connotation of rest cannot be eliminated from *šābat*, as the larger biblical tradition shows. Exod 20:11 urges observance of the Sabbath commandment for the reason that "in six days Yahweh made the heavens and the earth, the sea and all that is in them; but on the seventh day he rested (*wayyānaḥ*). Therefore Yahweh blessed the Sabbath and hallowed it." The linking of the Sabbath rest with the pattern established at creation demonstrates that the Israelites themselves understood God to have rested upon the completion of his work (see also Exod 23:12 and Deut 5:12–15).

Furthermore, *Chaoskampf* themes are not so absent from Gen 1:1–2:3 as is often asserted.[35] It is true that chaos (*tĕhôm* in Gen 1:1, cognate to "Tiamat") is presented less as a personal foe than as the raw material that the creator organized in causing the ordered cosmos to appear. But as demonstrated by Heidel and improved by Speiser, the structure of this P creation account corresponds to that of *Enuma Elish*.[36] One may, therefore,

---

33. So J. Morgenstern, "Sabbath," *IDB* 4, 135–41; cf. Westermann, *Genesis 1–11*, 173.

34. So *NEB* and *JPSV*. Note also the ambivalence of Vg in translating *šābat: requievit* (Gen 2:2) and *cessaverat* (Gen 2:3).

35. See my article, "Red Sea or Reed Sea?," *BAR* 10/4 (July/August 1984) 57–63, esp. p. 63.

36. A. Heidel, *The Babylonian Genesis* (Chicago: University of Chicago Press, 1951) 128–29; E. A. Speiser, *Genesis* (AB 1; Garden City: Doubleday, 1964) 9–13.

legitimately suggest that the rest of the deity (Gen 2:1–3) is more than the leisure appropriate to the divine craftsman satisfied with his completed masterpiece (as with Ptah in "the Theology of Memphis"). The theme of the divine king resting in his newly built temple-palace after his victory over the monster of chaos (cf. Baal on Mount Zaphon and Marduk in Esagila) seems to be present also. Proof of this may be found in Psalm 8, which is generally acknowledged to have close affinities with the P creation account. Precisely because of the presence of such creation motifs in Psalm 8, Dahood[37] appears to be correct in translating Ps 8:3 as "You built a fortress for your habitation,[38] having silenced your adversaries, the foe and the avenger" and in understanding this "fortress" (*'oz*) as the temple-palace of Yahweh from which he rules. Behind Gen 2:1–3 apparently lies this same pattern of the creator-victor retiring to his palace, except that here the emphasis is upon the motif of the divine victor *retiring to rest* in his new palace.

As with Baal's palace on Zaphon and Marduk's Esagila, Yahweh's "resting place" had both a geographical-historical referent and a mythic-heavenly referent, with the former being the physical manifestation of the latter. According to the royal Davidic/Zion theology, the temple on Mt. Zion was the earthly locus of Yahweh's dwelling. The Chronicler claimed that in proposing the temple David intended only to build this "house" as a "resting place" (*bēt měnûḥâ*) for the ark of the covenant, the footstool of Yahweh (1 Chr 28:2; cf. 2 Chr 6:41). This late tradition is patently sensitive to the theological problems in claiming that an earthly building built by human hands could be the authentic "resting place" (*māqôm měnûḥâ*, Isa 66:1; cf. Acts 7:48–49) of the divine sovereign whom the earth and the heavens cannot contain (1 Kgs 8:27). Nevertheless, earlier Zion traditions did not hesitate to say that the Jerusalem temple was authentically Yahweh's chosen residence, his eternal "resting place":

> For Yahweh has chosen Zion,
>   he desired it for his residence (*môsāb*).
> This is my resting (*měnûḥātî*) for ever;
>   here I will reside because I have desired it. (Ps 132:13–14; cf. v. 8)[39]

---

37. Dahood, *Psalms I*, 48–51.

38. Reading *lěmāʿōn* for MT *lěmaʿan*.

39. Within Ps 132 v. 8 may contain a slightly different thought than v. 14. As the *lectio difficilior* the reading of 2 Chr 6:41 *lěnûḥekā* "to your rest" is preferable to *limnûḥātekā* "to your resting place" of Ps 132:8, the latter likely being altered under the influence of *měnûḥātî* in v. 14. Accordingly, v. 8 should be an invitation to Yahweh to enter the temple so as to take his rest: "Arise, Yahweh, to your rest / You and the Ark of your Might." D. Hillers, "Ritual Procession of the Ark and Ps 132," *CBQ* 30 (1968) 48–55, followed by F. M. Cross, *Canaanite Myth and Hebrew Epic* (Cambridge, MA: Harvard University Press, 1973) 95, translates as "Arise O Yahweh from your resting-place." But as M. Dahood, *Psalms III* (AB 17A; Garden City: Doubleday, 1970) 245 notes, the parallelism between v. 7 and v. 8 requires one to translate *lě* as "to" and not as "from."

By extension the whole of Zion and the land surrounding it could be referred to as Yahweh's resting place. In Ps 95:11 Yahweh denies the rebellious Israelites entry into "my resting place." Reference here is to entry into
the promised land, analogous to the manner in which Exod 15:17 speaks
of Israel being planted on Yahweh's mountain sanctuary. The theme of
Yahweh's kingship following his victory over his foes present in this latter
text[40] is also implicit in the designation of Zion as Yahweh's resting place.

Chaoskampf motifs figure even more prominently in the composition of
other biblical writers (e.g., Pss 74:12–17; 89:10–15; 104:1–9; Job 3:8; 7:12;
9:5–14; 26:5–14; 38:8–11). Fortunately, there has been a plethora of monographs and articles on this topic.[41] We can, therefore, limit our consideration to passages involving the motif of divine sleep.

Nowhere do we find an actual description of God retiring to sleep after
his battle with the chaos monster. But the image is presupposed in several
passages. One of the most illuminating of such passages is Isa 51:9–11, the
so-called Ode to Yahweh's Arm.

> Awake! Awake! Robe yourself in Power,
>   O arm of Yahweh
> Awake as in primordial days,
>   (the) primeval generations.
> Is it not you who cleaves Rahab in pieces,
>   who pierces the Sea-dragon?
> Is it not you who dries up the Sea,
>   the waters of the great Abyss (*tĕhôm*)?
> The one who makes the depths of the Sea a road
>   for the redeemed to pass over?

Both the image of the battle against the chaos monster and the image of
the divine victor retiring to sleep lie behind this appeal for help.

However, an analysis of the context within Deutero-Isaiah reveals that
this Israelite adaptation of the motif of the sleeping deity was shaped by

---

40. F. M. Cross and D. N. Freedman ("The Song of Miriam," *JNES* 14 [1955] 237–50,
esp. pp. 249–50) rightly insist upon the enthronement connotations of *mākôn lĕšibtĕkā*,
"the dais of your throne," in v. 17. Note also "Yahweh will reign forever" (v. 18).

41. The most recent scholarly treatment of the subject is that of J. Day, *God's Conflict
with the Dragon and the Sea* (Cambridge, 1985). [More recently, in a major new study,
Rebecca S. Watson (*Chaos Uncreated: A Reassessment of the Theme of "Chaos" in the Hebrew
Bible* [BZAW 341; Berlin: de Gruyter, 2005]) has attempted to show that the Combat Myth
is absent from the Hebrew Bible. But in my own reassessment of Combat Myth motifs
in the Hebrew Bible, I find Watson's methodology to be defective and her conclusions
invalid, and that Combat Myth motifs are indeed present in a number of biblical passages; see my paper "The Combat Myth in Israelite Tradition Revisited," delivered at the
Joint Meeting of the Midwest Region of the Society of Biblical Literature, the Middle West
Branch of the American Oriental Society, and the American Schools of Oriental Research,
held at Olivet Nazarene University, Bourbonnais, IL, February 11–13, 2011; publication
forthcoming in *Creation and Chaos: A Reconsideration of Hermann Gunkel's Chaoskampf Hypothesis*, ed. JoAnn Scurlock (Winona Lake, IN: Eisenbrauns).]

her unique theological tradition and the catastrophe of exile. The larger contextual unit (Isa 51:9–52:3) is cast as a dialogue between the exiles and God.[42] Isa 51:9–11 is the community's lament to the effect that God has no thought for his people's plight in exile. This is followed by a series of divine assurances (51:12–16; 51:17–23; 52:1–3) that God has not forgotten his people but is even now in the process of returning them to their homeland.

In their lament the exilic community calls upon God—or more exactly, his mighty arm—to "wake up!" (*'ûrî*) and come to their rescue. They appeal to the tradition of his past saving acts as the reason why he should act in the present crisis. God's salvific power was most manifest in his victory over the chaos monster at the creation of the world and in his splitting of the (Red) Sea in order to allow his people to escape from Egypt. This is not a case of myth in one instance and history in the other. Rather, as was the case with other biblical authors, Deutero-Isaiah understood the two as essentially one and the same act of salvation. Egypt was viewed as an historical manifestation of the power of chaos (cf. Ezek 29:3; Isa 17:1; 30:7), while the exodus was seen as an extension of God's creative power. Just as God split the primeval sea to create dry land, so he split the sea again during the exodus to create a special people for himself.[43] It is worth noting that tradition credited Yahweh's victory during the exodus also to his mighty right arm/hand (Exod 15:6, 12, 16).[44]

The dependency of Isa 51:9–11 upon the old semitic *Chaoskampf* myth is patent. Not only is the victory over the chaos monster attributed to Yahweh, but it is even implied that he retired afterwards to his private chamber to sleep, as in the traditional story. But—so the exiles complain—Yahweh's "victory celebration" is premature, given the straits in which they, Yahweh's people, find themselves. The power of chaos is everywhere manifest. With the temple razed and Jerusalem in ashes, it was obvious that the monster of chaos was far from vanquished. Yahweh's work was even now being undone.

Not to be overlooked in Isa 51:9–11 is the grammatical tense. Practically every translation renders the action in the *past* tense, "Was it not you who *didst* cut Rahab? . . . *didst* dry up the sea?," etc. However, the use of participles rather than verbs in the grammatical perfect reveals that the Hebrew poet thought of God's saving actions as continuing into the present.[45] The appeal to Yahweh to wake up is therefore also a statement that Yahweh's

---

42. See C. Westermann, *Isaiah 40–66* (OTL; Philadelphia: Westminster, 1969) 239–40.

43. For a more detailed discussion of this topic see my article, "The Reed Sea: *Requiescat in Pace*," *JBL* 102 (1983) 27–35 [reprinted in this volume as chap. 6].

44. One may compare the frequent iconographic portrayals of the West Semitic storm god with an upraised right hand clutching a weapon and the descriptions in the Canaanite *Chaoskampf* myth of Baal's victory over Prince Yamm achieved by means of his club-wielding right hand (*CTA* 2 iv 11–27; 4 iii 40–41).

45. See C. Stuhlmueller, *Creative Redemption in Deutero-Isaiah* (AnBib 43; Rome: Biblical Institute Press, 1970) 49–51.

supreme authority is at stake. How can Yahweh sleep when his archfoe is even now challenging his dominion?

Yahweh's response (51:17–23) artfully reverses the tables. It is not Yahweh but Israel who is asleep and who needs to wake up. It is the exiles themselves who must rise from their own drunken stupor. To be sure, they have drunk deeply from the cup of Yahweh's wrath. But that cup, drained to the dregs, is now finished. The reversal is even more explicit in 52:1–3. Echoing 51:9, Zion is commanded to awaken and robe herself in power, because God is taking her home.

At the base of this dramatic dialogue lay Judah's conviction that Yahweh's creative power continued unabated into the present and that his absolute dominion has never been in doubt. Even in her darkest hour Judah was challenged to put her trust in "her maker Yahweh, who stretches out the heavens, who lays the foundations of the earth" (51:13; cf. 16). Stung by the taunts of his captors, the Babylonians who claimed that it was their god Marduk who slew the chaos monster and created the world, the exilic poet did not flinch at attributing these very powers to Yahweh. The recrudescence of chaos in this catastrophe of the exile, therefore, need not be feared. Although some may feel that Yahweh's authority has slipped away, in actuality Yahweh is very much in control, "stilling the sea when its waves rage" (51:15).[46]

This Isaian passage is instructive for understanding the imagery of those psalms which speak of God sleeping or arising from sleep (Pss 7; 35; 44; 59; and 74). All of these psalms belong to the category of laments. As universal prayers for times of duress, they employ stereotypical language and stock images as the vehicle within which to make their plea to God for help.[47] This makes their witness all the more valuable, for it reveals what was the "typical" thought in ancient Israel.

Psalm 44 was composed in nearly identical circumstances to Deutero-Isaiah. It also betrays an exilic origin when Israel was "scattered among the nations" (v. 12). The community laments that, in contrast to former days when God's saving acts were so manifest (vv. 2–4), God now seems to have cast off his people and made them the taunt of their enemies (vv. 10–17), and this despite their innocence and fidelity (vv. 5–9, 18–23). Having heard these complaints before, how the world is collapsing and reverting to chaos, one can almost anticipate the following appeal to God (vv. 24–25, 27):

> Awake! (*'ûrâ*) Why do you sleep (*tîšan*), O Lord?
> Wake up! (*hāqîṣâ*) Do not cast us off forever!

---

46. Similarly Jer 31:35; cf. Job 26:12. For *rg'* "to still" (not "to disturb" [BKB] or "to stir up" [RSV]), see M. Pope, *Job* (AB 15; Garden City: Doubleday, 1965) 166.

47. Note even the standardized language for awakening God: *hā'îrâ ǁ hāqîṣâ* (Ps 35:23), *'ûrâ ǁ hāqîṣâ* (Pss 44:24[23]; 59:5–6[4–5]), *qûmâ ǁ 'ûrâ* (Ps 7:7[6]), or *qûmâ* alone (Ps 74:22; cf. 44:27[26]).

Why do you hide your face?
Why do you forget our affliction and oppression?
Get up! (*qûmâ*) You must come to our rescue
And deliver us for the sake of your steadfast love.

Here again the motif of the sleeping deity is used to express Israel's belief in Yahweh's absolute kingship (cf. *malkî*, v. 5). But this very conviction gives her the confidence to appeal for help. Yahweh's reign is supreme and he can be counted on to "awaken" and to maintain that right order which he decrees as creator and sovereign of all.

Psalm 74 is in many respects similar to Psalm 44. It too is a community lament and obviously composed with the Babylonian destruction of Jerusalem and the temple fresh in mind (vv. 2–8). But the similarity to Isa 51:9–11 is even closer. The psalmist appeals to the strong arm of God to act (v. 11) as in the days of old, both at the exodus (v. 2; cf. Exod 15:12–13) and at creation (vv. 12–17). This reference to creation is particularly instructive, for it explicitly links God's eternal kingship (*malkî miqqedem*, v. 12) with his victory over the mythical chaos monster (vv. 13–14) and the creation of the cosmos (vv. 15–17), the traditional context of the sleeping deity motif. It comes as no surprise, therefore, when the psalmist calls upon God to "Get up!" (*qûmâ*, i.e., get out of bed, v. 22)[48] and do something about the enemy who scoffs at him and his people (vv. 18–23). The marauding Babylonian infidels were regarded as an historical extension of God's arch enemy, primeval chaos.[49]

Psalms 7, 35, and 59 are all laments of the individual. They are so stereotypical in content as to contain virtually no indications of the date or the occasion of their composition. There are the standard references to the unjust attacks of the "enemy"—whoever that may be. Though in dire straits, the psalmists are confident that God will vindicate his faithful servants. These psalmists appeal to an image of Yahweh as the ruler of the whole world (Ps 59:14; cf. vv. 6, 9) who dispenses justice upon all from his judgment seat on high (Ps 7:7–9). As supreme ruler and judge Yahweh has to be so outraged that he must surely "awaken" (*qûmâ* // *ʿûrâ*, Ps 7:7; *ʿûrâ* //

---

48. The presence of the phrase *rîbâ rîbekā* in the parallel colon here does not vitiate our thesis that *qûmâ* originates in a motif of the sleeping god. The root *rîb* is not restricted to a legal setting but can designate a conflict in which one's rights are defended with physical force (Gen 13:7; 26:20; Exod 21:18) and even military action (Deut 33:7; Judg 11:25). Similarities with Ps 35:1–2 (cf. v. 23) suggest that *rîbâ rîbekā* might be translated as "Fight for your rights!" Furthermore, the appeal *qûmâ YHWH* normally occurs in contexts involving military action rather than legal action (so J. Willis, "QÛMÂH YHWH," *JNSL* 16 [1990] 207–21).

49. The image of God awakening from sleep in Ps 78:65 may also derive from the sleeping deity motif; the allusion to wine and the possibility of a drunken stupor image make this uncertain, however. This text, despite its uncertainty, formed the principal support for Widengren's now discredited hypothesis concerning the origin of the cultic shout "Awake!"; see above, pp. 154–55.

ḥāqîṣâ, Ps 59:5–6) for the purpose of pronouncing judgment.[50] The thought
is expressed succinctly in Ps 35:22–24:

> You have seen, O Yahweh; do not remain silent.
> My Lord, be not far from me.
> Arise! Wake up! (*hāʿîrâ wĕhāqîṣâ*) for the sake of my justice,
>   My God and my lord, for the sake of my cause.
> Judge me in accordance with your righteousness
>   And let them not gloat over me.

Behind each of these psalms are vestiges of the ancient Near Eastern motif of the sleeping deity. The portrayal of Yahweh as asleep was a culturally
conditioned theological statement to the effect that Yahweh is the creator
and absolute king of heaven and earth. Likewise, the appeal to Yahweh to
"wake up," far from being a slur on the effectiveness of divine rule, was
actually an extension of Israel's active faith in Yahweh's universal rule even
in the midst of gross injustice and manifest evil.

Zech 2:17[13] is based precisely upon the belief that Yahweh does
awaken to judge in favor of his faithful. In the midst of eschatological visions about the advent of Yahweh comes the command for all flesh to keep
silence, "for Yahweh has roused himself from his holy dwelling" (*kî nēʿôr
mimmĕʿôn qodšô*). The proceeding and following context shows Yahweh
exercising his universal dominion on behalf of Zion and the high priest
while their accuser, the Satan, is rebuked. In stark contrast to this awesome
portrait of Yahweh stand the idols, who can be parodied precisely because
they have no power to awaken and arise for the benefit of their devotees
(Hab 2:18–20; cf. 1 Kgs 18:27).

Obviously, the motif could be inverted, with equal effect. In Psalm 121
the image of Yahweh as never slumbering nor sleeping (*lōʾ yānûm wĕloʾ
yîšān*, v. 4), like its opposite, functioned in Israel as an effective expression
of her faith in Yahweh as creator and absolute sovereign. The devotee could
walk in the confidence that his world would not collapse around him because "the keeper of Israel" is eternally vigilant in maintaining the order
which he has divinely ordained.

The final stage[51] in the biblical adaptation of the motif of the sleeping deity comes in the New Testament story of Jesus calming the sea. This

---

50. Appeals to the deity to act as universal judge are not incompatible with the motif
of the sleeping god, despite our rejection of the thesis that the expression "Arise, Yahweh!"
originated primarily within a forensic or courtroom setting (see above, pp. 139–140).
The role of the divine sovereign in establishing justice is implicit in the sleeping god motif. Accordingly, there may be yet additional allusions to this motif in other passages where
qûmâ lacks any parallel explicit reference to sleeping or awaking (e.g., Num 10:35; Pss 3:8;
9:20; 10:12; 12:6; 17:13; 68:2; Isa 14:22; 31:2; 33:10; Amos 7:9); see further n. 48. Similar
usage is attested at Qumran (1QM xii 9; xix 2).

51. The Talmud (*b. Soṭa* 48a) makes reference to Levites who, prior to the reforms of
John Hyrcanus, used to perform a daily ritual in which they cried, "Awake! Why do you
sleep, O Lord?" (Ps 44:24). It is likely that this "rite of the Awakeners" had nothing to do

incident is found in all three synoptic gospels (Matt 8:23–27; Mark 4:35–41; Luke 8:23–27). As with the related story of Jesus walking on the sea (Matt 14:22–33; Mark 6:45–52; John 6:15–21), the evangelists attached special significance to this story as revelatory of who Jesus is. From the manner in which the evangelists shaped these two stories using traditional biblical language and images of divine activity, it is evident that they regarded both stories as epiphanic, that is, as manifesting the divine presence.[52]

In the Old Testament the power both to still the raging sea (Job 26:12; Isa 51:15; Jer 31:35; cf. Pss 89:9[10]; 107:29) and to trample upon the back of the sea (Job 9:8; Hab 3:15; Ps 77:20) belongs to God alone, deriving ultimately from his victory over primeval sea.[53] Accordingly, it is not accidental that Jesus' walking upon the sea (Matt 14:25; Mark 6:48; John 6:19) is described in the language of Yahweh's walking or trampling on the back of the sea (note especially Job 9:8 LXX: *kai peripatōn hōs ep' edaphous epi thalassēs* "and (who) walks on the sea as if on ground"). Similarly, Jesus' calming of the sea borrows upon the terminology of Yahweh's stilling of the hostile sea, especially when this stilling is done through the divine rebuke (*gā'ar*, LXX: *epitimân*, Job 26:11). The sea is also the object of the divine rebuke in Pss 18:15[16] (= 2 Sam 22:16); 104:7; 106:9; and Isa 50:2; Satan is similarly rebuked in Zech 3:2. Whether Jesus' stilling of the sea still retained the age-old connotations of a battle against the chaos monster (as in Job 26:11–12; Ps 89:9–10[10–11]) or only the power of the creator to control his creatures (as in Ps 107:29), Jesus is clearly depicted as exercising divine control: "Who is this that even the wind and the sea obey him?" (Mark 4:41 & //s). The evangelists used the theophanic connotations of this language to suggest that Jesus possessed divine power.[54]

The matter of Jesus sleeping on the storming sea must be interpreted within this epiphanic context. Previous commentators have failed to appreciate the full significance intended by the evangelists. Some[55] have missed the point totally, taking Jesus' sleep as an indication of his humanness. Fatigued by the demands that the crowd had made upon him, Jesus was

---

with the motif of the sleeping deity, however. Since its suppression was justified by appeal to Ps 121:4, presumably the ritual was similar to the daily morning routine designed for the care and feeding of (anthropomorphically conceived) gods, common in ancient temples; see above, n. 14.

52. For a recent, comprehensive treatment, see J. Heil, *Jesus Walking on the Sea: Meaning and Gospel Functions of Matt 14:22–33, Mark 6:45–52 and John 6:15b–21* (AnBib 87; Rome: Biblical Institute Press, 1981).

53. For the mythic background of the deity trampling the back of the sea, see Pope, *Job*, 69–70.

54. 2 Macc 9:8 claims that Antiochus IV had thought himself capable of commanding the waves of the sea, only to find himself a lowly mortal indeed. Antiochus, as his name Epiphanes implies, regarded himself as an incarnation of the god Zeus.

55. So A. Plummer, *An Exegetical Commentary on the Gospel According to Matthew* (ICC; New York: Scribner, 1910) 130; and N. Geldenhuys, *Commentary on the Gospel of Luke* (NICNT; Grand Rapids: Eerdmans, 1979) 251–52.

forced to seek refuge in the boat where he promptly fell asleep, oblivious to developments around him. Closer but still wide of the mark are those[56] who interpret Jesus' ability to sleep peacefully and undisturbed in such circumstances as a sign of his perfect trust in the sustaining and protective power of God. However, it is not the faith of Jesus but of his disciples that is on trial here. Finally, despite obvious similarities between Jesus' calming of the storm and Jonah 1, the sleeping Jesus cannot be adequately explained as the evangelists' attempt to portray "one greater than Jonah."[57] Both the motive and the result of sleep are different in the two stories. Jesus' disciples do not awaken him to intercede with God as in Jonah 1:6. Rather, the disciples call upon Jesus even as the distressed sailors of Ps 107:23–30 called upon Yahweh to save them from the storm.

Since this is the only passage in the New Testament in which we read of Jesus sleeping, it appears that the evangelists attached special significance to it. Its function is most obvious in the original Marcan formulation of this scene.[58] Mark personified the sea and identified it with the demonic. Accordingly, the sea is rebuked (*epitimân*) by Jesus in almost identical terms (*siōpa, pephimōso* "Quiet! Be silent") as the demon in Mark 1:25 (*phimōthēti* "Be silenced!"). Even the reaction of the bystanders is similar (compare 4:41 with 1:27). The sea as an extension of the demonic is evident also in the following incident of the possessed man in the land of the Gerasenes (Mark 5:1–20). When Jesus cast the legion of demons out of the man, these entered the swine and rushed headlong over the cliff into the sea—appropriately to their rightful home, for the sea was considered to be the source of evil (Dan 7:2–3; Rev 13:1; contrast Rev 21:1).

Patently, Mark was drawing upon the long biblical tradition of the creator's battle with the chaos monster, though the latter is reinterpreted more specifically as the diabolic kingdom of Satan and his cohorts. Indeed, a major theme in Mark is the conflict between the kingdom of God and the kingdom of evil; it is a battle to the death. Just as the Israelites had called upon Yahweh to awaken and save them in their tribulation, so Jesus' beleaguered disciples wake Jesus for help against the sea which threatened to engulf them. And like Yahweh, Jesus arises and stills the demonic sea. Accordingly, the image of the sleeping Jesus is modeled after that of the sleeping divine king. His sleeping indicates not powerlessness but the possession

---

56. So D. Nineham, *Mark* (Baltimore: Penguin Books, 1963) 146–47; A. Oepke, "Καθεύδω," *TNDT* 3, 436; and E. Schweizer, *The Good News According to Mark* (Atlanta: John Knox Press, 1970) 109.

57. S. R. Pesch, *Das Markusevangelium* (2 vols.; HTKNT 2; Freiburg: Herder, 1980) 1.267–81. The superiority of Jesus to Jonah (Matt 12:41/Luke 11:32) is a Q saying and apparently unknown to Mark, the principal architect of the synoptic formulation of the calming of the sea.

58. Following the majority opinion within New Testament scholarship, the priority of Mark among the synoptic gospels is here assumed; the validity of this analysis is not dependent upon any particular order of composition among the gospels, however.

of absolute authority. The power of the demonic kingdom is only apparent, not real, as is evident when Jesus awakens and stills the raging of the sea.

Matthew, for his part, strengthens the epiphanic connotations in the scene. He speaks not of a "great windstorm" (*lailaps anemou megalē*) but of a "great earthquake" (*seismos megas*, 8:24). Earthquakes both in the Old and the New Testaments, and in various apocalyptic texts as well, are frequently associated with the end times. Since Matthew elsewhere employs earthquakes to great effect in evoking the eschatological significance of Jesus' death and resurrection (27:51, 54; 28:2), it may be that the evangelist wished to suggest here the advent of the eschatological times when the kingdom of God and the kingdom of Satan engage in the definitive battle (cf. Matt 24:7).[59]

Another change in Matthew's presentation may point in the same direction. Whereas in Mark 4:38 the disciples address Jesus as "Teacher" (*didaskale*)[60] and in Luke 8:24 as "Master" (*epistata*), in Matt 8:25 they call upon him as "Lord" (*kyrie*) and add "save us." (Note that in the similar story of Jesus walking on the sea Matthew has suppressed the Marcan statement that the disciples did not understand and instead has the disciples worship Jesus as the "Son of God"; compare Matt 14:33 with Mark 6:52.) Presupposing that this was an intentional alteration deriving from the post-resurrection faith of the evangelist, one concludes that Matthew intended his readers to associate Jesus closely with *kyrios*, the normal LXX rendering of the divine name Yahweh.

The Matthean reworking of this pericope made the adaptation of the motif of divine sleep to Jesus complete. The implication of Jesus' divinity suggested by the use of sleep motif was made explicit through the faith of the disciples in Jesus as Lord and Savior.[61]

---

59. See G. Bornkamm, "σείω, σεισμός," *TDNT* 7, 196–200, esp. p. 199; R. H. Gundry, *Matthew: A Commentary on His Literary and Theological Art* (Grand Rapids: Eerdmans, 1982) 154–55.

60. In Mark the title "Teacher" has christological significance not present in Matthew and Luke; see P. Achtemeier, "'He Taught Them Many Things': Reflections on Marcan Christology," *CBQ* 42 (1980) 465–81.

61. Luke may have tried to deemphasize some of the mythic overtones of the Marcan version by reinterpreting the incident as a "natural" event. He placed the incident on "the lake" (*hē limnē*, i.e., Gennesaret), thus avoiding all the mythic connotations associated with "the sea." For Luke the peril seemed to consist solely of unusually large swells caused by the "windstorm," rather than some demonic force per se. After the calming of the water, in Luke 8:25 the disciples exclaim, "Who then is this, that he commands the wind and the water [*kai tois anemois epitassei kai tō hudati*] and they obey him?," whereas in Mark and Matthew reference is to "the wind and the sea (*hē thalassa*)." Nevertheless, the demonic element has not been totally eliminated for Luke retains the verb "rebuked" (*epitimân*). In Luke 4:35, 39 as in Mark this verb often is used in a technical sense of solemnly commanding demons; see J. Fitzmyer, *The Gospel According to Luke I–IX* (AB 28; Garden City: Doubleday, 1981) 546 and 730.

Chapter 6

The Reed Sea: **Requiescat in Pace**

It is almost dogma with many modern biblical scholars that the sea of the exodus, through which the Israelites passed in their escape from Egypt (Exod 13:17–15:21), was not the Red Sea, as popularly supposed, but a lesser body of water further north known as the "Reed Sea." The identification of the sea as the Red Sea, it is alleged, dates only to the time of the Septuagint when the translators erroneously rendered Hebrew *yam sûp* into Greek as *Erythra Thalassa*. This mistake was perpetuated by the Vulgate (*Mare Rubrum*), whence it became firmly entrenched in Western tradition.

Despite its popularity, this Reed Sea hypothesis rests upon flimsy evidence indeed. A review of that evidence, plus new considerations, makes it clear that the hypothesis must finally be laid to rest.

The arguments for the hypothesis are so well known that they need not be repeated here.[1] The principal stay of this theory is the contention that *yam sûp* should be translated literally as "Sea of Papyrus" or "Sea of Reeds" because etymologically *sûp* is a loanword from Egyptian *twf(y)* "papyrus (reeds)."[2] However, despite the fact that *sûp* is used elsewhere in the Bible in this meaning (Exod 2:3, 5; Isa 19:6), there is good reason to doubt that *sûp* in the phrase *yam sûp* is related to this vocable. Most telling is the incontrovertible fact that every certain referent of the term *yam sûp* is to the Red Sea or its northern extensions into the gulfs of Suez and Aqabah

---

Originally published in *JBL* 102 (1983) 27–35. Debate about the meaning of *yam sûp* has continued in the ensuing three decades; I interact with recent scholarship in my postscript appended to this article (pp. 166–174), which I composed for this volume.

1. Convenient summaries of the hypothesis may be found in J. Bright, *A History of Israel* (3rd ed.; Philadelphia: Westminster, 1981) 122–23; J. Finegan, *Let My People Go* (New York: Harper & Row, 1963) 77–89; J. L. Mihelie, "Red Sea," *IDB*, 4.19–21; G. E. Wright, *Biblical Archaeology* (rev. ed.; Philadelphia: Westminster, 1962) 60–62; "Exodus, Route of," *IDB*, 2.197–99. A critical review of the evidence may be found in R. de Vaux, *The Early History of Israel* (Philadelphia: Westminster, 1978) 376–81.

2. For dissenting views see W. Helck, *Die Beziehungen Ägyptens zu Vorderasien im 3. und 2. Jahrtausend v. Chr.* (2. Aufl.; Ägyptologische Abhandlungen 5; Wiesbaden: Harrassowitz, 1971) 525; W. Ward, "The Semitic Biconsonantal Root *SP* and the Common Origin of Egyptian *ČWF* and Hebrew *SÛP* 'Marsh(-Plant),'" *VT* 24 (1974) 339–49.

(see especially 1 Kgs 9:26; Num 21:4; 33:10–11; Jer 49:21).[3] Furthermore, it seems fairly clear that every other attestation of the term *yam sûp* in the Bible for which a location can be determined from context, leaving aside for the moment those texts which have to do with the sea of the exodus miracle, has as its referent this same body of water (Exod 10:19; Num 14:25; Deut 1:40; 2:1). In every instance *yam sûp* can plausibly refer to the Red Sea. But as the name for the Red Sea, *yam sûp* clearly has nothing to do with papyrus because papyrus does not grow in these waters. Thus, even if one were to grant the validity of the Reed Sea hypothesis, the etymology of *yam sûp* = Red Sea would still be left unexplained. The burden of proof clearly falls upon those who would posit the existence of a second body of water farther north with the homophonous name of *yam sûp*, in addition to the well-known *yam sûp* = Red Sea.

Geographically, the main objection to equating the sea of the exodus miracle with the Red Sea is that those places named in the exodus itinerary prior to arrival at *yam sûp* would appear to be located in the eastern delta region of Egypt. It is claimed, therefore, that *yam sûp* should be located in that region. But this argument fails to reckon seriously with the literary character of the biblical sources involved.[4] The geographical framework of the received text of Exod 13:17–15:22 stems only from the latest (P) redaction of the narrative. Source-critical studies of the earlier traditions suggest at least two independent versions of the wilderness itinerary, a northern and a southern route.[5] Only the southern route implied passing by *yam sûp*—evidently understood as the Red Sea. This suggests that the wilderness itinerary was only secondarily joined with the deliverance at the sea tradition and cannot be utilized to determine the location and meaning of *yam sûp*.

Numbers 33 is especially instructive in this regard. It consists of a list of forty-two camping stations during the Israelites' journey from Egypt to the plains of Moab. The function of the list remains obscure. Frank Moore Cross rightly concludes that it was a tangible priestly document used by P to frame the redaction of the wilderness traditions now found in Exodus–Leviticus–Numbers,[6] rather than, as Noth supposed, a late redactional construction dependent in part on JEP.[7] The independent witness of Numbers 33 cannot be lightly dismissed, therefore, when it makes a sharp distinction between the sea of the miraculous passage through the water (v. 8) and *yam sûp* (vv. 10–11), at which the Israelites arrive after an interval of

---

3. See further de Vaux, *Early History*, 377.

4. See, among others, B. S. Childs, *The Book of Exodus* (OTL; Philadelphia: Westminster, 1974) 218–24.

5. See de Vaux, *Early History*, 370–88; J. T. Walsh, "From Egypt to Moab," *CBQ* 39 (1977) 20–33.

6. F. M. Cross, *Canaanite Myth and Hebrew Epic* (Cambridge: Harvard University Press, 1973) 308–21.

7. M. Noth, "Der Wallfahrtsweg zum Sinai," *PJ* 36 (1940) 5–28.

several camping stations. Cross violates his own conclusion concerning the independence of this text when he dismisses as "secondary" the notice of the second distinct station at *yam sûp*.[8] Given the careful manner in which P redacted the wilderness traditions on the basis of the list of stations in Numbers 33, as Cross himself has shown, one must conclude that in the exodus narrative P has deliberately suppressed the second station at *yam sûp* and telescoped the sea of the miracle and *yam sûp* into one (compare Exod 14:2 and 15:22 with Num 33:8–11). (We shall take up the reason for this deliberate telescoping by P later.) Quite obviously, Numbers 33 deals a mortal blow to the Reed Sea hypothesis.

It is also alleged that an Egyptian text actually speaks of a "Papyrus Marsh" or "Papyrus Lake" not far from the city of Ramesis (= Tanis?), the very place from where the biblical narrative says the Israelites began their journey out of Egypt (Exod 12:37). The text in question is Papyrus Anastasi III ii.11–12, an encomium on the residence of Ramesis II, which reads, "The papyrus-marshes [*pȝ-twfy*] come to it with papyrus reeds, and the Waters-of-Horus [*pȝ-š-Ḥr*] with rushes."[9] Despite Gardiner's contention that the connection between *pȝ-twfy* and biblical *yam sûp* is "beyond dispute," his own evidence indicates that this identification is far from certain. The use of *pȝ-twfy* in this and other Egyptian texts shows that the term referred to more than one locality in the eastern delta region where papyrus flourished, rather than to a specific body of water as desiderated by the biblical exodus narrative.[10] Furthermore, as H. Cazelles has pointed out, *pȝ-twfy* does not designate an expanse of water but rather a district or area where not only papyrus grows but also where pasturage for animals was found and agricultural enterprises undertaken. *Pȝ-twfy* [*pȝ* = definite article, *twf(y)* = "papyrus"] is always written with the determinative for plant and occasionally with the determinative for town, but is never written with the determinative for lake or water. Despite this problem Cazelles concluded nevertheless that biblical *yam sûp* referred to a body of water located at the border of the district of *twf(y)*, just as the Mediterranean could on occasion be called the sea of the Philistines (Exod 23:31) or the sea of Jaffa (Ezra 3:7).[11] It must be emphasized, however, that Cazelles' conclusion owes more to the desire to find confirmation for the hypothetical Reed Sea of the Bible than to the in-

---

8. Cross, *Canaanite Myth and Hebrew Epic*, 309.

9. Trans. R. Caminos, *Late-Egyptian Miscellanies* (London: Oxford University Press, 1954) 74; for another translation, see *ANET*, 471. H. Brugsch (*L'Exode et les monuments égyptiens* [Leipzig: Hinrichs, 1875]) was apparently the first to connect biblical *yam sûp* with Egyptian *pȝ-twfy*; see H. Cazelles, "Les localizations de l'Exode et la critique littéraire," *RB* 62 (1955) 321–64, esp. p. 323.

10. A. Gardiner, *Ancient Egyptian Onomastica* (2 vols.; London: Oxford University Press, 1947) 2.201–2. The identification of *pȝ-twfy* with biblical *yam sûp* is also espoused by R. Caminos (ibid., 79) and P. Montet (*Egypt and the Bible* [Philadelphia: Fortress Press, 1968] 64).

11. Cazelles, "Les localizations," 342. The caution of de Vaux (*Early History*, 377), who translates *pȝ-twfy* as "the land of the papyrus," is noteworthy.

ternal evidence of the Egyptian texts. While it is true that papyrus grows in marshy areas, Egyptian *pʒ-ṯwfy* would scarcely ever have been understood as referring to a body of water, apart from the biblical term *yam sûp*.

As observed above, the identification of the sea of the miracle as the Red Sea in the received text of Exod 13:17–15:21 results from the latest redaction. Given the careful manner in which P has arranged the exodus itinerary according to a precise chronology and specific geographical referents, it is clear that P consciously intended to historicize and localize the sea miracle at the Red Sea.[12] Crossing dry shod through the midst of that vast body of water split in twain was, in P's view, a positive display of Yahweh's saving power on Israel's behalf.

But if the latest stage of tradition has consciously historicized the tradition at the Red Sea, the same is not patently true of the earliest witness to *yam sûp*.[13] The Song of the Sea also has the Egyptians perish in *yam sûp* (Exod 15:4–5):

> Pharaoh's chariots and his army he cast into the Sea (*yām*);
> his picked officers are sunk in *yam sûp*.
> The abyss (*tĕhōmōt*) covered them;
> they went down into the depths (*mĕṣôlōt*) like a stone.

As has been observed many times, the Song of the Sea is heavily dependent upon mythological language—and it is this fact which provides the key to the correct interpretation of *yam sûp*.[14] The song reflects the same basic pattern as *Enuma Elish* and the Ugaritic Baal cycle. The creator god overcomes chaos, his watery foe, thus bringing order out of chaos and

---

12. The view of S. Norin (*Er Spaltete das Meer: Die Auszugsüberlieferung in Psalmen und Kult des Alten Israel* [ConBOT 9; Lund: Gleerup, 1977] 36–40, 205), namely that the tradition which localized the sea miracle at *yam sûp* postdates P, fails to reckon with the fact that it was P who framed the exodus narrative within the present series of camping stations, including the one at *yam sûp*; see n. 6 above.

13. I accept the thesis that the Song of the Sea is one of the most ancient pieces in the Hebrew Bible, dating perhaps to the pre-monarchical period in Israel; see F. M. Cross and D. N. Freedman, "The Song of Miriam," *JNES* 14 (1955) 237–50; F. M. Cross, *Canaanite Myth and Hebrew Epic*, 121–24; D. N. Freedman, "Strophe and Meter in Exodus 15," in *A Light unto My Path: Old Testament Studies in Honor of Jacob M. Myers* (ed. Howard N. Bream et al.; Philadelphia: Temple University Press, 1974) 163–203, esp. pp. 201–2; David A. Robertson, *Linguistic Evidence in Dating Early Hebrew Poetry* (SBLDS 3; Missoula: Scholars Press, 1972) 153–56. For the view that *yam sûp* in Exod 15:4 is a later deuteronomistic addition to the ancient poem, see S. Norin, *Er Spaltete das Meer*, 94 and 105.

14. The mythological background of the Song of the Sea is complex. On the one hand, W. Wifall ("The Sea of Reeds as Sheol," *ZAW* 92 [1980] 325–32) claims that the poem is dependent primarily upon Egyptian mythology. On the other hand, R. Luyster ("Myth and History in the Book of Exodus," *Religion* 8 [1978] 155–70) argues that the exodus story was composed after the pattern of the Babylonian *Enuma Elish*. However, in my opinion, Cross (*Canaanite Myth and Hebrew Epic*, 121–44) is correct in positing an immediate background in Canaanite mythology. The data of Wifall and Luyster point rather to the fact that ancient Near Eastern myths and mythological motifs were widely diffused and transcended national boundaries. All three authors continue to speak of *yam sûp* as the "Reed Sea."

creating a people in the process. The creator god then retires to his mountain sanctuary from where, as king, he rules his newly ordered cosmos.[15] It is not surprising, therefore, that the defeat of the historical pharaoh plays such a minor role in the poem. The struggle against pharaoh is portrayed as part of the larger battle of the deity against the powers. For this reason pharaoh is submerged in the sea and defeated along with the sea.

Such mythological motifs account rather patently for the presence of *yām* (= Sea-dragon) in the poem. What remains to be explained is why *yam sûp* is paralleled with *yām* in v. 4. In view of the fact that other early traditions did not connect the sea miracle with *yam sûp*,[16] it is unlikely that *yam sûp* in this case reflects the preservation of a historical memory that such a battle with pharaoh actually took place at *yam sûp* = the Red Sea. Even more improbable is the solution of those who invoke the Reed Sea hypothesis.

A way out of this impasse has been proposed by Norman Snaith. He clearly saw that the references to the abyss (*tĕhōmōt*) and the depths (*mĕṣôlōt*) in v. 5 require that the *yam sûp*, like *yām*, must refer to "the great primeval Sea, God's enemy since before the foundation of the world." Snaith would read *yam sûp* as the equivalent of *yam sôp* (< *sôp*, "end"), that is, as "that distant scarcely known sea away to the south, of which no men knew the boundary. It was the sea at the end of the land."[17]

Snaith's instinct was right. The difficulty has been in finding some confirmation that the ancient Israelites ever applied to *yam sûp* (or *sôp*) the connotations which Snaith proposed. Indeed, it has been objected that *sôp* is an Aramaic word which was introduced into Hebrew at a late date.[18] What has not previously been recognized is that *sûp* is attested in the Hebrew Bible in the precise meaning required by Snaith's thesis.

Jonah 2 contains a psalm of thanksgiving which apparently had an independent existence before acquiring its present context as a prayer placed on the lips of Jonah in the belly of the fish.[19] The psalm is especially appropriate in this context because it expresses separation from God in terms

---

15. See Cross, *Canaanite Myth and Hebrew Epic*, 138–44; P. Miller, *The Divine Warrior in Early Israel* (HSM 5; Cambridge: Harvard University Press, 1973) 113–17; Norin, *Er Spaltete das Meer*, 77–107.

16. J, like Num 33:8 (cf. Ps 114), identified the place of the miracle only as "the sea" (*hayyām*), apparently not the Red Sea. E, which had the Israelites flee from Egypt along the Red Sea road (Exod 13:18), in its present truncated form contains no certain reference to a sea miracle. Outside the exodus narrative those texts which link the exodus miracle to *yam sûp* (Deut 11:4; Josh 2:10; 4:23; 24:6; Neh 9:9; Pss 106:7, 9, 22; 136:13–15) are all late.

17. "יַם־סוּף: The Sea of Reeds: The Red Sea," *VT* 15 (1965) 395–98. See also J. A. Montgomery, "Hebraica (2) *yam sûp* ('The Red Sea') = Ultimum Mare?," *JAOS* 58 (1938) 131–32.

18. M. Wagner, *Die lexikalischen und grammatikalischen Aramaismen in Alttestamentlichen Hebräisch* (BZAW 96; Berlin: Töpelmann, 1966) 87. However, G. Ahlström (*Joel and the Temple Cult in Jerusalem*, VTSup 21 [1971] 2–3) points to several indications "that the root is not always or necessarily a late Aramaism."

19. See G. Landes, "The Kerygma of the Book of Jonah: The Contextual Interpretation of the Jonah Psalm," *Int* 21 (1967) 3–31; T. Fretheim, *The Message of Jonah: A Theological Commentary* (Minneapolis: Augsburg Publishing House, 1977) 58–59.

of being buried in the underworld (vv. 3 and 7) or engulfed in the sea (vv. 4 and 6). The latter two verses are especially relevant:

> You had cast me into the deep (*mĕṣûlâ*),[20]
>   in the midst of the Sea[21]
>   and River (*nāhār*) encircled me.
> All your breakers and your billows passed over me. . . .
> The waters encompassed me up to the throat;
>   the Abyss (*tĕhôm*) encircled me;
>   Extinction (*sûp*) was bound to my head.

The usual translation of *sûp* in v. 6, "(sea)weeds were wrapped round my head," or the like,[22] is demonstrably wrong. First, as implicitly recognized by these translators, if a plant is involved, it would have to be some kind of vegetation which is found in the depths of the sea, not the reeds from the marshy areas along the banks.[23] Such a meaning for *sûp* is otherwise unattested. Second, the image of being entangled in seaweed is patently inappropriate. All the other images concern the realm of the primeval chaos: Sheol, the Pit, and the Underworld (*'ereṣ*) as the abode of Death; the Sea-dragon under its twin names of Sea and River; the primeval Abyss (*tĕhôm*) and associated terms, "the deep," "breakers," "billows," "waters"; the foundations of the mountains in the underworld. Clearly, the context requires *sûp* to have something to do with a cosmic battle against chaos.

A comparison with Psalm 18 (= 2 Samuel 22), also a thanksgiving psalm, is most instructive. There, also, the psalmist cries out to God for deliverance from the present distress. Likewise, the psalmist's straits are conveyed in almost identical images of being trapped in the Underworld or engulfed in the watery Abyss. In Psalm 18, however, the image of what is involved in being rescued is clearer. When the psalmist's cry of distress reaches God in his temple, God rends the heavens, mounts his cherub, and flies down to rescue his servant. The rescue is told in images of the deity overwhelming

---

20. Many commentators omit either *mĕṣûlâ* or *bilbab yammîm* as a gloss; so BHK, BHS, and H. W. Wolff (*Dodekapropheton 3: Obadja und Jona* [BKAT 14/3; Neukirchen-Vluyn: Neukirchener, 1977] 101–2). Landes (*Int* 21 [1967] 13) prefers to delete only *bilbab* as the gloss; in this case the translation should read, "You cast me into the deep of the Sea." However, there is no compelling reason to emend the consonantal text; the extra-metrical length of the colon adds dramatic emphasis to the dire straits of the psalmist.

21. Consonantal *ymym* may be identified either as plural of majesty or as singular *yām* plus enclitic *mem*. Its mythological meaning as Sea is secured by the presence of *nāhār* in the next colon as the now familiar poetic pair; see M. Dahood, *The Psalms* (3 vols.; AB; Garden City: Doubleday, 1965–1970) 1.151 and 3.450. Another enclitic *mem* has been plausibly suggested elsewhere in this poem, reading *mĕšammĕrê* + *m* in v. 9; see H. Hummel, "Enclitic *Mem* in Early Northwest Semitic, Especially Hebrew," *JBL* 76 (1957) 85–107, esp. p. 99.

22. See for example among common English translations, *KJV*, *RSV* and *NEB*: "weeds"; *JB*, *NAB* and *NIV*: "seaweed."

23. So explicitly, H. W. Wolff, *Obadja und Jona*, 111.

the powers of chaos.[24] The Underworld (*'ereṣ*) is shaken (v. 7). The bottom of the Sea is revealed and the foundations of the world bared as Yahweh bursts the Sea asunder with a blast from his nostrils (v. 15, cp. v. 7). (The images are similar to those of the Song of the Sea.)

The mythological motifs could scarcely be clearer. In both Jonah 2 and Psalm 18 (as in the Song of the Sea), God rules from his holy temple. This rule is a continuation of his primordial battle against the nihilistic forces of chaos. The history of religions helps us to understand the mentality of the ancients here.[25] God's holy mountain, where his temple is located, is the center of the cosmos, or orderly creation. The farther away from the center of the cosmos one goes, the more one moves into the realm of chaos or non-creation. The spatial image is equally vertical and horizontal. Vertically, the heavens are the source of existence and creation; the underworld and the abyss are the place of death and non-existence. Horizontally, the land around the mountain of one's god is known and understood and therefore thought of as the most "created"; the sea which lay beyond the limits of the land was unsolid, non-formed—in other words, "uncreated." Thus, the sea and the abyss were simultaneously mythical and real to the ancient mind.

This brings me back to the use of *sûp* in Jonah 2:6. Given the context of images of non-existence and in parallelism with mythic waters and the Abyss, here *sûp* (or *sôp*) must be derived from the Semitic root *sûp*, "to come to an end," "to cease (to exist)." As a substantive *sûp* is attested in the meaning of "end," "edge," "border," and carries connotations of "non-existence," "extinction," and perhaps even "destruction."[26] Thus one may assert with confidence that *sûp* was a known term for the semi-mythic waters of the Sea. Indeed, such was the constant and univocal understanding of this vocable in Jonah 2:6 in all the ancient versions.[27]

---

24. The psalmists frequently employ this same mythological imagery to describe the epiphany of God to deliver; see B. W. Anderson, *Creation versus Chaos* (New York: Association, 1967) 96–99; C. Westermann, *The Praise of God in the Psalms* (2nd ed.; Richmond: John Knox, 1964) 93–98.

25. Compare M. Eliade, *The Myth of the Eternal Return* (Bollingen Series 46; New York: Pantheon, 1954) 9–17; *The Sacred and the Profane* (New York: Harcourt, Brace & World, 1959) 29–65; *Patterns in Comparative Religion* (New York: World, 1963) 367–85. Israel's neighbors also shared the conception that their own country, with one or other of its prominent sanctuaries, was the "center" of the cosmos; see E. Burrows, "Some Cosmological Patterns in Babylonian Religion," in *The Labyrinth* (ed. S. H. Hooke; London: SPCK, 1935) 41–70; S. Morenz, *Egyptian Religion* (Ithaca: Cornell University Press, 1973) 42–56. R. Clifford (*The Cosmic Mountain in Canaan and the Old Testament* [HSM 4; Cambridge: Harvard University Press, 1972]) defines "cosmic mountain" in a more circumscribed fashion but without contradicting the view presented here.

26. BDB, 692–93 s.v. *sûp* and *sôp*; J. Payne Smith, *A Compendious Syriac Dictionary* (Oxford: Clarendon Press, 1903) 369 s.v. *swp* and *swpn*. G. Ahlström ("Judges 5:20f. and History," *JNES* 36 [1977] 287–88) thinks along these same lines as he observes that *yam sûp* may mean "sea of destruction."

27. The *Tg. Neb.* saw here a reference to the Red Sea (*ym' dswp*), as did Aquila (*erythra*); the Vulgate (*pelagus*) reflects the same understanding. The Septuagint (*eschatē*, cf.

A word should also be said about the image of *sûp* being bound (*ḥābûš*) to one's head. As a symbol of threatening death it is closely paralleled by the twin motif of the binding cords of death and Sheol in Ps 18:5–6:

> The cords of Death encompassed me . . .
> The cords of Sheol encircled me.

The use of identical words (*'ăpāpûnî, yĕsōbĕbēnî/sĕbābûnî*) here and in parallel cola in Jonah 2:6 (cf. v. 4) further emphasizes the literary connections between these two compositions. Moreover, *ḥābaš* apparently had acquired a certain currency in the context of death and underworld imagery, as illustrated from Job 40:13:

> Hide (i.e., bury) them in the dust together,
> bind (*ḥăbōš*) their faces in the hidden place (i.e., the underworld).[28]

This image of death as a binding of the face/head may derive from funerary customs of shrouding the body for burial. If so, the aptness of "*sûp* was bound to my head" becomes all the more poignant as an expression of the threat of death or non-existence in Jonah 2.

I maintain that Snaith is correct. Literally, *yam sûp* means "Sea of End/ Extinction." Geographically, the Israelites applied this name to the Red Sea. But in accord with the practice of other ancients,[29] the Israelites did not distinguish the Red Sea from oceans further to the south. To their way of thinking the Red Sea—or as they called it, *yam sûp*—really was the sea at the end of the earth, a sea which in their minds was fraught with connotations of primeval chaos.[30]

These mythical associations explain the presence of *yam sûp* in Exod 15:4. *Yam sûp* stands simply as the B word in the poetic pair, *yām*//*yam sûp*; it has no more historical or geographical referent than does *yām* (= Sea-dragon). Rather here traditional mythical language is used to express the belief that the emergence of Israel as a people during the exodus was due to a creative act by Yahweh equal to that of the original creation of the

---

Syr. *wb'šth dym'*) and Symmachus (*aperantos*) either read *sôp* or connected the Hebrew term with that vocable.

28. It is tempting to translate the last colon as "Bind their faces with the Underworld," on the basis of Ezek 16:10 where the preposition *b* is used with *ḥābaš* to express not the locative but the material used for binding. In this case the connection with Jonah 2:6 would be even closer.

29. According to LSJ (s.v. *erythra* II), the Greeks applied the term *Erythra Thalassa* not only to the Red Sea proper but also to the Arabian Gulf, the Indian Ocean, and the Persian Gulf; it is also "used vaguely of remote and unknown places."

30. One is reminded that in the Israelite conception, the earth was an island of dry land surrounded on all sides by, and floating in, the primeval waters of chaos (Pss 24:1–2; 104:5–7; 136:6). E. Levine (*The Aramaic Version of Jonah* [Jerusalem: Academic, 1975] 75–76) relates that in later midrashic tradition Jonah, while in the belly of the fish, was shown the path of the Israelites through the Red Sea (*b. Soṭa* 45b; *Midrash Jonah, h.l.; Yal.* #551; Rashi, Comm. *ad h.l.*); this was possible, according to Ibn Ezra and Kimchi *ad h.l.*, because "the Red Sea extends to, and mingles with the waters of Jaffa."

cosmos itself. The Egyptians, the evil force which threatens the existence of this new creation, are appropriately cast into the Sea to perish. A more powerful symbol for non-existence can scarcely be found than submergence into the Sea of End/Extinction.

In contrast, by the time of P the exodus deliverance has been historicized and localized at, or better, in, the geographical body of water we know as the Red Sea. P literally has the Israelites pass through the Red Sea. The mythic elements have not been lessened any, however. On the contrary, P has *yam sûp* split and the Israelites, freed from the slavery of Pharaoh, emerge out of its midst as God's new creation (even as Marduk cleaved Tiamat in twain and out of her carcass created the cosmos).

In conclusion, at no period in Israelite history is there any evidence that *yam sûp* ever referred to a body of water other than the Red Sea. All occurrences of the term *yam sûp* fit adequately within either the geographical and historical or the mythological typology developed in this paper. There is no reason whatever to posit the existence of a second *yam sûp*.[31] In short, the hypothesis that the Israelites experienced deliverance from their Egyptian pursuers at some historical body of water, whose name was dimly but accurately preserved as the "Reed Sea," should be laid to rest forever. *Requiescat in pace!*

*   *   *   *   *

Postscript

The obituary for the Reed Sea hypothesis that I penned in 1983 was premature, apparently. There remain biblical scholars and Egyptologists who are unwilling to concede that the hypothesis has expired, nor are they ready to lay the "Reed Sea" to rest. The origin and meaning of the phrase *yam sûp* continue to provoke debate among biblical scholars, especially those who insist upon the basic historicity of the exodus narrative. Nevertheless, gone is the nearly ubiquitous confidence among biblicists that the biblical phrase literally means "Sea of Reeds" and that this sea was mentioned in Egyptian documents under the name *p3 twf(y)*. Instead, there is a trend back to rendering the phrase into English as the "Red Sea." My article played a major part in forcing a rethinking of the issue. The dust still has not settled, however, as additional scholars weigh in, both attacking my position, on the one side, and lauding my groundbreaking insights, on the other side. I am gratified for the part I have played in stirring up this renewed investigation. In my opinion, however, little new has come to the

---

31. Wifall ("Sea of Reeds as Sheol") has correctly seen that in Exod 15:4 *yam sûp* has more to do with the underworld than with a historical body of water. However, his attempt to interpret it as a mythological "sea of reeds" after the Egyptian "lake" or "field of reeds" fails for the same reasons as the standard Reed Sea hypothesis.

fore, and certainly nothing of significance to cause me to alter substantially the conclusions I reached some thirty years ago. In what follows I discuss only the major challenges to my 1983 article.

Using Papyrus Anastasi VI 51–56 as his primary evidence, Hans Goedicke proposes that Egyptian *pȝ ṯwf* "the reed/papyrus swamp" is indeed relevant to the exodus narrative, but not in the way scholars have traditionally assumed.[32]

First, Goedicke, in opposition to some other scholars, insists that P. Anastasi VI has nothing to do with the exodus event per se, despite the mention of some Asiatic nomads (*shasu*) from Edom who have been allowed to cross from Sinai into the western Wadi Tumilat to water their herds. Since this privilege was granted only for the day known as the "Birthday of Seth," Goedicke argues that these bedouin could not be from Edom, the ethnopolitical region located in the Arabah between the Dead Sea and the Gulf of Elath, since a journey of some 500 kilometers across barren desert just to graze and water their flocks for a single day would not be feasible. Rather, the solution lies in the meaning of the term *Edom* as "the red land." Edom is the Semitic equivalent of the Egyptian *dšrt* "the red land," i.e., any desert area. Thus, the *Shasu* in question must be from a desert area of Sinai just east of Wadi Tumilat. (J. Hoffmeier apparently does not accept Goedicke's thesis, as he continues to assert that in P. Anastasi VI 55–56, Edom refers to the same ethno-geographical group mentioned in the Bible.)[33]

Second, Goedicke proffers a two-part solution to the vexing question(s) concerning the Re(e)d Sea. If I understand his somewhat convoluted argument correctly, he maintains that behind the exodus narrative lay a correct historical memory that the Israelites did cross a reedy swamp in their escape out of Egypt, but not *yam sûp* "the Red Sea." P. Anastasi VI 51–56 and other Egyptian texts refer to a *pȝ ṯwf* "the reed/papyrus swamp." *Pȝ ṯwf* designates an area in the northeastern part of the Nile Delta whose "main characteristic, which gave it its name, is the growth of swamp vegetation, either reeds or papyrus." More specifically, it is to be identified with "the expanse now called Lake Menzalleh" (p. 97). Goedicke is not explicit at this point, but apparently his argument is that originally the exodus tradition simply referred to the Israelites crossing a reedy swamp—in Hebrew, (the) *sûp*—and not the vast Red Sea, known in Hebrew as *yam sûp* and in Greek as Erythra Thalassa.

The confusion of names was apparently caused by the biblical scribes themselves, Goedicke suggests. "The Egyptians called the Red Sea *Wȝḏ-wr*

---

32. Hans Goedicke, "Papyrus Anastasi VI 51–61," *Studien zur altägyptischen Kultur* 14 (1987) 83–98.

33. James K. Hoffmeier, *Ancient Israel in Sinai: The Evidence for the Authenticity of the Wilderness Tradition* (Oxford: Oxford University Press, 2005) 241. That Hoffmeier is well acquainted with Goedicke's article is evident from pp. 60, 62 with nn. 83, 96, and p. 84 with n. 51.

'the Great Green' (papyrus), *wȝd* being written with the papyrus plant. Those coming late to the Red Sea [namely, the Israelites] found an already established name and adopted it into their own language. The result is nothing else than *yam sûp* [= 'Sea of Reeds' = the Red Sea]. Needless to say, this adopted, originally Egyptian, term has nothing to do with the Exodus itinerary." The biblical confusion between *sûp* and *yam sûp*, Goedicke proposes, originated with Exod 15:4, where the original text mentioned just *sûp*, not *yam sûp*. "The immediately preceding mention of *yam* triggered an association with *yam sûp*, and ever since the Children of Israel have been assumed to have crossed the Red Sea." It should be noted that there is no textual or manuscript evidence for this proposal. Moreover, since Goedicke credits Exod 15:4–5 as the source of later Israelite mistaken belief that their ancestors crossed through the Red Sea; he apparently believes that this poem is relatively early.

This "solution" Goedicke thinks adequately answers what he labels Batto's "mythological tour de force," which Goedicke characterizes as proceeding from "the fashionable desire to remove the Exodus narrative from any physical implication."[34] Goedicke may be applauded for acknowledging that Egyptian *pȝ twf* designates an "area" first and foremost; but he can offer no textual evidence in support of his additional thesis that the Egyptian term specifically designates the body of water known as Lake Menzalleh— or any other body of water for that matter, as desiderated by the biblical references to the Israelites marching through the sea with the waters forming a "wall" on their right and their left (Exod 14:22; cp. Ps 78:13), while the pursuing Egyptian host "sank like lead in the mighty waters" (Exod 15:10). Furthermore, Goedicke's interpretation of the biblical data itself is hardly compelling. No scholar to my knowledge has accepted his thesis that Exod 15:4 is the source of a mistaken Israelite belief that their ancestors crossed through the midst of the Red Sea. For Exod 15:4 to be the source of a later Israelite mistake, Exod 15:4 must be itself among the earliest writings in the Hebrew Bible, as Goedicke correctly implies. Later compositions such as Pss 106:6–7; 136:11–15, the Deuteronomic History (notably Deut 11:2–4; Josh 2:9–11; 4:23–24), and the Priestly work (Exod 15:19, 22) are all likely derivative to some extent from Exod 15:4. The unified witness of these later compositions that the Israelites crossed through *yam sûp*—whether understood as Red Sea or some other body of water—as if on dry ground strongly suggests that, contrary to Goedicke, the phrase *yam sûp* was present in the source text (Exod 15:4) from the very beginning. Goedicke is hardly consistent, however, since he also argues that this text "would seem to be a confirmation of the historic tradition about the location of the Miracle of the Sea."[35] Granted that Goedicke is thinking of Lake Menzalleh; never-

---

34. Goedicke, "Papyrus Anastasi VI 51–61," 96.
35. Ibid.

theless his positing of a basis in historical memory necessitates that the phrase *yam sûp*—even if understood as Lake Menzalleh—be present already in the earliest layers of the exodus tradition, a proposition that Goedicke explicitly rejects. And if the phrase *yam sûp* was parallel to *yām* already in Israel's earliest textual witness to the exodus, then Goedicke's arguments for dismissing my mythological interpretation of Exod 15:4–5 crumble for lack of a foundation.

The most extensive and the most direct attack against my thesis has come from James K. Hoffmeier in two publications.[36] He attempts to defend the Reed Sea hypothesis principally through a two-pronged approach, first, by pointing to alleged weaknesses in my argument and, second, by adducing additional Egyptological data from recent archaeological activity in the eastern delta region and the Isthmus of Suez. Because of the severity of Hoffmeier's attack, it behooves me to assess his charges in some detail.

On the archaeological side, considerable progress has been made during the last three decades in the identification of Egyptian sites mentioned in the Hebrew Bible, including Hoffmeier's own contributions in this endeavor. He uses this new information to affirm the basic historicity of the biblical record, including the narrative of the Israelites' exodus out of Egypt. Hoffmeier's argument is that if archaeology can verify that the places named in the exodus narrative were actually located in the general vicinity of where the biblical story situates them, this is prima facie evidence of the historicity of the biblical narrative.

I have no quarrel with this aspect of Hoffmeier's argument, since I made no attempt to deny a historical core to the Israelite exodus—though I have much less confidence than he about the degree of historicity contained in the patently embellished biblical narratives concerning the Israelites' experience in Egypt.[37] Indeed, I consciously avoided the question of whether there is a historical incident behind the story of Israelites eluding their Egyptian pursuers that involved a lesser body of water other than the Red

---

36. In the first publication, Hoffmeier attempts an explicit refutation of my thesis ("The Problem of the Re[e]d Sea," chap. 9 in his *Israel in Egypt: The Evidence for the Authenticity of the Exodus Tradition* [Oxford: Oxford University Press, 1996] 199–222; see esp. subsection III: "The Etymology of *Sûp* and Bernard Batto's Thesis," pp. 204–10). In a second publication ("The Location of the Re[e]d Sea," chap. 5 in his *Ancient Israel in Egypt*, esp. pp. 81–87) Hoffmeier reiterates his major points from the earlier publication and also expands upon his criticism of my thesis.

37. Donald B. Redford ("An Egyptological Perspective on the Exodus Narrative," in *Egypt, Israel, Sinai: Archaeological and Historical Relationships in the Biblical Period* (ed. Anson F. Rainey; Tel Aviv: Tel Aviv University, 1987] 137–61) has argued that the vagueness of topographic material and the paucity of references to Egypt in the exodus narratives, together with anachronistic descriptions, point to a postexilic date for the writing of the exodus narratives. In a response to Redford in the same volume, Manfred Bietak ("Comments on the 'Exodus'," pp. 163–71) recognizes a historical basis to the exodus tradition, though the actual historical truth of the narratives continues to elude us.

Sea.[38] What I did explicitly challenge was the (then nearly ubiquitous) hypothesis that the Hebrew Bible actually names a body of water crossed by the Israelites during their exodus out of Egypt known as the "Reed Sea" (*yam sûp*), and that this (hypothesized, smaller) "Reed Sea" coincidentally has the same name as the Red Sea mentioned elsewhere in the Hebrew Bible. My claim was that always and everywhere in the Hebrew Bible the term *yam sûp* refers to that vast body of water we know as the Red Sea— including its northern extensions into the Gulf of Aqaba and the Gulf of Suez and to the south into the Indian Ocean and beyond—and that a correct reading of the biblical record itself voids any attempt to posit for the Hebrew scriptures a second, lesser body of water known as the *Reed* Sea. My basic thesis, I maintain, is as valid today as when I proposed it some thirty years ago.

Hoffmeier charged that my thesis was "reached without careful consideration of earlier sources," a charge based upon incomplete knowledge of my actual views. Hoffmeier apparently was acquainted only with my article "The Reed Sea: *Requiescat in Pace*," which appeared in *JBL* 102 (1983). That article was a shortened version—condensed at the request of the editors of the *Journal of Biblical Literature*—of a longer paper I presented in Dallas, Texas, at the 1980 Southwest Region meeting of Society of Biblical Literature. Some, but not all, of the excised matter found its way into a popularized version of that same paper.[39] Hoffmeier seemed unaware that in both my original paper and in the popularized version I noted that the suggestion that *yam sûp* refers to a "sea of reeds" or the like can be traced back at least to the medieval Jewish commentators Rashi and Ibn Ezra; I noted also that Martin Luther "translated *yam sûp* as *Schilfmeer* (meaning Reed Sea)." I did not cite Onkelos and Jonathan Ben Uzziel (ca. 200 C.E.) who render the phrase in Exod 15:4 and Num 33:10 as "sea of suph" because of the inherent ambiguity in interpreting their intentions concerning this matter.

Hoffmeier is correct in stating that I failed to note the witness of the Coptic Bohairic (or B) version of the Old Testament, which unlike the Sahidic version, apparently does not follow the LXX in rendering *yam sûp* as the Red Sea. Instead, the Bohairic version has *pyom n ša(i)ri*; which Hoffmeier argues is derived from an Old Egyptian phrase meaning "lake of reeds."

---

38. In my *Slaying the Dragon: Mythmaking in the Biblical Tradition* (Louisville: Westminster John Knox, 1993) 104–18, 128–52, I note that the older literary strands of the exodus narrative of J and E place the Israelites' deliverance vaguely at "the sea," without identifying this as *yam sûp;* moreover, the secondary motif of "crossing dry shod" through a body of water likely derives from the cult at Gilgal.

39. B. Batto, "Red Sea or Reed Sea?: How the Mistake Was Made and What *Yam Sûp* Really Means," *BAR* 10/4 (July/August 1984, 57–63; Hoffmeier seems unacquainted this article. In his second book (*Ancient Israel in Sinai*, 48 with n. 4), however, Hoffmeier does cite my later publication, *Slaying the Dragon*, although he does not engage any of my additional arguments made therein.

But as he himself notes, other etymologies have been proposed. Both the derivation and the precise meaning of the Coptic phrase are uncertain, as indicated by Hoffmeier's own careful phrasings: "it has been suggested that this means," and "if this is the meaning of (the Coptic phrase)."[40] Such hedging is hardly a firm foundation for the thesis of which Hoffmeier hopes to convince his readers.

Hoffmeier continues to insist that biblical *yam sûp* is the equivalent of *p3 twf* mentioned in several Egyptian texts of the Ramesside period and later. While acknowledging that "the biblical and Egyptological data do not allow for firm conclusions on the location of *yam sûp*,"[41] he argues that "the sea through which the Israelites passed most likely was one of the lakes in the Isthmus of Suez; most likely the Ballah Lakes, Lake Timsah, or Bitter Lakes region, and it could interchangeably be termed 'the sea' or *yam sûp*, the latter being a more descriptive name."[42] In his later book, *Ancient Israel in Sinai*, Hoffmeier argues that new archaeological and paleoenvironmental data allows for a more precise location in "the area between the north side of the el-Ballah Lake system and the southern tip of the eastern lagoon."[43]

In the earlier book, *Israel in Egypt*, Hoffmeier suggested why the name *yam sûp* could apply simultaneously both to a smaller marshy lake located somewhere in the Isthmus of Suez that is properly named "Reed Sea," the *p3 twf* of the Egyptian texts, and also to the vast Red Sea. There is evidence that in the second and first millennia b.c.e. the Bitter Lakes were larger and extended considerably farther to the south, while the level of the Red Sea was higher and extended much farther north, to the extent that these bodies of water actually connected at times. This, he suggested, could explain why the name *yam sûp* was also applied to Red Sea.[44] Hoffmeier appears to have abandoned this theory in his latter book, however, as he argues for a more northern location of *yam sûp*, in the area of el-Ballah Lake. But this leaves unexplained why this second sea (the Red Sea) should also bear the name *yam sûp*.

Hoffmeier acknowledges that *p3 twf* is written most often with the determinative for plants (reeds and rushes), occasionally with the determinative for a city, and once with the determinative for "papyrus and watery regions" (Gardner's sign M-15).[45] He does not explain why the term is never

---

40. Hoffmeier, *Israel in Egypt*, 204–5. Hoffmeier fails to take into consideration the possibility that the Coptic B translators may not have possessed any independent knowledge of a "Reed Sea" tradition, but, like Rashi and others, were simply relying upon the intra-biblical witness of Exod 2:3 and Isa 19:6 that the lexeme *sûp* refers to papyrus.

41. Ibid., 210; similarly in *Ancient Israel in Sinai*, 85–86.

42. Hoffmeier, *Israel in Egypt*, 215.

43. Hoffmeier, *Ancient Israel in Sinai*, 75–109; the quotation is from p. 108.

44. Hoffmeier, *Israel in Egypt*, 207–9.

45. Hoffmeier, *Ancient Israel in Sinai*, 82.

written with a determinative for a body of water per se, if that is its primary reference.

Rather, context makes it clear that *pȝ twf* refers to a geographic area located somewhere in the eastern delta or the Isthmus of Suez, though further specification has eluded Egyptologists. Context also makes it clear the Egyptian phrase refers to a region with abundant agricultural produce, including not only marsh plants such as reeds but also dry land plants such as oats and tamarisks.[46] What is not obvious is that *pȝ twf* ever designates a body of water per se, as required by the exodus narrative, which depicts the Israelites crossing dry shod through the middle of a sea split asunder, with the water forming "a wall to their right and to their left" (Exod 14:22; cf. Ps 78:13). This is a later embellishment to the narrative, to be sure, as I explained at length in my book *Slaying the Dragon*. But that is the point, I maintain. Whatever historical kernel may lie behind the exodus narrative, the received form of the narrative has the Israelites passing through the middle of the Red Sea, for the mythological motives I elaborate at length in *Slaying the Dragon*.

Sarah Groll also attempts to defend the Reed Sea hypothesis; indeed, she goes further, claiming that Papyrus Anastasi VIII provides an indirect Egyptian witness to the Israelite presence in Egypt and even to the exodus event itself.[47] She argues that the similarities between P. Anastasi VIII and the story of Exodus are apparent through a comparison of the following motifs: (1) the presence of numerous Semites in the delta of Egypt; (2) mention of a region called *pȝ twf* (P. Anastasi VIII iii.4, 12[48]), "in effect the Yam Suf 'Reed Sea' of the Exodus"; (3) troubled conditions, including the deaths

---

46. For example, James P. Allen ("Praise of Pi-Ramessu," *COS* 3:3 [p. 15]) translates the relevant phrase in P. Anastasi III ii.11, in a passage effusively recounting the abundance provided to the Ramesside capital Pi-Ramessu, the biblical Ramesses: "To it come the papyrus-marshes [*pȝ twf*] with rushes and the Lake of Horus with reeds." Among the produce of the region, P. Anastasi VIII lists reeds, fodder, birds, tamarisks, fish, and oats; so Sarah I. Groll, "The Egyptian Background of the Exodus and the Crossing of the Reed Sea: A New Reading of Papyrus Anastasi VIII," in *Jerusalem Studies in Egyptology* (ed. Irene Shirun-Grumachl; Ägypten und Altes Testament 40; Wiesbaden: Harrasowitz, 1998) 173–92, esp. pp. 190–91.

47. Sarah I. Groll, "Historical Background to the Exodus: Papyrus Anastasi VIII," in *Gold of Praise: Studies on Ancient Egypt in Honor of Edward F. Wente* (ed. Emily Teeter and John A. Larson; Studies in Ancient Oriental Civilization 58; Chicago: Oriental Institute, 1999) 159–62. Groll published virtually the same article earlier under the title "The Historical Background to the Exodus: Papyrus Anastasi VIII," in *Études égyptologiques et bibliques à la mémoire du Père B. Couroyer* (ed. M. Sigrist; Cahiers de la Revue biblique 36; Paris: J. Gabalda, 1997) 109–14; she made the same points, plus provided a copy, transcription, and commentary on this text in "The Egyptian Background of the Exodus and the Crossing of the Reed Sea" (see n. 46 above).

48. Why Groll here includes line 12 as evidence is unclear, as *twf* lacks the definite article; moreover, elsewhere ("The Egyptian Background of the Exodus and the Crossing of the Reed Sea," 185) she translated *twf* in this instance as a common noun "reed (handiwork)."

of several Egyptian crewmen from two boats who "died in apparently suspicious circumstances"; (4) a drought, apparent in the diminished agricultural produce from the delta region described in P. Anastasi VIII, to which may be compared the biblical notation "the LORD drove back the sea with a strong east wind all that night, and turned the sea into dry ground" (Exod 14:21); (5) P. Anastasi VIII can be dated to the middle years of the reign of Ramesses II, "which accords well with the period to which many scholars date the Exodus." Groll concedes that "no single motif provides indisputable 'proof' of the Exodus—there is no mention of an Egyptian prince of Hebrew origin whose brother turns staffs into serpents. Yet the sum of these motifs cannot be considered casual or insignificant."

In my opinion, none of these alleged "motifs" constitute anything more than ordinary occurrences that are documented in other texts on other occasions in ancient Egypt, particularly in the Prophecies of Neferti, as Groll herself acknowledges.[49] Moreover, I do not find any of the events noted in P. Anastasi VIII to parallel closely the "events" of the exodus as depicted in the Book of Exodus, even in their aggregate. Furthermore, Groll completely ignores the objections I raised in my 1983 article as to whether Egyptian *pꜣ twf* may be compared legitimately to biblical *yam sûp*. In my opinion, Groll's three articles contribute little to advancing the discussion.

Marc Vernenne[50] has again carefully reviewed the history of interpretation of *yam sûp* and *sûp* in the Hebrew Bible, from the time of the Septuagint translation to the present (1995). He is in agreement with me on most points, including that "the term סוף in the expression ים סוף cannot be explained by way of an appeal to the Egyptian *pꜣ twf*."[51] Vernenne differs on one significant point, however. I maintain that the name *yam sûp*, even when its referent was the Red Sea, was for the ancients heavily freighted with mythological connotations as the "Sea of End," that is, it was literally the sea at the end of the world/creation. Vernenne notes that Suph is a place name in Deut 1:1 and opines that *yam sûp* refers to a sea in the district of or adjacent to Suph. Accordingly, he concludes, "it would be best to render ים סוף as *Sea of Suph* or simply transliterate it as *Yam Suph*."[52] I have no problem with leaving the name untranslated, but doing so does not resolve the question of whether the ancient Israelites knew of a second, lesser body of water, in addition to our Red Sea, also known as *yam sûp*.

From this rapid survey of challenges to my 1983 article on the origin and meaning of the phrase *yam sûp* it is apparent that no solution has been

---

49. Groll, "In Praise of Gold," 159.

50. Marc Vernenne, "The Lexeme סוף (*sûph*) and the Phrase ים סוף (*yam sûph*): A Brief Reflection on the Etymology and Semantics of a Key Word in the Hebrew Exodus Tradition," *Immigration and Emigration within the Ancient Near East: Festschrift E. Lipinski* (Leuven: Peeters, 1995) 403–29; Batto's thesis is discussed in detail on pp. 424–25.

51. Ibid., 424–25; the quotation is from p. 427.

52. Ibid., 429.

proffered thus far that is convincing to all. Perhaps none is possible, given the ambiguity of the biblical record and the paucity of extrabiblical evidence available to us at present. At core, the debate turns on whether one understands the exodus narrative to be essentially historical in character. I remain convinced of the basic correctness of my thesis that the "Reed Sea" hypothesis should be laid to rest, and also, whatever its historical content, the exodus narrative in its present form is essentially a literary composition that has been greatly embellished through traditional ancient Near Eastern cultural and especially mythic motifs.

Chapter 7

The Covenant of Peace: A Neglected Ancient Near Eastern Motif

The phrase "covenant of peace" is found three times in biblical pro-phetic literature, always in the context of what may be termed eschatologi-cal visions (Isa 54:10; Ezek 34:25; 37:26). As far as this writer can determine, there does not exist any extrabiblical parallel to this phrase in the way used by the prophets.[1] Nevertheless, the prophets did not create the con-cept of an eschatological covenant of peace out of whole cloth. Rather this "covenant of peace" was the prophetic designation for an older biblical and ancient Near Eastern motif associated with the primeval era. The original function of the motif in primeval myth was to signify a cessation of hostil-ity toward humankind by the gods after the former revolted against the gods at creation. The gods ended their attempt to wipe out humankind by binding themselves under oath to maintain peace and harmony with humankind and even with the whole of creation. This oath, which in the Bible often is called a covenant, was then guaranteed by some permanent visible sign, symbolic of the perpetual character of this new alliance of peace.

The core primeval myth is attested in two distinct but overlapping pat-terns, here designated as Pattern A and Pattern B. Characteristic of Pattern A is an attempt to wipe out humankind through the sending of a flood. By contrast, Pattern B lacks a flood story but tells instead of a single goddess's bloody attempt to slay humankind with her sword. A submotif in Pattern B concerns the "planting of peace" as an image of the harmony achieved in the universe.

This article is an attempt to demonstrate that the covenant of peace is a distinct and identifiable motif with a specific content and a definite set of

---

Originally published in *CBQ* 49 (1987) 187–211. To my knowledge, there have been no significant challenges to the thesis presented herein, nor any studies which would incline me to change the conclusions I reached when writing this article.

1. To my knowledge there are no extrabiblical equivalents to the biblical usage; for a comparison of the phrase *rikilta šalāma* to designate a political treaty in Ugaritic Akkadian, see F. R. Knutson, "Literary Phrases and Formulae," *Ras Shamra Parallels II* (ed. L. R. Fisher; AnOr 50; Rome: Biblical Institute Press, 1975) 407–9.

characteristics. Furthermore, it will be argued that this covenant of peace was originally a primeval motif, which the biblical prophets have projected secondarily into the eschatological era.

1. The Biblical Covenant of Peace

The attempt to define the meaning of the term "covenant of peace" in the Bible centers on three prophetic texts, Isa 54:10; Ezek 34:25; 37:26.[2] The term also occurs in Num 25:12 but is not of a piece with the others and should be considered independently.[3] Common to all three prophetic passages is their setting within an exilic salvation oracle, wherein the prophets announce an end to exile and the advent of idyllic conditions associated with the restoration to their homeland.

The fullest description of the covenant of peace is found in Ezek 34:25–30. This passage is one of the series of oracles which announce a reversal of the judgment oracles of the early chapters of the book. In the judgment oracles, it was said that the wrath of God was being poured out upon the house of Israel and Judah. But here in chap. 34, with the wrath of his sword spent (cf. 5:1–2; 21:1–32; 33:2, 27), Yahweh turns as "the shepherd of Israel" to gather his torn and scattered flock and restore them to their land. It is within this context of reversal that the covenant of peace is announced.

> I will make with them a covenant of peace and banish evil beasts from the land, that they may dwell securely in the wilderness and sleep in the forest. And I will make them . . . a blessing(?)[4] and cause rain to fall in the proper time: they shall be showers of blessing. And the trees of the field shall give their fruit, and the earth shall give its produce. . . . And they

---

2. Within these texts the term occurs in slightly variant forms: *běrît šālôm* (Ezek 34:25; 37:26) and *běrît šělômî* (Isa 54:10). The term is also found in Num 25:12 in still a third variant, *běrîtî šālôm*.

3. The covenant of peace mentioned in Num 25:10–15 seems to have little in common with the prophetic passages just mentioned. In this passage, Phinehas is said to have turned back the wrath of God from consuming his people because of their sin in the Baal Peor incident. Phinehas' zeal for Yahwism was rewarded by God's granting to him and his descendants a perpetual priesthood: "Behold, I am giving him my covenant of peace; it shall be for him and his descendants after him a covenant of priesthood forever." Here the divine covenant of peace seems to be primarily a personal privilege and has no apparent connection with primeval events. However, there may be some eschatological connotations involved in that Phinehas' action purified Israel, poised to enter the promised land (for P an eschatological event), and allowed them to enter. Additionally, it is intriguing that here too the covenant of peace, as elsewhere, comes from a divine initiative after the deity's anger has been turned aside and that it is said to be an eternal covenant. Perhaps the author employed here a traditional expression because of its connotations of cessation of divine wrath and restoration of harmony between God and humanity.

4. The MT for v. 26a is almost certainly corrupt; see W. Zimmerli, *Ezekiel 2* (Hermeneia; Philadelphia: Fortress Press, 1983) 210.

shall dwell securely and none shall make them afraid. And I will cause a planting of peace[5] to spring up for them.

One cannot fail to notice that this description of the covenant of peace is extremely similar to the eschatological covenant of Hos 2:18–25, which God will make "with the beasts of the field, the birds of heaven, and the creeping things of the ground," when "bow and sword and war" will be "abolished from the face of the earth," and all will "dwell in security." And much like Ezekiel's showers of blessing, Hosea speaks of the heavens "answering" the earth and the earth producing harvest in abundance. Although Hosea does not specifically call his a covenant of peace, it is obviously the same covenant.[6] Both draw heavily from the paradise myth. The eschatological conditions described are nothing short of a restoration of the idyllic conditions of Eden. Every form of hostility will be removed from the face of the earth. Even the heavens and the earth will cooperate in producing abundance. Also not to be overlooked in these idyllic portraits is the implicit harmonious relationship that will exist between God and his people, far beyond anything that ever had been the reality in the historical period. Finally, the removal of hostility between men and beasts in the context of a covenant brings to mind the covenant "with all flesh" in the days of Noah (Gen 9:8–17). (That Ezekiel patterned the restoration upon primeval motifs is confirmed by 36:35: "This land that was desolate has become like the garden of Eden; the waste and the desolate and ruined cities are now inhabited and fortified.")

The second mention of the covenant of peace in Ezekiel (37:26) is an apocopated form of the first. It adds little to Ezekiel's preceding description, except to specify that the covenant of peace is to be an everlasting covenant—something already implicit in the previous passage.[7]

More instructive for our study is Isa 54:9–10. In this passage the connection between the covenant of peace and the Noachic covenant becomes explicit. And once again the covenant of peace involves the reversal of prior divine anger. In vv. 7–8 immediately preceding, under the metaphor of a deserted wife, Israel is informed that her exile was due to momentary anger on the part of God. That anger has now abated, however, and God henceforth will love Israel with everlasting fidelity. Then comes this illuminating statement:

5. For this translation ("a planting of peace") see below, Part 4. Please note the translations of biblical passages found in this study, although heavily dependent upon the *RSV*, are my own and reflect my interpretation of the texts under discussion.

6. For similarities between Hos 2:18–25 and Ezek 34:25–30 and also Lev 26:3–13, see H. W. Wolff, *Hosea* (Hermeneia; Philadelphia: Fortress Press, 1974) 51–52; W. Rudolph, *Hosea* (KAT XIII/1; Gütersloh: Mohn, 1966) 80.

7. Other themes here, such as God's promise to multiply his chosen people and to set his sanctuary in their midst forever, owe their origin to Ezekiel's priestly theology and can be omitted from discussion.

This is as the days of Noah[8] to me, when I swore that the waters of
Noah would never again trespass upon the earth; just so I have sworn
that I will not be angry with you and will not rebuke you.
Though the mountains may move
    and the hills collapse,
Yet will my steadfast love be unmoved,
    and my covenant of peace will never collapse,
    says Yahweh who has compassion on you.

A common interpretation of this passage is that the poet cites the Noah
incident for its value as an example of the steadfastness or reliability of
the divine word.[9] Reliability of the divine word hardly exhausts the poet's
meaning, however. Here the divine oath never again to flood the earth as
in the time of Noah is patently equivalent to the everlasting covenant with
all flesh in Gen 9:8–17 (P), in which God promised "never again shall there
be a flood to destroy the earth." Covenant and oath were frequently interchanged.[10] This is not to say that the author of Isaiah 54 was necessarily
familiar with the Priestly account of the flood. An equivalent divine oath is
found also in the Yahwistic version (Gen 8:21–22),[11] as well as in the Mesopotamian versions of the deluge (*Atrahasis* III vi 2–4; *Gilgamesh* XI 163–69).
This oath was, as will be seen, a standard feature of the flood story itself.

Given the appeal to the Noachic covenant, two additional points should
be noted in Isaiah 54. First, the reference to the abating of God's anger
(*qṣp*) against his people here (v. 10, cf. v. 8) seems to suggest that the poet

---

8. MT *kî-mê nōaḥ*; I omit the maqqef and read with the LXX, "like/as the days of
Noah." One could equally read with T and V, "for (this is) the waters of Noah." The meaning is substantially the same in either case. The *RSV* ("For this is like the days of Noah")
is a conflated reading.

9. So G. A. Knight, *Deutero-Isaiah: A Theological Commentary on Isaiah 40–55* (Nashville: Abingdon Press, 1965) 249; C. R. North, *The Second Isaiah* (Oxford: Clarendon Press,
1964) 248.

10. E. Kutsch ("Gottes Zuspruch und Anspruch: *běrît* in der alttestamentlichen Theologie," in *Questions disputées d'ancien testament: Méthode et théologie* [ed. C. Brekelmans;
BETL 33; Gembloux: Duculot, 1974] 71–90, esp. p. 81) maintains that in one meaning *běrît*
has reference to the deity unilaterally binding himself under oath to some obligation; he
calls attention to the frequent interchange in the Bible between covenant (*běrît*) and oaths
(*šěbûʿâ*). N. Lohfink (*Die Landverheissung als Eid* [SBS 28; Stuttgart: KBW, 1967]) maintains
that *běrît* means "oath," especially in its origins. Despite D. McCarthy's strictures (*Treaty
and Covenant* [rev. ed.; AnBib 21a; Rome: Biblical Institute Press, 1978] 16–22) about
Kutsch's and Lohfink's theses, McCarthy too acknowledges that the oath is an important,
if not always essential (p. 5), element of the covenant tradition. On the importance of the
oath in ancient Near Eastern treaties or covenants, see also D. R. Hillers, *Covenant: The
History of a Biblical Idea* (Seminars in the History of Ideas; Baltimore: The Johns Hopkins
University Press, 1969) 28.

11. L. Dequeker ("Noah and Israel: The Everlasting Divine Covenant with Mankind,"
in *Questions disputées d'ancien testament*, 115–29, esp. p. 116) maintains that J understood
this scene in the same sense as P, "although, in the Flood narrative, he did not use any
technical covenantal terminology."

understood the primeval deluge also to have been occasioned by divine anger against humankind; this is a point to which we must return later. Second, both in biblical and extrabiblical accounts of the flood, the divine oath/covenant never again to destroy all living beings with a deluge is always accompanied by some kind of sign which guarantees the divine oath, despite the fact that the sign is hardly ever the same in the different versions: a fly-necklace in *Atrahasis* (III v 46–vi 4, and its derivative[12] *Gilgamesh* XI 163–65), the (rain)bow in P (Gen 9:12–17), and the duration of the earth and its seasons in J (Gen 8:21–22).[13] One must, therefore, at least entertain the possibility that here in Isaiah the allusion to the steadfastness of the mountains and the hills may in one version of the deluge have served as the sign of the divine oath.[14]

Finally, mention should be made of Job 5:19–23 also. The poet lists six, nay, seven evils from which God delivers the just. Significantly, included among these are death, the sword, and famine. However, in the convention of wisdom literature, the emphasis falls upon the last named in the list, viz., fear from the wild beasts of the earth (*ḥayyat hāʾāreṣ*). Given the pattern of the prophetic passages we have examined, we will not be surprised to find that the absence of these specific evils is linked to the covenant involving all of creation.

> For with the stones of the field is your covenant,
> and the beasts of the field make peace with you.

Although the poet uses his license to play freely with traditional materials, the essential form of the covenant of peace is clearly recognizable. Moreover, the freedom of the poet to suggest by allusion, rather than being compelled by slavish explication, attests to the vitality of the concept for both the poet and his audience.

2. Primeval Pattern A

It is now time to follow the trail indicated by the prophets and explore the primeval myths to see why the prophets linked them with a covenant of peace. The first primeval pattern to be investigated involves an attempt

---

12. Although a Sumerian version of the flood story may have been known already in the Ur III Period (21st century B.C.E.), it circulated independently and likely became attached to the *Gilgamesh* tradition only after the Old Babylonian Period. Sometime before the end of the Middle Babylonian Period (ca. 1000 B.C.E.), the *Atrahasis* version of the flood story was incorporated into *Gilgamesh*, changing the third-person account into the first person to fit better the narrative structure of the *Gilgamesh* epic. For details see J. Tigay, *The Evolution of the Gilgamesh Epic* (Philadelphia: University of Pennsylvania Press, 1982), esp. pp. 240–41.

13. See below, pp. 182–184.

14. Cf. Isa 55:12–13, where the jubilation of *the mountains and the hills* is listed in a series of unnatural phenomena which will serve as an everlasting sign; note also the mention of *šālôm* in v. 12.

to annihilate humankind by means of a flood. The paradigm, if not the archetype, for this type is the Mesopotamian myth of *Atrahasis*. Although the flood myth is attested in other versions across the face of the ancient Near East, including the two biblical sources in Genesis 6–9 (J and P), *Atrahasis* seems to represent most accurately the original shape of the myth.

The interpretation of *Atrahasis* is still a matter of debate, especially because the ending of the myth is poorly preserved. Nevertheless, enough of the structure is preserved to allow us to determine that the myth is much concerned with the status and function of humankind vis-à-vis the gods. The opening scenes depict unsuccessful inchoative attempts to define cosmic order. The lesser gods rise in revolt against the high gods because of their excessive burdens. A first solution is attempted by the creation of humankind, who would do the work of the gods and especially bear the burden of providing sustenance for them. Accordingly, it was decreed that the ringleader of the rebellious gods should be killed and from his flesh and blood mixed with clay humans would be created.

But as humankind grew in numbers, so did the problems. Enlil, the king of the gods, was unable to sleep at night because of the din (*rigmu*//*ḫubūru*) raised by humanity. It is most unlikely, however, that the subsequent attempt of the gods to annihilate humankind should be interpreted, as is often done, as a capricious decision by the gods, simply because their king Enlil could not sleep at night because of noise issuing from an overpopulated earth.[15] Rather, the divine decision was taken in reaction to human transgression.[16] Humankind was created so that the gods might rest. Consequently, when Enlil's "sleep" (= rest) was disturbed by the humans' din, it was a violation of right order. The din (*rigmu*//*ḫubūru*) was not so much the noise generated by huge throngs of people as it was the cries of rebellion against divine rule. Enlil's ability to sleep (= rest) or not appears to have been tied up with his function as the ruler of heaven and earth. He could afford to rest only if his authority was unchallenged. One might compare this to OT descriptions of Yahweh, who does not sleep; if he did, the world

---

15. A. D. Kilmer, "The Mesopotamian Concept of Overpopulation and Its Solution as Reflected in Mythology," *Or* 41 (1972) 160–77; W. L. Moran, "Atrahasis: The Babylonian Story of the Flood," *Bib* 52 (1971) 51–61; T. Frymer-Kensky, "The Atrahasis Epic and Its Significance for Our Understanding of Genesis 1–9," *BA* 40 (1977) 147–55; V. Fritz, "'Solange die Erde steht'—Vom Sinn der jahwistischen Fluterzählung in Gen 6–8," *ZAW* 94 (1982) 599–614.

16. See R. A. Oden, Jr., "Divine Aspirations in Atrahasis and in Genesis 1–11," *ZAW* 93 (1981) 197–216; G. Pettinato, "Die Bestrafung des Menschengeschlechts durch die Sintflut," *Or* 37 (1968) 165–200. See further W. von Soden, "Der Mensch bescheidet sich nicht: Überlegungen zu Schöpfungserzählungen in Babylonien und Israel," *Symbolae Biblicae et Mesopotamicae Francisco Mario Theodoro de Liagre Böhl dedicatae* (ed. M. A. Beck, A. A. Kampman, C. Nijland, and J. Ryckmans; Leiden: Brill, 1973) 349–58; he maintains that the crime of humanity was to overreach the human realm and encroach upon the divine realm.

might revert to chaos as his archenemy gained an advantage.[17] It should also be noted that Enlil's rest was earlier disturbed by the cries of rebellion (*rigmu*) of the lesser gods (*Atrahasis* I 77). The humans are patently portrayed as carrying on in the spirit of the divine rebel(s). Not only is humankind created out of the flesh and blood of the slain divine ringleader, but also humanity is explicitly said to possess the slain god's ghost (*eṭemmu*) and his capacity to scheme or plot (*ṭēmu*).[18] Accordingly, the divine decision to destroy humankind by flood was just as much a punishment for sin in *Atrahasis* as it was in the biblical story.[19]

With this understanding, the conclusion of *Atrahasis* deserves another look. As the first of his acts upon emerging from the grounded ship, Atrahasis, like the "righteous" Noah, offered sacrifice to the gods. By this act Atrahasis displayed the virtues of a pious and faithful servant of the gods, unlike his fellow humans, who perished in the punishing deluge. But the deluge was likewise a lesson for the gods in that they learned the hard way of their dependency upon humankind for sustenance. The point is tellingly, if somewhat crudely, made in the scene of starving gods swarming like flies[20] around Atrahasis as he prepared his aromatic sacrifice. By defining the proper relationship of the human to the divine realm, the earlier inchoative attempt at creation by the gods was brought to completion and perfection. The divine regulations for human existence given at the conclusion of the myth have the same purpose, the establishment of correct order or harmony within the universe.[21]

The role of the mother goddess should not be overlooked. Having witnessed humankind, over whom she had labored at creation, die like flies in the deluge, Nintu vowed by Anu's fly-necklace around her neck never to forget.[22] But never to forget what?

---

17. Ps 121:3–4 describes Yahweh as never sleeping, i.e., he is eternally vigilant in keeping the force(s) of evil at bay. The image is reversed in other places, however. When the world appears to be collapsing around him, the devotee may call upon Yahweh to rouse himself from his sleep and to take up the battle against the power of chaos once again (Isa 51:9–11; Pss 7:7; 35:23; 44:24; 59:5–6; 74:22; cf. Isa 42:13–14; Ps 78:65; Zech 2:17). By contrast, the false gods can be parodied (1 Kgs 18:27) because they have no such power (Hab 2:19).

18. See Oden, "Divine Aspirations," 202–3; von Soden, "Der Mensch," 352; William L. Moran, "The Creation of Man in Atrahasis I 192–248," *BASOR* 200 (1970) 48–56, esp. p. 52. The concept is essentially the same as in Gen 6:5, where it is said of humankind "that every tendency of the scheming of his mind was for evil only."

19. That some sort of sin was involved is also clear from Ea's reproach of Enlil, preserved in *Gilgamesh* XI 180: "On the sinner lay his sin; on the transgressor lay his transgression."

20. Restored in the broken text of *Atrahasis* III v 35 from the parallel passage in *Gilgamesh* XI 161.

21. See Oden, "Divine Aspirations," 208, 214–15.

22. Unfortunately, the text of Atrahasis is partially broken at this crucial point. In the parallel text of *Gilgamesh* XI 164–65—which only partially replicates this damaged section of *Atrahasis*—Nintu says, "Ye gods here, as surely as this lapis upon my neck I shall be mindful of these days, forgetting (them) never."

Partially on the basis of the parallel in Genesis, I understand the mother goddess, as creatress of humankind, to speak for the assembled gods in swearing an oath that they will never again attempt to obliterate humankind. In Genesis 9 the Priestly conclusion to the flood joins the blessing of Noah and his sons with divine regulations for human conduct (vv. 1–7) and then links both of these with an "everlasting covenant" never again to destroy all flesh by the waters of a flood (vv. 8–17). The Yahwistic version likewise concludes with what apparently is a divine oath never again to curse the earth because of man's sin (Gen 8:21). Since the divine covenant and the divine oath were frequently interchanged, one is justified in assuming an equivalent typology for Atrahasis. Accordingly, in the end all the gods affirm Nintu's oath and even Enlil, the perpetrator of the ill-conceived plan, gives his blessing.[23] Moreover, given the common typology in all these flood stories, Nintu's fly-necklace can only be interpreted as the sign which guarantees this Mesopotamian "covenant of peace."[24]

But by the same token, the sign of the bow in Genesis 9 should be interpreted as God desisting from an act of hostility against humankind. This

---

23. *Blessing* is not a mere metaphor here. Blessing seems to be part and parcel of the vocabulary of the covenant of peace. At the conclusion of *Gilgamesh* XI 192, Utnapishtim tells how Enlil laid hands on him and his wife and "he blessed us" (*ikarrabannāši*). In *Gilgamesh* this blessing, which explicitly elevates Utnapishtim and his wife to the ranks of the gods, serves to advance the thesis of that epic, that immortality is a vain quest for any mortal. It appears unlikely that a comparable blessing should be posited for the fragmentary conclusion to *Atrahasis*. Nevertheless, it is not impossible that the regulations for postdiluvian humankind established by Enki and Nintu were connected with a blessing, as in the P version (Gen 9:1–7). The J account also knows the language of blessing, or at least its inverse: "I will no longer curse (*qallēl*) the ground because of humankind" (Gen 8:21). In Ezek 34:26b the benefits of the covenant of peace are called "showers of blessing" (and cf. 26a [MT; lacking in the LXX]). One is reminded, further, that blessings and curses are a prominent feature in the covenant/treaty tradition in the ancient Near East.

24. W. G. Lambert and A. R. Millard (*Atra-ḫasīs: The Babylonian Story of the Flood* [Oxford: Oxford University Press, 1969; reprinted Winona Lake: Eisenbrauns, 1999] 13) explain the fly-necklace differently: "Using her grief as a pretext, she [the mother goddess] appropriated some lapis lazuli flies which had been Anu's and insisted that she would wear them as a perpetual reminder of the time when her offspring were floating on the surface of the waters like flies. This is aetiological, to explain the actual necklaces of fly-shaped beads around the necks of statues of this goddess in the author's experience." This explanation ignores an explanation even closer at hand—in fact within the same context as the fly-necklace itself—viz., that the gods swarmed over the sacrifice like flies. But it is doubtful that either mention of flies is anything other than a literary pun on a preexisting fly-necklace motif in the flood story. Anne Kilmer ("The Symbolism of the Flies in the Mesopotamian Flood Myth and Some Further Implications," in *Language, Literature, and History: Philological and Historical Studies Presented to Erica Reiner*, ed. F. Rochberg-Halton [AOS 67; New Haven, CT: American Oriental Society, 1987], 175–80) demonstrates that the fly(-necklace) indeed served the same function as the rainbow; not only do the fly's wings act as a natural prism which shatters light passing through them into a rainbow of colors, but also the fly emblem was a prominent ancient Near Eastern symbol on weapons and in war contexts.

is hardly a novel idea. Since the days of Wellhausen, it has been common to point out that Hebrew *qešet* denotes the warbow of one or other of the gods.[25] Especially illuminating here is the similarity with Marduk's bow in the *Enuma Elish*. After his victory over Tiamat and her allies, Marduk literally "hung up" his bow. The bow, undrawn, is placed in the heavens to shine as the bowstar. One will not be far off the mark in interpreting this bowstar both as a sign of the definitiveness of Marduk's victory over the rebellious forces of chaos (in that he can afford to lay it aside) and as a guarantee that good order reigns within the cosmos. There is every reason to believe that the Genesis author understood the rainbow to function in a similar manner.[26] In the Priestly source the flood is an extension of *Chaoskampf*. Through human violence (*ḥāmās*, Gen 6:11–13), chaos (*tĕhôm*) had reentered the cosmos and threatened to undo God's initial victory over chaos (cf. Gen 1:2 and 7:11).[27] Thus we are justified in appealing to the parallel in *Enuma Elish* and in interpreting the rainbow as a sign that God's victory is total and that God has indeed hung up his bow used to subdue the enemy. With the reestablishment of divine rule, a new and more perfect order has been achieved. Humankind, in the person of righteous Noah, acknowledges its proper position before God. God binds himself to an everlasting covenant of peace with all creation. The rainbow now appears in the heavens to signal forevermore the advent of a new era of peace and harmony between God and the cosmos.[28]

---

25. J. Wellhausen, *Prolegomena to the History of Ancient Israel* (Cleveland: Meridian, 1957) 311; S. R. Driver, *The Book of Genesis* (10th ed.; Westminster Commentaries; London: Methuen, 1916) 98–99; J. Skinner, *A Critical and Exegetical Commentary on Genesis* (ICC; New York: Scribner's, 1910) 171–73; T. H. Gaster, *Myth, Legend and Custom in the Old Testament* (New York: Harper & Row, 1969) 130–31; E. Zenger, *Gottes Bogen in den Wolken: Untersuchungen zu Komposition und Theologie der priesterschriftlichen Urgeschichte* (SBS 12; Stuttgart: KBW, 1983) 11–21, 124–31. Among those who reject the idea of a warbow are B. Jacob (*The First Book of the Bible: Genesis* [New York: KTAV, 1974] 66 and C. Westermann (*Genesis 1–11* [Minneapolis: Augsburg Publishing House, 1984] 473). The image of God as a warrior who wields a bow and shoots arrows is clear in Lam 2:4 and Hab 3:9–11. That the LXX also understood *qešet* to have martial connotations is evident in the translation of Gen 9:13, 14, 16 as *toxon*, "warbow" (rather than as *iris*, "rainbow"; cf. Rev 4:3; 10:1; *Apoc. Pet.* 3:10); nevertheless, in time *toxon*, like *qešet*, came to mean little more than an arch or rainbow (Ezek 1:2; Sir 43:11–12).

26. On the drawn and the undrawn bow in Assyrian representations and on its parallel function in Genesis 9, see G. E. Mendenhall, *The Tenth Generation* (Baltimore: The Johns Hopkins University Press, 1973) 44–48.

27. See my article, "Red Sea or Reed Sea? How the Mistake Was Made and What *Yam Sûp* Really Means," *BAR* 10/4 (July/August 1984) 57–63, esp. p. 63.

28. P. A. H. de Boer ("Quelques remarques sur l'arc dans la nuée [Genèse 9,8–17]," in *Questions disputées d'ancien testament*, 105–14, esp. p. 111) likewise recognizes an ancient mythic background for the pericope in Gen 9:8–17. However, he misunderstands the bow in the clouds to be drawn and poised to shoot as a symbol of the deity's eternal vigilance against his enemies, chaos and death, lest these overwhelm humankind. Accordingly, de Boer misinterprets the divine battle as waged on behalf of humankind rather than

As indicated above, the Yahwistic account included a similar sign (Gen 8:21–22). The duration of the earth with its regularity of seasons is more than a metaphor for the stability of Yahweh's resolve. Based upon the comparative evidence, it seems to function as a sign guaranteeing a divine oath never again to cut off life from the face of the earth.

3. Primeval Pattern B

The second of the two primeval patterns involves an attempt by a goddess to slay humankind because of its rebellion against the gods. After an initial bloody carnage, the goddess is prevented from carrying out further killing through the intervention of the head god. The ending of the myth is not well preserved, but in my reconstruction there is a planting of peace on the earth and the attainment of cosmic harmony resulting from the establishment of divine rule. Finally, a special sign is created to signal the advent of this new age of peace. The primary witnesses to this primeval pattern are an Egyptian text known as "Deliverance of Mankind from Destruction"[29] and a Ugaritic text, *CTA* 3 of the Baal cycle. In addition, one can find in the biblical tradition, both in the Hebrew Bible and in the NT, vestigial reminiscences of the planting of peace motif.[30]

The similarities between the Egyptian and the Ugaritic texts have been studied previously by F. Charles Fensham[31] and need not be repeated here. Fensham has demonstrated that the two texts not only share a common pattern but also are in some way actually related.[32]

The beginning of the Ugaritic text is badly damaged; and so the reason for Anat's bloody rampage in the plain, "Smiting the people of the West, smashing the folk of the East" (*CTA* 3 ii 6–8), is uncertain. From the Egyptian account, however, we learn that Hathor's attack upon humankind was explicitly commissioned by the creator Re, in council with the other gods,

---

against it. For further critique of de Boer, see C. J. L. Kloos, "The Flood on Speaking Terms with God," *ZAW* 94 (1982) 639–42.

29. Translated by J. A. Wilson, *ANET*, 10–11. See also M. Lichtheim, *Ancient Egyptian Literature. Volume II: The New Kingdom* (Berkeley: University of California Press, 1976) 197–99; H. Brunner, "Die Vernichtung des Menschengeschlechts," in *Religionsgeschichtliches Textbuch zum Alten Testament* (Göttingen: Vandenhoeck & Ruprecht, 1975) 35–38. The complete text is found in C. Maystre, "Le livre de la vache du ciel dans les tombeaux de la vallée des rois," *BIFAO* 40 (1941) 53–115, the text being translated on pp. 53–73.

30. See below, Part 4.

31. "The Destruction of Mankind in the Near East," *Annali, Istituto universitario orientale di Napoli* n.s. 15 (1965) 31–37; see also C. Virolleaud, "La déesse Anat-Astarté dans les poèmes de Ras-Shamra," *Revue des études sémitiques* 1 (1937) 4–22, esp. pp. 8–9.

32. Both the literary and the artistic representations of the two goddesses involved, Hathor and Anat respectively, display a high degree of confusion and syncretism. Anat was goddess of both war and love. Hathor, normally regarded as a goddess of love, could also be portrayed as a goddess of war. In the Egyptian version, Hathor even changed into the form of the lioness Sekhmet, the mistress of war and sickness.

because humankind had rebelled against the creator. Hathor's initial massacre resulted in the annihilation of all humans who had fled into the desert. However, when Hathor returned to report this initial success to Re, the creator god experienced a change of heart and requested Hathor to refrain from further human destruction, apparently because he now believed that he could rule the remnant.[33] But Hathor was unwilling to desist, and Re was forced to resort to a ruse to prevent total annihilation. He sent messengers to obtain some red-colored substance, probably mandrakes,[34] which he then had ground and mixed with beer and poured onto the fields. When Hathor arrived in the morning to complete her work, she found the fields flooded with this red liquid. Believing it to be blood, she eagerly imbibed it and fell into a drunken stupor. Thus was humankind saved from total destruction.

The Egyptian version apparently dispensed with the original ending. In its present setting, written on the walls of three royal tombs, its purpose was a magical protection of the dead—the implication being "that the former deliverance of mankind from destruction will be valid also in this individual case."[35] For the original ending of this mythic pattern, we turn to the Ugaritic version.

The full significance of Ugaritic *CTA* 3 has not been recognized in the past because it has been erroneously considered as a fragment of a larger Baal cycle of texts. However, As R. J. Clifford has argued, *CTA* 3 is likely an independent duplicate of *CTA* 4–6.[36] Both versions of the Baal cycle concern the establishment of Baal's rule by a victory over his enemies and end with the building of a palace from which Baal governs the cosmos.

As mentioned previously, the beginning of *CTA* 3 is broken. The first preserved episode depicts Anat's bloody rampage against humankind; then the text again breaks off. When it resumes, Baal is sending a messenger to Anat with a command to desist from further carnage and to plant peace on earth instead:

> *qryy barṣ mlḥmt*
> *št bᶜprt ddym*
> *sk šlm lkbd arṣ*
> *arbdd lkbd šdm*

---

33. This reading is based upon my interpretation of the parallel Ugaritic account. The Egyptian text is capable of more than one reading; Wilson's (*ANET*, 11 n. 9) alternate translation, "I shall prevail over them. But do not diminish them any further," is remarkably similar to Baal's message to Anat.

34. The substance (*ddyt*) is usually identified as red-ochre or hematite. But the alternate interpretation as mandrakes (cf. West Semitic *ddy*), because of their reputed love-inducing qualities, seems more appropriate in view of the Ugaritic parallel; see Fensham, "Destruction of Mankind," 4–5. See further below, n. 38.

35. Wilson, *ANET*, 10.

36. R. J. Clifford, "Cosmogonies in the Ugaritic Texts and in the Bible," *Or* 53 (1984) 183–201.

> Remove war from the earth;[37]
>   set mandrakes [or love][38] in the ground,
> Pour peace into the heart of the earth;
>   rain[39] down love in the hearts of the fields. (*CTA* 3 iii 11–14)[40]

Baal also commands Anat to return immediately, for he has a new solution to propose.

Seeing the messenger approach, Anat cries in alarm that a new foe must have arisen to challenge Baal. But who can it be, since she herself had crushed Yamm, the dragon of chaos, and, according to our thesis, is even now in the process of wiping out the latest rebels, newly created human-kind. The messenger assures her that no new foe challenges Baal and delivers Baal's peace plan. Anat submits to Baal's will and returns to do his bidding. Together they plan a palace from which Baal will rule supreme. The text breaks off with Anat before El, demanding permission to build the palace. On the basis of the variant version (*CTA* 4–6), we may confidently assume that Anat's mission was successful and that the palace was built, thus securing Baal's rule.

On the basis of comparative evidence, one may attempt some initial conclusions. If Anat's carnage was occasioned by human rebellion and was carried out by a common divine decision to punish humankind, by the same token Baal's desire to plant peace and love in the earth should be understood as a statement of reconciliation. But it is a reconciliation not only with a chastened humankind but also with all the earth, which had become polluted by association with the "sinners"—the same situation as in Gen 6:5–7 (J) and 6:11–13 (P). Thus, with the abolishing of hostility between creator and creature and the planting of peace and love on earth, a new harmony between heaven and earth was achieved. One may suggest,

---

37. [There continues to be no agreement among recent translators about the meaning of this difficult line: "Present bread offerings in the earth" (D. Pardee, in *COS* 1:86 [p. 243, 252 et passim]); "Place in the earth war" (M. S. Smith, in *Ugaritic Narrative Poetry* [ed. Simon B. Parker; SBLWAW 9; Atlanta: Scholars Press, 1997] 93, 110 et passim).]

38. Ugaritic *ddym* has received a variety of interpretations. I opt for "mandrakes" on the basis not only of the Egyptian parallel *ddyt* (see n. 34) but also of the agricultural metaphor in these lines, which seem verified by my discovery of the motif of planting peace. Mandrakes were thought to have love-producing qualities and are therefore appropriately watered by peace and love (see following bicolons).

39. For this interpretation of *arb dd*, see M. Dahood (*Psalms I* [AB 16; Garden City: Doubleday, 1965] 281) on the strength of the agricultural metaphor (cf. my preceding note). It is equally possible to take *arb* as the aphel of *rby* and translate, "increase love (in the fields)"; see P. J. van Zijl, *Baal* (AOAT 10; Neukirchen-Vluyn: Neukirchener Verlag, 1972) 57–58. Note that *dd*, cognate to the Hebrew *dôdîm* ("love"), is a deliberate paronomasia upon *ddym* ("mandrakes") in the preceding bicolon.

40. This speech is not only repeated several times in our text but is also found in a very broken context in *CTA* 1 ii 19–21 and has been restored by the editor in the lacuna in *CTA* 7 II 14–20; the latter texts are too fragmentary to determine their relation to other texts in the Baal cycle.

as with the flood story, that this new achievement was considered the end
(*telos*)—i.e., both the conclusion and the goal—of creation. This is implied
in the statement that Baal reigns.

Until now I have deliberately omitted mention of the conclusion of
Baal's peace message to Anat. After the command to plant love and peace
in the earth, the message continues:

> *dm rgm iṯ ly wargmk*
> *hwt w aṯnyk*
> *rgm ʿṣ w lḫšt abn*
> *tant šmm ʿm arṣ*
> *thmt ʿmn kbkbm*
> *abn brq dl tdʿ šmm*
> *rgm ltdʿ nšm*
> *wltbn hmlt arṣ*

> For I have a word to tell you,
>   a message to recount to you:
> A word of tree(s) and a whispering of stone(s),
>   the answering of the heavens to the earth,
>   of the Abyss to the stars.
> I will create lightning[41] which the heavens know not;
>   thunder which humans know not,
>   which the earthly multitudes understand not. (*CTA* 3 iii 17–25)

Scholars have long puzzled over the meaning of these words. But the
presence of the planting of peace motif, which will be discussed shortly,
makes it clear that we have here a description of the attainment of cosmic
harmony. These are the same conditions which the Israelite prophets projected as characteristic of the eschatological age. The similarity of language
in "the answering of the heavens to the earth" to Hos 2:23–24, e.g., can
hardly be accidental.

There is a second element in Baal's message which has entirely escaped
the attention of scholars. I refer to the sign value of lightning. Baal proposes to "create lightning," a natural phenomenon hitherto unknown in
heaven and on earth. One of the reasons for the scholars' failure to understand the significance of this passage in the past has been their uncertainty
about how to translate *abn brq*.[42] But the uncertainty is cleared up when

---

41. The attempts to translate *abn brq* as "fire stone" or as "I understand lightning"
must now be given up; see below.

42. Three basic solutions have been proposed. U. Cassuto (*ha-Eleh ʿAnat* [Jerusalem: Bi-
alik Institute, 1951] 81) compared it to *ʾabnê ʾēš* ("stones of fire") in Ezek 28:14–15, which
produce lightning (cf. Ezek 1:13). R. J. Clifford (*The Cosmic Mountain in Canaan and the Old
Testament* [HSM 4; Cambridge: Harvard University Press, 1972] 68–70) proposed "I understand lightning." C. Virolleaud (*La déesse Anat* [Mission de Ras Shamra IV; Paris: Geuthner,
1938] 35–38) derived *abn* from *bnw* ("create" or "build") and translated the phrase as
"Je créerai l'éclair"; J. Gray (*The Legacy of Canaan* [rev. ed.; VTSup 5; Leiden: Brill, 1965]

one compares Anat's reply to Baal (*CTA* 3 iv 65–81) with his original message. Anat responds affirmatively to Baal's command to banish warfare and to plant love and peace by repeating his words exactly, except for changing the grammatical form from imperative to the first person imperfect: "*I will* banish war . . . *I will* plant mandrakes. . . ." There is, however, one significant departure in this pattern from Baal's original message. When it comes to the creation of lightning, Anat uses instead the precative: "*Let Baal set* [in the heavens(?)] *his bolt; let* [the cloud-rider(?)] *flash his ray*" (*CTA* 3 iv 69–71).[43] Anat's words confirm our interpretation. She will establish peace and love on earth and, simultaneously, Baal will create lightning to place in the heavens. But why?

Lightning seems to have a function in heaven parallel to Anat's actions on earth. In other words, it functions as a sign. We will thus be justified in comparing it to the function of Nintu's fly-necklace in *Atrahasis*, and in Genesis to God's bow in the Priestly account and to the duration of the earth with its seasons in the Yahwistic account, discussed above under Primeval Pattern A. Accordingly, lightning serves as the sign that reminds both gods and humans that hostility between them has ceased and that a new era of peace has begun. It is an era of cosmic harmony, of rejoicing between tree and stone, of heaven responding to earth, even of Abyss (*thmt*), that age-old enemy of good order, cooperating with the stars in producing universal love and peace. Accordingly, one may be so bold as to suggest that the iconographic representation of Baal wielding a lightning bolt in his hand is more than a portrayal of him as the storm god; it is also a depiction of Baal in his role as the guarantor of the continuation of the cosmos itself.

---

46) and G. R. Driver (*Canaanite Myths and Legends* [Edinburgh: Clark, 1956] 89) translate similarly. See further J. M. Sasson, "Flora, Fauna and Minerals," in *Ras Shamra Parallels I* (AnOr 49; ed. L. R. Fisher; Rome: Biblical Institute Press, 1972) 387–88. The words *abn brq dl td*ꜥ *šmm* are absent from the partially parallel communication of El to Kothar in *CTA* 1 iii 10–16. If this communication concerns the building of a palace for Yamm, then it is likely that the absence of a reference to lightning signifies "a datum about Baal that does not apply to Yamm"; so M. S. Smith, "Baal's Cosmic Secret," *UF* 16 (1984) 297. [Among recent translators of this Ugaritic text, D. Pardee (*COS* 1:86, (p. 252 et passim) and M. S. Smith (in *Ugaritic Narrative Poetry*, 110 et passim) continue to translate as "I understand (the) lightning."]

43. Unfortunately, the text is much damaged at this point, adding to the difficulty of interpretation. The precise meaning of *mdlh* is uncertain, but its general import as some weather phenomenon is determined by *CTA* 5 v 7, where it is listed as one of Baal's characteristic powers, along with clouds, wind, and rain (*qh* ꜥ*rptk rḥk mdlk mṭrtk*). My translation as "(lightning-)bolt" is certainly appropriate. A priori, one would certainly expect lightning to be included in this list since, in addition to the many literary ascriptions of lightning to him, Baal is frequently depicted in iconographic representations with the lightning bolt in his hand. In *CTA* 3 iv 70 *mdl* apparently is synonymous with "lightning" (*brq*), which Baal proposed to create, because of the parallel phrase *ybꜥr* . . . [*q*]*rn* in the following line. That *qrn* can designate a lightning bolt/ray is proved by Hab 3:4, which describes Yahweh marching forth in splendor carrying "bolts/rays" in his hand (*nōgah kāʾôr tihyeh / qarnayim miyyādô lô*). See further van Zijl, *Baal*, 67–69, 352–55; and D. Pardee, "The New Canaanite Myths and Legends," *BO* 37 (1980) 278.

4. The Motif of Planting Peace

As has already been stated, a submotif within Primeval Pattern B is the planting of peace in the earth. This motif deserves an exposition in its own right, since it is preserved in vestigial form in contexts other than the covenant of peace. Indeed, it is these additional passages that confirm that the planting of peace was a known, functioning motif in the ancient Near East.

Ezek 34:25–30 was discussed above (Part 1) as one of the principal witnesses for the covenant of peace. Within that context of the removal of every form of hostility from the land (or earth) and the concomitant advent of paradisiac conditions, there is reference to a planting of peace—although it has not been previously recognized. Ezek 34:29 in the MT reads *wahăqīmōtî lāhem maṭṭā lĕšēm*, i.e., "and I will raise up for them a famous plantation," or the like. This was not the original reading, however, as the versions make clear.[44] The LXX's *phyton eirēnēs* necessitates emending the text to *maṭṭa šālôm* (or a mere metathesis of the *lāmed* and the *šîn*) and translating, "and I will cause a planting of peace to spring up for them." If this interpretation is correct,[45] the planting of peace would appear to be more than just one of the conditions which will characterize the anticipated age; it is almost shorthand for the age itself. Such a suspicion is confirmed by the regularity with which the motif appears in related contexts.

The similarities between Ezek 34:25–30 and Hos 2:18–25 have already been noted. It is not surprising therefore to find in the Hosean passage reference to the motif of planting peace also. The words *ûzĕra'tîhā lî bā'āreṣ*, "and I will sow her for myself in the land [or earth]" (Hos 2:25), have long been an enigma to scholars.[46] Although the pun on the name Jezreel is obvious, the referent of the third person feminine singular pronominal suffix is problematic since the child Jezreel is a boy. In the context of a covenant of peace, one may suggest that what Yahweh will sow are all the eschatological conditions mentioned in the preceding verses of this salvation oracle.[47] In short, Yahweh will sow *šālôm* on the earth. Admittedly,

---

44. See the textual note on this verse in Zimmerli, *Ezekiel 2*, 211.

45. M. Dahood ("Emphatic *lamedh* in Jer 14:21 and Ezek 34:29," *CBQ* 37 [1975] 341–42) claims that the *lāmed* of *lšm* in the MT is emphatic; but his appeal to Ezek 39:25–26 is specious. The latter passage is not really parallel; and this use of *šēm* is well documented from other passages, both in conjunction with the root *qn'* and in the phrase *šēm / qodšî*; see BDB, 1028.

46. Most puzzling is the third feminine suffix of *ûzĕra'tîhā*, which appears to have no antecedent. Ever since Wellhausen, it has been popular to change the vocalization of the suffix to the masculine, so that the suffix refers to Jezreel in the preceding verse. Wolff (*Hosea*, 47, 54) suggested that the protasis of the sentence has been lost in transmission; v. 25a would then refer to the return of the population of Jezreel previously deported by the Assyrian. Closer to the mark is Rudolph's suggestion (*Hosea*, 83) that the sentence refers to the fertility of Israel—a kind of extension of the uninterrupted blessing of nature described in the preceding verses.

47. On the syntax of the third feminine singular pronominal suffix referring to ideas explicated in preceding sentences, see GKC, §122q and §135p.

this is a rather adumbrated reference to the motif of planting peace; but the likelihood of its correctness is increased by similarity of form and content not only with Ezek 34:25–29 but also with Lev 26:3–6.

Leviticus 26 clearly has some affinity to the two prophetic texts just discussed, especially to Ezekiel 34, although the exact nature of the relationship between the texts is controverted.[48] In language very similar to that of Ezekiel, Lev 26:3–6 speaks of nature cooperating to produce abundant harvests and the elimination of hostility between man and beast from the land within a covenant context, albeit this time as blessings for keeping the historical covenant of Sinai. Because of the close similarities in language and content, it behooves us to pay close attention to the phrase *wĕnātattî šālôm bāʾāreṣ* (v. 6). In the past, this has been understood to mean no more than "I will give peace over the land (of Israel)." However, since elsewhere *nātan* is used in the sense of "to plant" or "to sow" (Ezek 17:5), one can translate *nātattî šālôm bāʾāreṣ* equally well as "I will *plant* peace in/on the earth." The reappearance of the planting peace motif here, but with different vocabulary, confirms not only our emended reading of Ezek 34:29 but also our thesis that planting peace is part and parcel of a theme of idyllic conditions on earth resulting from a divine covenant.

Zech 8:12 contains yet another allusion to the motif of planting peace. If conventional scholarly wisdom is correct and Zechariah 9–14 is a secondary addition to the book, then it is likely that Zechariah 8 once formed the original conclusion to this prophetic book. In any case, the first half of the book appears to climax in chap. 8; its position gives chap. 8 great importance in a book concerned with the advent of the eschatological period. Zechariah 8 consists of a series of salvation oracles addressed to the remnant of Judah during the immediate postexilic period. But while the historical setting had to do with the rebuilding of Jerusalem and the temple, the oracles themselves, like so much of this prophetic book, are cast in eschatological and apocalyptic-like language. The sixth of these oracles (vv. 9–13) is patently an encouragement to complete quickly the rebuilding of the Jerusalem temple (vv. 9, 13) as a prelude to the advent of the eschatological age. Most interesting for our thesis is the manner in which the prophet contrasts "the former days," i.e., before the rebuilding had begun, with "the latter days," i.e., the idyllic future age when God will exercise his definitive rule over all the earth:

> For before those days there was no wage for man nor any wage for beast. To him leaving and to him entering there was no peace from the adversary, as I [Yahweh] set every man against his fellow. But I am not to the remnant of this people now as in those former days, oracle of Yahweh of

---

48. See Wolff, *Hosea*, 51; Zimmerli, *Ezekiel 1* (Hermeneia; Philadelphia: Fortress Press, 1979) 50–52; W. Eichrodt, *Ezekiel* (OTL; Philadelphia: Westminster, 1970) 479–84; K. Elliger, *Leviticus* (HAT 4; Tübingen: Mohr [Siebeck], 1966) 364–67. On Leviticus 26, see also D. R. Hillers, *Treaty-Curses and the Old Testament Prophets* (BibOr 16; Rome: Biblical Institute Press, 1964) 40–42.

hosts. *Surely*[49] *I will sow peace.*[50] The vine will give its fruit; and the earth will give its produce and the heavens will give their dew. (Zech 8:10–12)

Prominent here is the presence of several themes posited previously as part and parcel of the covenant of peace. Zechariah announces an end to some sort of hostility on the part of the deity toward man. This divine hostility has resulted in humans being set against their fellows and perhaps even humans against beasts (v. 10). The implication is that this divine hostility has ceased and the heavens and the earth will now cooperate in producing abundance upon the earth. Not to be overlooked is the fact that, in the prophet's mind, the advent of these conditions is somehow linked with the building of the temple, a theme present also in the Baal myth. Given this pattern of conjoined themes, one is justified in examining this oracle more closely as another instance of the motif of planting peace.

The key here is the correct reading of v. 12. Despite valiant attempts to retain the MT's reading, the phrase *kî zeraʿ haššālôm* is patently ungrammatical on context and yields little sense.[51] The LXX *Vorlage* apparently contained a first-person imperfect verbal form instead of a noun as in the MT.[52] Thus, on textual grounds alone, the balance already tilts toward the

---

49. Reading *kî* as emphatic; see Dahood, *Psalms* 1, 301. The meaning is not substantially altered, however, by the more conventional rendering of *kî* as the conjunction "for."

50. Reading *'ezrĕʿâ šālôm* (cf. the LXX: *deixō eirēnēn*) instead of the MT *kî zeraʿ haššālôm*; see *BHS*. This reading has been accepted by, among others, J. Wellhausen, *Skizzen und Vorarbeiten: Fünftes Heft: Die kleinen Propheten übersetzt, mit Noten* (Berlin: Reimer, 1892) 180; W. Nowack, *Die kleinen Propheten* (HKAT III/4; Göttingen: Vandenhoeck & Ruprecht, 1903) 372; and H. G. Mitchell, *A Critical and Exegetical Commentary on Haggai and Zechariah* (ICC; New York: Scribner's, 1912) 211, 214. In addition to the weight of the LXX reading, Wellhausen compares Hos 2:23–25; Mitchell notes the close parallel with Hag 2:9, where Yahweh says, "In this place [Jerusalem] I will put peace" (*'ettēn šālôm*).

51. The impossible reading of the MT is reflected in the variety of English translations: "For the seed shall be prosperous" (*KJV*); "there shall be the seed of peace" (*RV*); "for there shall be a sowing of peace" (*RSV*); "for they shall sow in safety" (*NEB*); "for it is the seed-time of peace" (*NAB*); "the seed will grow well" (*NIV*). Some interpret the phrase to imply prosperous harvests (so T. T. Perowne, *Haggai and Zechariah* [Cambridge Bible for Schools and Colleges; Cambridge: Cambridge University Press, 1886] 104; cf. *KJV*); but this would require at least a reading like *hazzeraʿ šālôm*, as in F. Horst, "Sacherja," *Die zwölf kleinen Propheten* (HAT 14; Tübingen: Mohr [Siebeck], 1954) 242. Ewald, Koehler, and Keil, among others, connect these words with the following context and consider *gepen* as an appositive of *zeraʿ*, approximately "the seed of peace, the vine, shall give its fruit." C. F. Keil (*The Twelve Minor Prophets* [2 vols.; Biblical Commentary on the Old Testament; Grand Rapids: Eerdmans, 1949] 2.316), following Koehler, explains the connection between peace and the vine. ". . . because the vine can only flourish in peaceful times, and not when the land is laid waste by enemies." Klostermann would retain the consonantal text of the MT; but transpose the *hē* from the beginning of the second word to the end of the first: *zarʿāh šālôm* "*h*er [the remnant's] seed shall be peace." For further discussion of the problems in the interpretation of this verse, see Nowack, *Die kleinen Propheten*, 372; F. C. Eiselen, *The Minor Prophets* (Commentary on the Old Testament 9; New York: Eaton & Mains, 1907) 644–45; Mitchell, *Haggai and Zechariah*, 214.

52. See above, n. 50. Nowack (*Die kleinen Propheten*, 372), following Wellhausen, entertains the possibility that the *'ālef* may have fallen out after the *yôd* because of the frequent

reading adopted here, "surely I will sow peace." With the accumulated weight of the pattern of the motif of planting peace, whose characteristic elements are here present, there can be little doubt that Zech 8:12 makes reference to the motif of the deity sowing peace, with all its connotations of the advent of the anticipated idyllic age.

Accordingly, we can now return to *CTA* 3 with renewed confidence in our earlier interpretation of Baal's message to Anat as a command to plant peace on earth. Although the actual vocables for "planting" or "sowing" are not used in this passage, it seems legitimate to understand it as an inchoative form of the motif. Inherent in Baal's command to "pour peace into the heart of the earth" is a patent agricultural image. But at this early stage in the development of the motif, it is not peace per se which is planted but rather mandrakes, the symbols of love. Also, all the essential themes of the later biblical motif are present, from the banishment of hostility from the face of the earth to the cooperation of heaven and earth in producing idyllic conditions described through agricultural images. It will be noted that in the Egyptian text, "Deliverance of Mankind from Destruction," despite other typological and verbal parallels, the mandrakes are not planted but ground up and poured onto the ground. The seminal agricultural image has not yet germinated. But by the time the Ugaritic text was composed, the image had already taken root, and by the time of the biblical prophets had achieved full blossom.

Moving to the opposite chronological end of the biblical period, one finds that the motif of planting peace survives in vestigial form even into the NT.[53] A Q saying of Jesus is preserved in the Gospels of Matthew and Luke in slightly varying forms. In Matt 10:34 Jesus is quoted as saying, "Do not think that I have come *to cast peace on the earth* (*balein eirēnēn epi tēn gēn*); I have not come to cast peace but a sword." The verb *ballō* ("to throw," "to cast") is used of scattering seed on the ground during the planting process in the LXX translation of Ps 125:6, in Mark 4:26 (the parable of the sower), and in Luke 13:19 (the planting of the mustard seed). Jesus' remark would appear to be an allusion to Lev 26:6, only in reverse. Instead of removing the sword and planting peace, Jesus claims his mission is to remove peace and to plant the sword! Jesus' apocalyptic mission to destroy evil necessarily involves turning topsy-turvy the eschatological peace motifs of an earlier tradition.

In Luke 12:51 the form of Jesus' words is, "Do you think that I have come to give (*didōmi*) peace on earth? No, I tell you, but rather division."

---

confusion of these two letters. More likely in my opinion is the possibility that the *ʾālef* was lost in oral transmission through a quiescing; the contiguous vowels *î* and *e* would have elided, resulting in the received MT.

53. Soon after the discovery of the Ugaritic texts, A. Goetze ("Peace on Earth," *BASOR* 93 [1944] 17–20) suggested that the angels' canticle at Jesus' birth, "Glory to God in the highest / and on earth peace / good will toward men" (Luke 2:14), is ultimately to be traced back to the Ugaritic myth about Baal's command to put peace on earth.

In the LXX version of Lev 26:6, Hebrew *nātan* is translated into Greek by the verb *didōmi*. Thus the Lucan form of Jesus' words makes the play on Lev 26:6 even more obvious. (One might note in passing that this variation between "giving" and "casting"/"sowing" confirms our interpretation, given above, of *nātattî šālôm bā'āreṣ* in Lev 26:6 as a reference to the planting of peace.)

The double form of Jesus' saying demonstrates, possibly more clearly than one could have expected, that the motif of planting peace is not simply the figment of an overly imaginative scholar's mind. That Jesus' words could be transmitted in two alternative but independent forms, each drawing upon different yet authentic formulations of the tradition, is proof positive that the ancients knew of the motif—and knew it sufficiently well that they could freely pun on it, even while preserving its essential character.[54]

If the NT preserved only vestiges of the motif, it is because the motif of planting peace was in its old age. Intertestamental literature is witness to the dissolution of the motif through a process of gradual metamorphosis and finally absorption into another agricultural metaphor, the plant of righteousness.

Already in Isaiah there is found a description of the people of Israel under the metaphor of some sprout or tree of righteousness which has been planted by God (Isa 60:21; 61:3, 11). Of course, the metaphor of the people of Israel as a tree or vine which is planted firmly around the mountain of God (e.g., Exod 15:17; 2 Sam 7:10; Isa 5:1–7; Ezek 17:22–24; Amos 9:15; Ps 80:7–13), but which may be uprooted or replanted (e.g., Jer 1:10),[55] is a frequent occurrence in the Bible; this plant metaphor had its own distinctive origins and history of development, unrelated to our motif of planting peace. The metaphor of Israel as the plant of righteousness represents yet a third plant/planting image, in addition to the planting of peace and the planting of Israel in her land. The plant of righteousness metaphor seems to be an internal Isaianic development out of the metaphor begun in Isa 6:13, of "a terebinth or oak whose stump remains standing after it is felled," and from whose stump will sprout a shoot (Isa 11:1, 10) which will form the stock of a new Israel. It is this renewed and restored Israel which "will be called oaks of righteousness, the planting of Yahweh" (Isa 61:3).[56]

---

54. James 3:18 ("the seed from which righteousness grows is sown in peace by those who make peace") may also be relevant here. However, the purport of this saying is uncertain; cf. M. Dibelius, *James* (rev. by H. Greeven; Hermeneia; Philadelphia: Fortress Press, 1976) 214–15.

55. See P. H. Williams, Jr., "Living Toward the Acts of the Savior-Judge: A Study of Eschatology in the Book of Jeremiah," *Austin Seminary Bulletin* 94/4 (1978) 13–39; Robert Bach, "Bauen und Pflanzen," in *Studien zur Theologie der alttestamentlichen Überlieferungen* (ed. Rolf Rendtorff and Klaus Koch; Neukirchen-Vluyn: Neukirchener Verlag, 1961) 7–32.

56. The expression in Jer 32:41, "I will plant you in this land in/with faithfulness (*be'ĕmet*)," is not related to the plant of righteousness but rather to the Jeremian reversal themes of tearing down and building up, uprooting and planting (Jer 1:10), and thus

In intertestamental literature this metaphor of the plant of righteousness achieved a measure of prominence. It became a frequent symbol in that apocalyptic milieu of the righteous elect, the authentic stock of Abraham. In the *Book of Jubilees* it is said that God created Abraham, "for He knew and perceived that from him [Abraham] would arise the plant of righteousness for the eternal generations, and from him a holy seed, so that it should become like Him who made all things" (*Jub.* 16:26; cf. 36:6 and 1:16). This metaphor is even more developed in *1 Enoch*. In "The Apocalypse of Weeks" Abraham appears in the third week as "the plant of righteous judgment," but the eternal plant of righteousness itself will appear only in the seventh week, or the final age of the earth (*1 Enoch* 93:2, 5, 9–10). Here the plant of righteousness is clearly an apocalyptic metaphor for the righteous elect who survive the catastrophic final judgment of the world. Similarly, among the sectarians at Qumran a derivative expression, "the eternal plant" (*mṭʿt ʿwlm*), was used as a term of self-designation (1QS viii 5; xi 8; 1QH vi 15; viii 6; cf. CD i 7).[57]

The planting of peace motif is, however, still preserved partially intact in *1 Enoch* 10:16–11:2. With the discovery of *1 Enoch* fragments among the Dead Sea scrolls, the theory popularized by R. H. Charles, that *1 Enoch* 6–11 is a fragment from an older Noah book, has now been abandoned.[58] Nevertheless, it is still likely that *1 Enoch* 6–11 once may have formed an independent unit of its own.[59] Accordingly, one is justified in considering this larger context in analyzing the presence of the planting of peace motif in 10:16–11:2.

This section of Enoch takes its departure from Genesis 6, especially the scene in vv. 1–4 in which "the sons of God" lusted after and married "the daughters of men." *1 Enoch* interprets this as the fall of certain rebellious angels. These fallen angels then proceed to teach every manner of evil and violence to humankind, thereby setting the stage for the deluge in the days of Noah. This section concludes with God sending one of his faithful angels to reveal to Noah what will happen and sending others to battle against and overcome the fallen angels. To the angel Michael, God gives the command: "Destroy injustice from the face of the earth. And every iniquitous deed will end, and the plant of righteousness will appear, and plant eternal

---

emphasizes God's fidelity to his covenantal word to establish Israel firmly in her own land (cf. Jer 18:7–9; 31:28).

57. On this phrase in each of these texts, see the comments of P. Guilbert, E. Cothenet, and J. Carmignac, respectively, in *Les textes de Qumran traduits et annotés* (ed. J. Carmignac et al.; 2 vols.; Paris: Letouzey et Ané, 1961, 1963) 1.56; 2.150–51; 1.222–23.

58. J. P. Lewis, *A Study of the Interpretation of Noah and the Flood in Jewish and Christian Literature* (Leiden: Brill, 1968) 11; see also E. Isaac, "1 (Ethiopic Apocalypse of) Enoch," *The Old Testament Pseudepigrapha* (ed. J. H. Charlesworth; Garden City: Doubleday, 1983) 1.5, 7.

59. George Nickelsburg, *Jewish Literature between the Bible and the Mishnah* (Philadelphia: Fortress Press, 1981) 49–52.

truth and joy" (10:16).[60] This command is reminiscent of Baal's command (in Pattern B) to remove hostility from the face of the earth. Moreover, the context is one of a rebellion against divine rule which results in a deluge (as in Pattern A). Consequently, it behooves us to examine further this episode in light of the mythic patterns established above.

Previous studies of *1 Enoch* 6–11 by George Nickelsburg and Paul Hanson have emphasized that the revolt against divine authority was instigated by heavenly beings and only secondarily involved humans. Nickelsburg[61] posits two cycles of tradition in these chapters: (1) an older story about rebellious angels led by Šemiḥazah, who, through intercourse with the daughters of men, give birth to certain giants responsible for the wickedness on earth; and (2) a secondary story (interpolated into the first) about the rebel angel ʿAśaʾel (Azazel), who taught men all manner of evil. Nickelsburg claims that only the second implies a human rebellion against divine authority and that this was itself heavily influenced by the Prometheus myth, mediated through Hellenistic culture. In contrast, Hanson[62] would trace the origins of *1 Enoch* 6–11 to second-millennium B.C.E. ancient Near Eastern mythic patterns, in which astral deities plot rebellion against the high god, are defeated, and finally are punished for their crimes. Cosmic disharmony was the result of this "rebellion in heaven" by certain members of the pantheon. Like Nickelsburg, Hanson also concludes that the theme of human rebellion and punishment is a misappropriation or secondary development in this pattern.[63]

Without denying the validity of many of the points made in these two studies, I think that Nickelsburg and Hanson have unfairly downplayed the theme of human rebellion both in *1 Enoch* 6–11 and in the myths on which it is dependent.[64] A primary consideration is the dependency of *1 Enoch*

---

60. One may also translate: ". . . and the plant of righteousness and truth will appear forever and he will plant joy." I have preferred Isaac's alternative translation, principally on the strength of "the plant of righteousness" theme; see below. Other MSS read: "Destroy all injustice from the face of the earth and let every evil work come to an end; and let the plant of righteousness and truth appear: and it shall become a blessing; the works of righteousness and truth shall be planted in truth and joy"; so Isaac, "1 Enoch," 18 n. b2. Michael A. Knibb (*The Ethiopic Book of Enoch* [2 vols.; Oxford: Clarendon Press, 1978] 1.90) translates: "And let the plant of righteousness and truth appear, and the deed will become a blessing; righteousness and truth will they plant in joy forever."

61. George Nickelsburg, "Apocalyptic and Myth in 1 Enoch 6–11," *JBL* 96 (1977) 383–405.

62. Paul Hanson, "Rebellion in Heaven, Azazel, and Euhemeristic Heroes in 1 Enoch 6–11," *JBL* 96 (1977) 195–233.

63. Even Hanson ("Rebellion in Heaven," 211) is forced to admit that in *1 Enoch* 6–11 the punishment of the divine rebels extends to their earthly counterparts.

64. Surprisingly, because of obvious connections through the deluge story, the *Atrahasis* myth plays a relatively insignificant role in Hanson's reconstruction of the rebellion-in-heaven pattern. When he finally does allude to *Atrahasis*, Hanson ("Rebellion in Heaven," 213–15) concentrates principally on the rebellion of the junior gods against the high gods

6–11 on Genesis. Despite the obvious fascination of the author with Gen 6:1–4 (the lusting of "the sons of god" after the daughters of men), the whole deluge story, including the corruption of the earth by humans, patently was a concern of the author. Accordingly, in my opinion it seems difficult to exclude the concept of human rebellion from any redactional stage of *1 Enoch* 6–11.

Moreover, reflexes of the dual mythic pattern noted earlier can be found also in *1 Enoch* 6–11. But it is characteristic of these late reflexes that the two patterns are no longer kept distinct. In common with Pattern A (especially in its principal witness, *Atrahasis*), the deluge follows upon a double rebellion: a first rebellion in heaven led by one deity acting as ringleader is followed by a second rebellion on earth by humans who have "inherited" the spirit of the heavenly rebel.[65] Whether in the *Šemiḥazah* or the *'Aśa'el* version, the spirit of the rebel angel spills over into wicked human conduct.[66] In keeping with Pattern B, a divine agent is dispatched to quell the rebellion on earth. As Anat/Hathor was sent by the ruler deity to destroy the rebels and establish peace on earth, so God directs the angel Michael to do something very similar.

It is not surprising, then, to find vestiges of the planting of peace motif also present. Once the challenge to divine authority is eliminated, the earth "will be filled with the blessing" of bountiful harvest (10:18–19). It would seem, as in the Baal myth and in various biblical covenant-of-peace passages, that such idyllic conditions are to be brought about through the cooperation of the heavens with the earth:

> And in those days I shall open the storerooms of blessing which are in the heavens, so that I shall send them down upon the earth, over the work and the toil of the children of man. And peace and truth shall become partners together in all the days of the world, and in all the generations of the world. (11:1–2)

There is even a reminiscence of the divine covenant/oath never again to attempt an annihilation of humankind: "And it shall not happen again that I shall send (plague and suffering) upon the earth from generation to generation and forever" (10:22). At first blush these words might be taken as an echo of the divine oath in the biblical flood story alone (cf. Gen 8:21 and 9:11, 15), rather than in the larger ancient Near Eastern covenant-of-peace pattern. But given the fact that the deluge itself is reduced to a minor

---

and on the issue of human creation. For the latter, moreover, he relies on an interpretation of the myth which sees it as concerned with the issue of overpopulation rather than with a challenge to divine authority, as discussed above.

65. See above, pp. 180–181.

66. Characteristic of an apocalyptic mentality is the portrayal of evil in the world as at once human and superhuman. Accordingly, the cry of earth to heaven against the perpetrators of violence (*1 Enoch* 8:4–9:11) is a protest not only against the fallen angels but also against the wicked on earth, who follow their lead.

theme in the story in *1 Enoch*, and given the presence of other elements from the larger pattern not in the biblical flood story (e.g., the removal of hostility, the blessing, and the cooperation of the heavens and the earth), it seems necessary to conclude that the writer of this section very likely had some direct acquaintance with the old mythic peace motif.

Nevertheless, the outlines of the planting of peace motif have become blurred. In God's words to Michael there is not a command to plant peace; instead, the plant of righteousness is to appear, and it (he) will plant eternal truth and joy (10:16). The planting theme is still there, but now it has become contaminated with the more common intertestamental "plant of righteousness" metaphor. Here the plant of righteousness seemingly refers to the eschatological elect of Israel. In this respect, the writer of *1 Enoch* has adopted the perspective of the biblical prophets; the time in which all these things happen is projected into the eschatological rather than the primeval age. Peace may no longer be the object planted, but it is still prominent. The effect of planting eternal truth and joy will be that the righteous can spend their days in absolute peace (10:17). Moreover, in this eschatological era, "peace and truth shall become partners together in all the days of the world, and in all generations of the world" (11:2). Undoubtedly, this description of the coming age owes as much to Isa 32:16–18 or Ps 85:10–11 as it does to the planting of peace motif. But that is the point. The motif of planting peace has ceased to be an operative concept.[67] With the blurring of the boundaries between the three planting themes, it was inevitable that the once distinctive motif of planting peace should be lost from sight and disappear from the literature forever.

5. Conclusion

This study has demonstrated the existence of an ancient Near Eastern motif in primeval myth which may appropriately be called the covenant of peace. It occurred in more than one pattern, but had a definite set of characteristics. It is grounded in the idea of an original offense (rebellion) against the creator which led to an attempt to annihilate humankind. However, once divine rule was (re)established, humankind was not only spared, but all of creation also participated in the benefits of the new and more perfect order characterized by peace and harmony between creator and creation. This new order manifested itself in the cooperation of heaven and earth in producing paradisiac conditions. Moreover—and this is the source of the name "the covenant of peace"—the divine wrath was forever put aside because the deity bound himself under oath (= covenant) to establish peace

---

67. Elsewhere in intertestamental literature, the planting/plant metaphor is almost completely unknown. There is considerable contamination both from the plant of righteousness metaphor (*1 Enoch* 84:6; *T. Judah* 24:4–5) and from the general theme of planting Israel in her own land, especially in the Jeremian form of a reversal of Israel's uprooting from her land (*Pss. Sol.* 14:2–3; *Jub.* 1:16; cf. Jer 32:41).

and harmony on earth. This oath was guaranteed by a sign, normally some natural phenomenon visible to deity and humankind alike.

Intimately associated with some expressions of the covenant of peace was a submotif of planting peace in the ground/earth. Understood in terms of ancient Near Eastern symbolism, planting peace was a powerful statement about divine rule and its implications. Set in the context of human rebellion against divine authority, the planting of peace in the earth was a statement of confidence in divine mercy to forgive human offenses and to take the initiative in bringing peace and harmony to a world disrupted by sin and violence. Especially in its biblical expression, the planting of peace is ultimately an expression of hope in divine power to transform this strife-torn world into the paradise for which humans have always longed.

The biblical prophets, operating out of a belief in the continuing wrath of Yahweh against his sinful people, projected the covenant of peace into the future. Perhaps applying the principle that *Endzeit wird Urzeit*, they envisioned a time when truly God and man would be reconciled and the conditions of peace would become a reality on earth. Thus, in prophetic literature the covenant of peace has become an eschatological hope rather than a primeval myth.

Chapter 8

The Malevolent Deity in Mesopotamian Myth

1. Introduction

The issue of "the malevolent deity" (or deities) in Mesopotamian literature is at core the age-old problem of evil: Why is there evil in our world
and what is its ultimate source? There have been numerous previous ex-
plorations of this issue, which I will not attempt to summarize or evaluate
here. Rather, my objective is to provide a basic overview of the concept in
Mesopotamian religion that I have termed "the malevolent deity." By this
I refer to any divinity, commonly understood to be a god, that displayed
hostility towards humans or caused them harm, rather than benevolence–
the latter being the presumptive attitude of the gods toward humankind.

We must be aware that the term malevolent deity is of our coinage,
derived from our philosophical world, and probably does not correspond
to ancient Mesopotamian thought categories. One normally does not find
statements in Mesopotamian literature that characterize a god as evil per
se.[1] Nevertheless, Mesopotamians were acquainted with a belief that individual gods may harbor hostile thoughts against humans and plot evil
actions against them, as in *Atrahasis* when Enlil decides to send a flood to
annihilate the whole human population: "Enlil committed an evil deed
(*šipra lemna*) against humankind" (*Atrahasis* II viii 35). Nergal, too, is described once as a god "who flits evilly around in battles(?)."[2] This theme
took many incarnations, varying both by chronological period and by geographical location. I will attempt to treat more or less systematically some
of the broader characteristics of this theme in Akkadian literature from the

---

Author's note: This chapter was originally presented as a paper for the "Divinity in Israel"
seminar at the annual meeting of the Catholic Biblical Association, August 5–8, 2006, held
at Loyola University Chicago.

    1. But note the isolated entry for "evil god" in a bilingual word list: d i n g i r   k i
š u . t a g . g a . n u . t u k = DINGIR *lem-nu* (Erimhuš I 215); *CAD* L 120.

    2. *ša ina annat lemniš iṣṣanarrara* (*BO* 6 166:11); see *CAD* L 119. Note also the accu-
sation against Nisaba, the wheat goddess: [*an*]*anta tabtanâ tušāḫaza l*[*em*]*uttu* "you have
created conflict and stirred up evil" (W. G. Lambert, *Babylonian Wisdom Literature* [Oxford:
Clarendon Press, 1960] 170:29.

Old Babylonian period on, ending with special attention to Neo-Assyrian and Neo-Babylonian periods, because in these late periods the problem of the malevolent deity takes on added poignancy because the development of a "near monotheistic" religion. The reader should be forewarned, however, that because of the enormity and complexity of the topic, what follows is perforce more of an exploratory essay than a full treatment.

For ease of understanding, I have divided consideration of the topic of the malevolent deity in Mesopotamian myth into three logically separable concepts: (1) proper gods who on occasion act as malevolent deities, but who otherwise may be considered benevolent figures; (2) the chaos monster tradition, which includes Tiamat, Apsu, Anzu, and other figures who threaten the very possibility of creation or ordered existence; and (3) the special problems associated with the inscrutable will of Marduk (or alternatively, Ashur), who in late, Neo-Babylonian (alternatively, Neo-Assyrian) thought was conceived in near monotheistic terms and could be considered responsible, therefore, for both good and evil. I will sidestep completely the category of demons, monsters, and ghosts, who were also considered a ubiquitous source of evil or misfortune in life.[3] But since these were not "gods," they will not be discussed in this paper.

2. Gods Proper Who on Occasion Act as Malevolent Deities

A common theme in Mesopotamian religious texts from earliest times is the capriciousness of the gods, whose actions mostly were assumed to be beneficial for humankind but who on occasion could turn against humans with little or no provocation. For most of its known history Mesopotamian religion followed for the most part the religious system worked out at least by the third millennium B.C.E. by the dominant Sumerians. Presumably because the Sumerians developed a political system of interdependent city-states, each with a local ruler, rather than a single political state or empire dominated by a monarch, the Sumerians imagined that the gods likewise were organized into a society of high gods and lesser gods distributed across the supernal and the infernal realms, as well as on earth. The high gods formed an assembly (*puḫru*) wherein decisions were reached collectively, under the leadership of the three (sometimes, four) highest ranking gods.

---

3. For synthetic treatments of demons, ghosts, and similar sinister figures, see J. Bottéro, *Religion in Ancient Mesopotamia* (Chicago: University of Chicago Press, 2001) 63–64, 109–10, 186–87, 192–94; Anthony Green, "Ancient Mesopotamian Religious Iconography," *CANE* 3.1847–49; F. A. M. Wiggermann, "Theologies, Priests, and Worship in Ancient Mesopotamia," *CANE* 3.1865–66; JoAnn Scurlock, "Death and the Afterlife in Ancient Mesopotamian Thought," *CANE* 3.1889–92; Walter Farber, "Witchcraft, Magic, and Divination in Ancient Mesopotamia," *CANE* 3.1896–98. Benjamin R. Foster (*Before the Muses: An Anthology of Akkadian Literature* [2 vols.; Bethesda, MD: CDL, 1993], 1.34–35) calls attention to texts in his collection concerning the warding off of demonic beings; he also cites several prior studies.

This triad consisted of the male gods Anu, Enlil, and Enki (known by the Akkadians as Ea); at times the female deity Inanna (Akkadian Ishtar) joined this august trio to form a supreme tetrad. Anu, the sky god, was (in some traditions) the father of Enlil, Enki, and Inanna. Originally Anu, whose sanctuary was at Uruk, was considered the chief deity, the head of the Sumerian pantheon. Increasingly, however, Anu came to be regarded as a kind of *deus otiosus* and was replaced by Enlil ("lord of the Earth") as the effective ruling god. Enlil's principal sanctuary was at Nippur. Enki-Ea, the wisest of the gods, always seemed to lag behind Enlil as far as authority was concerned, but nonetheless bested Enlil in the wisdom department. It was Enki-Ea who invariably came up with clever solutions to nearly every problem. Enki-Ea's cultic center was Eridu. Inanna-Ishtar, venerated as the goddess of war, sex, and fertility, had a more complex tradition. Inanna's cult center was originally in Uruk, where she was considered to be the daughter of Anu; but as her popularity under the name Ishtar spread, so did her cultic centers in other parts of Mesopotamia multiply, notably at Nineveh and Arbela. At one time or other, each of these gods in the supreme tetrad was guilty of action(s) against humans that justify consideration as a "malevolent deity."

A. *The Myth of* Atrahasis[4]

In *Atrahasis*, the so-called Babylonian Flood Story (composed during the Old Babylonian period), the most obvious candidate for a malevolent deity is Enlil. Although Anu is afforded the title "king" (*šarru*) in this myth (I 7), it is "Enlil, the counselor of the gods, the warrior" (*ᵈEnlil mālik ilī qurādu*, I 45) who throughout wields the principal power. When the lesser gods revolt against the heavy work that they are compelled to perform for the high gods, Enlil is at a loss about what to do. Wise Enki, however, devises a solution: kill the ringleader of the rebel gods, one Aw-ilu,[5] and from his blood mixed with clay create humankind to serve as substitute workers for the striking gods. At this stage the humans are not truly human, however, as no provision has been made for their natural death. Instead, they are

---

4. For the text, see W. G. Lambert and A. R. Millard, *Atra-ḫasīs: The Babylonian Story of the Flood* (Oxford: Oxford University Press, 1969; reprinted Winona Lake, IN: Eisenbrauns, 1999). For my interpretation of this myth and its relation to the Yahwistic primeval story in Genesis, see B. Batto, *Slaying the Dragon: Mythmaking in the Biblical Tradition* (Louisville: Westminster John Knox Press, 1992) 27–33, 41–72.

5. The name of this rebel deity is listed only once and its actual reading is uncertain; alternatively the name has been read as We-ilâ or We-ilu. Whatever the actual reading, there likely is a pun involved linking the Akkadian word for "human(kind)," *awīlu*, with the name of the rebel god Aw-ilu who furnishes the divine component in humankind; see K. Oberhuber, "Ein Versuch zum Verständnis von Atra-Hasīs I 223 und I 1," in *Zikir Šumim: Assyriological Studies Presented to F. R. Kraus on the Occasion of His Seventieth Birthday*, ed. G. Van Driel et al. (Leiden: Brill, 1982) 280; J. Bottéro, *Religion in Ancient Mesopotamia*, 100. This position is also adopted, in a modified form, by Jean-Jacques Glassner, "The Use of Knowledge in Ancient Mesopotamia," *CANE* 3.1820.

lullû, primeval humans, like Enkidu in his original, awesome condition. Full of vitality, the *lullû*-population quickly multiplies. Their "noise" (*rigmu* "cries" // *ḫubūru* "din") keep Enlil awake. Enlil attempts several times to diminish the human noise, by famine and disease. Each time his efforts are thwarted by Enki, who naturally does not want to see his handiwork destroyed. In desperation Enlil foolishly decides to annihilate the whole *lullû*-population. He persuades the council of gods to agree upon a flood to wipe the land clean.[6] Enlil's plan would have succeeded, had not crafty Enki managed to save one man, pious Atrahasis, and his family, from whom the world is repopulated. The disastrous consequences of the flood for the gods themselves soon become obvious to all the gods except Enlil. Eventually Enlil relents as well, but only on the condition that postdiluvian humankind be naturally mortal. Death is decreed for them, henceforth making them truly human (*awīlu*). Under these new conditions humankind is guaranteed a plan within the scheme of creation.

Enlil's actions deserve closer scrutiny. Granted that the myth makes it patent that the decision to send the flood was a mistake, was there any legitimate basis for Enlil's decision, or was his a purely capricious act? In Genesis the flood was necessitated by human wickedness. In *Atrahasis* the stated reason for the flood was human noise that prevented Enlil from sleeping. Moran's proposal that this myth is about the issue of overpopulation in the Mesopotamian plain has gained wide acceptance.[7] But there seems to be more at issue than mere demographics. Elsewhere I have argued that the sleep of the chief deity was a metaphor of divine sovereignty and that the noise which prevents such sleep is tantamount to rebellion against the sovereignty of the deity.[8] Before the idea of humans was even conceived, Aw-ilu and the other Igigi gods gathered in open rebellion before Enlil's palace to burn their work implements, the symbols of their oppression. On this occasion, too, it is said that the "noise" of these rebel gods—i.e., their *rigmu* "cries" // *ḫubūru* "din," the exact same language used later of the *lullû-awīlu* population—likewise prevented Enlil from sleeping. Patently, there is more involved than the mere inconvenience of too many humans. Whether there is a moral element ("sin") present or not, the

---

6. In the late (eight century B.C.E.?) text *Erra and Ishum* (for which see below), Marduk is credited with having sent the flood. This late text bears no independent mythic witness, reflecting instead the Neo-Babylonian "near-monotheistic" tendency to ascribe all divine powers to the national god Marduk. Significant, however, is the fact that *Erra and Ishum* maintains the mytheme that the chief deity in his anger acted rashly and unjustifiably, with disastrous cosmic consequences.

7. W. L. Moran, "Atrahasis: The Babylonian Story of the Flood," *Bib* 52 (1971) 51–61; reprinted in W. L. Moran, *The Most Magic Word: Essays on Babylonian and Biblical Literature* (ed. Ronald S. Hendel; CBQMS 35; Washington, DC: Catholic Biblical Association, 2002) 33–45.

8. B. Batto, "The Sleeping God: An Ancient Near Eastern Motif of Divine Sovereignty," *Bib* 68 (1987) 153–77; reprinted in this volume as chap. 5.

humans, like the rebel good Aw-ilu, whose divine blood coursed through their veins, seem to reject their divinely decreed role as servants of the gods. Enlil's actions, first of attempting to diminish the number of humans and then attempting to annihilate them completely, thus would appear to be partially justified due to humankind's rejection of its very raison d'être.

Nevertheless, there is also an element of divine capriciousness involved, as the attempt to wipe out the *lullû-awīlu* population is shown to be excessive and unwise. Too late the gods realized they needed the humans to "feed" them. The mother goddess Belit-ili, or Nintu, a form of Inanna-Ishtar, who earlier had aided Enki in the "manufacture" of humankind, speaks not just for herself in railing against Anu's and Enlil's audacity now, after having previously decreed the humans' destruction, at showing up at the conclusion of the flood for the feast, the flood hero's sacrifice:

> "Whatever came over Anu, the instigator of the plan?
> "Has Enlil come for the aromatic offering?
> "They who irrationally brought about the flood
> "And consigned the peoples to catastrophe?"
>   (III v 39–43)[9]

Submission, not annihilation, of humankind was required, and *Atrahasis* celebrates the triumph of Enki's moderating wisdom over Enlil's tyrannical rule.[10] Enlil's conduct, the Old Babylonian poet implies, was morally reprehensible: *šipra lemna ana nišī ipuš* ^d*Enlil* "Enlil committed an evil deed against humankind" (II viii 35).[11] To the extent that Enlil's actions were morally reprehensible, to that extent Enlil must be seen in the role of a malevolent deity.[12]

But while primary responsibility for the catastrophe lay with Enlil, all the gods to a greater or lesser extent were culpable in that they were

---

9. A few moments earlier Nintu had lashed out against Anu alone in nearly identical language (III iii 51–54).

10. At the conclusion of the flood, with all of humankind wiped out, save the solitary flood hero and his family, Enki belatedly accuses Enlil of indiscriminate destruction: "[On the guilty] impose your penalty" (III vi 25). B. Foster (*Before the Muses*, 2.182), however, reads this line as Enki's self-justification before Enlil for having aided the flood hero to escape destruction: "Impose your penalty [on a wrong-doer]." Foster suggests that "the thrust of [Enki's] argument may be that he had sworn not to tell mankind of the flood, but did not swear to annihilate life."

11. The translation of *CAD* L 123, "Enlil has wrought a fateful deed for mankind," misses the author's intended moral condemnation of the deity.

12. This is not the first time Enlil's "morals" have been called into question. In the Sumerian myth *Enlil and Ninlil*, Enlil violated the young virgin Ninlil, for which offense the divine council condemned him as a sex offender and banished him from the city. See Thorkild Jacobsen, *The Harps That Once . . . : Sumerian Poetry in Translation* (New Haven: Yale University Press, 1987) 167–80. See also J. Bottéro, *Religion in Ancient Mesopotamia*, 66–67.

complicit in the decision to send the flood: "All we great Anunnaki-gods resolved together on an oath" (III vi 7–8), they ruefully acknowledge after the
fact. Anu, in particular, is singled out for dereliction of duty. In addition to
Nintu's aforementioned blast, moments earlier she had already excoriated
Anu, father of the gods, in nearly identical language. In fact, Nintu apparently blames Anu more that Enlil for actually having conceived the idea
for a flood, as twice she names Anu as "instigator of the plan (*bēl ṭēmi*):[13]

> "Whatever came over Anu, the instigator of the plan
> "Whose sons, the gods, heeded his command?
> "He who irrationally brought about the flood
> "And consigned the peoples to ca[tastrophe]?"
>   (III iii 51–54)

But even Nintu, the mother goddess who helped Enki "birth" humankind,
was not exempt from blame. In her postdiluvian lament she castigates herself as well:

> "In the assembly of the gods,
> "How did I agree with them on annihilation?
> "Was Enlil so strong that he forced [me] to speak?
> "Like that Tiruru, did he make [my] speech confused?
> "Of my own accord, from myself alone,
> "To my own charge have I heard (my people's) clamor!
> "My offspring—with no help from me—have become like flies.
> "And as for me, how to dwell in (this) abode of grief, my clamor fallen
> silent?
>   (III iii 36–47)

In short, according to *Atrahasis*, the flood was one huge divine debacle. If
ever there was cause to question the wisdom and the justice of the gods in
the governance of the world, this was it. The gods did eventually resolve
the whole human question satisfactorily. But *Atrahasis*—from beginning to
end—serves as a reminder that the gods, like humans, are capable of mis-
takes, and even of wanton miscarriage of justice at times.

---

13. The import of the phrase *bēl ṭēmi* is missed by most translators, who render it variously: "the president" (Lambert and Millard, *Atra-ḫasīs*, 97, 99), "the chief decision-maker"
(Foster, *Before the Muses*, 1.180, 181). Earlier in *Atrahasis* the god Aw-ilu was killed and
from his blood mixed with clay humankind was formed. Aw-ilu was selected precisely because he was the ringleader of the rebellious Igigi-gods; he was the one "who had the plan"
ša išû ṭēma (I 223) and later is slaughtered "together with his plan" *qādu ṭēmīšu* (I 239); so,
correctly, W. L. Moran, "The Creation of Man in Atrahasis I 192–248," *BASOR* 200 (1970)
48–56; reprinted in Moran, *Most Magic Word*, 75–86. Since the author has already used
ṭēmu in the sense of "scheme" or "plot," it is difficult to believe that the phrase "owner of
the scheme" is not the intended meaning here also.

B. *Ishtar in* Gilgamesh[14]

The myth *Gilgamesh* was composed in Akkadian during the Old Baby-lonian period, though it incorporates stories from an older Sumerian cycle of legends about this semi-divine king of Uruk and his friend Enkidu. But our interest is less with Gilgamesh and Enkidu than with the manner in which the gods are portrayed in this epic.

In the flood story, Ishtar, the goddess of fertility, sex, and warfare (a form of Belit-ili/Nintu), fares perhaps better than the two chief male gods of the supreme divine tetrad. But in the myth of *Gilgamesh*, Tablet VI, it is Ishtar herself who comes across as the most capricious of the gods. After Gilgamesh and his inseparable friend Enkidu performed the Herculean task of killing the monster Humbaba, the pair returned to Uruk, bathed, put on their finest garments, and celebrated their superhuman feat before the admiring folk of Uruk. The pair must have appeared impressive indeed, catching even the eye of Ishtar, who was no novice when it came to choosing desirable lovers. Overcome with desire for Gilgamesh, Ishtar proposed instant marriage. Gilgamesh, no newcomer to amorous adventures himself, quickly assessed the risks of a liaison with the goddess of love and sex and summarily rejected her proposal. In declining, Gilgamesh recalled for Ishtar the long list of her previous marriages and affairs, ticking off the sordid manner in which she had treated each of her previous lovers or husbands. No, Gilgamesh would have nothing to do with such a fickle and volatile lover.

Unaccustomed to having her advances so thoroughly spurned, Ishtar in a rage flew to the throne of Anu her father and Antu her mother in heaven, demanding that she be given the Bull of Heaven to punish insolent Gilgamesh for his "tale of foulest slander." Anu was unwilling to hand over to Ishtar the Bull of Heaven, for as he reminded her, there was truth in Gilgamesh's "slanders" and "insults." Ishtar was not to be denied. When Ishtar threatened to smash the gates of the Netherworld and wreak havoc on earth, making "the dead to consume the living," Anu capitulated. Her victory was ephemeral, however. When Ishtar unleashed the Bull of Heaven upon Uruk, Gilgamesh and Enkidu easily discovered its vulnerable spot and slew it. Adding insult to injury, Enkidu wrenched a haunch off the Bull and hurled it in Ishtar's face. While Ishtar sulked, the two friends celebrated their triumph amid cries of approval from the streets of Uruk:

"Who is the finest among men?
Who is the most glorious of fellows?"

---

14. For a recent study and translation of *Gilgamesh*, see Andrew George, *The Epic of Gilgamesh: The Babylonian Epic Poem and Other Texts in Akkadian and Sumerian* (New York: Penguin, 1999).

"Gilgamesh is the finest among men!
[Gilgamesh the most] glorious of fellows!"
     (Standard Version VI 172–75)[15]

Thoroughly humiliated, Ishtar appeared before the divine council and, it would appear, demanded something be done about the hubris of the two upstarts, for in a dream Enkidu learns of his doom. In his dream Enkidu saw Anu, Enlil, Ea, and Shamash deliberating in council. Anu calls for the death of one of the two "because they slew the Bull of Heaven, and slew Humbaba that [guarded] the mountains dense-[wooded] with cedar." Enlil recommends that only Enkidu should die. At this, the sun-god Shamash reprimands Enlil, "Was it not at your word that they slew him, the Bull of Heaven—and also Humbaba? Now shall the innocent Enkidu die?" Enlil prevailed in the end, and Enkidu does die, setting his grieving friend Gilgamesh off on his famously futile search for immortality.

As was the case in *Atrahasis*, so also here in *Gilgamesh* the philosopher-poet has identified a grave problem in Mesopotamian religious tradition, namely, the apparent arbitrary nature of divine demands upon humans. The author uses celestial Shamash, traditionally the universal watchdog of justice, to voice this concern. Yes, Gilgamesh and Enkidu can be charged with a certain amount of hubris, but the gods have overreacted in decreeing death for "innocent" Enkidu at the insistence of Ishtar. If anyone is guilty in this whole sorry affair, it is Ishtar, whose unbridled lust and rage caused the death of an innocent person. Moreover, Anu and Enlil are complicit in this miscarriage of justice.

C. *The Myth of* Adapa[16]

The oldest extant—and most complete—copy of the Akkadian myth of *Adapa* comes from the fourteenth-century B.C.E. El-Amarna archive in Egypt. Later, less complete copies were found in the seventh-century B.C.E. Ashurbanipal library at Nineveh.[17] It has been suggested that the Akkadian tale of *Adapa* may derive from an older Sumerian prototype, but the basis for this claim is a recently published tiny Sumerian fragment in the British Museum that makes mention of the South Wind—hardly compelling evidence. At this point it seems best to assume that we are dealing with a composition dating to the Middle Babylonian period.

---

15. Trans. A. George, *Epic of Gilgamesh*, 54.

16. The most recent study of this myth, complete with a new edition of all known fragments, is Shlomo Izre'el, *Adapa and the South Wind: Language Has the Power of Life and Death* (Winona Lake, IN: Eisenbrauns, 2001); unless otherwise noted, all references to Adapa and translations of this myth are taken from this edition.

17. Henrietta McCall (*Mesopotamian Myths: The Legendary Past* [Austin, TX: University of Texas Press, 1990], 19) posits a fifteenth-century B.C.E. date for the composition of the Amarna recension of Adapa. A fourteenth-century date seems more probable, however; see S. Izre'el, *Adapa and the South Wind*, 47.

The interpretation of the *Adapa* myth is more difficult, in large measure because the ending has not been preserved. Once again, however, we are confronted with divine-human interaction that ends with the human getting "shafted." The story of "Adapa, the ancestor of humankind,"[18] seems to be a tale about the original "human" and how he lost the chance for immortality for all humankind. Adapa is thus the equivalent of Atrahasis in Mesopotamian tradition and of Adam in biblical tradition.[19]

Like Atrahasis, Adapa is a wise and pious devotee of Ea, and regularly performs the cult of this god in Eridu. But one day, when Adapa is fishing at sea, the south wind capsizes Adapa's boat. In desperation, Adapa curses the south wind, breaking its "wing," so that it could not blow. As the south wind is essential to the fertility of the southern Mesopotamian basin, the crops fail. Upon learning that Adapa is the culprit, Anu as head of the gods summons Adapa to account for his actions. Now Ea had prepared Adapa for his appearance before Anu, advising that Anu would offer Adapa food and drink, but that Adapa should refuse because these would be the "food of death" and the "water of death." Accordingly, when the chief god offered Adapa the "food of life" and the "water of life" and Adapa politely declined, Anu "laughed at him" for having missed the opportunity for immortality. At this point the main text (Amarna, Fragment B) breaks off, and we are left to speculate how the ancients understood this myth.

A number of questions arise. Was Ea correct in advising that Anu intended to offer Adapa "food of death" and "water of death"? Had Anu already prejudged Adapa as guilty but then changed his mind, perhaps at the encouragement of Anu's helper gods, Dumuzi and Gizzida, who were duly impressed with Adapa's contrite demeanor when they opened the gates of heaven to admit him? Or had Ea foreseen that Anu would offer Adapa (and thus all humankind) the "bread of life" and the "water of life," and so lied to Adapa on the assumption that immortality should be reserved to the gods alone and therefore was inappropriate for humankind?

It is difficult to think that an ancient Mesopotamian poet would imagine that wise Ea, always the first to assess correctly any situation, could have been so far off the mark in this instance. Add to this the fact that Ea was the creator of humankind and its chief patron—recall how in the flood story he stood up for humankind against the other gods—and one is almost compelled to conclude that Ea deliberately deceived Adapa, and with

---

18. *Adapa zēr amēlūti.* S. Izre'el (*Adapa and the South Wind*, 39) translates as "Adapa, a seed of humankind," which misses the point that Adapa is the source of humankind, not merely one human among others. It is true that *zēru* 'seed,' when used of humans, normally refers to "male descendant(s)" (*CAD* Z 89–97), but Adapa is a special case. The context in *Adapa*, Fragment D, where this phrase occurs, is an incantation; the apotropaic power of the incantation derives from the fact that Adapa stands at the head of the human line, and thus represents its progenitor or ancestor.

19. For more on the interpretation of Adapa as the original human, see B. Batto, *Slaying the Dragon*, 25–26 and 58.

him, all humankind. It appears that Ea was willing to grant humankind wisdom—itself a divine prerogative—but not immortality. In the words of one fragmentary text from Nineveh: *ana šuātu nēmeqa iddiššu napišta darīta ul iddiššu* "To him he gave wisdom, he did not give him eternal life" (Fragment A.4´).[20] To allow humankind immortality in addition to wisdom would erase all boundaries between the gods and humankind. In my view, then, *Adapa* is principally a myth about the proper limits of humankind, limits imposed by the very divine power that brought humankind into existence in the first place.

Even so, one cannot escape a nagging question that seemingly loomed large for the ancients: Did humankind *lose* immortality through some fault on its part, or was immortality *denied* to humankind through some kind of shenanigan (deceitfulness) on the part of the gods? One has to entertain the possibility that the poet in this instance was suggesting that the god(s) withheld mortality from humankind, for a reason not transparent to humans. Indeed, since devout Adapa dutifully followed his divine patron's instructions throughout, there may be more than a hint here that humans have been *cheated* out of immortality through no apparent fault of their own.

D. *The Myth of* Erra and Ishum[21]

The Akkadian poem *Erra and Ishum*, probably composed in Babylonia sometime during the eighth century B.C.E.,[22] is unusual for Mesopotamian literature in a number of ways, not the least of which is that the poet tells us his name, Kabri-ilani-Marduk. This author dares to try out new literary techniques and to explore challenging theological issues in novel ways. Indeed, one might think that the author was almost cognizant of and attempting to probe the very issue we are concerned with: the malevolent deity.

The poet gives lip service to the divine sovereignty of Marduk but then proceeds to undermine this motif. According to ancient Near Eastern convention, one of the chief functions of the divine sovereign is to keep the cosmos in order by overcoming chaos in all its manifestations, both primeval (e.g., the chaos dragon) and historical (e.g., warding off external threats to the state in the form of barbarian invaders, and suppression of internal threats to the realm in the form of evildoers).[23] The Babylonian Creation

---

20. S. Izre'el, *Adapa and the South Wind*, 9–10.

21. For a recent translation, see Foster, *Before the Muses*, 2.771–805, together with the literature cited therein.

22. Although the date of *Erra and Ishum* earlier was much controverted, recent scholars have adopted the revised position of W. von Soden (*UF* 3 [1971]: 255–56) in dating this poem to the period of 765–763 B.C.E. on the basis of precise historical, archaeological, and astronomical arguments.

23. I have explored the motif of the divine sovereign in several of my publications, most recently in my article "The Divine Sovereign: The Image of God in the Priestly Creation Account," in *David and Zion: Biblical Studies in Honor of J. J. M. Roberts* (ed. Bernard

Epic, *Enuma Elish* explicitly celebrated Marduk in this role. By contrast, *Erra and Ishum* is an exploration of a world in which Marduk seemingly has vacated his post, leaving the world to utter chaos.

The god Erra was associated with war, hunting, violence, and destruction; over time Erra was assimilated to Nergal, king of the netherworld, and therefore was also held responsible for plague and scorched earth. Erra is not an evil deity, however; he is usually placed among the Igigi- (alternatively, the Anunnaki-) gods who help the first-ranked gods in the governance of the world. In the prologue to Hammurapi's Law Code, for example, Hammurapi lists Erra as one of his divine patrons (ii 70). In *Erra and Ishum* "Nergal" on occasion alternates with "Erra" as the name of this god, but one sees here an intention to denigrate the character or status of Erra as a proper god.

In the narrative world of this poem, Erra feels slighted that his powers are not more widely celebrated. Erra then attempts to persuade Marduk to turn over the governance of the world to him, saying that Marduk needed to direct his attention to refurbishing his cult statue, now tarnished through age and neglect. Marduk senses that matters would not go well and resists, recalling,

> "Once long ago indeed I grew angry,
>   indeed I left my dwelling, and caused the deluge!
> When I left my dwelling,
>   the regulation of heaven and earth disintegrated:
> The shaking of heaven meant:
>   the positions of the heavenly bodies changed,
>   nor did I restore them.
> The quaking of netherworld meant:
>   the yield of the furrow diminished,
>   being thereafter difficult to exploit.
> The regulation of heaven and earth disintegrating meant:
>   underground water diminished, high water receded.
>   When I looked again, it was a struggle to get enough.
> Productivity of living offspring declined, nor did I renew it.
> Such that, were I a plowman,
>   I (could) hold (all) seed in my hand."
>   (I 131–138; trans. Foster, *Before the Muses*, 2.778–79).

This late text is unique in attributing responsibility for the flood to Marduk,[24] and it seems to reflect the Neo-Babylonian "near-monotheistic" tendency to consolidate all power in the national deity. (More on this in

---

F. Batto and Kathryn L. Roberts; Winona Lake, IN: Eisenbrauns, 2004) 143–86 (reprinted in this volume as chap. 4); see also "The Sleeping God: An Ancient Near Eastern Motif of Divine Sovereignty," *Bib* 58 (1987) 153–77 (reprinted in this volume as chap. 5).

24. Hymnic language such as "O warrior Marduk, whose anger is the deluge" (Foster, *Before the Muses*, 2.591) and "[Marduk's] rage [is] the deluge" (*Ludlul Bel Nemeqi* I 7; Foster, 1.310) is metaphorical and should not be interpreted as saying that Marduk decreed the flood.

Part 4, below.) In any case, Marduk vows never to repeat that calamitous mistake. But, unwittingly, he does. With further cajolement by Erra, who promised to maintain the very order Marduk himself established, Marduk turns over the governance of the world to Erra and retires to an isolated workshop.

Scarcely has Marduk left the scene, however, before Erra begins turning everything topsy-turvy. Erra's lieutenant, the god Ishum, attempts to dissuade and prevent Erra, but is reprimanded by Erra:

> "Keep quiet, Ishum, listen to what I say.
> "As concerns the people of the inhabited world,
>   whom you would spare . . .
> "I am the wild bull in heaven, I am the lion on earth,
> "I am the king in the land, I am the fiercest among the gods . . .
> "I am the smiter of wild beasts,
>   battering ram against the mountain,
> "I am the blaze in the reed thicket,
>   the broad blade against the rushes,
> "I am the banner for the march,
> "I blast like the wind, I thunder like the storm."
>   (I 106–115; trans. Foster, *Before the Muses*, 2.776–77)

In short, Erra says, it is his nature to be violent and destructive. He cannot do otherwise.

Still later, in a long monologue, Erra boasts of the havoc he wreaks both in heaven and on earth: The sun and the moon lose their light. Storm and drought scourge the land. Cities lie in waste, while the sea convulses. Beast and human alike perish. Father, son, mother, daughter all turn on one another. Demons haunt the cult centers. Neighbor loots neighbor. Shepherds desert their flocks. The Sutaean barbarians roam freely throughout Babylonia. And more still.

All of this, of course, is a miscarriage of justice. Ishum tries once more to convince Erra to stay his hand:

> "Why have you plotted evil against god and man?
> "And why have you remorselessly plotted evil
>   against the black-headed folk [the Mesopotamians]?"
>   (I 102–103 & Fragment C 36–37; trans. Foster, *Before the Muses*,
>   2.791)

Ishum eventually assuages Erra's inferiority complex by pointing out that both humankind and the gods are duly impressed by his power—or more precisely, they are terrified of him. Satisfied, Erra agrees to return governance of heaven and earth back to Marduk, but not before havoc has been wreaked on the world. Ishum's role in the restoration of order is celebrated in this poem. The author claims, moreover, that he has received divine confirmation in a dream that he has written well of these matters, with the implication that the recitation of his poem has apotropaic value for warding off future catastrophes in the land.

It would appear that one of the purposes of the author is to explore the question of evil. Why is there evil in the world? The answer, surprisingly, is not one of the usual stock answers: vestigial influence of the (primeval) chaos dragon, human malfeasance that angers the deity,[25] the presence of demons who inflict pain and suffering on unwitting humankind, or the like. Rather our author dares to propose a more radical answer: abuse of divine power. First and foremost, of course, Erra-Nergal, whose function is to regulate the potentially harmful elements like plague, drought, and the ghosts of the dead, clearly went too far in this instance. He is divine power out of control. But how is that possible, given Erra-Nergal himself was supposed to be under the control of the divine sovereign and the council of gods? The divine sovereign has clearly suffered a major mental lapse in abdicating his primary function. Also, the other gods of the divine council have cowardly refused to challenge one of their own who abused his divine privilege. So the real problem is with the gods themselves. In some sense, all the gods could be considered malevolent in bad times like this, when "the world has gone to pot." Fortunately, the second-ranked Ishum refused to be cowed, and by his persistence he saved the day—rescuing at least partially the belief that there is a (capable) god in heaven.

E. Countering the Capriciousness of the Gods

As has been seen, a theme of capriciousness of the gods clearly runs through Mesopotamian literature. Nearly every major deity is implicated at one time or other. But there is another, countertheme present as well, namely, that the gods are themselves just and watch to see that justice prevails on earth. The high gods were thought to uphold justice by rewarding the righteous and punishing wrongdoers.

Shamash, in particular, was regularly invoked as the overseer of justice. As the sun god, Shamash traverses daily the whole earth, illuminating even its darkest corners. No act escapes the watchful eye of this god, so he is in a unique position to scrutinize the actions of humankind and ensure that justice is done, even for the lowliest of society.[26] Hammurapi in the

---

25. Early in the poem, when the Sibitti-demons are trying to incite Erra to raise havoc in heaven and on earth, they cite the stock motif about the noise of humankind that the gods, including Erra himself (I 41) along with all the Anunnaki-gods (I 81–83), found offensive. The Sibitti here are troublemakers, however, and their charge in this case is completely unwarranted. Moving beyond this poem, one encounters frequently an assumption that humans bring divine wrath upon themselves by their sins, even unwitting sins. This assumption has resulted in numerous "confessions" of unknown sins, such as in a prayer to Marduk: "O great lord Marduk, merciful lord! Men, by whatever name, what can they understand of their own sin? Who has not been negligent, which one has committed no sin?" (Foster, *Before the Muses*, 2.591). See below, about the "Sun Disk" tablet of Nabu-apla-iddina, for similar sentiments applied to Shamash.

26. See, for example, "The Shamash Hymn," in Foster, *Before the Muses*, 2.536–44.

epilogue to his famous law code professes to carry on this divine mandate, whereby "the strong might not oppress the weak, and that justice might be dealt the orphan (and) the widow" (Epilogue, xlvii 59–61). Shamash, "the great judge of heaven and earth," is invoked multiple times to make "justice prevail in the land" (xlvii 85–89, et passim).

The so-called boundary stone, or "Sun Disk" tablet, of Nabu-apla-iddina[27]—whether an ancient fraud as some think, or not—is witness to the belief that Shamash vigorously enforced justice, even to the extent that he abandoned his own temple over infraction done there: "Shamash, the great lord, who, for many days, had been angry with the land of Akkade and had wrathfully shown his neck, in the term of Nabu-apla-iddina, king of Babylon, became placated, and turned towards (him) his face."[28] The inscription records the privileges supposedly granted by King Nabu-apla-iddina to the priest responsible for restoring (the image of) Shamash to his rightful place.

In the myth *Etana*, the snake invokes Shamash to right an injustice done by the eagle. Previously the snake and the eagle had coexisted peacefully at a certain tree; they had sworn not to harm each other or the other's young. So the eagle made a nest in the upper branches of the tree, without fear that the snake would snatch its eggs or emerging eaglets while the eagle was away. Likewise, the snake dwelt at the base of the tree, secure in the knowledge that its offspring were safe. But one day the eagle broke the pact and devoured the snake's young while the snake was away. Although the myth is much more involved, for our purposes it is enough to note that, when the snake discovered the treachery, it was to Shamash that the snake turned to obtain justice against the perfidious eagle.

Similarly, the whole of the *Tukulti-Ninurta Epic* depends upon an assumption that the gods enforce justice and defend the righteous against the unrighteous. This Middle Assyrian text, composed very close to, if not during the reign of Tukulti-Ninurta I in the thirteenth century b.c.e., cast its titular hero as engaging in a righteous battle against his antagonist, Kashtiliash, the Kassite ruler of Babylon.[29] Not only Ashur but even the gods of Babylon join on the side of Tukulti-Ninurta because Kashtiliash broke his treaty with the Assyrian king. Characteristically Shamash is invoked to judge between the two warring kings. Within the narrative framework of the poem, Shamash obviously decides for the Assyrian king, as

---

27. For additional discussion and a photograph, see above, chap. 1, pp. 8–10 with fig. 1.

28. Trans. V. Hurowitz, *COS* 2:135 (p. 366); see also Michael B. Dick, ed., *Born in Heaven, Made on Earth: The Making of the Cult Image in the Ancient Near East* (Winona Lake, IN: Eisenbrauns, 1999) 58–63. For a discussion of the iconographic issues regarding this tablet, see Tallay Ornan, *The Triumph of the Symbol: Pictorial Representation of Deities in Mesopotamia and the Biblical Image Ban* (OBO 213; Fribourg: Academic Press/Göttingen: Vandenhoeck & Ruprecht, 2005) 63–66.

29. For a translation, with literature, see Foster, *Before the Muses*, 1.209–29.

Tukulti-Ninurta decisively defeats Kashtiliash and his army. Tukulti-Ninurta carted the cult statues of Marduk and other Babylonian gods off to his own capital as booty, where he lavishly installed them in Assyrian sanctuaries. In the impeccable religious logic of the day, the Babylonian gods voluntarily abandoned their Babylonian sanctuaries because of the sin (i.e., breach of treaty) of the Kassite ruler.

The preceding discussion has highlighted a fundamental dichotomy within Mesopotamian religious thought. On the one side, the experience of rampant injustice was so ubiquitous that it engendered a deep-seated suspicion, if not the conviction, that the gods were either inattentive to human affairs or at times even allied against humankind. On the other side, however, were stories of Shamash diligently overseeing both the divine and the human realms—witness to a persistent belief in an ultimate system of divinely administered universal justice. A resolution to the underlying human dilemma was anything but obvious to these ancients.

3. The Chaos Monster Tradition

The Mesopotamians were extremely conscious of the manifold presence of "evil" (*lemuttu*) in their world, from devastating invasions by foreign marauders, to loss of property and wrongful personal injury at the hands of unscrupulous persons, to loss of property and even life from natural disasters, to sickness and disease that sometimes decimated whole populations. These were sometimes attributed to the gods, as in the preceding discussion. Oftentimes such evils were attributed to the ubiquitous presence of malevolent spirits, demons (which we are excluding from discussion in this paper).

Yet another common explanation for evil was the vestigial influence of the chaos dragon (monster), now kept in check by the divine sovereign.[30] The two primary myths of the "slaying" of the chaos dragon are *Anzu* and *Enuma Elish.* It might be more accurate, however, to speak of two variants of the same myth, since the latter is literarily dependent upon the former. Our interest here in not with the myth per se, the storyline, but with the portrayal of the chaos dragon itself—Anzu or Tiamat, respectively—and how this figure is seen as the embodiment of the power of evil, as well as with the portrayal of gods allied with the chaos dragon.

A. Anzu in the Myth of Anzu[31]

The myth we call *Anzu* was known in Akkadian as *bin šar dadmē,* from its incipit. A fragmentary copy of an Old Babylonian version exists, but the

---

30. For a discussion of the seven-headed chaos monster tradition and associated iconographic images, see above, chap. 1, §3.3, "The Ancient Near Eastern Context for the Hebrew Ideas of Creation."

31. See the convenient translation of *Anzu,* with bibliography, by Foster, *Before the Muses,* 1.461–85; or by Marianna Vogelzang, *COS* 3:147 (pp. 327–35).

myth was completely rewritten late in the second millennium B.C.E., resulting in a substantially different version, the so-called Standard Babylonian
(SB) version. The wide dissemination of the latter version gave it a kind of
canonical status.

Anzu is not really a god, and its name, when written syllabically (e.g.,
an-zu-ú), was written without the divine determinative dingir, normal for
any god. As its Sumerian equivalent (an.imdugud.mušen) indicates, it
was thought of as an eagle-like bird; Anzu is actually described as a gigantic
"thunderbird" in the Sumerian *Epic of Lugalbanda*, though in that cycle
Anzu is a benevolent figure. A wall relief from Nineveh depicts the warrior
god with lightning bolts as weapons pursuing a fleeing monstrous bird-like
figure, probably correctly identified as Ninurta attacking Anzu.[32]

Like other cosmogonic myths, *Anzu* is set at or near the beginning of
creation. The cosmos is in its inchoate stage, with the ranks of the gods still
being worked out. During this critical juncture Anzu is born. Though the
text is very fragmentary at this point, enough is preserved to see that the
inexperienced gods are both fascinated and alarmed; they are unsure what
to make of this grotesque figure, born of Earth and the primeval flood. So
horrible was Anzu's appearance that Enlil, when he first glimpsed Anzu,
recoiled in horror. Ea, however, with his superior intelligence surmised Anzu's identity and, perhaps in an effort to keep this dangerous being under
surveillance, recommends that Enlil as supreme ruler make Anzu his personal attendant. That decision would have disastrous consequences.

As Enlil's personal attendant, Anzu was able to observe Enlil's daily routine, which included a ritual bath, during which time Enlil would remove
the Tablet of Destinies. In Mesopotamian tradition the Tablet of Destinies
(*ṭuppi šīmāti*) represented the power to determine the nature and fate of all
things; this tablet was worn by the ruling deity like a garment or perhaps,
better, like a jewel or royal insignia.[33] The sight of the unguarded Tablet
of Destinies kindled in Anzu an irrepressible desire for supreme control.
So one day, while Enlil was performing his regular ablutions, Anzu seized
the Tablet of Destinies for himself and fled to far-off mountains—to the
very boundary of creation, according to the mythic geography of the story.
In great consternation at the looming catastrophe of universal chaos, the
terrified gods met in council with Anu, the father of the gods, presiding.
None of the established gods was willing to go forth to challenge Anzu.
One by one the great warrior gods, Adad, Girra, Shara, all declined. With
no champion in sight, Belet-ili (Mami) urged her young son Ninurta to
volunteer and win fame for himself. Ninurta confidently set off, only to
have his arrows repulsed by Anzu. But armed with additional advice from

---

32. Fig. 16 (and note also fig. 15) in chap. 1, above. For a recent discussion of this
relief, see Ornan, *Triumph of the Symbol*, 87–88.

33. For a discussion of the role of "Tablet of Destinies" and the related Sumerian me
in the governance of the world, see J. Bottéro, *Religion in Ancient Mesopotamia*, 90–95 and
103–5.

Ea on how to outmaneuver Anzu, Ninurta eventually returned to battle, and this time was successful in killing Anzu. Having tasted supreme power himself, Ninurta was reluctant, however, to return the Tablet of Destinies to his father Enlil, the rightful owner. The tablet is damaged at this point, so what happened next is uncertain. When the text becomes legible again, the gods are praising Ninurta in terms reminiscent of Marduk's fifty names at the conclusion of *Enuma Elish*, after Marduk's defeat of Tiamat and the establishment of cosmic order.

B. *The Myth of* Enuma Elish

Enuma Elish, the so-called Babylonian Creation Myth, is difficult to date but probably was composed during the Middle Babylonian period late in the second millennium B.C.E. It may have taken shape during or shortly after the reign of Nebuchadnezzar I (1126–1104 B.C.E.), a native Babylonian king who succeeded in restoring the prestige of Babylon by ending foreign Kassite domination and restoring the captured statue of Marduk, patron deity of Babylon, to its rightful place. *Enuma Elish* appears to be the work of a single author who melded prior mythic traditions together for his own purpose.[34] Clearly, the composition is literarily dependent on *Anzu*, from which it borrows many motifs and even much of its plot. Essentially it is an encomium for Marduk: during the course of the narrative Marduk, hitherto strictly a local deity, is promoted over the ruling triad of established gods to the position of divine sovereign by virtue of his primordial victory over the chaos dragon, Tiamat. Since this myth is about ranking among the gods, humans play no role in the narrative, though their creation by Marduk from clay mixed with the blood of a slain god is recounted in familiar terms, borrowed from the myth of *Atrahasis*.

The issue of the malevolence or the benevolence of the gods takes on a different cast in *Enuma Elish*. In this narrative the gods divide themselves into two camps, one malevolent and the other benevolent, or in a contemporary idiom, on the one side are the "good guys" and on the other side are the "bad guys," with the two sides engaged in a battle for total victory over the other. (If this conjures up mental images of the later "Christian myth" concerning a primordial battle between good angels and bad angels that led to the downfall of the latter, which John Milton so magisterially orchestrates in *Paradise Lost*, the allusion is intentional!)[35]

As is well known, in *Enuma Elish* at the very beginning there is only Apsu, primeval underground water, and Tiamat, primeval ocean. From their coupling waters are born all the gods in a kind of progressive ascendancy, with

---

34. See W. G. Lambert, "Mesopotamian Creation Stories," in *Imagining Creation* (ed. Markham J. Geller and Mineke Schipper; IJS Studies in Judaica 5; Leiden: Brill, 2008) 15–59.

35. See Bernard F. Batto, "Paradise Reexamined," in *The Biblical Canon in Comparative Perspective: Scripture in Context IV* (ed. K. Lawson Younger, Jr., W. W. Hallo, and Bernard F. Batto (Lewiston, NY: Edwin Mellen, 1991) 33–66; reprinted in this volume as chapter 2, above.

each successive generation of gods being superior to the preceding generation. In Mesopotamian thought, creation consisted of a steady progression from inchoate beginnings to its apex in the great Sumero-Akkadian civilization.[36] Accordingly, this series of divine generations climaxed in the great triad of gods, Anu, Enlil, and Ea, traditionally the highest gods of the Sumerian pantheon. (The myth later progresses by one additional generation, of course, to allow for the latecomer Marduk, who within the narrative will emerge as the culmination of this dramatic evolution of the gods.)

At first, the traditional Sumerian gods served their function well, as Ea is able to dispatch Apsu—the first head, so to speak, of the seven-headed chaos dragon. Following this initial victory over the chaos dragon, Anu, Enlil, and Ea each assumed his traditional place in the governance of heaven, earth, and the underworld, respectively. But there came a time when the traditional Sumerian gods proved inadequate. A new crisis arose when the chaos dragon reemerged, stronger and more dangerous than ever. A recrudescent Tiamat promoted one of her own children, the god Qingu, as her lover and champion. Many of the other gods apparently found this duo so formidable that they joined this coalition of "the bad guys." This left the ranks of the "good gods" depleted and powerless against a superior force.

Fortunately, in the meanwhile, Ea had fathered Marduk, who, in keeping with the Mesopotamian rule of progression, turns out to surpass all previous gods. As Anu notes, from birth Marduk was endowed with four eyes and four ears; that is to say, his perception and his intelligence was twice that of other gods, surpassing even his father Ea, renowned among the gods for wisdom, ingenuity and accomplishment.[37] Marduk agrees to challenge Tiamat and her coalition on the condition that the gods make him, Marduk, the divine sovereign. In a terrific cosmic battle, Marduk succeeds in slaying Tiamat, and from her carcass creates an ordered cosmos. Apparently, the poet intends the reader to recall—and supplant—the myth of *Atrahasis*, wherein it was Ea who conceived the plan to create humankind, formed out clay mixed with the blood of the chief rebel god, to serve as substitute laborers for the lesser gods, thereby allowing them the leisure of rest. The author of *Enuma Elish* (Tablet VI 1–38) specifies that it was Marduk, however, rather than Marduk's father Ea, who thought up the plan to create humankind. After Marduk kills the "rebel" Qingu, he directs his father Ea to fashion humankind out of clay mixed with Qingu's blood. Marduk pardons the remaining rebel gods and allows them the divine privilege of "rest" along with the other gods. Unity among the gods is restored and right order prevails. And so all ends well, with the seven-headed chaos dragon (Tiamat) finally subdued and Marduk securely enthroned as the

---

36. Ibid.
37. J. Bottéro, *Religion in Ancient Mesopotamia*, 60.

divine sovereign. The gods in gratitude sing Marduk's praises in the form of his fifty incomparable names.

The story of *Enuma Elish* is well known, of course. But I want to return to the issue of benevolent and malevolent deities, and the fluidity between the two, as this aspect of the myth is normally overlooked.

Apsu and Tiamat are the principal antagonists in the narrative, and as such come off as "bad guys." But a couple of observations are in order. First, although Apsu and Tiamat are the progenitors of all the gods (*ibbanûma ilū qerebšun* "the gods were created inside them" I 9), Apsu and Tiamat are not themselves gods. The scribe never employs the divine determinative (dingir) when writing their names. Second, as the primordial matrix from which the gods sprang, Apsu and Tiamat exhibit many of the same characteristics as gods because the gods, as their offspring, are of the very same substance.[38] Moreover, originally the gods all had their home inside Tiamat, until Ea killed Apsu and made his new domain within "apsu," and until Marduk killed Tiamat and from her body fashioned the heavens and earth as new homes for the various gods. Accordingly, the gods themselves, as descendants of Tiamat and Apsu, bear within "genes" which make them susceptible of turning to "the dark side."

The myth begins before there was heaven and earth, before there were any gods, when existed "only Apsu, the foremost, their begetter, (and) creator Tiamat, the one who bore them all" (*Apsûma rēštû zārûšun* || *mummu Tiāmat muallidat gimrišun*, I 3–4). The poet introduces this pair to the reader using epithets that elsewhere are applied to the highest gods. Apsu's epithet has been translated as "primeval Apsu."[39] Akkadian *rēštû* can have that meaning, especially when applied to cities and sanctuaries; but its basic meaning is "first" and normally is associated only with the highest-ranking gods, e.g., Marduk, Anu, Dagan, Ishtar, and Ninlil. Hence it carries the connotation of "preeminent, foremost, supreme, outstanding."[40] The implication is that Apsu is no mean figure. Similarly, Tiamat's epithet, *mummu* "craftsman, creator," is an epithet given later in *Enuma Elish* to Marduk (VII 86), and in other texts it is also applied to Ea, Ishtar, and other gods.[41] So there does not seem to be any attempt on the part of the poet to denigrate the character of either Apsu or Tiamat at the beginning. Their turn to "the dark side" would seem to come only later, when they oppose their

---

38. Contrary to my interpretation here, most commentators underscore a difference in kind between Tiamat and Apsu (primordial matter, the ancestor generation) and their offspring (the gods, the generation of "brother-gods"); so Jean-Jacques Glassner, "The Use of Knowledge in Ancient Mesopotamia," *CANE* 3.1819–20. See also W. G. Lambert, "Myth and Mythmaking in Sumer and Akkad," *CANE* 3.1829–30.

39. So Foster, *Before the Muses*, 1.354.

40. *CAD* R 274–76.

41. *CAD* M 197. W. G. Lambert (*CANE* 3.1830) translates "Demiurge Tiamat."

offspring, the younger, "good" gods, thus violating the standing rule of Mesopotamian creation stories, which is progression—a progression from inchoate beginnings to its climax in high Mesopotamian culture.

If Apsu and Tiamat were not characterized as full gods, those who joined them certainly were as much *gods* as were Anshar, Anu, Ea, and the others. We are not told how Mummu, Apsu's "vizier" (*sukkallu*, I 48) came into being, but since his name is always written with the divine determinative (dingir) and since he addressed Apsu as "father" (I 49), his origins must be assumed to be the same as that of the other gods. The difference is that Mummu was something of a tattler and a climber, thereby ingratiating himself with his "father." Thus, when the "clamor" (*nāṣiru*) of the youthful gods disturbed Apsu's and Tiamat's sleep, Mummu sided with his "father" against Tiamat:

> "Put an end here and now, father, to their troublesome ways!
> "By day you should have rest, at night you should sleep."
> Apsu was delighted with him, he beamed.
> On account of the evils he plotted against the gods, his children,
> He embraced Mummu, around his neck,
> He sat on his knees so he could kiss him.
> (I 49–54; trans. Foster, *Before the Muses*, 1.355–56)

Ea, however, was able with ease to kill Apsu and imprison Mummu because they were only two. Even Tiamat did not join their plot, since she opposed killing her own offspring. (If Tiamat can be faulted up to this point, it would be for being an overly indulgent mother, but hardly a sinister figure.)

But with the next generation of gods, a second and more desperate crisis developed, occasioned by Ea's own rambunctious young son Marduk playing with his four winds, "toys" given him by his grandfather Anu. This time it is not just Tiamat whose sleep is disrupted. The text recounts how "the gods," so discomforted by Marduk's disruptive winds that they cannot sleep, converge on Tiamat and urge her to put an end to the disturbance (I 110–124). From the context, it is clear that "the gods" intend to do away not only with Marduk but also with all the younger gods, "for they have been concocting evil against (us) gods, their begetters" (I 128). We are not told the composition of Tiamat's new alliance, but it appears to have been a considerable force, even without the additional monsters Tiamat will create shortly to augment her army. Anshar is informed, with some exaggeration, "All the gods have rallied around [Tiamat]. Even those you sired are going over to her side" (II 11–18, repeated in III 15–22 and III 74–80).

One of these "rebel" gods was Qingu, whom Tiamat made her new husband and promoted to rank of commander of her army:

> "I make you the greatest in the assembly of the gods,
> "Kingship of all the gods I put in your power.
> "You are the greatest, my husband, you are illustrious,

"Your command shall always be greatest, over all the Anunna-gods."
She gave him the tablet of destinies, had him hold it to his chest . . .
(I 152–56; trans. Foster, *Before the Muses*, 1.360)

These "rebels," then, were not some small cell of guerrillas; they constituted a major contingent, perhaps even the majority, of the divine council,
i.e. the Anunnaki-gods and the Igigi-gods. At the very least, this was a full-
scale civil war among the gods.

The author seemingly adapted the theme of a civil war among the gods
from the *Atrahasis* myth, wherein the majority lesser gods (the Igigi-gods),
burdened with the task of provisioning the fewer elite gods (i.e., Enlil, Ea,
and the Anunnaki-gods), rose up to challenge the authority of the latter.
The rebellion ended only when a compromise was worked out, whereby
the ringleader of the rebellion was slain and from his blood mixed with
clay, humankind was created to take over the burden of provisioning not
just the elite gods but all gods. The author of *Enuma Elish* took over from
Atrahasis this motif of humankind created from the blood of the slain ringleader so as to provide all the gods with leisure. So it requires no stretch of
imagination to think that our author also incorporated from *Atrahasis* the
auxiliary motif of a majority of gods rebelling against a minority of elite
gods—even though the relative position of the Igigi-gods and the Anunnaki-gods is reversed, in keeping with normative Mesopotamian tradition.

In *Enuma Elish* it is sometimes difficult to distinguish the "good gods"
(those who sided with Anshar, Anu, Ea, and Marduk) from the "bad gods"
(those who sided first with Tiamat and Apsu and later with Tiamat and
Qingu). Both camps are referred to as "the gods" or even "all the gods."
In preparation for the coming conflict, it is said that "Tiamat assembled
her creatures and organized for battle *against the gods*, her (own) descendants" (II 1–2), here referring to the group we would designate as the "good
gods." But only a few lines later, following Tiamat's elevation of Qingu to
kingship, he attempts to decree "destinies for the gods, [their] offspring"
(II 45–46), apparently referring to all the gods, including the Igigi-gods and
the Anunnaki-gods—some of whom are assembled before Anshar and Ea at
that very moment (II 121). Although Anshar had requested "all the gods"
to convene before him (III 7) in order to swear allegiance to Marduk, manifestly many of them were conflicted and chose to assemble with Tiamat
and Qingu, no doubt in part because of Tiamat's own powerful magic that
she used to create monstrous creatures to aid her in her bellicose endeavors.

Even setting aside for the moment Tiamat's powers, one may discern
that the "good gods" were a minority, and hard pressed in this unfair contest to field an army adequate to match the awesome and powerful Tiamat
and her horrific horde. No wonder that first Ea and then Anu prove no
match for Tiamat and her league. Urged on by his father Ea, Marduk ultimately volunteers to challenge Tiamat and put down her force. Success in
battle was not assured, however, as not only the allies of Marduk cowered

before the awesome—and apparently superior—enemy force confronting them, but even the mighty Marduk's courage faltered, if only momentarily (IV 65–70). Victory, however—if it happens—will come with a huge price tag: Anshar will have to cede kingship to Marduk, and the other gods will have to acknowledge Marduk's supreme authority. Given that Anshar and his allies have no alternative, they quickly accede to Marduk's demands. Ultimately, the contest came down to single combat between Marduk and Tiamat, while their minions, in both camps, stayed on the sidelines "whetting their blades" (IV 92–94), apparently through procrastination happy to evade battle themselves.

In the end, then, one needs team uniforms and a scorecard to keep the "good gods" separate from the "bad gods." Apart from a few "superstars," most of the players are indistinguishable one from the other. There is no discernible reason why the lesser gods ally with one side or the other, other than personal advantage. The lack of a firm boundary between the "good gods" and the "bad gods" is demonstrated at the conclusion of the battle, when, apart from Tiamat and Qingu who are killed, all of the "bad" gods are forgiven and all swear allegiance to their new sovereign Marduk as "Lugaldimmerankia" ("King of the gods of heaven and earth"). Marduk acknowledges their new-found loyalty by giving them rank among the Igigi-gods and the Anunnaki-gods, including seats in the divine assembly. So in the end there is no difference between the two camps. Apart from Qingu, all end up as "good" gods. What this myth reveals is that the gods' loyalty often can be unpredictable, fickle even.

As a postscript, one may note that the author of *Enuma Elish*, like Mesopotamians generally, was quite conscious that the seven-headed chaos dragon is never completely eliminated from the scene, that it is always lurking somewhere in the distance, ready to rear another of its ugly heads if given the chance. Tucked away in Marduk's forty-ninth title is a prayer that the divine sovereign keep Tiamat perpetually at bay, since the battle against the seven-headed chaos monster is a never-ending struggle: "May he vanquish Tiamat, constrict and shorten her life. Until the last days of humankind, when even days have grown old, may she depart, not be detained, and ever stay away" (VII 132–134).[42] Marauding barbarian hordes and wicked enemies could be understood as historical incarnations of the chaos dragon, similar to the way the Israelites viewed their Babylonian and Egyptian captors.[43]

4. Marduk: The Inscrutable Divine Sovereign

All along we have been flirting with the suspicion that ultimately the malevolent deity may be indistinguishable from the benevolent deity, and

---

42. See Batto, *Slaying the Dragon*, 85.
43. Ibid., 144–67.

that in fact these may be but two faces of the same god (or gods). In this final section I want to address this issue head on, in an examination of the role of Marduk in the wisdom piece *Ludlul Bel Nemeqi*, also known as "The Poem of the Righteous Sufferer."[44] This composition has been dubbed "the Babylonian Job" because, like Job, the speaker—Shubshi-meshre-Shakkan is his name (III 43)—has experienced all manner of suffering that he is at a loss to explain.[45] He assumes that his suffering ultimately comes from Marduk, but he is unaware of any wrongdoing on his part that would cause the deity to be angry at him. Unlike Job, however, in *Ludlul* there is no omniscient narrator, so that neither the reader nor the sufferer knows the actual reason for all this terrible suffering.

We surmise that prior to the onset of Shubshi-meshre-Shakkan's troubles, he had been a wealthy and powerful official in the royal court. But then, without warning, everything began to go wrong. In the idiom of the day, his personal god deserted him. The signs are: he has lost favor with the king and his associates have conspired against him; ostracized by society, his family has shunned him and even his slaves disrespect him; he is consumed with numerous horrible diseases; he is so weak that he even has lost bladder and bowel control, with the result that nightly he must wallow in his own excrement; so near death is he that he has already made his own funeral arrangements.

Shubshi-meshre-Shakkan knows that all this is from the hand of Marduk but is unaware of any sin that would warrant such punishment. In contrast to Job, however, our Babylonian sufferer does not protest his innocence or rail against the deity for his unjust treatment. Rather, in typical Mesopotamian fashion, he acknowledges the possibility of unconscious sin.[46] He

---

44. All recent treatments of *Ludlul* rely on the critical edition of this text by W. G. Lambert (*Babylonian Wisdom Literature*, 21–62). Since then, numerous new fragments have been found, which supply most of the text that was lacking at the time of Lambert's publication, especially the long introduction of Tablet I. The most recent edition of this poem, by Amar Annus and Alan Lenzi (*Ludlul bēl nēmeqi: The Standard Babylonian Poem of the Righteous Sufferer* [SAACT 7; Publications of the Foundation for Finnish Assyriological Research 2; Helsinki: The Neo-Assyrian Text Corpus Project, 2010]), engages all known fragments to reconstruct a single composite text—with the cuneiform text provided both in a computer-generated font (thus reproducing the signs without attempting to recreate the scribal hand) and in transcription—together with a new translation, brief introduction, and glossary. For another recent translation, with literature, see Foster, *Before the Muses*, 1.308–25.

45. Because the narrator at times speaks in the first person, some have assumed that the speaker and the author of the poem are identical. More likely, however, the author is an anonymous scholar consciously imitating various forms and styles for literary effect; see Annus and Lenzi, *Ludlul bēl nēmeqi*, xvii–xviii. The fact that the speaker reveals his name within the context of the poem is not particularly significant. With justification, Moran ("The Babylonian Job," in his *Most Magic Word*, 186) characterizes the speaker as "Mesopotamian Everyman."

46. For another confession of unconscious sins, see "Dialogue between a Man and His God," 12–14 (Foster, *Before the Muses*, 1.75). Other Mesopotamian writers take the

does a rapid "examination of conscience" that yields only acts of piety, but then ends ambiguously, "Who knows?"

> I wish I knew that these things were pleasing to a god!
> What seems good to oneself could be an offense to a god,
> What in one's own heart seems despicable could be good to one's god!
> Who knows the will of the gods in heaven?
> Who understands the plans of underworld gods?
> Where have mortals learned the way of a god?
> (II 31–38)[47]

In the depths of Shubshi-meshre-Shakkan's misery, abandoned by family and friends, he experiences a series of comforting dreams of restoration, including a messenger from Marduk that he will be healed. Once recovered, his troubles are not ended, however, for then he must undergo a series of ordeals to establish his innocence before the community. Apparently Shubshi-meshre-Shakkan is successful in this, for the fragmentary ending has him making a thanksgiving offering in the temple to Marduk and his consort Zarpanitu for having graciously restored him to life.

Many of these themes are common in ancient Near Eastern wisdom literature, of course. What is somewhat unusual about *Ludlul* is the portrayal of Marduk as alternating between anger and mercy, without any apparent reason. I say *somewhat* unusual because this portrayal of Marduk is alluded to elsewhere. In *Enuma Elish* (VI 137), one of Marduk's names is Mershakushu 'savage, (yet) relenting'—an apt characterization of Marduk in *Ludlul*. W. G. Lambert opines that the ancients no doubt stressed Marduk's mercy as a way of inducing him to be less savage.[48]

In 1992, in an address to the Catholic Biblical Association, William L. Moran developed a new interpretation of *Ludlul*. Moran's insights were facilitated by D. J. Wiseman's publication in 1980 of a new fragment, which supplied the until-then missing introduction to the composition. Moran's address, which remained unpublished during his lifetime, provides the basis for my own observations here.[49]

---

opposite tack: humans by nature are imperfect, so sin is inevitable; see "Who Has Not Sinned?" (Foster, *Before the Muses*, 2.644–45); note also the statement in "The Babylonian Theodicy," lines 276–80: (When the gods created humankind, they) "gave twisted words to the human race; they endowed them in perpetuity with lies and falsehood" (Foster, *Before the Muses*, 1.813). For a fuller discussion of conscious and unconscious sin, see J. Bottéro, *Religion in Ancient Mesopotamia*, 188–92.

47. Cf. Bottéro, *Religion in Ancient Mesopotamia*, 61; Foster, *Before the Muses*, 1.314–15; Annus and Lenzi, *Ludlul bēl nēmeqi*, 35.

48. W. G. Lambert, "Studies in Marduk," *BSOAS* 47 (1984) 1–9. See also Foster, *Before the Muses*, 1.389 n. 2.

49. See now William L. Moran, "The Babylonian Job," in *Most Magic Word*, 182–200; see also Moran, "Notes on the Hymn to Marduk in *Ludlul Bēl Nēmeqi*," *JAOS* 103 (1983) 255–60. The supplementary fragment was published by D. J. Wiseman in his article "A New Text of the Babylonian Poem of the Righteous Sufferer," *AnSt* 30 (1980) 101–7.

The poet, dissatisfied with conventional religion, directly challenged current religious conceptions, which depended heavily upon a belief that personal well-being is intimately connected with one's relationship with one's personal god: one prospers when one's personal god is attentive to the devotee, and one languishes when the personal god has been offended and no longer intercedes on behalf of his devotee before the great gods and no longer keeps the demons of disease and misfortune at bay. The poet intimates that such religious practice is worthless because personal gods know nothing and are powerless in any case. [50] If not personal gods, then who? The answer: Marduk, and Marduk alone!

The poem, as we now know from the restored opening lines, is really a hymn of praise to Marduk and his inscrutable wisdom. In Moran's translation:

1   I will praise the lord of wisdom, judicious god,
     Enraged in the night, in the daylight calming,
     Marduk, the lord of wisdom, judicious god,
     Enraged in the night, in the daylight calming,

5   Whose fury, like a storm blast, makes a wasteland,
     Whose breath is, like the dawn wind, pleasing.

     In his rage he's irresistible, a very deluge is his wrath,
     His is a pardoning mind, his a forgiving heart.

     The *full weight* of whose hands the heavens cannot support,
10   Whose soft palm saves a man about to die,
     Marduk, the *full weight* of whose hands the heavens cannot
          support,
     Whose soft palm saves a man about to die.

     When he is angry, many are the graves to be opened,
     When he pities, from the tomb he raises the fallen.

15   He frowns, and Life-force and Lady Fortune go far away.
     He looks with favor, and to the one he had rejected his god comes
          back again.

     Terrible is his . . . punishment to the one *still not* absolved.
     He is moved to mercy, and suddenly *the god is like* a mother,
     Hastening to treat his loved one tenderly,
20   And behind, like a cow with her calf, back and forth, round about
          he goes.

     Sharp are the barbs of his whip, the body pierce and pierce.
     His bandages are cool, giving life to death itself.

---

50. In our own time, one is reminded of the "Death of God" theology popularized just a few decades back.

He *commands* and makes one give offense.
On his day of redress, absolved are guilt and sin.
25   It is he who ever saves, provides that a case be heard.

Through his holy spell are shivers and chills released–
Healer of *Adad's* thrusts, of Erra's wound,
Reconciler of god and goddess enraged.

The *exalted* lord sees into the heart of the gods,
30   *Never* does *a god* know his way.
Exalted Marduk sees into the heart of the gods,
No god, whoever he be, can learn his plan.

As heavy as is his hand, so merciful is his heart.
As savage as are his weapons, so healing is his spirit.

35   Against his will, who could cool his wound?
Would he not, which one relieve his *thrusts*?

I will glorify his fury, which like . . .
He took pity on me, and suddenly how he gave me life.

I will have the people learn adoration . . .
40   His good invocation *I will teach the land.*

The poet alternates between almost incompatible images of "the Lord" (Bel): fierce and angry, on the one side, and gentle and merciful, on the other. The stark contrast between the two faces of Marduk is new in our study of the gods. Granted that we have encountered angry gods before— for example, Enlil who wanted to annihilate humankind because of their noise that prevented his sleeping. Countering an angry Enlil, however, was another deity (Ea, in this example), who would mollify the angry deity and so mediate on behalf of defenseless humans. But having one and the same deity embody both qualities, anger and mercy, and at the same time, is a new development in the Neo-Babylonian/Neo-Assyrian period.[51]

Some years ago, W. G. Lambert called attention to an almost monotheistic impulse in the Late Babylonian period to attribute to Marduk the traits of the other gods (with the possible exception of Marduk's spouse Zarpanitu and the demons):

---

51. As A. Annus and A. Lenzi (*Ludlul bēl nēmeqi* [SAACT 7; Helsinki: Neo-Assyrian Text Corpus Project], xviii–xix) note, a firm date for the composition of *Ludlul Bel Nemeqi* cannot be established. On the one side, the mention of the Kassite king Nazimurutas within the poem itself establishes the terminus post quem (earliest possible date) as ca. 1300 B.C.E. On the other side, the earliest manuscripts of the poem come from the Neo-Assyrian period, establishing the terminus ante quem (latest possible date). Some argue that the exalted role of Marduk implies that the poem was composed ca. 1100 B.C.E. under the aegis of the Second Dynasty of Isin, perhaps during the reign of Nebuchadnezzar I. But the recovery of more than 52 manuscripts from seven different Neo-Assyrian and Neo-Babylonian sites attests to the widespread fascination with—and influence of—the poem during the eighth to sixth centuries B.C.E.

Urash (is)	Marduk of planting.
Lugalidda (is)	Marduk of the abyss.
Ninurta (is)	Marduk of the pickaxe.
Nergal (is)	Marduk of battle.
Zababa (is)	Marduk of warfare.
Enlil (is)	Marduk of lordship and consultations.
Nabu (is)	Marduk of accounting.
Sin (is)	Marduk who lights up the night.
Shamash (is)	Marduk of justice.
Adad (is)	Marduk of rain.
Tishpak (is)	Marduk of troops.
Great Anu (is)	Marduk of . . .
Shuqamuna (is)	Marduk of the container.
[(is)]	Marduk of everything.

(*CT* 24, 50, BM 47406, obverse)[52]

By consolidating all divine functions in the national deity, Babylon's theologians were, in effect, positing the divine sovereign, Marduk, as the only god, with absolute authority and control over heaven, earth, and the netherworld. There is no other. Moran sees this as part of a "movement in the late second millennium B.C. to exalt Marduk to a unique position in the Mesopotamian pantheon. In this movement Marduk becomes absolutely supreme and, in some sense, the only god, for he alone, apart from the remote figure of the sky-god, enjoys autonomy."[53] A parallel theological development was going on to the north, as the Assyrians were making similar claims for Ashur, their national deity. This development has been called henotheism.[54] I prefer to use the term "near monotheism." With all other divinities, including demonic ones, effectively eliminated from having any power or function, logically it became necessary to attribute responsibility for evil, as well as for good, to Marduk (alternatively, Ashur), the universal lord. Everything must come from the hand of Bel.

---

52. W. G. Lambert, "The Historical Development of the Mesopotamian Pantheon: A Study in Sophisticated Polytheism," in *Unity and Diversity: Essays in the History, Literature, and Religion of the Ancient Near East* (ed. Hans Goedicke and J. J. M. Roberts; Baltimore: The Johns Hopkins University Press, 1975) 191–200, translation on pp. 197–98.

53. Moran, "Babylonian Job," 198.

54. Lambert, "Historical Development," 191–200; W. von Soden, "Das Fragen nach der Gerechtigkeit Gottes im Alten Orient," MDOG 96 (1965) 49; J. Bottéro, *Religion in Ancient Mesopotamia*, 55–58. Batto (*Slaying the Dragon*, 36–39) finds a "monotheistic impulse" in late Mesopotamian religion. The reluctance of many scholars to employ the terminology of *monotheism* in connection with Mesopotamian religion—even a diminutive phrase such as "near monotheism" or "monotheistic impulse"—seems rooted in the same religious prejudice that Tallay Ornan posits among scholars assessing parallel aniconic tendencies in Israel and Mesopotamia with regard to the depiction of deities: "it may be that a Judeo-Christian heritage of many scholars subconsciously prevented them from acknowledging a link with non-monotheistic religious expressions, when dealing with such a fundamental issue as the image of God" (*Triumph of the Symbol*, 182).

This is the dilemma of "the righteous sufferer." If he attributes the good things that happen to him to Bel, then he must also conclude that the misfortunes that have befallen him also come from the hand of Bel. And Shubshi-meshre-Shakkan certainly has had his share of misfortune—overwhelming misfortune. Not able to discern any correlation between his fate and his moral behavior, Shubshi-meshre-Shakkan concludes that, if there is logic involved here, it is known only to Bel himself. Even "the gods" do not know. Marduk's will is inscrutable.

In the face of the absolute sovereignty of Marduk, the best one can do is to praise him, as Shubshi-meshre-Shakkan does in this poem, as "the lord of wisdom" (*bēl nēmeqi*). Moran notes that Akkadian *nēmequ* "is not concerned with the abstract. It is a quality of mind in the experiential and practical order that is a guide to action in all its manifold forms. It conceives of goals and determines the means to achieve these goals." Citing the *CAD* definition of *nēmequ* as "the body of experiences, knowledge, skills, and traditions, which are the basis of a craft or occupation, or form the basis of civilization as a whole,"[55] Moran posits that our poet attributes to Bel a wisdom whereby the world is governed according to a well-defined plan. "We may not understand the plan. No one can. Not even the other gods. But there is a plan, there is meaning, behind what can only seem not just mysterious but even willful and capricious."[56]

In praising Marduk as "the lord of wisdom," the righteous sufferer accepts his inherent limitation as a mere human standing before the inscrutable divine sovereign. Like Job, he gets no answer to the question of why he suffers; he can only acknowledge the mystery, not solve it. That, in short, is what it means to "praise the lord of wisdom."

In the final analysis, *Ludlul* implies that there is no distinction between "malevolence" and "benevolence" in human existence. Both come from the same divine will. The attempt to designate some experiences as malevolent and others as benevolent is a vain, foolish, human attempt to control our own destiny. The author of *Ludlul* would approve of the attitude of his biblical compatriot in suffering: "Shall we receive the good at the hand of God, and not receive the bad?" (Job 2:10).

5. Conclusions

This essay makes no claim to be a comprehensive study of the motif of "the malevolent deity" in Mesopotamian literature. Rather, the goal has been to outline with broad strokes some of the main contours of a development in Mesopotamian religious thinking about the problem of evil—a problem involving the deity, whether "deity" be conceived as many gods, each with discrete divine functions, or as a single god incorporating the totality of divine power. The former is commonly labeled polytheism and

---

55. *CAD* N/2 160.
56. Moran, "The Babylonian Job," 192.

was characteristic of the Sumero-Akkadian culture from the very beginning. The latter, which may be labeled "near monotheism," developed only during the late stages of Mesopotamian culture, more exactly, during the Neo-Babylonian/Neo-Assyrian period.[57]

The foundations of Mesopotamian religious belief were set in the Sumerian period. Within that system the functions of good and evil were thought to be distributed broadly among distinct supernatural beings, with good generally being associated with a tetrad of highest gods who are aided by a larger number (traditionally given as seven hundred) of lesser gods. Evil was attributed to several sources, among them personal sin, demons, ghosts, and the like, and residual influence of the chaos monster. A more troubling source of evil was the capriciousness of the gods themselves. The latter was the subject of this essay, under the designation of "the malevolent deity."

I must confess that I started this investigation with the assumption that "malevolence" among the gods was rare and that the "problem cases" would be few and far between—the act(s) of a few isolated deities. During my review of literary texts, however, I discovered that the theme of malevolence on the part of the gods was far from rare and certainly not restricted to a few "rogue elements" among the gods. Literary texts probably should not be taken as representative of popular religion. But literary works are the expressions of the best thinkers of a society, especially in Mesopotamia, where the complexity of the writing system perforce made the written word the exclusive domain of the educated. The Mesopotamian intellectuals who composed these literary texts belonged to this elite group, of course. They may well have dared to explore issues that were considered taboo to a less intellectually sophisticated populace. But the frequency of the theme of malevolence among the gods within Mesopotamian literature is prima facie evidence that ancient Mesopotamian intellectuals found the issue theologically troubling; it was "a problem that just would not go away," so to speak.

Even though Mesopotamia's theologians were troubled by the apparent capriciousness of gods, their polytheistic religious system precluded any serious "crisis of faith." The malevolence of one god was canceled out by the benevolence of another god. An angry Enlil could be outmaneuvered by a wise Ea, an out-of-control Erra could eventually be pacified by a reasonable Ishum. Should even the majority of the gods become irrationally hostile, the gods of justice would be even more powerful in restoring right order. That was the "virtue" of polytheism.

But this comforting system of religious checks and balances was gradually eroded away by the rise of empires in Babylonia and Assyria, and the

---

57. A similar movement away from polytheism and toward monotheism was happening in Israel at about this same time. These simultaneous developments were not unrelated—nor surprising—as contact between these two regions was considerable during the first half of the first millennium B.C.E.

concomitant development of a new religious system centered on the national god, Marduk in Babylonia and Ashur in Assyria. In this system, the national god was understood to be the absolute or universal divine sovereign. All divine power was consolidated in this one god. The king (in Assyria or Babylonia, respectively) is the designated agent (viceroy) of the divine sovereign to administer affairs on earth. Though the movement's roots are evident already in the Old Babylonian kingdom under Hammurapi, the full flowering of the movement came only some thousand years later in the Late Babylonian period.

This religious system served the political agenda of the Assyrian and Babylonian kings very well. But it created strains in the piety of individuals. With all power consolidated within one divine figure, logically, both good and evil had to be attributed to the divine sovereign—a conclusion from which the ancients shrank back. In fairness to the ancient Mesopotamians, however, it must be acknowledged that subsequent theologians and philosophers have not fared much better in finding a satisfactory solution to "the problem of evil."

Perhaps the most honest, as well as the most profound, Babylonian attempt to address this conundrum is that of Shubshi-meshre-Shakkan in *Ludlul Bel Nemeqi*. Unwilling to castigate Marduk as a malevolent deity, the poet acknowledges his inability to comprehend the mystery, and therefore concludes simply, "I will praise the lord of wisdom."

Index of Authors

Index of Scripture

233

New Testament

Apocrypha

Index of Ancient Sources